COASTAL EROSION AND THE ARCHAEOLOGICAL ASSESSMENT OF AN ERODING SHORELINE AT ST BONIFACE CHURCH, PAPA WESTRAY, ORKNEY

CHRISTOPHER LOWE

with contributions from Sheila Boardman, Stephen Carter, Ann Clark, Ruby Cerón-Carrasco, Anne Crone, Magnar Dalland, Dianne Dixon, Sheila Hamilton-Dyer, Daphne Home Lorimer, Finbar McCormick, Gerry McDonnell, Ann MacSween, David Mann, Jenny Shiels, Richard Tipping & Graeme Wilson

SUTTON PUBLISHING
HISTORIC SCOTLAND

First published in 1998 by
Sutton Publishing Limited · Phoenix Mill
Thrupp · Stroud · Gloucestershire · GL5 2BU
in association with Historic Scotland, Longmore House, Salisbury Place, Edinburgh EH9 1SH

British Library Cataloguing in Publication Data
A catalogue record for this book is available from the British Library

ISBN 0 7509 1755 5

Jacket illustrations: *front*: Excavation of Area 1 'farm mound'; *back*: The whalebone weaving baton (SF122).

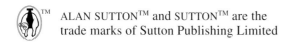 ALAN SUTTON™ and SUTTON™ are the
trade marks of Sutton Publishing Limited

Typeset in 10/11pt Times
Typesetting and origination by
Sutton Publishing Limited
Printed in Great Britain by
Bookcraft, Midsomer Norton, Somerset.

Contents

LIST OF ILLUSTRATIONS   xi

LIST OF TABLES   xv

ABSTRACT   xvii

ACKNOWLEDGEMENTS   xix

ABBREVIATIONS   xx

LIST OF CONTRIBUTORS   xxi

PART 1	**PHYSICAL, HISTORICAL AND ARCHAEOLOGICAL BACKGROUND**	1
1.1	**Introduction**	1
1.1.1	*Physical Background*	
1.1.2	*The Threat*	
1.2	**Archaeological and Historical Background**	3
1.2.1	*Introduction*	3
1.2.2	*The Later Medieval Ecclesiastical Site*	3
1.2.21	Introduction	
1.2.22	St Boniface Church	
1.2.23	Hogback stone	
1.2.24	Saga reference	
1.2.25	Summary	
1.2.3	*The Early Medieval Ecclesiastical Site*	6
1.2.31	Introduction	
1.2.32	Cross-inscribed stones	
1.2.33	Shrine panel fragment	
1.2.34	Toponymy	
1.2.35	The pre-Norse episcopate in Orkney and the *Life* of St Findan	
1.2.36	Summary	
1.2.4	*The 'Farm Mound'*	9
1.2.41	Introduction	
1.2.42	The stockfish model	
1.2.43	The structure model	
1.2.44	'Farm mounds' on Sanday, Orkney	
1.2.45	Chronology of farm mounds	
1.2.46	Summary and application of the models in Orkney	
1.2.5	*The Iron Age Settlement*	10
PART 2	**METHOD AND SURVEY**	13
2.1	**Project Design**	13
2.1.1	*Introduction*	13
2.1.2	*Research Objectives*	13
2.1.3	*Excavation Strategy*	13
2.1.4	*Recording System*	16
2.1.5	*Sampling Strategy*	16
2.2	**Archaeological Survey**	17
2.2.1	*Introduction*	17
2.2.2	*The Cliff-Section*	17
2.2.3	*Other Located Structures*	18
2.2.4	*Binnas Kirk*	19

PART 3   **THE CLIFF-SECTION EXCAVATION**   21

3.1   **Introduction**   21
3.2   **Excavated Structures, Features and Deposits**   23
3.2.1   *Phase 1: Early Funerary Activity*   23
                  Blocks 108, 118 & 119: Sandy loam soils
                  Blocks 251:308, 310 & 312: Sand
                  Block 306: Cairn
                  Block 309: Pit or possible cist
                  Block 311: Cist
3.2.2   *Phase 2: The Earliest Settlement*   27
                  Block 255: Structure 1b
                  Block 307: Structure 1a
3.2.3   *Phase 3: Windblown Sand*   30
                  Blocks 247 & 248: Sand
                  Block 250:305: Sand
3.2.4   *Phase 4: The Settlement of the Late Second Millennium BC* 31
                  Block 240: Rubble
                  Block 241: Orthostat
                  Block 242: Rubble
                  Block 243: Structure 5
                  Block 244: Post-abandonment deposits in Structure 3
                  Block 245: Structure 4
                  Block 246: Structure 3
3.2.5   *Phase 5: Unenclosed Roundhouse Settlement*   37
                  Block 114: Structure 22
                  Block 115: Linear cut feature
                  Block 116: Buried ground surface
                  Block 117: Mound
                  Block 208: Linear cut feature
                  Block 215: Shell midden
                  Block 237: Primary post-roundhouse deposits
                  Block 249:304: Structure 2
                  Block 302: Secondary refurbishment of Structure 2
                  Block 303: Primary collapse of Structure 2
3.2.6   *Phase 6.1: Enclosed Roundhouse Settlement*   50
                  Block 109: Rubble and midden dumps
                  Block 110: Structure 24
                  Block 111: Structure 23
                  Block 112: Stone path or causeway
                  Block 113: Post-abandonment deposits in Structure 22
                  Block 204: Drain
                  Block 206: Primary paving at entrance
                  Block 210: Structure 18, primary enclosure wall
                  Block 213: Fills of primary ditch
                  Block 214: Structure 16, primary enclosure ditch
                  Block 220: Extra-mural roundhouse passage
                  Block 221: Stone platform
                  Block 229: Structure 11
                  Block 234: Structure 8, south side of primary entrance façade
                  Block 235: Rubble
                  Block 236: Structure 7
                  Block 239: Structure 6
3.2.7   *Phase 6.2: Enclosed Roundhouse Settlement and Secondary Enclosure* 66
                  Block 205: Structure 20, secondary paving at entrance
                  Block 209: Structure 19, secondary enclosure wall
                  Block 212: Structure 17, secondary enclosure ditch
                  Block 219: Stone buttress and blocking of extra-mural passage
                  Block 225: Structure 13
                  Block 226: Post-abandonment deposits in Structure 12
                  Block 227: Structure 12
                  Block 228: Rubble and burnt stones
                  Block 230: Post-abandonment deposits in Structure 10

           Block 231: Structure 10
           Block 232: Post-abandonment deposits in Structure 9
           Block 233: Structure 9
           Block 238: Post-abandonment deposits in Structure 6
           Block 252: Primary fills of secondary ditch
           Block 253: Stone-robbing and abandonment of extra-mural passage
3.2.8   *Phase 6.3: Abandonment of Enclosure*   83
           Block 207: Post-abandonment deposits in Structure 19
           Block 211: Fill deposits of secondary enclosure ditch
           Block 224: Post-abandonment deposits in Structures 7 & 11
3.2.9   *Phase 7: Late Iron Age Deposits*   86
           Block 105: Late Iron Age ground surface
           Block 106: Linear cut feature and possible post-hole
           Block 107: Late Iron Age ash deposits
3.2.10   *Phase 8: The 'Farm Mound' and Final Structures on Area 2*   88
           Block 102: Upper 'farm mound' deposits
           Block 103: Secondary 'farm mound' deposits
           Block 104: Primary 'farm mound' deposits
           Block 203: Structure 21
           Block 216: Drain
           Block 217: Rubble, final collapse of Structure 2
           Block 218: Structure 15
           Block 222: Structure 14
           Block 223: Hearth
           Block 254: Mound of ash residues
3.2.11   *Phase 9: Modern Turf and Topsoil, Rubble and Erosion Horizon*   96

PART 4   CHRONOLOGY, SEQUENCE AND PHASING   97

4.0   **Introduction**   97
4.1   **Radiocarbon Dating, Calibration and Statistical Analysis**, by Magnar Dalland   97
4.1.1   *The Radiocarbon Dates*   97
4.1.2   *Statistical Analysis*   99
4.1.21   Introduction
4.1.22   Method
4.1.221   The duration of Structure 22 (B114)
4.1.222   Contemporaneity of Structure 2 (B249:304) and the primary enclosure ditch (B214)
4.1.223   The duration of the primary enclosure ditch (B214)
4.1.224   The duration of the secondary enclosure ditch (B212)
4.1.225   The duration of Structure 10 (B231)
4.1.226   The duration of the Late Iron Age ash mound (B107)
4.1.227   The duration for the formation of the Late Iron Age buried ground surface
                        (B105)
4.1.228   The duration for the formation of the 'farm mound'
4.1.229   The terminal date for the accumulation of deposits in the 'farm mounds' (B103)
4.2   **The Artefactual Sequence**   108
4.2.1   *Introduction*   108
4.2.2   *Pottery*   108
4.2.21   Aceramic phases
4.2.22   Tempered and untempered wares
4.2.23   Surface treatment
4.2.3   *Querns*   108
4.2.4   *Metal*   108
4.3   **Anthropogenic Content and the Ecofactual Sequence**   109
4.3.1   *Introduction*   109
4.3.2   *Mammal Bone*   109
4.3.3   *Fish Bone*   109
4.3.4   *Shell*   110
4.3.5   *Fuel Ash*   111
4.3.6   *Burnt Peat*   112
4.3.7   *Charcoal*   112
4.3.8   *Cereals*   113
4.3.81   Introduction

4.3.82	Hulled barley	
4.3.83	Naked barley	
4.3.84	Oats and flax	
4.4	**The Architectural Sequence**	113
4.5	**Correlation of Dating Evidence**	114
4.6	**Phasing and Connected Account**	114
4.6.1	*Introduction*	114
4.6.2	*Connected Account: The stratigraphic and chronological sequence*	115
4.6.3	*Summary*	124
PART 5	**MATERIAL CULTURE**	125
5.1	**The Coarse Pottery**, by Ann MacSween, with catalogue with Jenny Shiels and geological identifications and comment by Dianne Dixon	125
5.1.1	*Introduction*	125
5.1.2	*Technology*	125
5.1.3	*Morphology*	125
5.1.31	Late Bronze Age/Early Iron Age	
5.1.311	Catalogue of illustrated pottery	
5.1.312	Pottery thin-sections	
5.1.32	Middle Iron Age	
5.1.321	Catalogue of illustrated pottery	
5.1.322	Pottery thin-sections	
5.1.33	Medieval	
5.1.331	Catalogue of illustrated pottery	
5.1.4	*Conclusions*	133
5.2	**The Coarse Stone, Flint and Pumice**, by Ann Clark	133
5.2.1	*Coarse Stone Artefacts*	133
5.2.2	*Flint*	135
5.2.3	*Pumice*	135
5.2.4	*Coarse Stone, Pumice and Flint Catalogue*	135
5.2.41	Coarse stone	
5.2.411	Cobble tools	
5.2.412	Pounders/grinders	
5.2.413	Stone discs	
5.2.414	Querns	
5.2.415	Pivot stones	
5.2.416	Perforated stones	
5.2.417	Ard point	
5.2.418	Miscellaneous	
5.2.42	Flint	
5.2.43	Pumice	
5.3	**The Worked Bone and Antler**, by Graeme Wilson	139
5.3.1	*Introduction*	139
5.3.2	*Bone Points* 139	
5.3.3	*Handle*	139
5.3.4	*Perforated Pin*	139
5.3.5	*Comb Fragment*	140
5.3.6	*Weaving Swords*	140
5.3.7	*Tool Fragment*	141
5.3.8	*Utilized Long Bone*	141
5.3.9	*Waste or Raw Material*	142
5.3.10	*Catalogue of Worked Bone*	142
5.4	**Metal Artefacts and Metalworking**, by Ann MacSween and Gerry McDonnell	142
5.4.1	*Metal Artefacts*, by Ann MacSween	142
5.4.11	Copper alloy artefacts	
5.4.12	Iron artefacts	
5.4.2	*Metalworking*, by Gerry McDonnell	143
5.4.21	Fired and vitrified clay	
5.4.22	Mould fragments	
5.4.3	*Catalogue*, by Ann MacSween	143
5.5	**Lime Mortar**, by Christopher Lowe	144

PART 6	**THE PALAEOENVIRONMENTAL EVIDENCE**	145
6.1	**Human Bone**, by Daphne Home Lorimer	145
6.1.1	*Summary*	145
6.1.2	*Skeleton 1*	145
6.1.21	Inventory	
6.1.22	Sex	
6.1.23	Non-metrical variations	
6.1.24	Pathology	
6.1.3	*Skeleton 2*	146
6.1.31	Inventory	
6.1.32	Sex	
6.1.33	Non-metrical variations	
6.1.34	Pathology	
6.2	**Mammal Bone**, by Finbar McCormick	146
6.2.1	*Introduction*	146
6.2.2	*General Results*	146
6.2.3	*Domesticates*	147
6.2.4	*Ageing Data*	147
6.2.5	*Butchery/Pathology*	148
6.2.6	*Metrical Data*	148
6.2.7	*Red Deer*	148
6.2.8	*Area 1: intra-site variation*	148
6.2.9	*Conclusion*	149
6.3	**Fish Bone**, by Ruby Cerón-Carrasco	149
6.3.1	*Methods*	149
6.3.2	*Results*	149
6.3.3	*Comment and Phase Distribution*	150
6.3.31	Phases 1–5	
6.3.32	Phase 6.1	
6.3.33	Phase 6.2	
6.3.34	Phase 6.3	
6.3.35	Phase 7	
6.3.36	Phase 8	
6.3.37	Phase 9	
6.3.4	*Exploitation of Fish Resources*	152
6.3.41	Origins of the fish bone	
6.3.42	Fishing	
6.3.43	Fish processing	
6.3.431	Cut-marks	
6.3.432	Element representation	
6.3.433	Other processes	
6.3.434	Conclusion	
6.3.5	*Comparison with other Iron Age and Norse Fish Bone Assemblages in the North of Scotland*	154
6.4	**Bird Bone**, by Sheila Hamilton-Dyer	155
6.4.1	*Methods*	155
6.4.2	*Results*	155
6.5	**The Crustacean Remains**, by Sheila Hamilton-Dyer	155
6.6	**Mollusc Shell**, by Stephen Carter	156
6.6.1	*Methods*	156
6.6.2	*Marine Shells*	156
6.6.21	Results	
6.6.22	Discussion	
6.6.3	*Non-Marine Shells*	157
6.6.31	Results	
6.6.32	Discussion	
6.6.321	Terrestrial	
6.6.322	Fresh water	
6.6.323	Brackish water	
6.7	**The Charred Plant Remains**, by Sheila Boardman	157
6.7.1	*Introduction*	157
6.7.2	*Species Represented*	158
6.7.21	Cultivated plants	

6.7.22	Wild species	
6.7.3	*Discussion*	158
6.7.31	Distribution and composition of the charred plant samples	
6.7.311	Areas 2 and 3	
6.7.312	Area 1	
6.7.32	Origins of the crops	
6.7.33	Other sites	
6.7.4	*Conclusions*	160
6.8	**Carbonized Wood**, by Anne Crone	161
6.8.1	*Introduction*	161
6.8.2	*Results*	161
6.8.3	*Discussion*	162
6.8.4	*Conclusion*	162
6.9	**Pollen Analysis of the Late Iron Age Buried Soil**, by Richard Tipping	162
6.9.1	*Introduction*	162
6.9.2	*Methods*	162
6.9.3	*Results*	164
6.9.4	*Interpretation*	164
6.9.41	Sedimentological data	
6.9.42	Soil pollen data	
6.9.43	Reliability of pollen spectra for palaeoecological interpretation	
6.9.44	Possible contributing sources to the turf-line pollen assemblages	
6.9.45	Palaeoecological interpretation of the turf-line	
6.10	**Diatoms**, by David G. Mann	169
6.10.1	*Introduction, Material and Methods*	169
6.10.2	*Results and Discussion*	169
6.10.21	General features of the diatom assemblages	
6.10.22	Comparisons between blocks	
6.11	**Soil Micromorphology**, by Stephen Carter	172
6.11.1	*Introduction*	172
6.11.11	Samples	
6.11.12	Methods	
6.11.13	Results	
6.11.2	*The 'Farm Mound'*	173
6.11.21	Basic mineral and organic components	
6.11.22	Fabric and microstructure	
6.11.23	Composition and sources of the 'farm mound' sediments: part 1	
6.11.231	Mineral sediment	
6.11.232	Laminated organo-mineral sediments	
6.11.233	Uncarbonized organic bands	
6.11.234	Other components	
6.11.235	Conclusion	
6.11.24	Composition and sources of the 'farm mound' sediments: part 2	
6.11.241	Modern reference samples	
6.11.242	Methods	
6.11.243	Results	
6.11.244	Comparison with archaeological material	
6.11.245	Percentage mineral content	
6.11.246	Basic mineral components	
6.11.247	Basic organic components	
6.11.248	Structure	
6.11.249	Discussion	
6.11.2410	Conclusion	
6.11.25	Accumulation of the 'farm mound'	
6.11.26	Comparison of Blocks 103 amd 104	
6.11.27	The 'farm mound': conclusions	
6.11.3	*The Late Iron Age Sediments*	183
6.11.31	Basic mineral and organic components	
6.11.32	Fabric and microstructure	
6.11.33	Comparison of the composition and accumulation of the 'farm mound' (Blocks 103 and 104) and the Late Iron Age sediments (Block 107)	
6.11.4	*The Late Iron Age Buried Soil*	184
6.11.41	Micromorphology	

6.11.42   Interpretation
6.11.5   *The Pre-Iron Age Buried Soil*   184
6.11.6   *'Farm Mound' Type Sediments on Area 2*   185
6.11.61   Micromorphology
6.11.62   Comparison with the Area 1 sediments

PART 7   DISCUSSION   187

7.1   **'Farm Mounds' and the Formation of the Area 1 Sediments,** by Stephen Carter 187
7.1.1   *Introduction*   187
7.1.2   *Area 1 Sediments*   187
7.1.21   Stratigraphy and extent
7.1.211   Introduction
7.1.212   Development of the site topography
7.1.213   Depth and extent of the 'farm mound'
7.1.214   Summary
7.1.22   Composition
7.1.221   Mineral grains
7.1.222   Biological and cultural components
7.1.23   Sources
7.1.24   Mode of deposition
7.1.241   Blocks 103 and 104 (Phase 8)
7.1.242   Blocks 105 and 107 (Phase 7)
7.1.243   Block 119 (Phase 1)
7.1.25   Volume ratio of organic fuel to ash deposits
7.1.251   Introduction
7.1.252   Materials and methods
7.1.253   Results
7.1.254   Discussion
7.1.255   Conclusion
7.1.26   Volume and rate of accumulation of the 'farm mound'
7.1.27   Post-depositional alteration
7.1.271   Chemical processes
7.1.272   Physical processes
7.1.28   Conclusions
7.1.3   *The 'Farm Mound' in Orkney*   197
7.1.31   Summary of previous research
7.1.32   The Norwegian farm mounds
7.1.33   Comparison of the evidence from Norway and Orkney
7.1.34   Formation of the Orkney mounds
7.2   **The Settlement Complex: Discussion and Overview**   199
7.2.1   *Introduction*   199
7.2.2   *The Second Millennium BC and Earlier*   199
7.2.3   *The Iron Age Settlement*   200
7.2.31   Introduction
7.2.32   The roundhouse
7.2.33   Structural development and use of space
7.2.34   Ritual aspects
7.2.4   *The Early Medieval Ecclesiastical Site*   203
7.2.41   Introduction
7.2.42   The spatial association of Iron Age and ecclesiastical sites
7.2.43   The plaggen soil: an 'ecclesiastical artefact'?
7.2.44   The buried ground surface
7.2.5   *The Later Medieval Ecclesiastical Site*   206
7.2.51   Introduction
7.2.52   Ecclesiastical monuments of the eleventh century
7.2.53   Ecclesiastical monuments of the twelfth century
7.2.54   The fish-processing station
7.3   **Conclusion**   209

BIBLIOGRAPHY   211

Illustrations

Illus 1	Location map	2
Illus 2	Survey plan	3
Illus 3	St Boniface church, from SW, prior to restoration	4
Illus 4	Shrine panel fragment	6
Illus 5	The Area 1 cliff-section prior to excavation	14
Illus 6	Detail of features exposed in Area 1 cliff-section (cf. Illus 66)	14
Illus 7	The Area 2 cliff-section, from S, prior to excavation	15
Illus 8	The Area 2/3 cliff-section, from N, prior to excavation, showing the breaks of slope which were utilized during the excavation and recording of the site	16
Illus 9	Detail of roundhouse wall exposed in section, from W, prior to excavation, with outer passage wall to south	17
Illus 10	The 'farm mound', from N, seen against the horizon, to the north of St Boniface church, with the site samples processing station in foreground	18
Illus 11	Site plan of excavated structures: unphased	22
Illus 12	Stratigraphic phase matrix	between pp. 22–3
Illus 13	Phase 1 funerary features	24
Illus 14–16	Stratigraphic matrices: Blocks 108, 118 & 119	25
Illus 17–19	Stratigraphic matrices: Blocks 251:308, 310 & 312	25
Illus 20	Block 306 stratigraphic matrix	26
Illus 21	Block 309 stratigraphic matrix	26
Illus 22	Block 311 stratigraphic matrix	27
Illus 23	Phase 2 structures	28
Illus 24	Structure 1a (B307)	29
Illus 25	Structure 1a (B307), from N, with floor of roundhouse exposed to S	29
Illus 26	Block 307 stratigraphic matrix	29
Illus 27–28	Stratigraphic matrices: Blocks 247 & 248	30
Illus 29	Block 250:305 stratigraphic matrix	31
Illus 30	Phase 4/5 structures	32
Illus 31	Composite middle & lower section (Area 2)	between pp. 32–3
Illus 32	Block 240 stratigraphic matrix	33
Illus 33	Structure 5 (B243), showing primary (right) and secondary (left) floor levels	33
Illus 34	Structure 5 (B243), from SW, with primary floor (F2094) exposed	34
Illus 35	Block 243 stratigraphic matrix	34
Illus 36	Block 244 stratigraphic matrix	35
Illus 37	Structure 4 (B245)	35
Illus 38	Block 245 stratigraphic matrix	36
Illus 39	Structure 3 (B246)	37
Illus 40	Block 246 stratigraphic matrix	37
Illus 41	Structure 22 (B114)	38
Illus 42	Structure 22 (B114), from NW, with wall F1092 in foreground and wall F1101 beyond	38
Illus 43	Block 114 stratigraphic matrix	39
Illus 44	Composite section (Area 1)	between pp. 38–9
Illus 45	Block 115 stratigraphic matrix	39
Illus 46	Block 116 stratigraphic matrix	40
Illus 47	Block 117 stratigraphic matrix	40
Illus 48	Block 208 stratigraphic matrix	41
Illus 49	Block 215 stratigraphic matrix	41
Illus 50	Block 237 stratigraphic matrix	41
Illus 51	Block 249:304 stratigraphic matrix	42
Illus 52	Structure 2 roundhouse	44
Illus 53	Section across south wall of roundhouse	45
Illus 54	Section through south side of roundhouse (Structure 2), from W, showing secondary internal refacings (B302) to the north	46
Illus 55	Detail section showing secondary inserted refacing walls (Walls 2a and 2b: B302), against primary internal wall-face F3036 located adjacent to ranging rod	46

Illus 56   Interior of roundhouse (Structure 2), from S, with entrance and orthostat to east:
             inserted wall-faces (F3001, Wall 2b & F3002, Wall 2a exposed)   47
Illus 57   Interior to roundhouse (Structure 2), from N, Wall 2b (F3026) partially excavated, with
             secondary inserted wall-face (Wall 2a: F3028) behind   47
Illus 58   Block 302 stratigraphic matrix   48
Illus 59   Phase 6.1 structures   49
Illus 60   Block 109 stratigraphic matrix   50
Illus 61   Detail of Area 1 section, from W, showing Structure 24 (B110) to left, Structure 22
             (B114) to right and rubble/midden dump (B109) at centre   50
Illus 62   Block 111 stratigraphic matrix   51
Illus 63   Structure 23 (B111)   52
Illus 64   Stone causeway (B112) from S, with ruins of Structure 23 (B111) to north   53
Illus 65   Block 113 stratigraphic matrix   53
Illus 66   Structure 22 (B114) and infill dumps (B113), from W   53
Illus 67   Block 204 stratigraphic matrix   54
Illus 68   Block 206 stratigraphic matrix   54
Illus 69   Primary paving at entrance (B206)   55
Illus 70   Block 210 stratigraphic matrix   56
Illus 71   Structure 18 (B210)   56
Illus 72   Block 213 stratigraphic matrix   57
Illus 73   Block 214 stratigraphic matrix   57
Illus 74   Structure 16: primary ditch (B214)   58
Illus 75   Block 220 stratigraphic matrix   58
Illus 76   Superimposed floor levels in extra-mural passage (B220)   59
Illus 77   Section across passage between Structures 2 and 7   60
Illus 78   Block 221 stratigraphic matrix   61
Illus 79   Structure 11 (B229)   61
Illus 80   Structure 11 (B229) from E, abutting Structure 7 (B236)   62
Illus 81   Interior elevation view of north wall of Structure 11 (B229)   62
Illus 82   Block 234 stratigraphic matrix   63
Illus 83   Structure 8, south side of entrance façade (B234)   63
Illus 84   Block 235 stratigraphic matrix   64
Illus 85   Block 236 stratigraphic matrix   64
Illus 86   Structure 7 (B236)   64
Illus 87   Structure 7 (B236), from W, with Structure 15 (B218) over and exterior face of
             roundhouse (Structure 2) in foreground   65
Illus 88   Block 239 stratigraphic matrix   66
Illus 89   Structures 6 and 10 (B239 & B231)   66
Illus 90   Phase 6.2 structures   67
Illus 91   Block 205 stratigraphic matrix   68
Illus 92   Structure 20, secondary paving and entrance façade (B205)   68
Illus 93   Secondary paving (F2060: B205) and orthostatic walls (F2052 & F2098: B205) at the
             enclosure entrance, from SW   69
Illus 94   Block 209 stratigraphic matrix   69
Illus 95   Structure 19 (B209), secondary enclosure wall and north-west side of entrance façade   70
Illus 96   Structure 19 (B209), secondary enclosure wall and north-west side of entrance façade,
             from E: with post-abandonment collapse and dump deposits (B207) to west   70
Illus 97   Block 212 stratigraphic matrix   71
Illus 98   Structure 17, secondary enclosure ditch (B212)   71
Illus 99   Section across secondary enclosure ditch   72
Illus 100   Secondary enclosure ditch (Structure 17: B212), from W, with primary fills and
             buttress (B252) overlain by B211 infill   73
Illus 101   Block 219 stratigraphic matrix   73
Illus 102   Blocking (B219) of extra-mural passage, from S, with roundhouse (Structure 2) to west
             and Structure 7 to east   74
Illus 103   Block 225 stratigraphic matrix   75
Illus 104   Structure 13 (B225)   76
Illus 105   Block 227 stratigraphic matrix   77
Illus 106   Structure 12 (B227)   77
Illus 107   Structure 12 (B227), from N   78
Illus 108   Block 231 stratigraphic matrix   79
Illus 109   Elevation of Structures 10 and 6 (B231 & B239)   79
Illus 110   Block 233 stratigraphic matrix   80

Illus 111	Structure 9 (B233)	81
Illus 112	Block 238 stratigraphic matrix	81
Illus 113	Block 252 stratigraphic matrix	82
Illus 114	Detail of section through extra-mural passage, from N: showing B253 debris overlying a series of superimposed floor surfaces (B220) and underlying external buttressing (F2115: B219) of the roundhouse to west	82
Illus 115	Block 207 stratigraphic matrix	83
Illus 116	Block 211 stratigraphic matrix	84
Illus 117	Block 224 stratigraphic matrix	84
Illus 118	Upper section: Structures 11, 13 & 14	85
Illus 119	Block 106 stratigraphic matrix	86
Illus 120	Block 107 stratigraphic matrix	87
Illus 121	Phase 8: Area 2 structures only	88
Illus 122	Block 102 stratigraphic matrix	89
Illus 123	Block 103 stratigraphic matrix	90
Illus 124	Block 104 stratigraphic matrix	90
Illus 125	Block 203 stratigraphic matrix	91
Illus 126	Structure 21 (B203)	91
Illus 127	Structure 21 (B203) from W, with Structure 14 (B222) in background	92
Illus 128	Block 216 stratigraphic matrix	92
Illus 129	Structure 15 (B218) and drain (B216)	93
Illus 130	Structure 15 (B218), from W, with floor (F2003) extending over earlier blocking wall (B219) in foreground	94
Illus 131	Block 218 stratigraphic matrix	94
Illus 132	Structure 14 (B222) and hearth (B223)	95
Illus 133	Block 254 stratigraphic matrix	96
Illus 134	Probability distributions of the radiocarbon dates	98
Illus 135	PD diagram of Blocks 113 & 115	102
Illus 136	PD diagram of Blocks 215 & 213	103
Illus 137	PD diagram of Blocks 113 & 211	104
Illus 138	Cumulative PD diagram of Blocks 230 & 238	104
Illus 139	PD diagram of GU-3063 & GU-3065	105
Illus 140	PD diagram of Blocks 107 & 104	106
Illus 141	Cumulative PD diagram of Blocks 103 & 104	106
Illus 142	Cumulative PD diagram of GU-3069c	107
Illus 143	Correlation table of various attributes to phase	115
Illus 144	General view across the LBA and IA settlement (Area 2), from NW	116
Illus 145	Structure 4 in foreground, from W, with roundhouse (Structure 2) to south and Structures 6 and 7 higher up the section	117
Illus 146	General view, from N, across Area 2, with Structure 10 in foreground	120
Illus 147	View, from SW, towards the enclosure entrance façade	121
Illus 148	The Area 1 'farm mound' section, from N, together with the IA causeway and settlement beyond. The prominent dark band of the LIA ground surface (B105) is clearly visible in section	123
Illus 149	V61, SF87A, F2071, A2, B 237, Phase 5	126
Illus 150	V85, SF11A, 0, A1, u/s	127
Illus 151	V103, SF25A, 0, A2, u/s	127
Illus 152	V55, SF162Y, F2166, A2, B 233, Phase 6.2	128
Illus 153	V197, SF42, F2033, A2, B 225, Phase 6.2	128
Illus 154	V262, SF20A, 0, A2, u/s	128
Illus 155	V32, SF162A, F2166, A2, B 233, Phase 6.2	129
Illus 156	V34, SF162C, F2166, A2, B 233, Phase 6.2	130
Illus 157	V52, SF162V, F2166, A2, B 233, Phase 6.2	130
Illus 158	V36, SF162E, F2166, A2, B 233, Phase 6.2	130
Illus 159	V35, SF162D, F2166, A2, B 233, Phase 6.2	131
Illus 160	V12, SF4, 0, A1, u/s	131
Illus 161	V80, SF45A, F2037, A2, B 202, Phase 9	131
Illus 162	V28, SF8A, F1080, A1, B 109, Phase 6.1	132
Illus 163	V13, SF5, A1, u/s (B 103 / 104: 'farm mound' deposits)	132
Illus 164	Pounder / grinder SF159	133
Illus 165	Cobble tool SF166	134
Illus 166	Cobble tool SF34	134
Illus 167	Grinder with quern SF123	135

Illus 168	Dish quern SF123	136
Illus 169	Bone pin SF198	139
Illus 170	Comb fragment SF6	140
Illus 171	Weaving baton SF122	141
Illus 172	Copper alloy strip decorated with lozenge motifs SF102	143
Illus 173	Mould for a decorative boss SF178	143
Illus 174	Impressed mortar from F1063, B104 primary 'farm mound'	144
Illus 175	Area 1 section at Sample Column C	163
Illus 176	Sediment stratigraphy, soil micromorphological stratigraphy, sample numbers and thicknesses and sedimentological data	165
Illus 177	Pollen concentration data, concentration and taxonomic ratios, and preservation data for determinable and indeterminable pollen grains	166
Illus 178	Pollen percentage data, concentrations of major taxa (inset within bars of *Calluna*, Gramineae <8 µm anl-D, Compositae Liguliflorae), pollen sums and microscopic charcoal counts.	168
Illus 179	Diatom diagram	170
Illus 180	Contour model of natural surface of till	188
Illus 181	Contour model showing depth of LIA and earlier deposits	189
Illus 182	Contour model of the LIA ground surface	190
Illus 183	Orthographic projection showing depth of Norse and later deposits	191
Illus 184	Expanded view of past and present ground surfaces	192

Tables

Table 1	Block-Phase Concordance	23
Table 2	Comparison of anthropogenic inputs to Blocks 248 & 250:305	31
Table 3	Comparison of anthropogenic inputs to surface deposits (B231) and post-abandonment deposits (B230) inside Structure 10	79
Table 4	Radiocarbon dates from St Boniface and calibration	97
Table 5	Summary PD curves at 100 years resolution	100–1
Table 6	Summary of the probability distribution of the age difference between Blocks 113 and 115	102
Table 7	Summary of the probability distribution of the age difference between Blocks 215 and 213, adjusted for stratigraphy	103
Table 8	Summary of the probability distribution of the age difference between Blocks 113 and 211, adjusted for stratigraphy	104
Table 9	Summary of the probability distribution of the age difference between Blocks 230 and 238, adjusted for stratigraphy	105
Table 10	Summary of the probability distribution of the age difference between GU-3063 and GU-3065, adjusted for stratigraphy	105
Table 11	Summary of the probability distribution of the age difference between Blocks 107 and 104	106
Table 12	Summary of the probability distribution of the age difference between Blocks 103 and 104, adjusted for stratigraphy	107
Table 13	Cumulative probability distribution for the age of GU-3069c	107
Table 14	Summary of phase distribution of pottery fabric types	108
Table 15	Volume of samples processed by phase	109
Table 16	Anthropogenic inputs to blocks, ordered by phase	110
Table 17	Phase summary of anthropogenic inputs	111
Table 18	Five point scale of relative abundance per 10 l sediment	111
Table 19	Comparison of radiocarbon-dated samples of limpet and winkles	112
Table 20	Vesicular fuel ash content of Area 1 ash deposits	112
Table 21	Summary of excavated structure types	114
Table 22	Sherds and vessel numbers	125
Table 23	Summary of fabric by phase (contexted sherds)	125
Table 24	Summary of surface finish by phase (contexted sherds)	125
Table 25	Metal fragments recovered from samples sorting	144
Table 26	Percentage distribution of bone fragments by phase	147
Table 27	Relative percentages of principal species from pre-Norse and Norse period sites in Orkney	147
Table 28	Cattle measurements	148
Table 29	Sheep measurements	148
Table 30	Cat measurements	148
Table 31	Average fragment weight (g) from bulk sample residues	149
Table 32	Fish bone elements by phase	150
Table 33	Total Gadidae element representation by size and phase	151
Table 34	Cod element representation by size and phase	151
Table 35	Saithe element representation by size and phase	151
Table 36	Block 103 (Phase 8) Gadidae element frequency	152
Table 37	Block 104 (Phase 8) Gadidae element frequency	152
Table 38	Phase 8, Gadidae commonest element representation	154
Table 39	Marine shell: frequency of each taxa by phase	156
Table 40	Carbonized wood	161
Table 41	Summary of micromorphological characteristics: composition	174
Table 42	Summary of micromorphological characteristics: fabric, microstructure and pedofeatures	175
Table 43	Soil thin-section analysis of burnt peat fragments larger than 1 mm in STS 102–111 (Area 1, sample column C) and STS 31–32 (Area 2): (a) Total number in 5 × 7.5 cm section, fragment length (% in each size class) and total length in 5 × 7.5 cm section	176

xvi

Table 44   Soil thin-section analysis of burnt peat fragments larger than 1 mm in STS 102–111
(Area 1, sample column C) and STS 31–32 (Area 2): (b) Percentage mineral content
and maximum grain size of minerals (% in each class)   177
Table 45   Results of soil physical and chemical analyses from selected contexts   178
Table 46   Modern reference samples of organic sediments: summary table of micromorph-
ological characteristics of carbonized residues   180
Table 47   Summary of biological components in selected blocks from Area 1   182
Table 48   Summary of biological components in Blocks 103 and 104 from the four sampling
columns   182
Table 49   Ratio of fuel bulk density to ash bulk density for a range of organic sediments from
Orkney   195
Table 50   Summary of sediment formation in Area 1   197
Table 51   Radiocarbon dates for Early Iron Age roundhouses in Orkney and Caithness   201
Table 52   Early Iron Age roundhouses in Orkney and Caithness   202

Abstract

The excavation assessment at St Boniface church was undertaken by Historic Scotland in May and June 1990 in response to the continuing threat of coastal erosion of the exposed cliff-section adjacent to the church. Coastal erosion represents one of the most serious threats to the archaeological resource, not only in Orkney where the threat is particularly acute, but also elsewhere in Scotland. Although the occasion of the archaeological assessment was specific to this site, a broader specification for the project was the creation and development of a methodology and an approach which would be cost-effective and cost-efficient in tackling other, similarly exposed sites. This report describes the development and execution of the approach which was adopted at St Boniface church.

The results of the assessment clearly demonstrate the chronological depth and physical extent of a site which, over time, has witnessed at least four or five major changes or shifts in its core function from cemetery or Bronze Age settlement to Early and Later Iron Age settlement, from early ecclesiastical site to fish-processing station, to medieval and modern graveyard and church.

The development of the modern-day archae-ological palimpsest at St Boniface church, now most openly manifested in the refurbishment and re-roofing of the medieval church as a local community and ecumenical centre (1994), amid its ancient and modern graveyard, is but the latest facet of a site which extends back at least 5000 years. The formation of the site, as revealed by the excavation assessment, however, is neither a linear nor a chronologically regular progression, but rather one which is temporally diverse, with periods of accelerated change concomitant with others of stability or gradual decline. It is clear, for example in the change from funerary to domestic site, or from domestic to ecclesiastical, that changes in the core function of the site were, seemingly, abrupt, to the extent that such events can be measured archaeologically. At other times, however, particularly with regard to the relationship of the early medieval ecclesiastical site, its medieval and modern successor and the establishment and subsequent demise of what was essentially an adjacent fish processing 'station', it is clear that these core functions must have overlapped like interconnected cogs in an antique chronometer, physically and even functionally discrete but, nonetheless, each a chronologically linkable, and in part contemporary, aspect of the movement.

Possibly from its early beginnings as a settlement site or its use as a burial ground in the second or late third millennium BC, but certainly from the period of the Early Iron Age and Iron Age settlement, in all its phases of development and superimposition, and the early ecclesiastical and 'farm mound' complex, the site appears to have been one of high status, at least within its local island context. On at least two occasions in its development, in its early ecclesiastical and 'farm mound' phases, the site is likely to have been of importance outwith its immediate locality. This report traces the development of the settlement complex at St Boniface church and describes the project design and its execution, against the archaeological and historical background to the site, together with discussion and synthesis of its results. This report supersedes the earlier interim accounts (Lowe 1990; 1993a).

This volume is published with the aid of a grant from Historic Scotland

Acknowledgements

The project was funded and arranged by Historic Scotland and undertaken by archaeologists from Historic Scotland Archaeological Operations & Conservation, formerly the Central Excavation Unit (Scotland). The project was directed by the principal author, assisted by Alan Duffy, Jane Hewitt and the excavation staff: Gillian Carpenter, Jon Hall, Scott Kenney, Bridget Peacock, Rob Schofield and Alan Stapf. Samples processing, on site, was undertaken by Phil Miller. The survey was conducted by Magnar Dalland and Stephen Carter. Additional help on site was also provided by Jocelyn Rendall and special thanks are due to the Rendalls of Holland and Micklegarth for assistance with the transportation of the equipment to and from the site. Thanks are due too to the landowners, Mr Bill Irvine of Links and Messrs Rendall of Whitecraig, for permission to excavate on their land. Thanks also to Paul and Maggie, Jocelyn and Neil and all the folk of Papay for making our stay on the island so enjoyable and memorable. By way of return, it would seem that our container, brim-full of equipment and samples, which proved too much for the winches on the *Orcadia*, and our marquee, which served as our 'tea-hut' and sieving station, have entered local folklore (Hewitson 1996, 38).

The post-excavation analysis, undertaken at HS-AOC and subsequently at AOC (Scotland) Ltd, was coordinated by Dr Stephen Carter and Dr Coralie Mills. The artefact reports were coordinated by Dr Ann MacSween. Specialist analyses were undertaken by the authors of the various reports. I am particularly grateful to Stephen Carter for his specialist contributions (shells and soils) and for his palaeoenvironmental synthesis.

The principal illustrators were Emma Carter (plans) and Christina Unwin (artefacts). Additional illustrations and amendments were also provided by Sylvia Stevenson, to whom I am also grateful for her fine drawing of the weaving baton (Illus 171).The stratigraphic matrix diagrams were drawn by David McAleese. Site photographs were taken by the excavation team. The photograph of the possible shrine panel fragment (Illus 4) was kindly provided by Raymond Lamb. Thanks are due to the whole project team, to all the excavation staff who laboured in not the best of weather that Orkney can offer and to all the illustrators, post-excavation specialists and technicians who have made this report possible. The text was copy-edited by Duncan McAra.

Parts 5 and 6 were written by the various contributors over the period 1992–93. Parts 1 and 2 were completed over the winter of 1993, Part 3 (spring 1994), Part 4 (summer 1994) and Part 7 was finally completed over the autumn and winter of 1994. The text was brought to first full draft in March 1995. The final copy-edited text, together with amended illustrations, was completed, prior to publication submission in December 1996.

I am grateful to the Historic Scotland inspectors, particularly Olwyn Owen, who managed the project for Historic Scotland, Patrick Ashmore, Noel Fojut and Ian Armit, who kindly commented on the text. Sections of the report were also read by Dr Raymond Lamb. I am also grateful to my colleagues at Headland Archaeology, Stephen Carter, Magnar Dalland and Timothy Holden, not only for their patience during the final preparation of this text, but also for their discussions and comments, particularly on the Orcadian Iron Age and aspects of the palaeoenvironmental evidence. Any errors that remain are my own.

Lastly, my thanks go to my wife, Jane, for all her help during the fieldwork and for her forbearance over the months and years that this report has been in the making.

Headland Archaeology Ltd, Edinburgh.
24 December 1996.

Specialist acknowledgements

Sheila Boardman (macroplants) wishes to thank the following for their assistance in the processing and sorting of the samples: Sarah Aldred, Patricia Allan, Galo Cerón-Carassco, Mary Hunter, Robin Johnston, Richard Jones, Phil Miller, Andrea Riedl, Sarah Whitehead, and particularly Ruby Cerón-Carassco and Jennifer Thoms. I am also grateful to Mrs Camilla Dickson, Department of Botany, University of Glasgow, for some useful tips regarding the identification of sedge seeds.

Richard Tipping (pollen) is grateful to Richard Kynoch for the care and patience in developing the fine-resolution techniques employed here, and for the pollen preparations and sedimentological analyses. Stephen Carter helpfully discussed many aspects of the site.

Abbreviations used in this report

B	block number
c	corrected for marine reservoir effect (suffix to radiocarbon laboratory codes)
F	context number
LCR	Long Continuous Range (of radiocarbon dates)
OD	Ordnance Datum
ON	Old Norse
PD	Probability Distribution (of radiocarbon dates)
PTS	pottery thin-section
Rt	Retent (used of artefacts recovered from samples processing)
SCR	Short Continuous Range (of radiocarbon dates)
SF	small find
STS	soil thin-section
V	vessel

Contributors

Sheila Boardman	c/o Historic Scotland, Longmore House, Salisbury Place, Edinburgh EH9 1SH.
Stephen Carter	Headland Archaeology Ltd, Albion Business Centre Unit B4, 78 Albion Road, Edinburgh EH7 5QZ.
Ann Clark	Rockville Lodge, Kingston, East Linton, East Lothian.
Ruby Cerón-Carrasco	Department of Archaeology, University of Edinburgh.
Anne Crone	AOC (Scotland) Ltd, 4 Lochend Road, Leith, Edinburgh EH6 8BR.
Magnar Dalland	Headland Archaeology Ltd, Albion Business Centre Unit B4, 78 Albion Road, Edinburgh EH7 5QZ.
Dianne Dixon	170 Newbattle Abbey Crescent, Dalkeith, EH22 3LS.
Sheila Hamilton-Dyer	5 Suffolk Avenue, Shirley, Southampton SO15 5EF.
Daphne Home Lorimer	Scorradale House, Orphir, Orkney KW17 2RF.
Christopher Lowe	Headland Archaeology Ltd, Albion Business Centre Unit B4, 78 Albion Road, Edinburgh EH7 5QZ.
Finbar McCormick	Department of Archaeology & Palaeoecology, Queens University, Belfast.
Gerry McDonnell	Department of Archaeological Science, University of Bradford.
Ann MacSween	2 Eden Terrace, Edinburgh.
David Mann	Royal Botanic Garden, Inverleith Row, Edinburgh.
Jenny Shiels	57 Brunswick Street, Edinburgh.
Richard Tipping	Department of Environmental Science, University of Stirling FK9 4LA.
Graeme Wilson	EASE, Unit 8 Abbeymount Techbase, 2 Easter Road, Edinburgh EH7 5AN.

PART 1

Physical, Historical and Archaeological Background

Christopher Lowe

1.1 Introduction

1.1.1 Physical Background

Papa Westray, known locally as Papay, is one of the outermost of the northern isles of the Orkney archipelago (Illus 1). It is a small island, roughly 7 km long and 2 km wide, and generally low lying but bounded by high cliffs to the north and south-east. The shoreline is punctuated by a series of broad sandy bays on the south and east but, in the main, the west side of the island, particularly in the vicinity of the excavated site, is now only poorly accessible by boat.

The island is a rich landscape, with fertile soils and an abundance of available and easily split flagstone for building. In the later medieval rentals or *skat* (tax) registers (Peterkin 1820; Thomson 1996), a series of documents that provides a basis on which to compare the relative productive wealth of the different islands, Papay was assessed as 4 urislands, in comparison with roughly 13 and 36 urislands, respectively, for the much larger islands of Westray and Sanday. In terms of its local resources and the extent of good cultivable land, relative to its size, Papay is one of the most fertile and agriculturally productive of the Orkney islands. In the *Old Statistical Account* entry for 1794, in testimony to the island's economic status as implied in the much earlier rental evidence, Papay was considered to contain

> some of the best pasture and arable lands in the whole country; and, to appearance, there is a greater proportion of this island under cultivation than that of the island of Westray.
> (Withrington & Grant 1978, 357)

The soil parent material of the island comprises, in the main, drift derived from flagstones, sandstones and mudstones of the Stromness, Rousay and Eday Flags groups of Middle Old Red Sandstone rocks, interspersed with shell sand (Mykura 1976). The hill ground at the north end of the island, beyond the hill-dyke, comprises thin soils, peaty gleys, occasional thin peat and rock outcrops. Elsewhere, to the south

of the hill-dyke, the local soils are characterized by freely drained brown calcareous soils on the shell sand areas at the south end of the island and along much of the central coastal region. Inland, although the term is relative, given the size of the island, the soils are dominated by freely or imperfectly drained podzols. Much of the land below the hill-dyke constitutes good pasture, with potential for arable cultivation.

The only notable deficiency on the island, aside from the lack of trees, a factor common to much of Orkney in both the historic and prehistoric periods, is the lack of any significant peat resource. In this respect, Papay most closely resembles, not the adjacent island of Westray, but the islands of Sanday and North Ronaldsay, two of the north-easternmost of the outer isles group. The archaeology of these three islands also has in common a monument type which is otherwise restricted in its distribution. 'Farm mounds' and associated landforms are discussed below (Part 1.2.4).

1.1.2 The Threat

The old medieval parish church and graveyard stand above an eroded shoreline on the north-west coast of the island (Illus 1) where erosion, caused by the wind and the action of the sea, is active. The problem is exacerbated by the craggy nature of the local offshore topography which has the effect of channelling the full force of the Atlantic into parts of the cliff-section. The similarly exposed Neolithic farmstead of Knap of Howar (Ritchie 1983) lies roughly 2 km to the south of St Boniface church.

An extensive Iron Age settlement, known locally as *Munkerhoose* (RCAHMS 1946, ii, 184, no. 526), is located under and to the west of the church. The church is dedicated to Boniface, a saint traditionally associated with the Northumbrian mission to the Picts in the early eighth century.

A large mound, previously described as a 'farm mound' (Lamb 1983a, 7, 18), lies to the north of the church. The 'farm mound' has been identified as the *Binnas Kirk* (< ON *boen-hus*, prayer house, chapel) of the local oral tradition and has been postulated as the

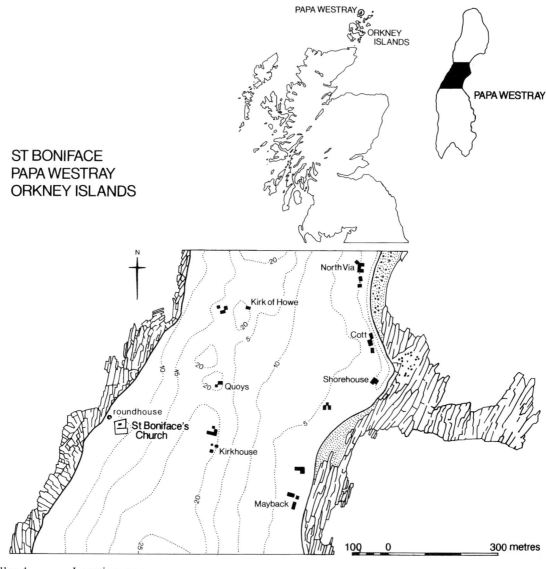

ST BONIFACE
PAPA WESTRAY
ORKNEY ISLANDS

Illus 1   Location map

site of a separate ecclesiastical building (Marwick 1925, 34; Lamb 1983a, 18). An alternative identification for the Binnas Kirk site is explored below (Part 2.2.4).

Prior to excavation, the exposed cliff-section, roughly 125 m long, was characterized as basically consisting of a series of outbuildings, clustered around a large roundhouse or broch, with further outbuildings to the north, and the 'farm mound' beyond. Superimposed structures and deposits were clearly evident in the area immediately adjacent to the roundhouse. None, however, could be discerned at the north end of the exposed cliff-section where the 'farm mound' sediments predominated. The two settlement mounds, one dominated by stone, the other composed almost wholly of fine mineral sediments, were exposed, to varying degrees, in the eroded cliff-section. The worst affected areas were those in the vicinity of

the roundhouse and at the north end of the exposure where the 'farm mound' and roughly a 2 m depth of till and rock below were being actively undercut.

The purpose of the excavation assessment of the exposed cliff-section was not simply to record the archaeological remains in advance of their destruction, although the action taken in 1990 was seen to be fully justified when large parts of the section in the vicinity of the remains of the roundhouse were swept away in the violent storms of January and February 1993. More important, given the extensive nature of the threat of coastal erosion to the archaeological resource, particularly around the coasts of Scotland, Historic Scotland was concerned to develop a cost-effective means of tackling the assessment of large, extensive, deep sites with complex stratigraphy. The methodology adopted at St Boniface is described in Part 2.

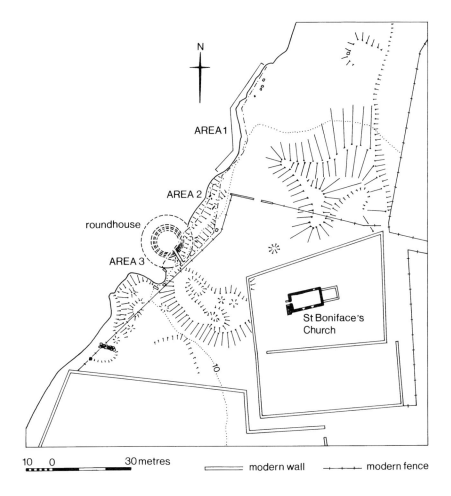

Illus 2   Survey plan

1.2 Archaeological and Historical Background

1.2.1 Introduction

In all, the settlement complex at St Boniface church (Illus 2) extends roughly 100 m inland, nearly 200 m along the coast and is up to 4 m deep in places and, as such, represents one of the largest and deepest archaeological sites known in Orkney. The excavation assessment has also demonstrated the great chronological depth which the present-day landform conceals (Part 4.6).

As individual elements of an archaeological palimpsest, St Boniface church, the 'farm mound' and the Munkerhoose settlement complex are impressive monuments in their own right. Together, however, they have been described as 'an assemblage of the greatest historical importance' (Lamb 1983a, 8), in large measure a reflection of the hypothesis that the site was the premier ecclesiastical missionary centre for Orkney, and beyond, in the pre-Viking period, and one that had been appended to or developed out of a high status settlement of the Late Iron Age (Lamb

1993). In this context, the appreciation of the chronological position or association of the 'farm mound' complex, with regard to the Iron Age or later ecclesiastical settlement on the site, and the investigation of what is a rare and poorly understood monument type in the British Isles, could well be considered something of a bonus.

It was anticipated, therefore, prior to the start of the field project, that the assessment was likely to clarify the structural and depositional site sequence in terms, at least, of the early medieval and later ecclesiastical site, the 'farm mound' and the underlying Iron Age settlement complex, the latter dominated by a substantial roundhouse or broch. These four themes are now considered in more detail, in roughly reverse chronological order.

1.2.2 The Later Medieval Ecclesiastical Site

1.2.21 Introduction

The archaeological and historical context for the later medieval ecclesiastical site at St Boniface rests with the church itself, a coped stone of the hogback series

Illus 3   St Boniface church, from SW, prior to restoration

and an allusion to the island, tentatively the site itself, in a reference in the *Orkneyinga Saga*.

1.2.22 St Boniface church (Illus 3)

The church, recently re-roofed and refurbished, is largely an early eighteenth-century rebuild of an originally twelfth-century nave and chancel church (RCAHMS 1946, ii, 179, no. 518; Marwick 1925, 33). In its present form a unicameral building with an external western staircase, the church is reported to have been extended to the west in 1700 (RCAHMS 1946, ii, 179) or *c*. 1720 (Marwick 1925, 33), an event which Marwick has suggested may have been contemporary with the abandonment and demolition of the old chancel and its subsequent utilization as a burial plot for the Traill family, the former lairds of the island. The site of the old chancel arch is visible in outline as a void in the plaster on the building's eastern exterior wall-face, suggesting that much of the east gable, at least, preserves the medieval fabric of the church.

1.2.23 Hogback stone

A coped stone lies to the east of the old chancel. It is oriented and has a plain upright slab set at its west end. Carved from sandstone, a deep channel has been cut along the ridge of the stone, to either side of which are three rows of rectangular tegulae. The stone is considered to be related to the Scottish series of hogback monuments and has been assigned, on typological grounds, to the twelfth century (Lang 1974, 220, 230). According to local tradition, current earlier this century but referring to the period *c*. 1800 (Kirkness 1921, 132), the stone is said to have been recovered, from Herti Geo, a rocky inlet on the coast 400 m to the north of the church, whence it was brought to serve as a grave cover. It seems unlikely, however, that the stone has ever been in the sea and the tale has thus generally been discredited (Kirkness 1921, 132; Lang 1974, 230). Interestingly, however, as Morris (1985a, 240) has pointed out, the tradition would seem to confirm that the stone was still then perceived as a grave monument.

1.2.24 Saga reference

The murder of Rognvald Brusison, Earl of Orkney, on Papa Stronsay and his subsequent burial on Papa Westray is recorded in the *Orkneyinga Saga* (cap XXX: Taylor 1938, 185). The event occurred *c*. AD 1046 and his removal effectively left Thorfinn, his uncle, the sole earl in Orkney.

The history of Orkney in the first half of the eleventh century is essentially that of rivalry and the consolidation of power by Thorfinn, overturning an earlier arrangement whereby the sons and, in turn, the grandsons of Earl Sigurd the Stout had shared the earldom between them (*Orkneyinga Saga*: Thomson 1987, 43–53). The basis upon which the islands were divided and shared by the contemporary earls is poorly understood. The only explicit reference in the *Orkneyinga Saga* (cap XX) concerns Earl Brusi, whose share is said to have comprised 'the northernmost part of the islands'. Indeed, it is the same part of Orkney in which Rognvald, his son and successor, is seen to have been active (Thomson 1987, 45).

By having Rognvald Brusison's body returned to Papay for burial, it is clear that his family would have been seen as re-establishing their links, not only with the island itself but with the outer isle estates which had belonged to Earl Brusi. The site of the burial, however, is not known. Taylor (1938, 367) has suggested that Rognvald would have been buried at St Tredwell's chapel, a small promontory site in the Loch of St Tredwell. If, on the other hand, there was an established missionary bishopric or similar high-status ecclesiastical site at St Boniface church, as seems possible (Part 1.2.35), this and not St Tredwell's chapel would seem the more appropriate place for Rognvald's interment.

It is many years since R. W. Southern (1953, 133) pointed out:

> The most revealing map of Europe [in the medieval period] would be a map, not of political or commercial capitals, but of the constellation of sanctuaries, the points of material contact with the unseen world. The resting places of the saints were the chief centres of ecclesiastical organisation and of spiritual life.

In a similar vein, the chosen resting places of kings and earls can be seen to be equally significant. Rognvald's burial at St Boniface church, like Thorfinn's later burial in his church, Christchurch, at Birsay (*Orkneyinga Saga* cap XXXI: Taylor 1938), would have been a clear political statement to contemporaries of matters concerning inheritance and birthright. In this light, the contest between Thorfinn and Rognvald for the earldom may have reflected, and its outcome ultimately have decided, the fate of their two churches and, indeed, the Orcadian bishopric.

The late eleventh-century account (Part 1.2.35) in Adam of Bremen's *History of the Archbishops of Hamburg–Bremen* of Turolf's appointment to the Orcadian episcopate,

> Ad easdem insulae Orchadas, quamvis prius ab Anglorum et Scothorum episcopis regerentur, noster primas iussu papae ordinavit Turolfum episcopum in civitatem Blasconam, qui omnium curas ageret
>
> (*Gesta hammaburgensis ecclesiae pontificum* IV,34)

> For these same Orkney Islands, *although they had previously been ruled by English and Scottish bishops*, our primate on the pope's orders consecrated Throlf bishop for the city of Birsay, and *he was to have the cure of all*.
>
> (Tschan 1959, 216 [my italics])

is probably one of the most significant passages, for Orkney, in the work. It not only acknowledges the presence of a much earlier stratum of ecclesiastical activity in Orkney (discussed below, Part 1.2.35), but more importantly, in the present context, confirms that Throlf, at Birsay, 'was to have the cure of all', the implication being that another or other candidates were or had been in contention for the appointment. Political and episcopal rivalry, the claims and counter-claims of appointed bishops, supported by rival candidates for the earldom, is a recurrent theme in the history of Orkney for the later eleventh and early twelfth centuries (Crawford 1983; Lowe 1987, i, 27–32).

There seems, moreover, to be a clear correspondence, both chronologically and in the events described, between Adam's *Gesta* and the *Orkneyinga Saga* account of Thorfinn's establishment of the bishopric and minster church at Birsay:

> Hann sat jafnan í Byrgisheraði ok lét þar gera Kristskirkju, dýrligt musteri, þar var fyrst settr byskupsstóll í Orkneyjum.
>
> *Orkneyinga Saga* (cap XXXI)

> He [Thorfinn] lived usually in Birsay, and had Christ's Kirk built there, a magnificent church. The Episcopal seat in the Orkneys was first established there.
>
> (Taylor 1938, 189)

The link between the earldom and the episcopate in eleventh-century Orkney, whether expressed in physical or political terms, is exemplified by Thorfinn's establishment of the bishopric at Birsay. In this light, his victory over Rognvald could be interpreted as not only a political, but also as an ecclesiastical, watershed. Indeed, the ecclesiastical repercussions of Rognvald's defeat at the hands of Thorfinn in 1046 and the subsequent establishment of the Orcadian episcopacy at Birsay might well have been the demise of a rival and more ancient episcopate centre on Rognvald's estates in the Outer Isles, most arguably the site at St Boniface church itself.

1.2.25 Summary

The archaeological and historical assemblage for the later medieval ecclesiastical site at St Boniface church is fragmentary and its elements diverse in kind. The twelfth-century church, a building of some sophistication, and the hogback-type monument, together indicate access to patronage and some degree of contact with developments further afield. The earldom connection with Papay in the eleventh century, with Brusi and his son Rognvald, is particularly important. In many ways, this connection could be considered to form a plausible link between the earlier and later medieval ecclesiastical phases of the site's history.

1.2.3 The Early Medieval Ecclesiastical Site

1.2.31 Introduction

The archaeological and historical context for the early medieval ecclesiastical site at St Boniface church rests with the discovery of two cross-inscribed stones, a third stone, ostensibly part of a composite corner-post shrine of Early Christian type, the place-name and dedication evidence, and a possible allusion to the site in an early Irish *Life*.

Also of this early period, although not explicitly ecclesiastical, are a number of bone comb fragments which were recovered from an exposed midden section in 1975. The grid reference would place the discovery at the southern end of the 'farm mound',

although whether above or below the Late Iron Age ground surface (Block 105: Part 3.2.9) is not known. Block 107 deposits (Part 3.2.9), comprising mixed midden material would seem the most likely source for these artefacts. The fragments have been likened to combs of seventh- or eighth-century date (Arnold 1975).

1.2.32 Cross-inscribed stones

An early ecclesiastical presence on the site is indicated by discoveries, during grave-digging, of two cross-inscribed stones of pre-Norse type (Kirkness 1921, 134; Radford 1962, 169; Lowe 1987, ii, 122–6).

The first (RMS: IB 200) was found in 1920, on the north side of the church, 0.9 m below ground. The slab was broken during grave-digging, the remaining part being left in the ground. The extant piece displays on one face a cross-pattée within a circle. The circle is surmounted by a small incised cross with crescentic terminals and a pedestal base (Kirkness 1921, fig. 3). Radford (1962, 169) has suggested that the stone is unlikely to be much later than *c*. AD 700.

Illus 4   Shrine panel fragment (1:1)

The second stone, unearthed in 1966 or 1967 and now in Tankerness House Museum, Kirkwall, was also found on the north side of the church, close to the north-east corner of the medieval nave and roughly 0.3 m below ground (W. Irvine, pers comm). The stone is a worn beach boulder and displays on one face a square-armed cross set above an encircled cross-pattée (Lowe 1987, ii, pl. 37). Faintly incised figures or designs are visible to the left of the square-armed cross and there are traces of a rectilinear pattern, possibly representing a robed human figure, on the reverse (Lamb 1983a, 18). The stone probably dates to the last quarter of the first millennium AD.

1.2.33 Shrine panel fragment (Illus 4)

A small fragment (136 × 94 mm) of what has been identified as part of a panel from a composite corner-post shrine (R.G. Lamb, pers comm), the first known from Orkney, was recovered from the beach below the excavated cliff-section in June 1992. A number of pecked and smoothed grooves on the face of the panel, forming a cross, suggest that it was originally divided into at least four fields. The width of the panel, on the basis of symmetry, could be reconstructed as approximately 200 mm. As such, the slab, although small, would have most likely formed an end panel.

A rectangular design, possibly the Pictish 'rectangle' or 'comb-case' feature, is set in the upper right-hand field. The only surviving original edge is rebated, ostensibly for insertion into the mortice of a corner-post.

On the basis of decoration, aspect and references preserved in various of Bede's writings, Thomas (1973a, 20; 1983, 287–92) has cogently argued that such shrines would normally have been erected against the east wall of the church, to the south of the altar or in the south-east corner. On this basis, the decoration on the St Boniface panel would have been visible to celebrants on entering the church.

The remains of four composite corner-post shrines have been identified at Papil, and another two at St Ninian's Isle, both in Shetland (Thomas 1973a). Overall, the corner-post shrine has an essentially eastern Scottish or 'Pictish' distribution and this, together with art-historical links, has led Thomas (1971, 150–63; 1973a; 1973b; 1983) to consider the type as an essentially Northumbrian-inspired monument form, dating principally to the eighth century.

1.2.34 Toponymy

The toponymy of the island, with its *papar* place-name element, and the dedication evidence for Saints Boniface and Tredwell, together, provides a wealth of significant place-name evidence of early type. Add to this the possible St Moluag dedication, which was proposed by Marwick (1925, 35–6) for the ecclesiastical site at Kirk of Hoo (Lowe 1987, ii,

127–30), 450 m to the north-east, and the traditional nunnery site on the Holms of Aikerness (Brand 1701, 51; Lowe 1987, ii, 155–8), a series of small skerries and islets in Papa Sound immediately south-west of St Boniface church, and the island's Early Christian past seems almost tangible.

The *papar* place-names have traditionally been viewed as the sites of an Irish eremitical clergy. This was certainly the case in Iceland, as is made explicit in the opening sections of *Landnámabók* (Benediktsson 1968), compiled *c.* 1097 x 1125, and Ari Thorgilsson's slightly later *Islendingabók* (Benediktsson 1968). *Papae* are also identified in the late twelfth-century *Historia Norwegiae* (Storm 1880, 88–9) as one element in the pre-Norse population in Orkney.

The tendency to view the Orkney and Shetland papar place-names as the sites of an eremitical clergy has been put most forcefully by MacDonald (1977, 109) who, in considering their distribution and location, concluded that 'a strong eremitical element among the *papar* seems to be indicated by this emphasis on small islands and extreme marginal areas'. Close examination of the local setting in which these place-names are found, reinforced by the evidence of the later rental documents (Peterkin 1820; Thomson 1996), however, makes this argument untenable (Lowe 1987, i, 351–4). In the later medieval period, the farmsteads and districts with *papar* names were among the largest and most heavily taxed areas in the parish. Far from being established in marginal areas, it is clear that the *papar* place-names are closely associated with agriculturally productive and thus populated districts and as such can hardly reflect the settlements of eremitical groups and individuals. In other words, the *papar* place-names, as Lamb (1983a; 1993) has also remarked, are clearly related to missionary, and not eremitical, activity.

Marwick (1925, 35) was the first to point out the significance of the unique occurrence together, and especially on a small island like Papay, of dedications to both St Boniface and St Tredwell, traditionally members of the Northumbrian mission to the Picts (Skene 1867; MacKinley 1914, 476; MacDonald 1992), recorded by Bede (*HE* v, 2: Colgrave & Mynors 1969, 532–53) in *c.* 710 x 715.

The cult of St Tredwell was certainly popular in medieval Orkney (Lowe 1987, ii, 144–7). However, the Northumbrian association and the later obscurity which surrounds St Boniface suggest strongly that the dedications, together, would have been out of place in a Norse Christian cultural milieu, and, on this basis, would belong most appropriately to the period prior to the Norse settlement of the islands. Indeed, Lamb (1983a, 8) has suggested the dedications commemorate the Northumbrian mission to the Picts, and, on a broader scale, reflect the re-alignment of the Early Christian Church in Scotland along a Roman-based ecclesiastical orthodoxy. At the very least, as Thomson (1987, 10) has pointed out, the dedications demonstrate the presence of a cult which had its base in Northumbrian territory and, as such, is suggestive of a link between the Orkney papae, the early bishops of the pre-Norse episcopate (Part 1.2.35) and the Northumbrian mission to Pictland.

1.2.35 The pre-Norse episcopate in Orkney and the *Life* of St Findan

Historical documentation for the pre-Norse episcopate in Orkney is slight and, in part, obscure. Most of what does survive comes down to us, almost as asides, in the records compiled on behalf of the later, established Norse episcopate.

Adam of Bremen's *Gesta hammaburgensis ecclesiae pontificum*, written in *c*. 1072 x 1076 and later revised in *c*. 1076 x 1085 (Tschan 1959, xvi), is a virtually contemporary record for the development of the Church in Orkney for the period *c*. 1035–72, a time which almost coincides with Thorfinn's rise and consolidation of power.

The Church at Hamburg–Bremen under Archbishop Adalbert (1042–72) had become, according to Adam, 'like Rome, known far and wide and was devoutly sought from all parts of the world' (*Gesta* III, 23). Indeed, legates with requests for priests came from Iceland, Greenland and Orkney. Barbara Crawford (1983, 103), for example, has suggested that the *Orkneyinga Saga* (cap. XXXI) account of Thorfinn's journey to Rome, via Denmark and Germany, in *c*. 1050 may have been undertaken as such a delegation. In any event, it is clear that Hamburg–Bremen was certainly making episcopal appointments to Orkney from the mid-eleventh century (*Gesta* IV, 34: Part 1.2.24).

The association of the Orcadian Church with the archiepiscopacy in Hamburg–Bremen in the second half of the eleventh century, and after 1103 with Lund, did not go unchallenged. Rival appointees were nominated by York throughout the eleventh and early twelfth centuries. Indeed, the archiepiscopacy at York had long claimed authority over all the bishops of Scotland, and Crawford (1983, 105) has suggested that York would have appointed bishops to Orkney long before the Viking Age. The traditional association with York was certainly appealed to in 1073 when Earl Paul Thorfinnsson sent Bishop Ralph to Thomas Archbishop of York, urging him to consecrate his bishop 'antecessorum tuorum ordine custodito' (Haddan & Stubbs 1873, ii, (i), 162). Heinricus, described by Adam of Bremen (*Gesta* IV, 8) as having previously been a bishop in Orkney, may, from his association with Canute (*ob.* 1035), have been an early eleventh-century York appointment. The names of other, earlier appointments, however, are not known. That such existed, however, is clearly implied in Adam's acknowledgement that English and Scottish bishops had previously been appointed to Orkney (*Gesta* IV, 34: Part 1.2.24).

A listing of references to putative early bishops of Orkney, clearly unrelated to the later Norse Church in Orkney, has been collated by Kolsrud (1913). The material, however, is derived from various late, obscure and disparate sources. Nonetheless, possibly of some significance is the reference to a feast day on 6 April which was observed in Kirkwall in commemoration of *Berthami episcopi Orcadum sanctissimi*, possibly the same figure as 'S Bercham bishop and confessor in scotland under king kennede' (Kolsrud 1913, 377); the latter evidently a reference to Kenneth MacAlpin, king of the Picts and Scots in the mid-ninth century.

Early bishops in Orkney are also referred to in another, seemingly reliable source, independent of Adam's *Gesta*, the *Vita Findani* (Holder-Egger 1887; Thomson 1986; Omand 1986). The *Life*, which was probably composed in an Irish house on the Continent in the latter part of the ninth century by a fellow Irishman and acquaintance of the saint (Holder-Egger 1887, 502; Thomson 1986, 279), is a virtually contemporary record of the events described. Saint Findan himself was admitted to holy orders in 851 and his sojourn in Orkney can be dated no later than the period 840 x 850. He is believed to have died in 878, his entire religious life having been spent on the Continent (Thomson 1986, 279).

The early sections of the *Life* describe a local feud in his native Leinster, Findan's subsequent betrayal to a Viking slave-raiding party and his intended transportation back to Norway. During an enforced sojourn in Orkney, during which the raiding party rested and awaited a fair wind, Findan was able to make good his escape from an uninhabited island. On meeting a group of strangers, he was subsequently taken to a bishop whose episcopal seat was nearby (*tunc illi susceptum eum ad vicinae civitatis duxerunt episcopum*: Holder-Egger 1887, 505), and with whom he stayed for two years. Interestingly, the *Life* goes on to remark that the bishop:

> had been instructed in the study of letters in Ireland and was quite skilled in the knowledge of this language.
>
> (Omand 1986, 287)

from which it has been inferred that the bishop was a native Pict (Thomson 1986, 280). An English origin, however, might be equally appropriate and, perhaps, more likely. Nonetheless, the fact that, seemingly, only the bishop could converse with Findan suggests quite strongly that the other members of the community might well have been native Picts. In any event, as Thomson (1986, 283; 1987, 40) has stressed, the significance of the *Vita Findani* is that it provides good evidence for the survival of an episcopally organized Christian community in Orkney as late as the mid-ninth century.

The *Vita Findani* corroborates Adam's acknowledgement in the *Gesta* that earlier, pre-eleventh-century bishops had been appointed to the Orcadian bishopric from outwith and prior to the assumption of ecclesiastical jurisdiction by the archiepiscopacy of Hamburg–Bremen. Indeed, the physical presence of Findan's episcopal ally suggests strongly that such appointments, perhaps the majority, were by no means necessarily nominal. On this basis, the late references to early bishops in Orkney, as collated by Kolsrud (1913), may in part provide some evidence for an episcopally organized church in Orkney, prior to the eleventh century, as anticipated in the *Vita* and reflected in Adam's *Gesta*.

The site of the bishop's seat to which Findan was taken is not explicitly stated. Thomson (1986, 280–3) has advanced the suggestion, based principally on topographical evidence in the *Life*, that the island on which Findan was disembarked during the voyage may well have been the Holm of Papay, a small island on the east side of Papay opposite South Wick, itself a favourable landing site in the bay. On this basis, the neighbouring island to which Findan escaped would be Papay itself and the bishop's seat could most appropriately be identified, albeit speculatively, as the site of St Boniface church.

1.2.36 Summary

The archaeological and historical evidence for the earlier, pre-Norse ecclesiastical assemblage at St Boniface church, although fragmentary, seems to reflect an association with a Northumbrian cultural milieu. Such a connection is most clearly demonstrated in the dedication evidence and the possible shrine panel fragment, and, more generally, in the historical notices regarding York's ancient ecclesiastical link with Orkney.

The idea that St Findan was taken to St Boniface church and met with its bishop, possibly the Bishop Bercham who is identified in Kolsrud's (1913) collation of records of the early bishops of Orkney, can only be advanced as speculation. Nonetheless, it is not inconceivable, as Lamb has advocated in a series of articles and presentations, that the site of St Boniface church, the Munkerhoose of the local oral tradition, was one of the principal ecclesiastical settlements associated with an eighth-century Northumbrian-based Christian mission to the north of Scotland (Lamb 1983a; 1993; 1995). Moreover, and perhaps significantly, this is an idea which can be inferred from both ends of an Early Christian chronology, from Thomson's (1986) speculative interpretation of the *Vita Findani* for the ninth century and earlier, and the historical reconstruction of the political and ecclesiastical implications of Rognvald Brusison's career in the early eleventh century (see above).

In summary, a case exists that St Boniface church was an important early ecclesiastical centre, possibly the seat of a pre-Norse bishopric, which was associated with the eighth-century Northumbrian mission to Pictland.

1.2.4 The 'Farm Mound'

1.2.41 Introduction

The large mound (Illus 2), immediately to the north of St Boniface church, and also exposed in the adjacent cliff-section to the north of the Iron Age settlement focus, has been described as a typical 'farm mound' (Lamb 1983a, 18). The monument type has also been identified on Sanday and North Ronaldsay (Davidson, Lamb & Simpson 1983; Davidson, Harkness & Simpson 1986). In Arctic Norway, where the monument type has been most extensively explored and where the type has been defined, two basic causation models have been advanced to account for their formation. In one, the stockfish model, the site formation processes have been considered as a gross accumulation of deposits which would otherwise have been dispersed. In the second, the structure model, the formation of the farm mound has been considered as an accumulation of deposits created by *in situ* rebuilding on the site over time.

1.2.42 The stockfish model

One of the earliest farm mound excavations was undertaken at Grunnfarnes by Munch in the early 1960s. It was this excavation that prompted an initial hypothesis that farm mounds accumulated as a result of a major shift in the economy of northern Norway, involving a move away from stock-raising towards an economy in which fishing and stockfish production became dominant (Munch 1966). The stockfish trade, a response to the demand for dried white meat, is a well-documented historical phenomenon (Sandnes 1977, 170–6), associated with demographic changes, in particular the rise of urban centres in England and on the Continent, and the lenten fare regulations of the Catholic Church.

Bergen was the principal Norwegian entrepôt for the trade throughout the medieval period, receiving dried fish from production areas such as Vågan, Lofoten (Bertelsen 1985a; Bertelsen & Urbanczyk 1988) in northern Norway for onward transmission to England and the Continent. The hypothesis that a causal link exists between the stockfish trade and the formation of farm mounds rests heavily on the assumption that dung and other fertilizers, being no longer needed on the fields, were allowed to accumulate in the farmyard. On this model, fish were sold in exchange for grain, a commodity which had either previously been grown at the settlement, in those places where conditions were favourable, or purchased in exchange for cattle and meat products.

1.2.43 The structure model

An alternative model has been proposed by Bertelsen (1979; 1985b; 1989; 1990), based on the preliminary results of a large number of small-scale investigations of farm mounds in northern Norway. This work has suggested that the key factor affecting the formation of these landforms is probably architectural, mound accumulation being the result of the decay and replacement of turf buildings, with some input from midden, manure and windblown sand (Bertelsen 1989; Holm-Olsen 1981). The farm mound, according to this interpretation, is thus a type of settlement mound, composed of structures and other associated occupation detritus. The subject has been discussed most recently by Bertelsen & Lamb (1993).

1.2.44 'Farm mounds' on Sanday, Orkney

Three of the Sanday 'farm mounds' have been partially investigated (Davidson, Harkness & Simpson 1986). The results of this earlier work are considered elsewhere in connection with the site at St Boniface church (Part 7.1). It was suggested that the Sanday mounds had formed as a result of the gradual accumulation of midden material, together with inputs from hearth debris and turves, which for one reason or another was left *in situ* (Davidson, Harkness & Simpson 1986, 58). The implication of this study was that the inherent fertility of the local soils obviated any need for improvement.

1.2.45 Chronology of farm mounds

Most of the Norwegian examples (Bertelsen 1979, 50), like the 'farm mound' at Langskaill on Sanday (Davidson, Harkness & Simpson 1986, 52), have been radiocarbon dated to the medieval period. A post-seventh-century AD date was obtained, by radiocarbon dating, for the formation of the mounds at Skelbrae and Westbrough, also on Sanday (Davidson, Harkness & Simpson 1986, 52). Some of the Norwegian sites, however, have been assigned on the basis of radiocarbon dating to the Iron Age (Bertelsen 1979, 50). Indeed, the argument has been made, in Norway in those places where optimal climatic conditions exist for stable agricultural settlement, that 'farm mound' accumulation extends as far back as the beginnings of sedentary agriculture and settlement (Bertelsen 1979, 53).

1.2.46 Summary and application of the models in Orkney

The current, and most widely accepted, view of the Norwegian farm mounds is that they essentially represent a type of settlement mound, a landform principally composed of organic building material and, as such therefore, not dissimilar from a mound which has been formed by the repeated construction of buildings in stone. On this interpretation, the monument is an artefact of its architecture, its form dependent on the locally available or preferred building medium and its creation the result of similar site formation processes. This structural definition is also prevalent in Icelandic archaeology where it has been applied, for example, to the excavation of the farm mound and later church and graveyard at Stóraborg (Snaesdóttir 1990).

Whether the monument type, as defined in its Norwegian homeland, exists in Orkney, however, is a matter of some debate. Lamb (1980a, 7–8) initially described the Orcadian examples which he found on Sanday as settlement mounds, characterized by the superimposition of stone structures interspersed with periods of sand-blow. Morris (1985a, 226), similarly, has likened the type to mounded sites such as those investigated at Beachview in Birsay, and Skaill (Morris 1985b) or the sites excavated at Saevar Howe (Hedges 1983) and Pool (Hunter *et al* 1993; Hunter *et al* forthcoming). In a later paper, however, Lamb (1983a, 7) has characterized the monument type in a very different way, laying stress on the soil and sediment and 'loamy earth' content and deliberately discounting any element of a stone architecture as an integral part of the mound's formation.

In part, the problem of the Orcadian 'farm mounds' is one of defining the monument type and, that done, of further defining the formation processes which predicated its accumulation. Indeed, the central problem is to resolve the riddle of 'when is a farm mound not a farm mound?' This study's contribution to this debate is considered in detail below (Part 7.1), in the context of the monument type as it is found in Orkney.

1.2.5 The Iron Age Settlement

Extensive, deep remains of an Iron Age (and earlier) settlement, known locally as Munkerhoose, are exposed in the cliff-section on the shore, immediately west of St Boniface church (Illus 2).

The earliest known, comprehensive description of the site dates to 1928, the time of Corrie's visit which was undertaken during the course of the compilation of the Orkney Inventory by the RCAHMS (1946, ii, 184, no. 526):

> The mound at Munker Hoose . . . lies on the sea bank adjoining the Kirk of St. Boniface and the whole area appears to be riddled with remains of stone buildings, the character of which cannot be satisfactorily determined without excavation. All along the edge of the sea bank where the storms and tides lash against the shore there are fragmentary traces of these buildings and at one time within recent years I am told that it was possible to gain an entrance for some distance into the mound through a lintelled passage. . . . Partial excavations have at times been carried out but no definite information as to the results of these efforts is available.
> *RCAHMS Notebook (Orkney) 2 (9 July 1928)*

Previously unrecorded excavations at the site were also noted by Marwick (1925, 33). Indeed, accounts of a Victorian period excavation are still current on the island today (J. Rendall, pers comm). Recent research, based on the results of the fieldwork reported here and post-excavation analysis in the archives of the National Monuments Record of

Scotland (NMRS) and the Society of Antiquaries of Scotland, has tentatively identified Captain Thomas as the likely excavator of the site around the middle of the nineteenth century. A plan of the site, previously credited as the 'Castle of Bothican' (RCAHMS 1946, ii, fig. 226; Hedges 1987, iii, pl.;3.15), a site on the links at the south end of Papay, is also now known (Lowe 1994). The drawing (NMRS: ORD/17/2), by George Petrie, clearly demonstrates that a substantial roundhouse or broch lay at the centre of the Iron Age complex, an idea first anticipated by Marwick (1925, 33) but discounted by Corrie (RCAHMS Notebook (Orkney) 2, 1928) and given only a luke-warm appraisal by the compilers of the Orkney inventory (RCAHMS 1946, ii, 184).

The exposure of the roundhouse and other buildings in the cliff-section forms only one facet of the visible extent of the Iron Age settlement. Structural remains are also known to underlie the churchyard and its modern extension to the south. Several 'cart-loads' of stone are said to have been removed from the churchyard as a result of grave-digging (W. Irvine, pers comm). Sections of dry-stone walling have also been recorded up to 1.5 m below ground along the line of the south wall of the churchyard, near the south-west corner, and another feature, described as a 'passage', was encountered during grave-digging in February 1982 on the west side of the new extension (W. Irvine, pers comm).

Clearly the settlement remains visible in the exposed cliff-section formed only a small part of an extensive Iron Age settlement, centred on a substantial roundhouse or broch. A major element of the assessment was to determine the boundaries of the site, assess its development over time and determine its relationship to the 'farm mound' and the later ecclesiastical site. The chronology of roundhouses, brochs and the enclosure of Iron Age settlements are discussed elsewhere (Part 7.2).

PART 2

Method and Survey

Christopher Lowe

2.1 Project Design

2.1.1 Introduction

The cliff-section at St Boniface church is but one of over a hundred sites in Orkney where coastal erosion has been identified as a major threat to the survival and long-term integrity of the archaeological resource (R.G. Lamb, pers comm). Thus, while the occasion of the archaeological assessment of the cliff-section at St Boniface church was particular to this site, a broader specification for the project was the creation and development of a methodology and an approach which would be both cost-effective and cost-efficient in tackling other, similarly exposed sites.

2.1.2 Research Objectives

Prior to excavation the cliff-section was characterized as basically consisting of a series of outbuildings, clustered around a possible broch or roundhouse, with further outbuildings to the north, and the 'farm mound' beyond (Illus 5–8). Superimposed structures were clearly evident, both in section and on plan, in the area immediately adjacent to the roundhouse. None, however, could be discerned at the north end of the exposed cliff-section where the 'farm mound' sediments predominated. The seemingly better preserved and stable area to the south of the roundhouse was surveyed but otherwise was not investigated by this project. The principal research objectives of the assessment were:

- to determine the horizontal and vertical extent of the site;

- to record the surface remains, their relationship to each other and to the features exposed in the cliff-section;

- to record and characterize the nature of the structures and deposits in the cliff-section, and to retrieve datable and environmental material from appropriate contexts;

- to determine the relationship between the 'farm mound' and the Iron Age settlement;

- to identify the formation processes and date of the 'farm mound';

- to identify the formation processes, date and chronological range of structures in, under and over the Iron Age settlement mound.

The purpose of the assessment was thus to clarify the nature, date, quality and extent of the archaeological deposits and features at the site and, thereby, provide the basic data on which future management decisions could be made.

2.1.3 Excavation Strategy

The exposed cliff-section was roughly 125 m long, with the most acute erosion located at the north and south ends of the exposure (Illus 2). Much of the area between the roundhouse, at the south end of the exposure, and the 'farm mound' to the north, was grass-covered, inclined at roughly 45° to the shore and effectively stable. The first principle of the fieldwork design was thus to adopt an excavation strategy which minimized the extent of any intrusive investigation while at the same time maximizing the quality and integrity of the data recovered, and satisfying the research aims of the project.

The site was visited in March 1990, prior to the start of the assessment, by the author and Olwyn Owen, Historic Scotland's Project Manager. Examination of the author's earlier survey records of the site, dating from 1982 and 1983, and that undertaken by Graham Ritchie (RCAHMS) in the mid-1980s, confirmed that erosion was most acute in those areas adjacent to the roundhouse and along the length of the exposed 'farm mound' to the north.

Various excavation and recording techniques were considered during the pre-fieldwork planning stage. It was important, however, that the strategy eventually adopted should not only realize the aims of the project but, also, that it should neither

Illus 5   The Area 1 cliff-section prior to excavation

Illus 6   Detail of features exposed in Area 1 cliff-section (cf. Illus 66)

compromise the landowner nor impact upon the movement of livestock at the site.

A necessary requirement, before any of the research objectives of the project could even begin to be satisfied, was the creation of a continuous section line along the exposure. It was clear from the outset that this would not be an easy task to achieve, given the configuration of the coastline and adherence to the first principle of the evaluation which precluded any large-scale intervention on the site.

A particular logistical difficulty was posed by the north end of the site where the 'farm mound' deposits, some 2.5–3 m deep, were exposed above a further 2 m deep erosion zone of weathered till and rock. Scaffolding would have been neither desirable nor feasible in such conditions, and would have adversely affected the project budget, both in terms of materials and additional time or manpower. Trench excavation behind the standing section, in a manner similar to the area excavation strategy adopted at Pool (Hunter *et al* forthcoming), was briefly considered but abandoned as too intrusive and potentially damaging to the stability of the cliff-edge.

In the event, the strategy adopted was minimalist, conforming as closely as possible to the configuration of the coastline and principally involving the removal of only slippage and slumping of the section face. The 'farm mound' (Area 1) section was cut back between, on average, 0.5 m and 1 m and the spoil deposited on the shore below, to form a 'raft' from which the recording and sampling of the section could be conducted. The 'farm mound' section was cut vertically for most of its height, the section-line being pulled back on deposits and features at the very base of the section. Structures and features located during the cutting back of the cliff-face were recorded and sampled prior to removal.

A different strategy was adopted on the Iron Age settlement complex (Areas 2 & 3). It was clear from the outset that the creation of a single vertical section through the stabilized and inclined, turf-covered area (Area 2), between the roundhouse (Area 3) and the 'farm mound' (Area 1) to the north, would be neither feasible nor archaeologically desirable. The area was roughly 6–7 m wide horizontally, from its lower edge at the shore to the uppermost break of slope. Instead, the assessment of Areas 2 and 3 was conducted by means of a combination of horizontal excavation and vertical section, utilizing the natural breaks of slope on the site, roughly at the top ('upper section line'), centre ('middle') and front ('lower') of the bank, as subsidiary section lines. By this means, the area between the roundhouse and the

Illus 7   The Area 2 cliff-section, from S, prior to excavation

Illus 8   The Area 2/3 cliff-section, from N, prior to excavation, showing the breaks of slope which
                 were utilized during the excavation and recording of the site

'farm mound' was deturfed and excavated from the
top down, the section line being pulled back across
floor surfaces or other clearly defined deposits
whose upper surface could be seen to be sealed by
deposits or structures higher up in the section. The
stratigraphic record of the site was thus compiled, in
effect, three-dimensionally, in both its horizontal and
vertical planes. In all, three major section lines
were utilized, each individual line linked
horizontally by structures and deposits above and
below it.

2.1.4 Recording System

A single-context recording system was employed by
the project. All deposits in the 'farm mound' (Area 1)
were recorded in section. Structures and features
removed during the cutting back of the section face
were also recorded on plan.

Structures and deposits on the Iron Age settlement
complex (Areas 2 & 3) were recorded both on plan
and in section, via a single-context planning system.

The stratigraphic record was compiled and
checked on a daily basis using a computer-based
analytical package and error-checker. Stratigraphic

groups or 'blocks' were identified and tested for their
archaeological integrity in the field as the assessment
progressed.

2.1.5 Sampling Strategy

The sampling strategy was designed to recover
datable and environmental samples for the purpose of
clarifying the chronology of the site and the
processes of its formation.

The 'farm mound' (Area 1) section was intensively
sampled. Four sampling columns (A, B, C & D),
0.5 m wide and 0.5 m deep, were established at
points along the face of the section and all contexts,
from the modern ground surface to the surface of the
till, were sampled, including any 'repeat' contexts
which appeared in more than one sampling column.
The location of the column sites was governed by
two criteria. The column sites were selected to
encompass as many of the identified contexts as
possible; and they were spaced in such a way as to
provide the optimum amount of spatial information
on the mound's formation, allowing an assessment of
both inter- and intra-context and context-group or
'block' variability. The identification of context-

groups or 'blocks', the term used in this report, is discussed elsewhere (Part 3.1).

Standard bulk samples (20 l) for sieving, for the recovery of artefacts, charcoal, and plant remains, and a 500 g routine soil sample for physical and chemical analyses were taken from every soil and sediment context which constituted the 'farm mound' (Area 1). The majority of the bulk and routine samples were taken from the sampling columns. Where volume allowed, 10 l samples, to test for the presence of insects and parasitic ova, were also recovered from each context in the sampling columns. In addition, small column samples for soil micromorphological and pollen analyses were also taken in 0.25 m and 0.5 m monolith tins and Kubiena tins, at points within and adjacent to the sampling columns.

A less intensive, but equally thorough, sampling strategy was adopted on the Iron Age settlement complex (Areas 2 & 3) to the south, where the majority of contexts comprised stone structures or rubble deposits. Standard bulk and routine samples were retrieved from all soil and sediment contexts. Kubiena tins, for soil micromorphological and pollen analyses, were used for the recovery of specific samples of the pre-roundhouse and late, post-roundhouse land-surfaces.

Samples for radiocarbon dating, on all areas, were taken on an *ad hoc* basis, their selection determined by an on-site assessment of the context taphonomy and site stratigraphy (Part 4.1). The standard bulk samples also represented an additional, potential source of dating material.

2.2 Archaeological Survey

2.2.1 Introduction

The horizontal and vertical extent of the site was determined by augering. The work clearly demonstrates that archaeological deposits, associated with the Iron Age settlement and the 'farm mound', extend roughly 175 m along the coast and 125 m inland. The results and implications of this work for the palaeotopography and structural development of the site, over time, are considered elsewhere (Part 7.1).

A topographic contour survey, to record the disposition of the features in the cliff-section and the form and surface extent of the 'farm mound' and the ground between the churchyard and the sea, was also undertaken. This work was recorded on a Total Station EDM as non-gridded data.

2.2.2 The Cliff-Section (Illus 2)

Clear evidence of stone structures was traced in the area immediately adjacent to the roundhouse. A

Illus 9   Detail of roundhouse wall exposed in section, from W, prior to excavation, with outer passage wall to south

series of protruding edge-set stones, part of a small curvilinear structure, was subsequently exposed and partially excavated during the course of the assessment as Structure 12 (Part 3.2.7). Other structures were also traced in the area to the south of the roundhouse, outwith the scope of the assessment.

The area immediately south of the roundhouse has been heavily eroded by the action of the sea, which has created a broad inlet into the cliff-section, and the narrow cliff-edge path which survives here has been further eroded by cattle trample. Several rectilinear wall-fragments, possibly medieval in date, together with midden material and a small mound of burnt stones are visible at the top of the section. Lower down the exposure, near its base, a fragment of curved drystone masonry is visible. This wall, presumably part of an outbuilding associated with the roundhouse settlement, appears to follow the line of the exterior wall-face of the roundhouse and is set concentric to it at a distance of roughly 1 m (Illus 9). The passage, thus formed, was also traced on the east side of the roundhouse (Part 3.2.6) and can be paralleled at Gurness (Hedges 1987, ii, 37, fig. 2.10), Lingro (RCAHMS 1946, ii, no. 406, 152–3) and Midhowe broch on Rousay (RCAHMS 1946, ii, no. 553, 193–200). Other examples have been listed by Hedges (1987, iii, 14).

A large oval, stony mound, roughly 7 m by 4 m and now grass-covered, possibly a spoil heap from the nineteenth-century excavations, lies to the south of the roundhouse, near the fence. A number of exposed wall fragments and many edge-set stones are visible to the west, lower down the grass-covered sea-bank. No coherent structures, however, can be discerned. However, these features, like those exposed and partially excavated to the north of the roundhouse, almost certainly form part of the Iron Age and later settlement.

2.2.3 Other Located Structures (Illus 2)

The 'farm mound', outside the north wall of the churchyard, is a dominant feature of the local landscape (Illus 10). A second, smaller mound with a rectangular stone building on its summit, its footings traced below the turf, was located in the area to the west of the churchyard. The evidence for this site, possibly the Binnas Kirk of the local oral tradition, is considered below.

A second, roughly square platform, with sides 12–13 m long and raised 0.5–0.7 m above the surrounding land surface, was located on the north flank of the 'farm mound'. No surface trace of a

Illus 10   The 'farm mound', from N, seen against the horizon, to the north of St Boniface church, with the site samples processing station in foreground

structure was apparent. Augering and a small soil pit excavation across the western side of the platform, however, indicate that it almost certainly post-dates the formation of the 'farm mound'.

A length of drystone walling, 1.5 m wide and 5.5 m long, was located near the south end of the settlement mound. It appears to form the north side of a small sub-rectangular structure, represented by a distinct hollow, roughly 7 m long and 3–4 m wide. The possible structure narrows to the east, its end rounded, and is open to the west. Identified as a possible boat naust, it has to be admitted, however, that the extremely rocky nature of the off-shore topography might well preclude such an interpretation. No local knowledge of the structure was traced and the feature was not included in Bowman's (1990) survey of Papay boat naust sites.

Several circular depressions, possibly kelp pits or, perhaps more likely, the effect of subsidence into voids and structures below ground, were traced on the south-west flank of the site, a few metres to the north of the possible naust. Two further circular depressions were recorded on the north-west and south-west flanks of the 'farm mound', close to its summit. All are roughly 2.5 m in diameter and up to 0.4 m deep.

Quarry sites, presumably for the removal of soil, were traced on the north side of the churchyard wall, in the 'farm mound' and in the area immediately adjacent and to the south of the possible Binnas Kirk structure.

Clear evidence of a field edge, created by cultivation, is apparent on the north-east flank of the 'farm mound'. It stands 0.3–0.6 m high for much of its course.

2.2.4 Binnas Kirk

The name Binnas Kirk (<ON *boen-hus*, prayer-house, chapel) was considered by Marwick (1925, 34) to be an old name for the church site, otherwise known as St Boniface church. This usage, as Lamb (1983a, 18) remarked, may have come about as a result of some confusion in popular etymology with the name Boniface. However, Marwick has also recorded an alternative and, seemingly, ancient tradition which applies the name Binnas Kirk specifically to the 'farm mound', and refers to it as a separate church from St Boniface:

> According to one old Papey man, Binnas Kirk was supposed to be a separate structure from the present church of St Boniface, and was situated on the mound outside the churchyard wall.
> (Marwick 1925, 34)

Lamb (1983a, 18), and possibly Marwick too, seem to have identified the 'mound' with the large 'farm mound' outside the north wall of the churchyard, a conspicuous feature of the local landscape. It has not, however, been previously recognized that there is a second, smaller mound to the west of the

churchyard, on the summit of which can be traced the outline of a small rectangular stone building, aligned north-west to south-east. Interestingly, this seems to be the selfsame site which is referred to in Petrie's notes:

> Old house said to have stood near Established Church between that and sea and was called Bannies Kirk.
> *Petrie 1863, 63: Notebook 7 (MSS 26: SAS 550)*

Dated 25 July 1863, this is the earliest known reference to Binnas Kirk and it would seem to confirm this study's suggestion that this structure may well be the Binnas Kirk of the local oral tradition.

The structure is marked by a distinct sub-rectangular hollow, roughly 7 m by 3.3 m and 0.2–0.3 m deep, within turf-covered walls roughly 1 m wide. The wall-lines, clearly of stone, were traced by probing. The mound, on which this structure has been built, stands about 0.5 m above the surrounding ground surface to the north and is elevated 1 m or more above the ground to the south. A sub-rectangular platform, roughly 15 m by 4 m and possibly a quarry site for the formation of the upper levels of the mound, is located on the south side of the building. The building and mound, as upstanding surface features, are probably indicative, here, of a medieval or later date.

Two pieces of folklore have been recorded by Marwick (1925, 34) in connection with the site of Binnas Kirk:

> An old tradition . . . had it that the people in St Boniface one day heard the folks singing in Binnas Kirk a short distance away. And another fragment told how a woman lived there who was so irreverent as to bake bread on Sundays. These facts I record as bits of genuine tradition, but I confess myself utterly unable to offer any probable explanation of their origin.

Their significance, as Marwick confessed, is obscure. Speculatively, the bread-baking woman could represent an allusion to a nunnery on the site, reinforcing, perhaps, the local tradition of a nunnery on the nearby Holms of Aikerness (Part 1.2.34).

It is, however, by no means clear that the structure identified on the mound, even if it is the Binnas Kirk of the local oral tradition, is necessarily an ecclesiastical building. Although of a size and proportion compatible with ecclesiastical buildings in the Northern Isles (Lowe 1987, i, 124–7, fig. 55), its orientation might militate against a church interpretation. Equally speculative, but perhaps more prosaic, the bread-baking woman might merely reflect a memory of medieval or post-medieval occupation on the site, and the structure, if related, could simply be a contemporary dwelling. It is, perhaps, of interest that Petrie (above) should have recorded the building as an 'old house'. Possible associations for the building are explored elsewhere (Part 7.2.54).

PART 3

The Cliff-Section Excavation

Christopher Lowe

3.1 Introduction

The cliff-section was excavated as three contiguous areas. Area 1, at the north end of the exposure, was centred on the 'farm mound'. Area 3, at the south end of the eroded shoreline, was used as a unit of record for the site occupied by the substantial roundhouse or broch. The zone between the north wall of the roundhouse and the south end of the 'farm mound', the latter coincident with the southern limit of the major active erosion zone and marked topographically by a slight spur in the course of the cliff-face, was recorded as Area 2 (Illus 11).

The recording of contexts in these three areas used a series of four-figure numbers, the first digit identifying the area code (1, 2 or 3). In all, 390 contexts were identified during the course of the excavation. Context-groups or blocks, identified on site, were subsequently tested and refined as part of the programme of post-excavation analysis. Blocks have been recorded as three-figure numbers, again with the first digit identifying the area code. In all, 87 blocks were identified. However, 3 of these (B249:304, B250:305 & B251:308), essentially blocks associated with the roundhouse and features beneath it, are common to both Areas 2 and 3, reducing the number of blocks reported here to 84.

The excavation of what was essentially a standing section, by its very nature, cut across a vast range and depth of structures and deposits, testament to the intensity of past activity on the site. The whole, with a chronological depth that is typical of multiperiod sites, displays a physical depth that is rarely seen outside the urban situation. Discussion of the different excavation strategies adopted on different parts of the site is presented elsewhere (Part 2.1). Essentially constructed as part excavation in plan and part excavation by section, the cumulative effect of the work and, indeed, the principal aim of the project, was to establish a clear stratigraphical sequence for the deposits and structures on this part of the site. Thus, while the sequence of deposits and structures is clear, our understanding of their extent, function and sometimes their association with other located features in the cliff-face is less certain. In blocking the contexts, therefore, the overriding aim has been

to rationalize the excavation record and to identify clearly coherent and meaningful groups of contexts.

In all cases, the blocking procedure has been done on the basis of the context stratigraphy. Two essentially different kinds of blocks may be seen to emerge as a result of this analysis.

The first, and most clearly defined blocks, are, for example, the buildings and their associated occupation horizons or floors, dumps of midden material, rubble demolition horizons or infill dumps of abandoned buildings. Such blocks are spatially discrete and the constituent contexts comparable in kind with one another and clearly referable to the action or actions which led to their formation. These have a common depositional history.

A second type of blocking procedure, by default but nonetheless founded purely on stratigraphical considerations, has been used in those cases where contexts, perhaps deriving from different formation processes, seem only loosely connected but cannot be associated with either an overlying or underlying block. Economy of interpretation suggests that our appreciation of such contexts would be better served in a single block, rather than a multiple block entry per context. A similar economy, to preclude the fragmentation of the interpretative record, has also been applied to Block 220, a series of superimposed floor levels which occupy and constitute the passageway between the roundhouse and a later building to the east.

The blocks identified in this report are units of interpretation and are central to the resolution of the excavation record to manageable proportions. However, in drawing a 'ring-fence' around each group of contexts or block, and assigning it, on the basis of the site stratigraphy and dating, to one particular phase (Part 4.6) or another, it is important to appreciate that the blocks can have duration and that this will vary from block to block. Soil-horizon blocks and some structures, for example, can have a considerable longevity.

The justification, coherence and interpretation of each block are presented in Part 3.2. The accompanying context-matrix diagrams illustrate the detailed intra-block associations and the broader inter-block relationships. The radiocarbon dates,

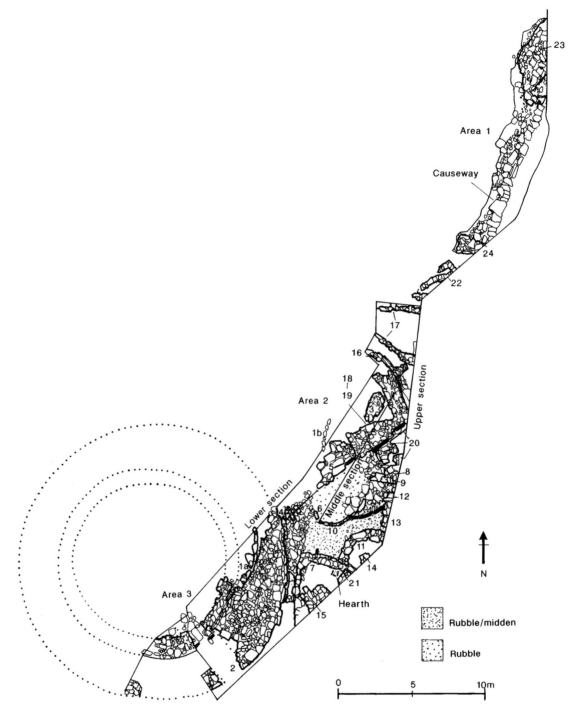

Illus 11   Site plan of excavated structures: unphased

referred to in this report, are quoted as calibrated LCR dates (equivalent to 2-sigma: Part 4.1) and have been corrected, where necessary, for the marine reservoir effect. The radiocarbon dating evidence and an overview of the stratigraphical, artefactual and ecofactual sequences, and their correlation, commented upon briefly here where appropriate, are discussed in detail in Parts 4.1–4.4. Comment upon anthropogenic content, the extent to which the blocks

have been modified by human agency and expressed as a concentration of different inputs per 10 l of sediment, is cross-referenced to the overview presented elsewhere (Part 4.3). These data are summarized in Table 16.

Detailed discussion of the criteria adopted in the phasing of the site is presented elsewhere (Part 4.6). Each phase is prefaced with a summary, which outlines the content and theme of the grouping and its justification, and a note on the order of composition. This reflects the order in which this report was compiled and essentially follows the vertical chains through the stratigraphic hierarchy. The blocks are presented here in block number order by phase and should be read in conjunction with the overall stratigraphic sequence for the site (Illus 12) or the order of composition. A concordance of block to phase is listed below (Table 1).

TABLE 1: BLOCK-PHASE CONCORDANCE

Block	Phase	Block	Phase	Block	Phase
1	9	209	6.2	237	5
101	9	210	6.1	238	6.2
102	8	211	6.3	239	6.1
103	8	212	6.2	240	4
104	8	213	6.1	241	4
105	7	214	6.1	242	4
106	7	215	5	243	4
107	7	216	8	244	4
108	1	217	8	245	4
109	6.1	218	8	246	4
110	6.1	219	6.2	247	3
111	6.1	220	6.1	248	3
112	6.1	221	6.1	249:304	5
113	6.1	222	8	250:305	3
114	5	223	8	251:308	1
115	5	224	6.3	252	6.2
116	5	225	6.2	253	6.2
117	5	226	6.2	254	8
118	1	227	6.2	255	2
119	1	228	6.2	301	9
201	9	229	6.1	302	5
202	9	230	6.2	303	5
203	8	231	6.2	306	1
204	6.1	232	6.2	307	2
205	6.2	233	6.2	309	1
206	6.1	234	6.1	310	1
207	6.3	235	6.1	311	1
208	5	236	6.1	312	1

3.2 Excavated Structures, Features and Deposits

3.2.1 Phase 1: Early Funerary Activity (Illus 13)

Summary

Phase 1 blocks, at the base of the exposed cliff-section, constitute a series of soil and relic sand-blow deposits, the latter surviving on site only in those places where sealed beneath later buildings. Funerary activity, clearly identified in one case and postulated in two others, has also been assigned to this phase. Such activity clearly predates deposits associated with Phase 3. The assumption is made that funerary activity also predates the structures associated with Phase 2.

Radiocarbon dates, from cattle bone in a basal sand horizon (B312) and an overlying windblown sand horizon (B250:305) assigned to Phase 3,

indicate that the Phase 1 deposits and structures were laid down within the period 3020–2700 cal BC (AA-9561) to 1610–1320 cal BC (AA-9560).

Order of composition

Block sequence: 108, 118, 119, 251:308, 310, 312, 306, 309 & 311

Blocks 108, 118 & 119: Sandy loam soils (Illus 14–16)

Blocks 108, 118 and 119 consisted of basically sterile sandy loam deposits over till and bedrock. The deposits represent an *in situ* soil, developed in glacial till with some admixture of windblown sand which survives as a layer 0.5 m deep elsewhere on the site (B251:308, B310 & B312, Phase 1 and B247, B248 & B250:305, Phase 3) where it has been protected by the construction of Phase 4 and earlier buildings. Chronologically, these soil blocks span several millennia. Block 119, for example, remained at the surface from its development during the first 5000 years of the Holocene. At an unknown date, but possibly within the period 3500–2700 cal BC (Part 7.1: and see B312), the soil was covered by at least 0.5 m of windblown sand. The sand was then partially eroded, decalcified and mixed into the underlying soil, and subsequently buried in the Iron Age.

Chemical and physical analyses of contexts F1037, F1038 and F1049 (all B119) show it to be a non-calcareous, poorly sorted sandy loam. Particle size analysis (Part 6.11) indicates that F1037 and F1038, by comparison with the local till, were relatively deficient in fine sand and rich in medium sand. This pattern was reinforced by the thin-section analysis of F1085 where medium sand was shown also to be relatively abundant. The presence of moderately sorted medium sands (B251:308, B310 & B312, Phase 1) beneath Area 3 structures to the south suggests that the medium sand enrichment of these early Area 1 soils is due to the deposition and incorporation of windblown sand. The Area 1 sediments are non-calcareous and thus the presence of marine shell can neither confirm nor refute this suggestion. However, analysis of the quartz/rock ratio in F1085 is closer to that observed in F3018 (B310, Phase 1) sand than to deposits that clearly have no windblown sand component (Part 6.11).

Context F1036 (B108) formed an uppermost horizon to Block /119, distinguished from it only on the basis of its darker colour, and interpreted in the field as a buried A horizon. No thin-sections of these deposits were taken but an equivalent Block 118 deposit (F1085) was thin-sectioned (Part 6.11). The fabric and microstructure of F1085 (B118), which are indicative of biological activity, support its identification as a soil A horizon.

A small inner chunk of flint (SF161), from F1077 (B119), was the only artefact recovered from these deposits. Trace amounts of mammal and fish bone, burnt peat, charcoal and cereal grains were recovered from the upper horizons of the sand but are likely to represent contamination from mixing with overlying deposits, the result of deflation.

Blocks 251:308, 310 & 312: Sand (Illus 17–19)

Blocks 251:308, 310 and 312 consisted of sand, up to 0.5 m deep, over till. Blocks 310 and 312 of this sand horizon were cut by a number of possible funerary structures (B306, B309 & B311, Phase 1). Block 251:308, effectively an upper horizon of Block 312, was overlain by Structures 1a and 1b (B307 & B255 respectively, Phase 2).

Chemical and physical analyses (Part 6.11) demonstrated that the sand deposits comprised a calcareous, moderately well-sorted medium sand. Soil thin-section analysis (STS 27) of sands F3014 and F3018 (both B310), beneath the later roundhouse, was also undertaken. The sand was found to consist of a mixture of sand-sized single-grain quartz, sedimentary rock fragments and marine shell with limited evidence for sedimentary banding, and is clearly identifiable as a windblown shell sand. This sand horizon survived only in those places in the cliff-section where it had been protected by the construction of Phase 4 and earlier buildings. No evidence survived for a developed soil profile in these sands, and the sediments are interpreted as an eroded shell sand accumulation which partly decalcified in the Iron Age (Part 6.11).

Some mammal (120 g/10 l) and fish bone (12 g/10 l), occasional shell (14 g/10 l) and trace amounts of charcoal (1 g/10 l) were recovered from these deposits. Cattle bone from F3056, a basal sand over till, has been radiocarbon dated to 3020–2700 cal BC (AA-9561) and provides a *terminus ante quem* date for the presence of windblown sand on the site.

Block 306: Cairn (Illus 13, 20 & 53)

Block 306 constitutes a small cairn and the remains of a disturbed cist-like structure which was subsequently incorporated into the south sector of the roundhouse wall. The north side of the cairn was truncated by the interior wall of the roundhouse; the exterior wall of the roundhouse, to the south, was founded on deposits covering the cairn.

The cist (F3057), roughly 0.45 m wide and the same deep, was cut into sand (B310). The cut for the pit, although obscured, was seemingly straight-sided and preserved by the line of a thick cemented iron/manganese pan which also passed beneath the stone-lined base of the chamber. A brown sandy silt (F3013) filled the chamber thus formed. No finds or anthropogenic materials were recovered from the cist. Part of a capping stone survived to the south, but none to the north where the feature had clearly been

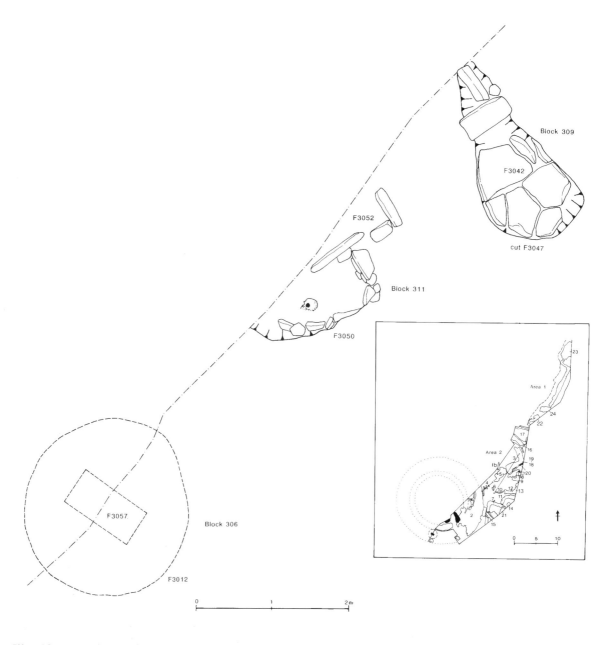

Illus 13   Phase 1 funerary features

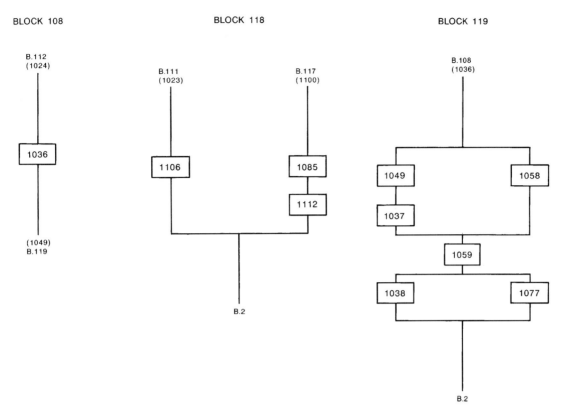

Illus 14–16   Stratigraphic matrices: Blocks 108, 118 & 119

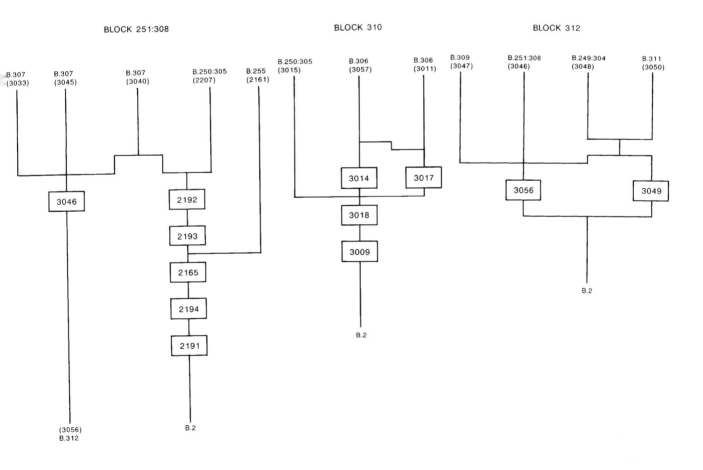

Illus 17–19   Stratigraphic matrices: Blocks 251:308, 310 & 312

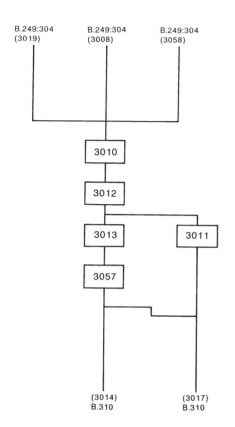

Illus 20   Block 306 stratigraphic matrix   Illus 21   Block 309 stratigraphic matrix

disturbed by later building. The absence of cairn material (F3012) in the chamber and its fill suggests that the latter filled the chamber prior to the disturbance of its capping stones.

Large angular flagstones, presumably cut from nearby outcrops on the shore, were laid on the surface, whence the pit for the chamber had been cut, to form a broad *annulus*. Pockets of shell sand (F3011) were also identified at this level. Over this was piled the cairn material (F3012), a dark sandy loam with small to medium rounded stones. A shelly sandy loam (F3010) subsequently formed over the cairn.

Reconstruction of the cairn, on the assumption that the cist-like structure was located in the centre of the structure, would indicate a small monument, roughly 2 m in diameter, upon an *annulus* roughly twice as wide. The cairn stood roughly 0.5 m above its contemporary land surface.

Block 309: Pit or possible cist (Illus 13 & 21)

Block 309 is a large pit and its fills. The pit was poorly stratified and its upper levels badly disturbed. The blocking together of the pit and its fills may encompass more than one period of activity. The pit, like the funerary structures discussed at Blocks 306 and 311, was cut into the underlying sand (B312, Phase 1) and till. However, unlike these features which were variously stratified beneath pre-roundhouse demolition horizons and roundhouse construction levels, the Block 309 pit was sealed only by rubble deposits (B303, Phase 5) associated with the primary collapse of the roundhouse.

The pit (F3047), aligned north-west to south-east, was 0.4 m deep, 1 m wide and 1.6 m long but eroded at its seaward end. The sides and base of the pit, away from the exposed cliff-section, were carefully lined with large flagstones (F3042). A single side-

slab and capstone also survived at the cliff-face. Clayey silt (F3044), midden-rich loam (F3043) with cattle, sheep/goat and pig bones (86 g/10 l) and trace elements of shell, fuel ash, burnt peat, charcoal and charred grains of naked barley filled the pit. Large angular stones (F3024), possibly part of Block 303 or the rubble foundations for Block 302 (Phase 5) walls, filled the top of the pit.

The clay, loam and midden fills clearly have little association with the surviving surface (B312) into which the pit was cut and, if contemporary with the pit, would indicate severe truncation of that feature. Such truncation is most likely to have occurred as a result of construction activity associated with the roundhouse or earlier structures on the site. As a rubbish pit, associated with domestic occupation on the site, Block 309 could range between Phase 2 and Phase 4. Indeed, the pit lay adjacent, to the south-west of Structure 1a (B307, Phase 2). No stratigraphical relationship between the pit and the structure, however, survived. Alternatively, identifying the fills as potentially secondary deposits filling an earlier existing structure, the stone-lined pit may represent a funerary structure associated with Blocks 306 and 311. The careful lining of the pit may negate any interpretation of the feature as a domestic rubbish pit.

A radiocarbon date of 3020–2700 cal BC (AA-9561) from Block 312 provides a *terminus post quem* date for the construction of the Block 309 pit.

Block 311: Cist (Illus 13 & 22)

Block 311 comprises the partial remains of two cist-like structures, sealed beneath a later demolition horizon (B250:305, Phase 3). One was cut into sand, the other into till. Both lay at the base and seaward edge of the exposed cliff-section where they had been partially eroded.

BLOCK 311

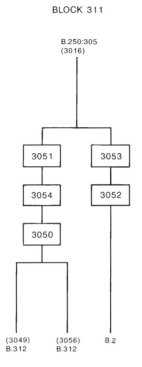

Illus 22   Block 311 stratigraphic matrix

The two structures, both uncapped and aligned north-east to south-west, differed in their architecture. One (F3052) was formed of slabs set edge-wise. Only the north-east and part of the longer south-east sides survived, indicating a structure at least 1.2 m long and 0.4 m wide. Loose brown loam with patches of burning (F3053), containing a small amount of fuel ash, burnt peat and charcoal (all densities in the range 1–2 g/10 l), filled the structure. Charred grains of naked barley were also present.

The second structure lay adjacent, to the south-east, and in part appeared to share with the first structure a long edge-set stone in common. Elsewhere, however, the cist was constructed of crudely coursed drystone walling, of beach pebbles in the main (F3054). The chamber (F3050), thus formed, was approximately 1.5 m long, 0.7 m wide and 0.35 m deep. Brown loam and stones (F3051), with low concentrations of midden-type debris (sheep/goat bone 4 g/10 l, fish bone 1 g/10 l and shell 9 g/10 l), presumably derived from later disturbance on the site, filled the cist. From beneath the fill were recovered the frontal and right parietal bones of a single human skull, identified as belonging to an adult male (Part 6.1). No artefacts or other human remains were found in the cist. The absence of other bone and, in particular, tooth enamel may indicate that the skull alone was transferred to the chamber some time after death.

Insufficient collagen was present to date the bone. Radiocarbon dates from above (1610–1320 cal BC, AA-9560: B250:305, Phase 3) and below (3020–2700 cal BC, AA-9561: B312, Phase 1) these features would indicate a second or late third millennium date for their construction.

3.2.2 Phase 2: The Earliest Settlement (Illus 23)

Summary

The fragmentary remains of two separate structures (Structures 1a & 1b) have been assigned

to Phase 2. Both were erected over the primary sand horizon of Phase 1 but have different upper stratigraphies. Structure 1b is sealed by later sand-blow and demolition deposits associated with Phase 3; Structure 1a predates only the construction of the roundhouse (Structure 2) in Phase 5. The structures could be contemporary with the funerary activity recorded at Phase 1. Structure 1a, on the other hand, could be contemporary with the settlement of the late second millennium BC (Phase 4). The significance of the pottery associated with this structure is discussed below (B307).

Order of composition

Block sequence: 255 & 307

Block 255: Structure 1b (Illus 23)

Block 255 comprises a single context (F2161), a line of angular stones which protrude from the base of the cliff-section. The feature, aligned roughly north to south, was at least 2.6 m long and 0.3 m wide. The structure, possible a wall-line or kerb, was founded on sand (F2165: B251:308, Phase 1) and overlain by windblown sand and demolition debris (F2162: B250:305) associated with Phase 3. No artefacts, related structures or surfaces were found in association with this fragmentary feature.

Like the underlying Phase 1 deposits, Structure 1b also lies within the chronological range, 3020–2700 cal BC (AA-9561) to 1610–1320 cal BC (AA-9560), provided by the radiocarbon dating of Phase 1 (B312) and Phase 3 (B250:305) deposits.

Block 307: Structure 1a (Illus 23–26)

Block 307 comprises the vestigial remains of an early building which was traced beneath the walls of the later roundhouse (Structure 2, B249:304, Phase 5). Previously exposed in 1849, the structure has been identified as 'Chamber K' on George Petrie's drawing (ORD/17/2: RCAHMS 1946, ii, fig. 266) of the 'Castle of Bothikan' where the structure was misinterpreted as an intramural feature within the wall of a broch (Lowe 1994, 181).

Only one or two courses remained of what appears to have been part of a free-standing cellular building, the feature (F3040) forming an arc 5.4 m long and 0.6 m wide below the primary roundhouse wall (F2039, B249:304, Phase 5) and continuing below the later thickening of the wall-base (F3003: B302, Phase 5). No trace of an exterior face, possibly of dump construction, was located. A patch of burnt clay (F3033), roughly 0.9 m by 0.6 m, possibly the base of a hearth, and remnants of a paved floor (F3045) lay within the alcove formed by the wall-line.

Trace amounts of fish bone (2 g/10 l), shell (15 g/10 l), charcoal (1 g/10 l) and charred grains of naked barley (10/10 l) were recovered from the burnt clay. A single sherd of heavily tempered pottery (PTS2, V1), of Late Bronze Age or Early Iron Age type and similar in fabric to sherds of that period from Tofts Ness on Sanday (Part 5.1), was also recovered from the same deposit. However, pottery of this type was also recovered from the core deposits filling the wall of the later roundhouse (Structure 2, B249:304, Phase 5). Its presence here, therefore, may represent contamination from later deposits.

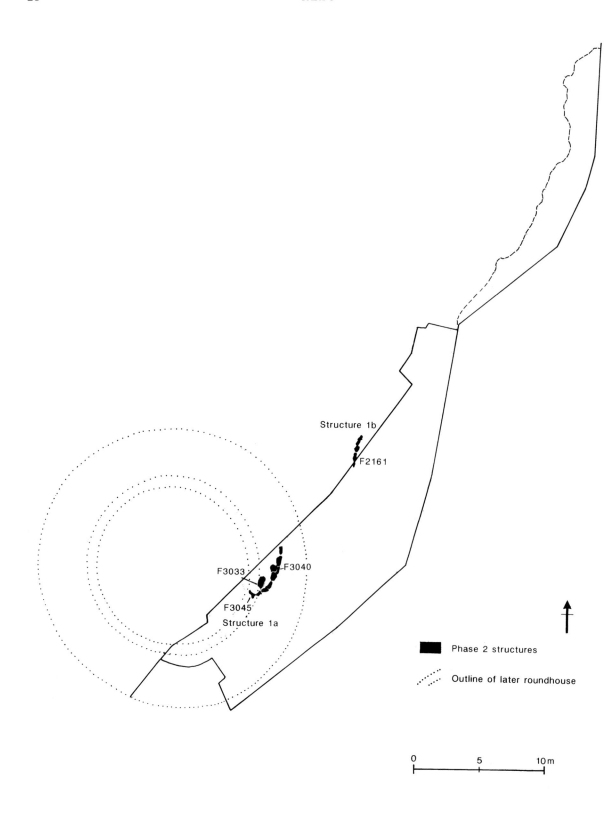

Structure 1b

F2161

Structure 1a

F3033

F3040

F3045

Phase 2 structures

Outline of later roundhouse

0   5   10 m

Illus 23   Phase 2 structures

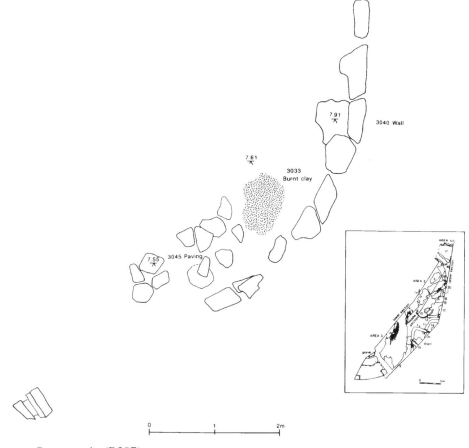

Illus 24   Structure 1a (B307)

Illus 25   Structure 1a (B307), from N, with
                  floor of roundhouse exposed to S

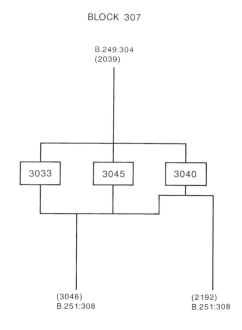

Illus 26   Block 307 stratigraphic matrix

3.2.3 Phase 3: Windblown Sand

Summary

Phase 3 blocks constitute an amalgam of windblown sand and rubble deposits which accumulated over the remains of Structure 1b (B255) and were, themselves, in turn sealed by the construction of Phase 4 buildings, Structure 3 (B246) and Structure 4 (B245), and the later roundhouse (Structure 2: B249:304, Phase 5).

No upstanding remains of buildings seem to survive from this phase. The single post-hole (B248), cut into Block 250:305 sand, like the rubble deposits which permeate this horizon, however, is presumably testament to some degree of building activity at this time.

Radiocarbon dates, from cattle and pig bone in the sand and rubble horizon (B250:305, Phase 3) and cattle and deer bone from an occupation horizon inside Structure 4 (B245, Phase 4), indicate that the Phase 3 deposits accumulated within the period 1610–1320 cal BC (AA-9560) to 1535–1115 BC (AA-9562).

Order of composition

Block sequence: 250:305, 247 & 248

Blocks 247 & 248: Sand (Illus 27 & 28)

Blocks 247 and 248, in effect, both represent those upper levels of the underlying block, Block 250:305, which are coincident,

respectively, with two overlying buildings, Structure 3 (B246) and Structure 4 (B245), both assigned to Phase 4.

Block 247 (F2179 & F2180) comprised deposits of brown to dark brown windblown sand with occasional clay and charcoal inclusions. These deposits immediately underlay and were delimited by an area of paving (F2131: B246, Phase 4) associated with Structure 3.

Block 248 comprised a series of rubble and windblown sand deposits which underlay and were delimited by the extent of Structure 4. A small, and seemingly isolated, post-hole has also been assigned to this group.

The post-hole (F2160) was cut into sand (F2163: B250:305, Phase 3). It was roughly 0.3 m in diameter and 0.15 m deep, with vertical sides and a flat base. The sides of the cut were lined with stones, as packing for a post, and the feature was filled with orange ashy silt (F2159). It was overlain by a rubble spread (F2146) of medium to large angular stones in a matrix of clean brown sand. Further windblown sand deposits (F2140 & F2141) covered this rubble horizon.

Six sherds of coarse pottery (V64, V170 & V171) were recovered from these overlying sands. All were heavily tempered (Fabric types 1.2 & 3.2) and, although undiagnostic, are typical of the early assemblage at the site. In terms of fabric and technology, the sherds are comparable to Late Bronze Age or Early Iron Age wares from Tofts Ness on Sanday (Part 5.1). Other anthropogenic indicators were rare (Table 2) by comparison with the assemblage recovered from the underlying Block 250:305 deposits.

Block 250:305: Sand (Illus 29 & 31)

Block 250:305 deposits were identified at two main locations on the site: in the Lower Section line (Part 2.1), at the front seaward edge of the cliff-section, and at the base of the deep sondage in the passage area between the roundhouse and Structure 7. The

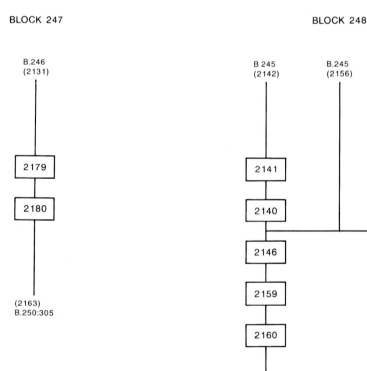

Illus 27–28   Stratigraphic matrices: Blocks 247 & 248

TABLE 2: COMPARISON OF ANTHROPOGENIC INPUTS TO BLOCKS 248 AND 250:305

Block	Mammal	Fish	Shell	Fuel ash	Burnt peat	Charcoal	Cereal	Seed
248	12g	0	4g	1g	3g	2g	13	0
250	73g	2g	15g	0g	5g	7g	74	1
305	23g	2g	19g	1g	8g	4g	60	0

Standardized as weight/frequency per 10 l sediment

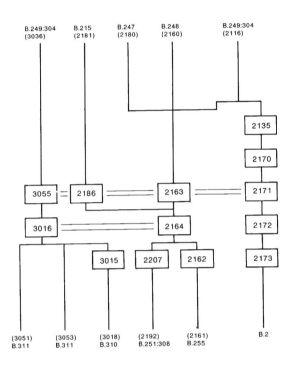

Illus 29   Block 250:305 stratigraphic matrix

deposits extended the length of the Area 2 cliff-section, overlying the windblown sand deposits of Phase 1 and the fragmentary remains of Structure 1b (B255, Phase 2). The upper levels of the block were sealed by those contexts (B247 & B248) coincident with and immediately underlying Structures 3 and 4, and overlain elsewhere by deposits associated with the construction of buildings of Phase 5 and earlier.

Soil thin-section analysis of sand F3015 (STS 28: Part 6.11), like that of the underlying sands associated with Phase 1 deposits, showed that it consists of a mixture of sand-sized single grain quartz, sedimentary rock fragments and marine shell, and is clearly a windblown shell sand. Other sand layers (F2163, F2170–2173, F2186, F2207 & F3055) in the block, some of them multiple numberings of the same deposit, were distinguished only by colour and visible variability in anthropogenic content. Four sherds of heavily tempered coarse pottery (V 96), of Late Bronze Age or Early Iron Age type (Part 5.1), were recovered from F2170. Fragments of a cetacean bone implement (SF183), tentatively described as a possible weaving sword (Part 5.3), were also recovered from this deposit.

Rubble layers were present under (F2162), within (F2164 & F3016) and over (F2135) these windblown sand horizons. Of these rubble horizons, only F2162, which lay along the northern side of the wall-line or kerb of Structure 1b (B255, Phase 2), may be referable to a known structure. The other rubble deposits are considered to represent demolition debris associated with buildings which were constructed in or after Phase 2 but prior to Phases 4 and 5.

Block 250:305 deposits, by comparison with the upper levels (B248) beneath Structure 4, were relatively rich in anthropogenic remains (Table 2). The charred cereal grains from Block 250:305, where identifiable, were all of naked barley.

These differences are interpreted as the result of the differential deflation of the unstable sand horizon, which was only in part protected by the superimposition of Structure 4 (B245, Phase 4), with greater mixing and enrichment of the sand occurring in those areas which were not securely sealed until a later date.

3.2.4 Phase 4: The Settlement of the Late Second Millennium BC (Illus 30)

Summary

The principal elements of Phase 4 consist of three buildings (Structures 3, 4 & 5), together with their occupation levels where they survive, and infill deposits following their abandonment. Two of the buildings were broadly contemporary, the third (Structure 5) being constructed over and between the ruins of Structures 3 and 4. All three buildings were situated in the area to the north of the (later) roundhouse and all were located, principally in section, in the Lower and Middle Section lines (Illus 31), along the seaward edge of the exposed cliff-section. Radiocarbon dating of debris from a floor inside Structure 4 (B245) indicates that the earlier buildings of this phase were occupied in the period 1535–1115 cal BC (AA-9562).

Order of composition

Block sequence: 245, 246, 244, 243, 242, 241 & 240

Block 240: Rubble (Illus 31 & 32)

Block 240 constitutes a 0.5 m deep deposit of compacted soil and rubble (F2046 & F2148). In effect, Block 240 represents a lower element of the 'rubble raft' discussed at Blocks 221 and 235, both Phase 6.1.

The deposits sealed Structures 4 and 5 and formed part of a 'rubble raft' on which a series of later buildings, including Structure 6 (B239, Phase 6.1) and Structure 10 (B231, Phase 6.2), were built. Stone size varied from small to medium, with occasional large stones, in a matrix of dark grey and brown silty loam soils, with shells, occasional mammal bones, burnt peat and other anthropogenic indicators.

The deposits are interpreted as demolition debris associated with the construction, occupation, abandonment and reconstruction of buildings on the site over some considerable period of time. The deposits are most likely to represent demolition debris associated with the buildings of Phase 4 or the primary extra-mural roundhouse settlement of Phase 5. No *in situ* structural remains were apparent within this horizon.

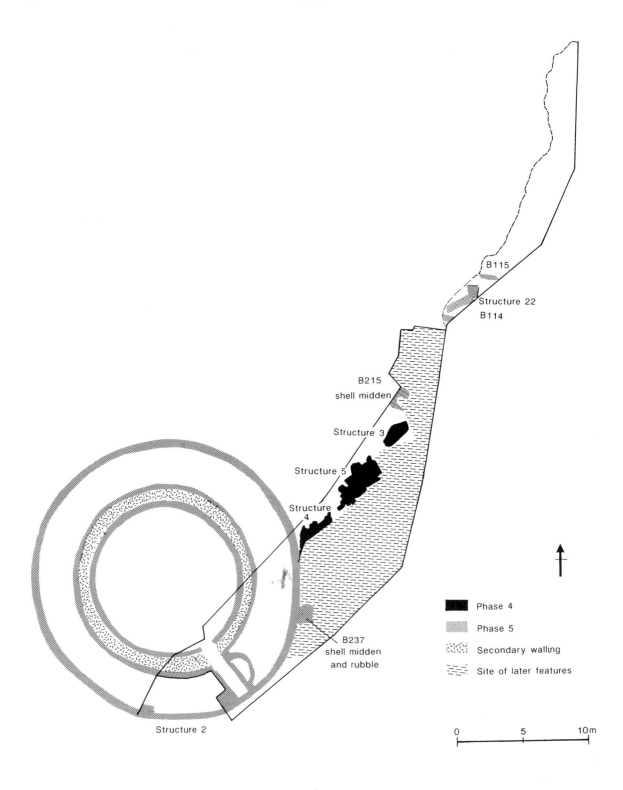

B115

Structure 22
B114

B215
shell midden

Structure 3

Structure 5

Structure
4

Phase 4

Phase 5

Secondary walling

Site of later features

B237
shell midden
and rubble

Structure 2

0   5   10m

Illus 30   Phase 4/5 structures

Block 241: Orthostat (Illus 31)

Block 241 is an orthostat (F2147), formed from a large rounded boulder set on edge. Its associations are unclear.

The stone was traced only in section but may have formed part of a second orthostatic wall, set at right angles to wall F2154 (B243) and slightly off-set from the line of wall F2158 (B243). The stone, however, was clearly set into demolition levels (B242) which post-date the construction of the partition walls associated with the secondary occupation of Structure 5 (B243).

Block 242: Rubble (Illus 31)

Block 242 relates solely to a spread of dark brown silt and medium rubble (F2025), roughly 0.2 m deep, which accumulated against the south side of the partition wall (F2158: B243, Phase 4) of Structure 5, sealing the primary floor (F2094) of that building beyond the partition.

Block 242 deposits are interpreted as demolition deposits associated with the abandonment of the southern end of Structure 5 (B243, Phase 4), subsequent to its internal refurbishment and the rearrangement of its interior space, marked by the erections of walls F2154 and F2158 (both B243, Phase 4).

Block 243: Structure 5 (Illus 31 & 33–35)

Structure 5 is a large rectilinear drystone building, seemingly aligned with its longer axis roughly parallel to the cliff-section. It was erected over the abandoned remains of Structures 3 and 4, its north wall (F2155) cut into underlying deposits (F2185: B244, Phase 4) and faced internally. Only part of the north wall, 2 m

BLOCK 240

Illus 32   Block 240 stratigraphic matrix

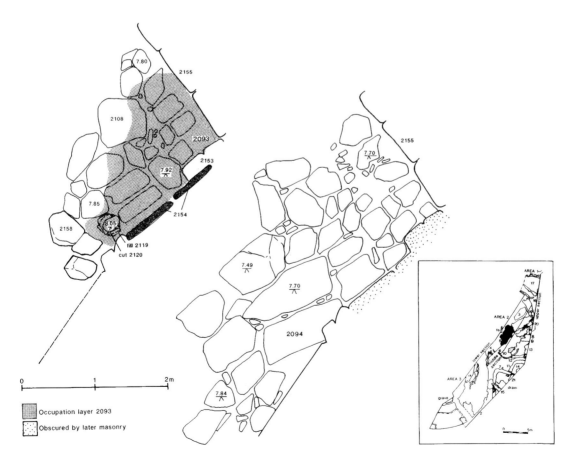

Illus 33   Structure 5 (B243), showing primary (right) and secondary (left) floor levels

Illus 34   Structure 5 (B243), from SW, with primary floor (F2094) exposed

BLOCK 243

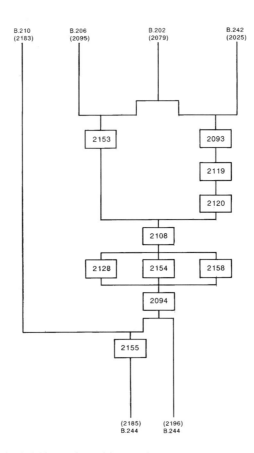

Illus 35   Block 243 stratigraphic matrix

BLOCK 244

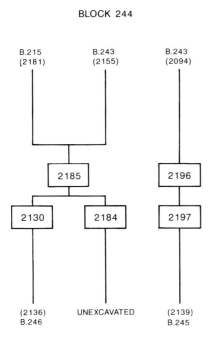

Illus 36   Block 244 stratigraphic matrix

long and 0.6 m high, terminating in a possible entrance jamb to the west, and its primary paved floor (F2094), were exposed in plan. Together, they define a building which was at least 5 m long. The building lay buried beneath rubble (B240, Phase 4) to the east, and had been removed through erosion of the sea-bank to the west. No trace of any corresponding walls survived to the south, the structure having been demolished during later building activity on the site. Significantly, the only substantial wall to survive was later utilized as a foundation for Structure 18 (B210, Phase 6.1).

Two internal partition walls were subsequently erected over the primary floor (F2094), an event which may have signified the abandonment of the southern end of the building (see B242). A short stub of coursed, drystone masonry (F2158) lay parallel to wall F2155. A second wall, formed of orthostats (F2154), lay at right angles to both, forming a small cell 2.2 m wide. A post-hole (F2120), 0.3 m in diameter and 0.3 m deep, was traced close to the junction of the two internal walls, where it may have functioned as a support for the orthostatic screen. The stone packing of the post-hole included a discarded dish quern and grinder (SF123a,b). To the north, the orthostatic wall was supported by a pillar or buttress of coursed drystone masonry (F2153).

The area within the cell formed by the erection of walls F2154 and F2158 was re-paved at this time. This upper level of paving (F2108) sealed a thin spread of dark brown loamy soil (F2128), from which were recovered two sherds of heavily tempered pottery (V63). This sealed deposit may represent debris associated with the primary occupation of the building or a layer of make-up associated with the laying of floor F2108.

A spread of dark grey sandy silt (F2093), rich in charcoal and peat ash, survived in the corner of the building formed by walls F2155, F2154 and F2158, overlying the secondary paved floor

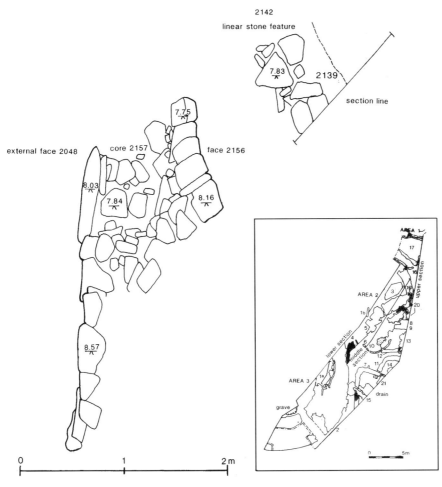

Illus 37   Structure 4 (B245)

F2108. Two sherds of tempered pottery (V31), of Fabric Type 3.1, and a small quantity (18/10 l) of charred grains of barley type were recovered from this deposit, possibly the remains of debris associated with the secondary occupation of the building.

Block 244: Post-abandonment deposits in Structure 3 (Illus 36)

Block 244 constitutes a series of sediment and windblown sand deposits which overlay Structure 3 and abutted the internal partition wall of Structure 4 to the south. Structure 5 (B243) was erected over these deposits.

The deposits were brown silty sands, with charcoal and peat ash flecks, fragments of shell and occasional rubble. A single large boulder (F2197), which lay adjacent to the robber trench (F2139: B245, Phase 4) in Structure 4, may have originally formed part of a partition wall in that building.

Four sherds of coarse tempered pottery (V117, V145 & V148), of Fabric Types 1 and 1.1, were recovered from F2130. A single sherd (V192), also of Fabric Type 1, was found in F2185. The sediments are interpreted as mixed man-made and windblown sand deposits which accumulated over Structure 3 after its abandonment.

Block 245: Structure 4 (Illus 31, 37 & 38)

Structure 4, part of a free-standing, cellular or lobate building, lay immediately to the north of the later roundhouse. It was constructed on sand (F2141 & F2146: B248, Phase 3). The cell, as defined in the Middle Section, was up to 1.4 m across. Only the south wall, 1.7 m wide, survived *in situ*. It was constructed of coursed drystone masonry, faced on both sides (F2048 & F2156) with an earth, midden and rubble core (F2157). The line of a corresponding wall to the north, however, did not survive, its site marked only by a robber trench (F2139) and, on its outer lip, a large boulder (F2197: B244, Phase 4), possibly part of the wall or later debris. Clearly less substantial than the wall to the south, the north wall was at most only 0.45 m wide and presumably represents an internal partition wall.

The primary floor surface inside the cell was scooped into the underlying sand, by design or wear, and a large angular stone (F2142), raised up on a plinth adjacent to the partition wall to the north, may represent the remains of a low bench along this side of the building. This stone feature was overlain by all but the primary deposit (F2144) inside the building.

A series of well-stratified and distinct surfaces was preserved inside this building, abutting the external wall to the south and cut by the robber trench (F2139) to the north. Consisting of alternate layers of compacted brown and dark grey sandy silt, the deposits (F2132, F2134, F2138 & F2144), 50 mm to 100 mm thick, are interpreted as mixed occupation and sand-blow deposits which were allowed to accumulate inside the building.

Two sherds of heavily tempered coarse pottery (V 99 & V 169), a crude bone point (SF135) and a flaked flint pebble (SF149) were recovered from the primary deposit (F2144) inside the building. A piece of pumice (SF150), with a groove 5 mm wide and 2 mm deep on one surface, and a carved handle (SF134), of antler perforated at both ends, were recovered from secondary deposits (F2138). Analysis (Part 5.3) of the use-wear marks on the handle has suggested that it may have formed part of a bradawl-type tool. Cattle, sheep/goat, pig, red deer, seal and cetacean bones were present in these contexts in low densities (65 g/10 l). Only naked barley was identified among the cereal assemblage (13/10 l). Fragments of burnt peat were also present in some quantity (10 g/10 l), the concentration ranging from 4 g/10 l (F2144) to 24 g/10 l (F2134). Charcoal (3 g/10 l) was present, at context level, in concentrations of up to 16 g/10 l (F2144). Fuel ash counts, however, were uniformly low (1 g/10 l).

Cattle and red deer bones from a charcoal-rich ashy floor deposit (F2134), the third in the sequence, has been radiocarbon dated to 1535–1115 cal BC (AA-9562). A single oyster shell, the only example recovered from the site, was found in the uppermost, surviving deposit (F2132). This layer may represent make-up material for a paved floor. The latter, not separately identified during excavation, may be represented in section by a single, large flat slab which was recorded as part of an overlying context (F2046: B240, Phase 4).

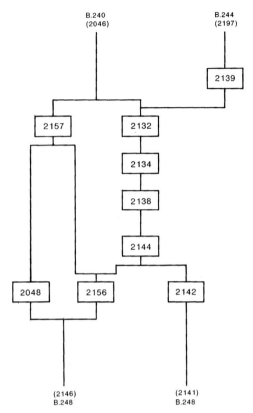

BLOCK 245

Illus 38   Block 245 stratigraphic matrix

Two antler tines (SF144a,b), their tips worn, part of an indeterminate bone tool (SF144c) carved from cetacean bone and eight sherds (V101, V152, V167 & V168) of coarse pottery of Fabric Types 1.1, 1.2 and 3.2 were recovered from the back-fill of the robber trench (F2139). The surfaces inside the building and the robber trench, which cut through the uppermost floor deposits (F2132, F2134 & F2138), were sealed by rubble (F2046: B240, Phase 4) up to 0.55 m deep.

Block 246: Structure 3 (Illus 39 & 40)

The fragmentary remains of Structure 3, marked only by an area of paving, lay towards the northern end of Area 2, roughly within the angle formed by a later building, Structure 18 (B210, Phase 6.1). No associated walls were located.

The paving (F2131), formed of large flat, rounded stones, extended over an area roughly 4 m by 2 m and was set directly over sand F2179 (B247, Phase 3). A spread of peat ash and charcoal (F2143), mixed with sand, overlay the paving. The deposit was rich in charcoal (5 g/10 l), principally heather and some willow (Part 6.8). From it were recovered two sherds of heavily tempered pottery (V93 & V179), one a rim-sherd from a flat-rimmed vessel. Occasional fish bones (12 g/10 l) were also present.

The disturbed remains of a stone feature (F2129) lay roughly in the centre of the floor. It comprised edge-set stones on two sides, with capping stones over, and was set within a slight gulley (F2209), 0.15 m deep, 0.5 m wide and at least 0.8 m long. Beneath the capping was preserved a brown crumbly silt (F2136), extremely rich (363/10 l) in charred grains of naked barley and a single cereal straw node. Lumps of burnt peat (34 g/10 l) were abundant. A single sherd of coarse tempered pottery (V137), of Fabric Type 1, was also found in this deposit (F2136). Trace quantities (2/10 l) of naked barley were recovered from the

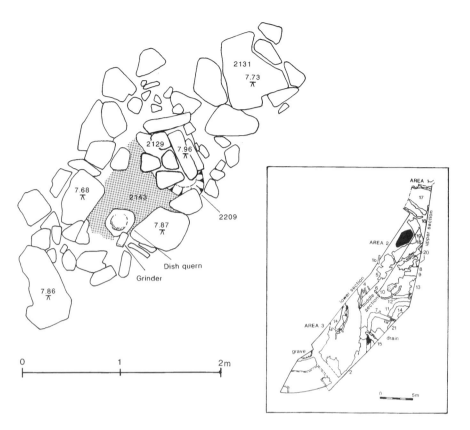

Illus 39   Structure 3 (B246)

BLOCK 246

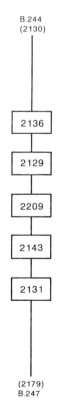

Illus 40   Block 246 stratigraphic matrix

adjacent ash spread (F2143). A dish quern (SF124), with an accompanying grinder, was set into the floor (F2131), on the south side of the stone-built feature.

The presence of the nearby quern, the dense concentration of charred grain, abundant fragments of burnt peat and relatively high levels of charcoal may indicate that the central stone-built feature represents the remains of a flue or hearth associated with the drying of grain. Stratigraphically associated with Structure 4 (B245), Structure 3 may be broadly assigned to the latter half of the second millennium BC.

3.2.5 Phase 5: Unenclosed Roundhouse Settlement (Illus 30)

Summary

The principal element of Phase 5 relates to the construction of a substantial roundhouse or broch (Structure 2, B249:304) on Areas 2 and 3. Activity at the south end of Area 1 and the north end of Area 2, represented by accumulations of shell midden material, some of it backfilled into pits, has also been assigned to this phase on the basis of the radiocarbon dating evidence. Structure 22, a cell of a larger lobate building, has also been assigned to this phase. It may, however, belong to Phase 6.1.

In very broad terms, Phase 5 spans the period between roughly 750 and 250 BC, the latter part of the Late Bronze Age and the Early Iron Age periods.

Order of composition

Block sequence: 249:304, 303, 302, 237, 117, 116, 115, 114, 215 & 208

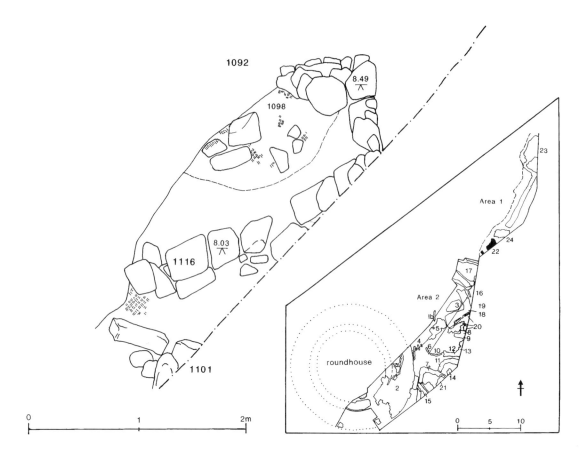

Illus 41   Structure 22 (B114)

Illus 42   Structure 22 (B114), from NW, with wall F1092 in foreground and wall F1101 beyond

Block 114: Structure 22 (Illus 41–44 & 66)

Structure 22 was erected over the surface deposits of Block 116 and the low mound (F1094: B115, Phase 5) which was deposited over the Block 115 pit. It was excavated in plan, prior to cutting back the lower part of the section. Only a fragment of the structure, which is clearly part of a larger building, was revealed during the course of the excavation. Eroded in the sea-bank to the west, the eastern part of the structure survives behind the standing cliff-section.

The south wall (F1101), of mixed coursed drystone and orthostatic construction, was cut into, and was partly revetted by, earlier deposits (F1103: B117, Phase 5). It was 0.45 m wide and stood 0.5 m high. An associated coursed drystone wall (F1092), caught obliquely in section, lay to the north. It was constructed of medium to large rounded and angular stones, forming a free-standing wall 0.25 m wide and 0.4 m high. Constructed as a single width of stones, presenting a face on both sides, the north side of the wall was slightly concave on plan. A fragment of a return wall also survived. Overall, the walls defined an irregular space, roughly 2–2.5 m across.

The slightness of the north wall (F1092) and its concave north face, together, clearly indicate that it was neither a load-bearing nor external wall to the building. Wall F1092 is interpreted as a partition wall between Structure 22 and a second cell which may survive within the standing cliff-section.

A line of flat stones (F1116: recorded as F1122 in section) extended across the interior of Structure 22. Although resembling a covered drain, no cut was traced and the feature is interpreted as a paved area within the building. A scatter of flat stones, in part overlain by a black and yellowish red sandy peat ash spread (F1098), lay immediately adjacent. The arc formed by the disposition of this material suggests that its centre lay to the west, in an area which had been removed through erosion of the cliff-face. A few charred barley grains and fragments of heather were recovered from the ash spread (F1098). It is interpreted as dispersed hearth material. A single piece

of pumice (Rt, F1098), with a U-shaped groove 10 mm wide and 4 mm deep, was also recovered from this deposit. Other anthropogenic indicators were present only in trace amounts.

Radiocarbon dates from the pit (B115, Phase 5) and the mound of demolition debris (B117, Phase 5), beneath Structure 22, provide a *terminus post quem* date of 620–190 cal BC (GU-3060c & GU-3268c) for its construction. Radiocarbon dates (340 cal BC–cal AD 75, GU-3275c & 235 cal BC–cal AD 115, GU-3061c) from a late infill deposit (F1091: B113, Phase 6.1), which filled the building after its disuse, may provide *termini ante quo* dates for its occupation and abandonment. Statistical analysis (Part 4.1) suggests that there is a 68 per cent probability that the age difference between the dates from Blocks 113 and 115 is between 205 and 435 years. This reflects the potential duration of the building's occupation.

Structure 22 lay outwith the primary roundhouse enclosure (B214: Phase 6.1). The structure clearly post-dates the construction of the roundhouse (Structure 2: B249: 304, Phase 5) and, indeed, the construction and occupation of Structure 22 would seem to lie towards the latter end of Phase 5, possibly within the third or fourth quarter of the first millennium BC. It is interpreted, however, as an outlying part of the unenclosed roundhouse settlement of Phase 5 which possibly defined the northern limit of the Iron Age settlement of the late first millennium BC. This is discussed further below (Part 4.6.2). The structure has been previously identified as a possible boat naust (Bowman 1990, 321–2, fig. 7).

Block 115: Linear cut feature (Illus 44 & 45)

Block 115 comprises a linear cut feature, its fills and a series of dump deposits which were mounded over the cut. The feature was excavated in plan, prior to the cutting back of the lower part of the cliff-section.

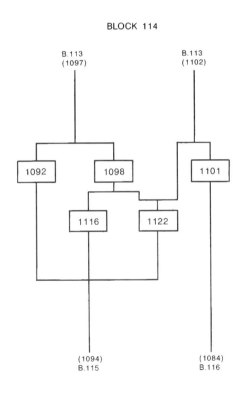

BLOCK 114

Illus 43   Block 114 stratigraphic matrix

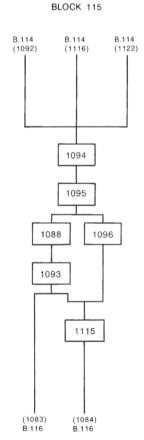

BLOCK 115

Illus 45   Block 115 stratigraphic matrix

The linear cut feature (F1115), aligned roughly east to west, was 0.55 m wide and at least 1.4 m long. Although the east end was preserved, the west sector of the feature had been eroded in the sea-bank. The cut was U-shaped, up to 0.7 m deep on the seaward side but falling to only 0.55 m deep at its eastern end.

Limpet shells (1782 g/10 l) were abundant throughout all infill deposits (F1088, F1093, F1095 & F1096). Mammal (62 g/10 l) and fish (4 g/10 l) bones were also present in low concentrations. The fill material also contained small to large angular and subangular stones in a matrix of dark brown sandy loam The deposits spilled out over the top of the cut, and the whole was sealed by a low mound of sandy loam and stones (F1094). Two sherds of heavily tempered coarse pottery (V59), of Fabric Type 3.2, were recovered from this uppermost deposit.

Limpets from the fill (F1095) have been radiocarbon dated to the period 625–190 cal BC (GU-3060c). This provides a *terminus post quem* date for the construction of Structure 22 (B114, Phase 5), and, in conjunction with an identical radiocarbon date from underlying Block 117 (Phase 5) deposits, provides a broad date for activity associated with the cutting of the linear feature and its infilling.

Superficially resembling, on plan, a cut for a grave, the longitudinal inclined profile is not easily paralleled in grave architecture. The feature is interpreted as a rubbish pit. A seemingly similar feature is discussed at Block 215 (Phase 5).

Block 116: Buried ground surface (Illus 44 & 46)

Block 116 comprises an extensive, and roughly level, layer of dark greyish brown clay loam, up to 0.2 m thick. It is interpreted as a ground surface. It lapped over the lower, northern side of the Block 117 mound and, to the north, directly overlay the pre-Iron Age soil (F1085: B118, Phase 1). The upper part of the deposit (F1083) was distinguished from its lower element (F1084) only by

a darkening in colour and a raised stone content. Fragments of shells and worm burrows were present throughout both deposits.

Three sherds of slightly tempered pottery (V14 & V15) and a pointed bone implement (SF96), made from the tip of an antler tine, were recovered from F1084. A piece of pumice (Rt, F1083), with a possible groove 4 mm wide and 2 mm deep on one side, was recovered from F1083. Mammal bones (10 g/10 l) and shells (64 g/10 l) were present in low concentrations. Other anthropogenic indicators, such as fish bones, fuel ash, burnt peat, charcoal, charred barley grain and wild seeds, were present only as trace amounts.

Identical radiocarbon dates (625–190 cal BC: GU-3268c & GU-3060c) from Block 117 deposits below, and Block 115 deposits cut into this surface indicate that Block 116 deposits were also laid down within this period.

Block 117: Mound (Illus 44 & 47)

Block 117 constitutes a mound of medium to large angular and subangular stones in a matrix of dark brown sandy loam, rich in shells (545 g/10 l). The mound was deposited over the pre-Iron Age soil (F1085: B118, Phase 1), and tip lines, falling to the north, were clearly evident in section. The upper levels (F1103 & F1104) of the mound were characterized by the presence of abundant thin, angular stone splinters. Up to 1 m high and 1.5 m wide, fanning out to the north to a width of 4.5 m, the mound had been removed on the south by the cut for the secondary enclosure ditch (F2122: B212, Phase 6.2).

Three sherds of tempered pottery (V7 & V8), of Fabric Types 1.1 and 3.2 respectively, were recovered from the basal sandy loam deposit (F1100). Limpet shells from this layer were radiocarbon dated to 625–190 cal BC (GU-3268c).

Block 117 is interpreted as a mound of demolition debris mixed with midden material and windblown sand. The frequency of

BLOCK 116

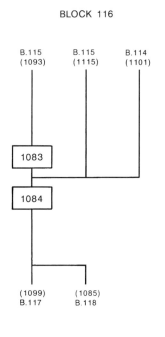

BLOCK 117

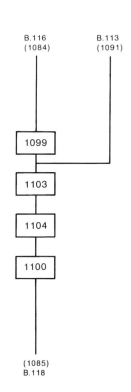

Illus 46   Block 116 stratigraphic matrix

Illus 47   Block 117 stratigraphic matrix

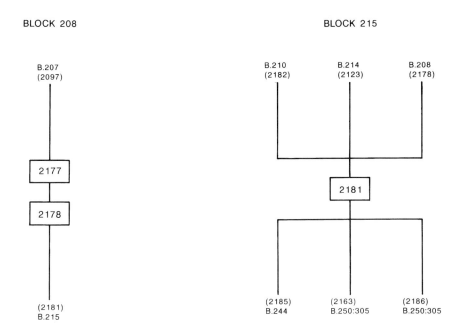

BLOCK 208

B.207
(2097)

2177

2178

(2181)
B.215

BLOCK 215

B.210   B.214   B.208
(2182)   (2123)   (2178)

2181

(2185)   (2163)   (2186)
B.244   B.250:305   B.250:305

Illus 48   Block 208 stratigraphic matrix

Illus 49   Block 215 stratigraphic matrix

splintered shale fragments in the upper levels of the mound is presumptively good evidence for the stone robbing of structures in the vicinity. The evidence of the tip lines and the fanning out of the mound to the north would be conducive with the idea that the mound was formed as a result of activities which originated from the south or east. Any associated structures in this area, of Phases 4 or 5, however, would have been removed by the cutting of the later enclosure ditch (Structures 16 & 17: Blocks 214 & 212, Phases 6.1 & 6.2).

Block 208: Linear cut feature (Illus 31 & 48)

Block 208 comprises the fill (F2177) and cut (F2178) of a feature, possibly a pit, which was cut into the shell midden deposits recorded at Block 215. The fill (F2177), of limpet shells (4960 g/10 l) in a matrix of loose brown sandy loam, was differentiated from the midden layer (F2181: B215, Phase 5) only by its lighter colour and looser texture. Observed only in section, the feature, 0.5 m deep and 1.4 m wide, may represent a pit or part of a linear feature, similar to that recorded at Block 115 (Phase 5).

Block 215: Shell midden (Illus 31 & 49)

Block 215 constitutes a localized spread of shells in a matrix of dark brown sandy loam (F2181), which was cut by the primary enclosure (B214, Phase 6.1) and overlain by the footings of Structure 18 (B210, Phase 6.1). In its turn, it was deposited over the post-abandonment deposits (B244, Phase 4) filling Structure 3. The deposit is interpreted as a shell midden.

The midden consisted mainly of limpets (4766 g/10 l), with cockles also present in significant numbers, and trace amounts of mammal bone (17 g/10 l) and occasional charcoal (2 g/10 l). A sample of the shell has been radiocarbon dated to 770–375 cal BC (GU-3273c). This provides a *terminus post quem* date for the construction of the primary enclosure ditch (B214, Phase 6.1).

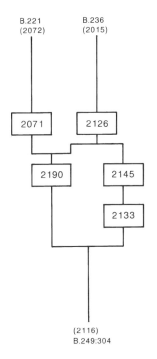

BLOCK 237

B.221   B.236
(2072)   (2015)

2071   2126

2190   2145

2133

(2116)
B.249:304

Illus 50   Block 237 stratigraphic matrix

BLOCK 249:304

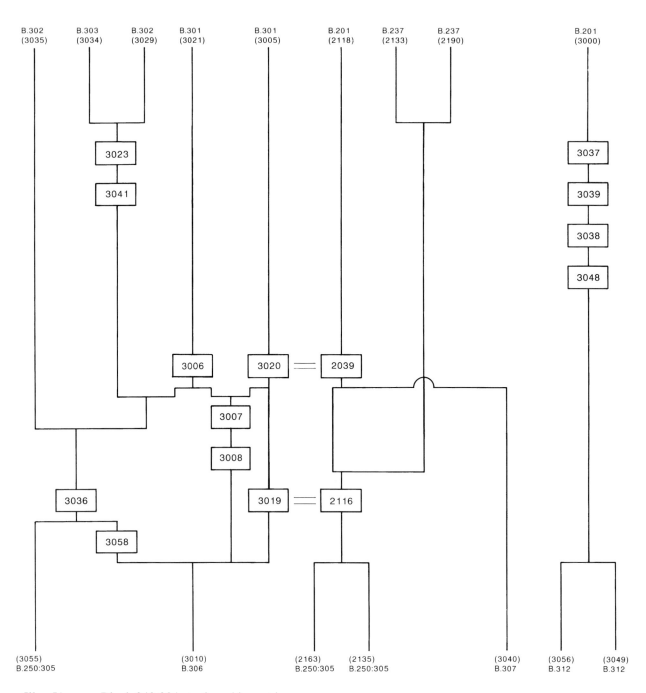

Illus 51   Block 249:304 stratigraphic matrix

Block 237: Primary post-roundhouse deposits (Illus 50 & 77)

Block 237 constitutes a series of deposits which accumulated against the east side of the roundhouse. The deposits were recorded in the deep sondage between Structures 2 and 7 and have been blocked together on a locational basis, rather than on the basis of any shared depositional history.

The basal deposit (F2133) was a localized spread of splintered stone fragments. This abutted the plinth of Structure 2 and is interpreted as debris associated with the construction of the building. A complete cetacean bone implement, interpreted as a weaving sword (SF122), was recovered from this deposit.

Overlying this, and abutting the exterior face of Structure 2, was a 0.3 m deep deposit (F2145) of dark grey silt and small stones, rich in shells (1496 g/10 l), overwhelmingly limpets but with cockles also present in significant numbers. Occasional cattle and pig bones (51 g/10 l) and a single cobble tool (Rt, F2145) were also present. The deposit extended across the width of the sondage (0.75 m) and was recorded in section to the north as contexts F2071 and F2190. Its eastern extent is unknown. It is interpreted as an *in situ* midden. The deposit has been radiocarbon dated to the period 800–390 cal BC (GU-3059c & GU-3271c) and provides a *terminus ante quem* date for the construction of Structure 2 and the manufacture and use of the weaving sword. The earliest diagnostic pottery (V61), a heavily tempered vessel with a splayed rim, was recovered from these deposits (F2071). It is likened to Late Bronze Age or Early Iron Age wares from elsewhere in Orkney (Part 5.1), an ascription which would not be inconsistent with the radiocarbon dates from this deposit.

The midden was overlain by a dump of medium to large angular stones (F2126). These extended beneath the walls of Structure 7 (B236, Phase 6.1) and may represent demolition debris associated with adjacent structures, of Phases 4 or 5, or a foundation for a pavement (B220, Phase 6.1) which extended around the outside of Structure 2.

Block 249:304 Structure 2 (Illus 51–57 & 77)

Block 249:304 comprises the construction and primary fittings of a substantial thick-walled roundhouse or broch. The preparation of the site involved considerable truncation of earlier structures, features and deposits. The space occupied by the interior of the roundhouse, in particular, was reduced to the level of the Phase 1 sand horizon and truncation of the Block 309 pit (Phase 1) is likely to have occurred at this time. The interior and exterior wall faces were erected on sand deposits (B250:305, Phase 3) to the west and over rubble (F2135, B250:305, Phase 3) to the east. Structure 1a (B307, Phase 2) was sealed beneath the north wall sector of the roundhouse. A cairn (B306), part of the Phase 1 funerary assemblage, was incorporated into the south wall sector, and was partially truncated by the cut (F3058) for the emplacement of the primary interior wall-face (F3036). The exterior wall-face (F3019=F2116), in its south sector, was erected over a shelly, sandy loam (F3010: B306, Phase 1) which covered the cairn.

The differential nature of the underlying deposits over which the roundhouse was constructed, with sand to the west and rubble to the east, may have contributed to the instability of the building. Later subsidence, for example, may be indicated by the pronounced outward lean of the wall in the east sector and its subsequent external buttressing (B219, Phase 6.2), and possibly by the incidence of *in situ* crazing of the primary and secondary extra-mural roundhouse passage surfaces (B220, Phase 6.1).

The wall of the roundhouse was constructed of large to very large angular stones, the exterior face set upon a projecting plinth, 0.15 m wide, formed by the basal course. The lowermost metre, observed in the deep sondage between Structures 2 and 7 (B236, Phase 6.1), was battered at an angle of roughly 10° to the perpendicular. The wall was 3.2–3.8 m wide and, on the south-east, where best preserved, stood just under 3 m high. In general, the wall was 1–2 m high externally, less internally, and was constructed with a solid soil (F3006 & F3007) and rubble core (F2039, F3008 & F3020). A

0.1 m deep layer of shattered and splintered stones (F3008), located in the section through the south wall sector, is most likely to represent debris associated with the crude dressing of the facing stones. If this is the case, it would indicate that the wall-faces were worked on and laid from within the core of the wall, the core subsequently being raised in a series of 'building lifts'.

Ten sherds of tempered coarse pottery (V62, V98, V100, V106 & V124), of Fabric Types 1 and 3.2, two fragments of pumice (SF40 & Rt, F3020) and a cut fragment of cetacean bone (SF39) were recovered from the wall-core deposits. The pottery is of Late Bronze Age/Early Iron Age type (PTS5: Part 5.1) and presumably represents extant material which was incorporated into the building at the time of its construction. Mammal bones (66 g/10 l), fish bones (6 g/10 l), shells (235 g/10 l) and charred barley grains (64/10 l), of the naked variety where identifiable, all similarly derived from extant deposits, were also present.

Only part of the south and east sectors of the building survived. Projection of the wall-lines, however, suggests that the building measured roughly 17.6 m externally, with an internal diameter of roughly 10.6 m. The building was entered from the south-east along a stone-flagged passage (F3037), covering a drain which extended into the interior of the building, its cut (F3048) exposed in the cliff-section. The drain, falling to the north-west, was 0.4 m wide, 0.25 m deep and its base and sides, incorporating a reused pivot stone (SF197), were lined with stones (F3038). A live field-mouse, its nesting material and a plastic flower, probably from a discarded brown wreath, were found in the fill (F3039), a crumbly and vacuous brown silty loam.

The entrance to the roundhouse was checked at the line of the primary interior wall-face by two large orthostats, that on the north side of the passage measuring 1.4 m high, 0.5 m wide and 0.1 m thick. A stone, originally of similar proportions but now broken, stood opposite, and traces of a bar-hole were preserved on the interior side of the check. The much-disturbed remains of a 'guard-cell' (not excavated) lay outwith the checks, on the north side of the passage. The 'guard cell' was roughly 2 m by 1.5 m and had been constructed within the thickness of the wall. It was filled with rubble and detritus (B201, Phase 9) from the nineteenth-century excavations.

The interior of the roundhouse was neatly paved with large flagstones (F3023), on a level with and incorporating the paving which extended along the entrance passage. Any deposits or later floor levels which may have once existed were removed during the course of the nineteenth-century excavations.

A midden-rich brown loam with small to medium stones (F3041) underlay the paving, and abutted the interior wall-face. The deposit contained cattle, sheep/goat, pig and bird bones and is interpreted as a make-up deposit for the floor. A perforated bone pin (SF198), with a rectangular head and highly polished shank, was recovered from this make-up deposit. It may have derived from earlier deposits on the site or represent a chance loss at the time of construction.

Radiocarbon dating of Phase 3 sand deposits (B250:304) clearly demonstrates that the building was constructed after 1610–1320 cal BC (ΛΛ 9560). A *terminus ante quem* date is provided by a radiocarbon date from an extensive shell midden (F2145: B237, Phase 5) which accumulated against the exterior of the building, overlying the plinth. This would indicate that the building was constructed at or around the middle of the first millennium BC, prior to the period 800–390 cal BC (GU-3059c & GU-3271c). The dating implications of a sample from a deposit which was sealed beneath an inserted secondary internal wall-face are discussed below (F3022: B302, Phase 5).

Block 302: Secondary refurbishment of Structure 2 (Illus 52–58)

Block 302 constitutes a secondary refurbishment of the interior wall-face of Structure 2 and a thickening of the wall-base. Two drystone masonry fragments (Walls 2a & 2b) were constructed against the primary interior wall-face (F3036: B249:304, Phase 5). Both were traced on either side of the entrance passage and, with the exception of the core (F3003) to Wall 2a, to the north of the entrance, were dismantled during the course of the excavation.

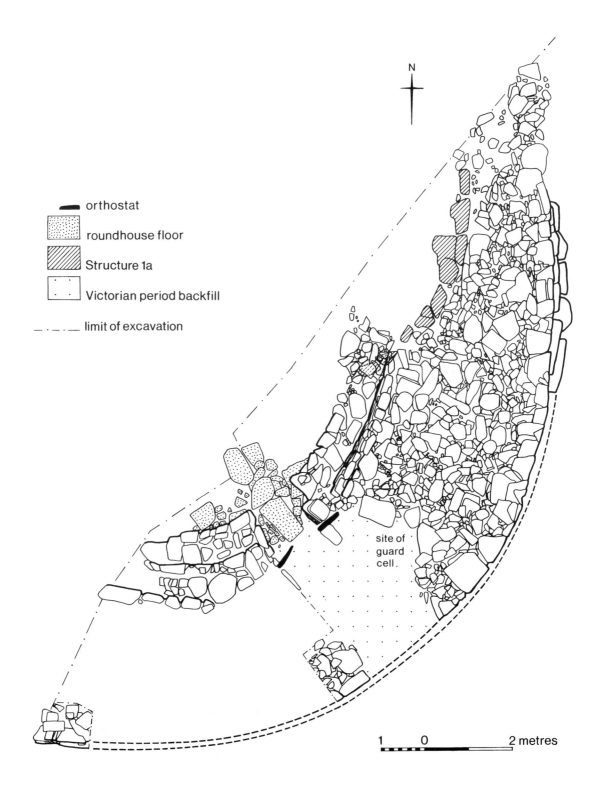

N

orthostat

roundhouse floor

Structure 1a

Victorian period backfill

— . — . — limit of excavation

site of
guard
cell.

1   0   2 metres

Illus 52   Structure 2 roundhouse

Illus 53   Section across south wall of roundhouse

Illus 54   Section through south side of roundhouse (Structure 2), from W, showing secondary internal
                refacings (B302) to the north

Illus 55   Detail section showing secondary inserted refacing walls (Walls 2a and 2b: B302), against
                primary internal wall-face F3036 located adjacent to ranging rod

Illus 56   Interior of roundhouse (Structure 2), from S, with entrance and orthostat to east: inserted wall-
faces (F3001, Wall 2b & F3002, Wall 2a exposed)

Illus 57   Interior to roundhouse (Structure 2),
from N, Wall 2b (F3026) partially
excavated, with secondary inserted
wall-face (Wall 2a: F3028) behind

The walls were erected over a spread, 0.1 m to 0.3 m deep, of loamy clay with stones. This was recorded as F3022 to the north of the entrance and F3029 to the south. This deposit lay directly over Block 303 rubble deposits and the primary paved floor (F3023: B249:304, Phase 5). Four sherds of heavily tempered pottery (V3 & V4), a fragment of pumice (SF194), three pounders or grinders (SF171, SF195 & SF196) and four cobble tools (SF169, SF170, SF172 & SF173) were recovered from this deposit (F3022). It was also relatively rich in fish bones (32 g/10 l) and extremely rich in fuel ash (70 g/10 l). Shells from this deposit have been radiocarbon dated to 970–790 cal BC (AA-9563c). The radiocarbon date clearly provides a *terminus post quem* for the construction of the walls. As a relic occupation horizon, associated with the primary occupation of the building, it would also provide a *terminus ante quem* date for the building's primary construction. The absence of any diagnostically late finds, such as burnished wares, may reinforce this interpretation. The fact, however, that F3022 overlay rubble deposits (F3034: B303, Phase 5), which in turn were deposited over the primary floor (F3023: B249:304, Phase 5), indicates strongly that F3022 constitutes a derived deposit, presumably from a pre-existing site-midden deposit, which was brought into the building as a foundation or make-up layer for the construction of the Block 302 walls. The dating of this material, therefore, has no *terminus ante quem* value for the dating of the primary construction of Structure 2.

The absence of accumulated deposits against the inserted wall-faces, at differing levels, and the observation that they were both constructed over F3022:3029 suggests that the wall-skins were inserted at the same time.

Wall 2a (F3002 & F3028) was roughly 0.5 m wide and 0.4–0.75 m high. It was constructed with a laid stone (F3003 & F3032) and soil and rubble core (F3030, F3031 & F3035). In two places, the core was tied in with the face by means of transverse key-stones. Wall 2a was composed of large to very large angular stones, laid in courses with occasional pinnings.

Wall 2b (F3026), to the south of the entrance, was roughly 0.8 m wide and 0.7 m high. It was constructed with a soil and rubble core (F3027). Nine sherds of tempered coarse pottery from a short-necked, plain-rimmed vessel with a flat base (V261), of Fabric Type 1.1, were recovered from this deposit. The drystone masonry of Wall F3026, unlike that of Wall 2a, was arranged in thick and thin courses, formed of large angular stones alternating with thinner slabs. Part of the basal course was formed by thin stones, set on edge and cut into the underlying primary floor (F3023: B249:304, Phase 5).

Wall 2b (F3001), to the north of the entrance, was of similar dimensions but stood only 0.4 m above the floor. Constructed of medium to large subrounded stones, the quality of the facing was poor by comparison with Wall 2a (F3002).

The Block 302 masonry fragments are interpreted as wall-skins or buttresses. This thickening of the wall-base, from 3.2–3.8 m to 4.9–5.3 m, resulting in an internal diameter of 7.5 m, effectively reduced the internal area of the building by half.

The wall fragments may have been added for reasons of stability, after what is interpreted as its partial collapse (B303, Phase 5), or in connection with the construction of a secondary roundhouse inside the building. Their original heights are unknown. It is possible, however, that the wall fragments may have served as raised areas within the building or acted as masonry supports for upper floors. Wall 2b (F3001), to the north of the entrance, for example, may have functioned as a low bench around the interior of the building.

The period between the primary construction of Structure 2 and the secondary insertion of the Block 302 wall fragments is of unknown duration. The absence of any primary occupation floor deposits and diagnostically late material from wall-core deposits, however, may indicate that the period was of negligible duration. It is unlikely, therefore, that the inserted interior walling associated with Block 302 is contemporary with the later erection of one or two external buttresses (B219, Phase 6.2) which clearly post-date the construction of Structure 2 by some considerable period of time.

Block 303: Primary collapse of Structure 2

Block 303 is represented by a single context (F3034), a tip deposit of large angular stones set over the primary floor (F3023: B249:304, Phase 5) of Structure 2 and overlain by a series of secondary internal wall-faces (B302, Phase 5). The deposit was confined to the area to the north of the entrance passage and is interpreted as collapse from the primary wall-head.

BLOCK 302

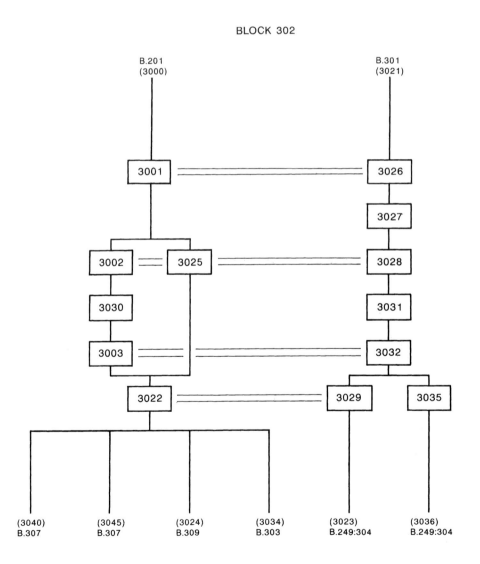

Illus 58   Block 302 stratigraphic matrix

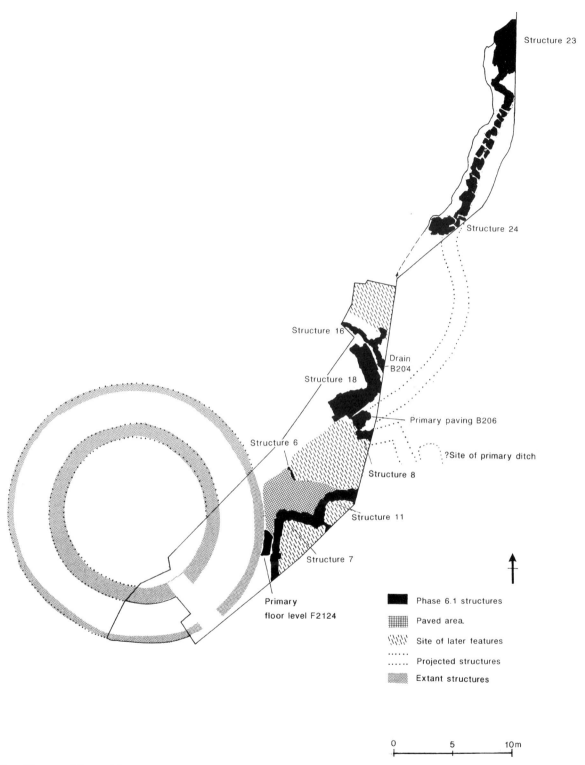

Illus 59   Phase 6.1 structures

3.2.6 Phase 6.1: Enclosed Roundhouse Settlement (Illus 59)

Summary

Phase 6.1 accommodates several structures and features which are either demonstrably post-roundhouse in date, for stratigraphic or chronological reasons, or are likely to be so because of their spatial relationships with buildings and deposits whose stratigraphic position in the hierarchy is fixed.

The principal criteria which have governed the identification of Phase 6.1 blocks are the cutting of the primary enclosure ditch (B214) and the construction of buildings and features relative to or in association with it. In very broad terms, Phase 6.1 spans the last quarter of the first millennium BC.

Order of composition

Block sequence: 214, 206, 234, 210, 204, 213, 113, 112, 111, 110, 109, 236, 239, 220, 221, 235, & 229

Block 109: Rubble and midden dumps (Illus 44, 60 & 61)

Block 109 constitutes a series of dumped rubble and midden-enriched deposits which abutted the north and south sides of Structure 24 (B110, Phase 6.1), an east to west aligned wall which may represent an outer enclosure wall to the Iron Age settlement to the south.

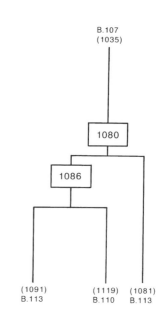

BLOCK 109

Illus 60   Block 109 stratigraphic matrix

Illus 61   Detail of Area 1 section, from W, showing Structure 24 (B110) to left, Structure 22 (B114) to right and rubble/midden dump (B109) at centre

BLOCK 111

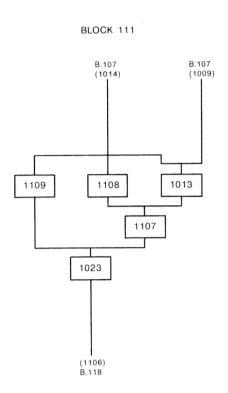

Illus 62   Block 111 stratigraphic matrix

The deposit (F1086) to the south of the wall comprised dark brown sandy silt-loam, with many subangular and angular, small to large stones, and shells. It was dumped over the midden and infill deposits (B113, Phase 6.1) which filled the abandoned remains of Structure 22, the whole forming a sizeable mound to the south of the wall and seaward of the entrance causeway (B112, Phase 6.1).

The deposit (F1080) to the north of the wall was of similar composition but was also relatively rich in pottery. It contained sixty sherds from a flat-based vessel (V28) with a rounded shoulder and short neck, similar in form to vessels from the Iron Age roundhouse settlement at Clickhimin (Part 5.1). Two further vessels (V29 & V89) were represented by single sherds. Two fragments of pumice (SF24 & Rt, F1080), one with a deep U-shaped groove on one face, were also recovered from this deposit. Shells (340 g/10 l), mammal bones (12 g/10 l) and fish bones (1 g/10 l) were also present in low concentrations in Block 109 deposits.

Shells from context F1080 have been radiocarbon dated to 400–70 cal BC (GU-3062c). A basal date of cal AD 285–670 (GU-3063) from overlying sediments (B107, Phase 7) indicates a hiatus in the use of this part of the site during Phase 6.2, dated activity during this period being concentrated within the enclosed settlement to the south.

Block 110: Structure 24 (Illus 44 & 61)

Block 110 constitutes the remains of a free-standing wall (F1119), aligned east to west. It lay on the seaward side of the causeway F1024 (B112, Phase 6.1) and, likewise, was constructed over deposits (F1081 & F1082: B113, Phase 6.1) which post-date the abandonment of Structure 22. It was abutted by deposits (B109, Phase 6.1) which have been radiocarbon dated to the period 400–70 cal BC (GU-3062c).

The wall was revealed in plan over a distance of roughly 2 m. Faced with edge-set stones on the south, a low heap of stones, immediately adjacent to the north, may represent collapse or an outer face of simple dump construction, the whole forming a wall roughly 1.5 m wide. At the standing section face, however, the wall was of crudely coursed drystone construction and was only roughly 0.35 m wide and 0.4 m high.

Wall F1119 is spatially coincident with the return angle of the causeway (F1024: B112, Phase 6.1), as the latter turns beneath the standing section. It may be associated with the causeway, either as an outer boundary wall to the enclosure or as a retaining wall for the mound of deposits (B113, Phase 6.1) which formed over and around the abandoned remains of Structure 22 to the south.

Block 111: Structure 23 (Illus 44, 62 & 63)

The fugitive remains of a possible building or an open paved area lay at the north, exposed, end of the path or causeway (B112, Phase 6.1). Eroded on the west, the feature was overlain by deposits which have been radiocarbon dated (GU-3063) to the second quarter of the first millennium cal AD (B107, Phase 7).

The feature comprised an area of paving (F1108), roughly 4.5 m by 2.5 m across, formed of large subangular and subrounded flat stones. The paving was revetted on the west by a line, 4 m long, of large subrounded stones (F1013). Seven flat stones (F1109), laid to form a right angle, on the south side of the paving, adjacent to the paved causeway, may represent additional revetting or a basal course for a building. The paving and revetment overlay a layer of rounded and angular, medium to large stones (F1023) in a matrix of brown sandy loam (F1107). These deposits are interpreted as make-up for the overlying paving and revetment. Seven sherds (V5, V9-11, V92 & V120) of tempered pottery, of Fabric Types 1.1, 1.3 and 3.1, were recovered from these deposits. The feature, although clearly poorly preserved, is interpreted as a constructed terminal to the path or causeway.

Block 112: Stone path or causeway (Illus 44 & 64)

A substantial stone-built linear feature (F1024), 0.8 m wide, lay roughly parallel to the exposed cliff-section and was aligned north-east to south-west. The feature disappeared beneath the standing section a few metres to the north of the ruins of Structure 22 (B114, Phase 5). It was formed of massive angular and subangular flat stones, with sides up to 0.9 m long, and their upper surfaces worn. It was exposed over a distance of roughly 11 m. Datum levels on the feature ranged from 7.98 m OD at its north end, where it was founded on bedrock, to 8.06 m OD in its middle course where it was founded over primary sandy soil deposits of Block 108 (F1036, Phase 1) and to 8.12 m OD where exposed to the south where it overlay the spread of dump material (F1081 & F1082: B113, Phase 6.1), post-dating the abandonment of Structure 22.

The feature is interpreted as a stone path or causeway, associated with the entrance to the roundhouse enclosure. To the north it appeared to be associated with the fugitive remains of a small building or open paved area (Structure 23: B111, Phase 6.1). A reconstruction outline of the course of the causeway is shown in Illus 59. Datum levels on the primary entrance paving (B206, Phase 6.1), at 8.75 m OD, indicate that the causeway must rise 0.6 m over a distance of roughly 16 m, a gradient of roughly 1:26. Such a gradual gradient would suggest that the causeway was inclined, not stepped.

A radiocarbon date from shell midden material (F1080: B109, Phase 6.1) which accumulated against the north wall of Structure 24 (B110, Phase 6.1) and partially overlay the stone causeway would indicate that both structures were in place prior to the period 400–70 cal BC (GU-3062c). The fact that the causeway was not finally sealed until the formation of the Late Iron Age ash mound (B107, Phase 7) would suggest that the feature continued in use through to the abandonment of the Iron Age settlement in Phase 6.3. The radiocarbon-dated horizon from the uppermost fill

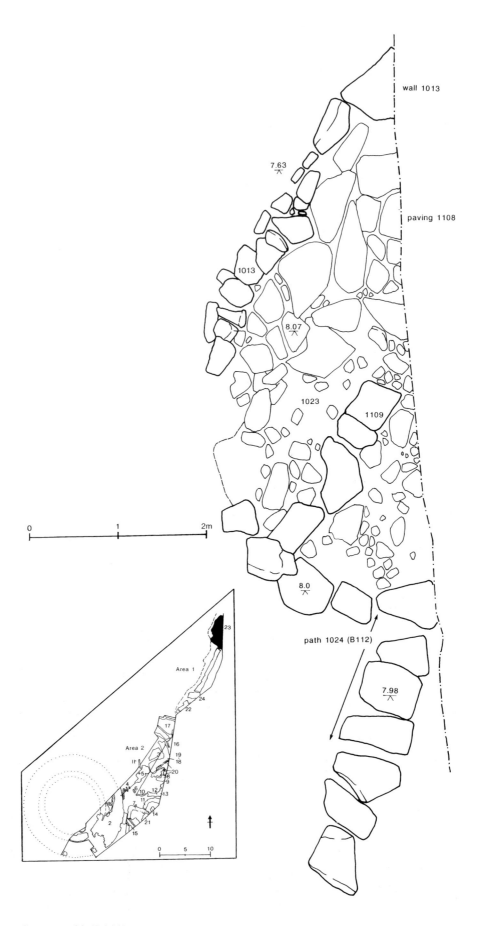

Illus 63   Structure 23 (B111)

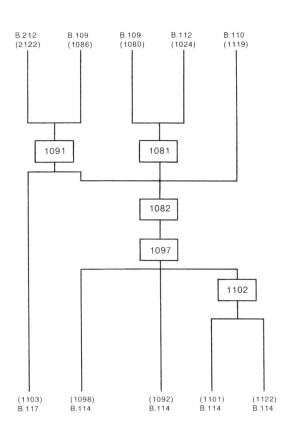

BLOCK 113

Illus 64   Stone causeway (B112) from S, with   Illus 65   Block 113 stratigraphic matrix
               ruins of Structure 23 (B111) to north

Illus 66   Structure 22 (B114) and infill dumps (B113), from W

(F1091: B113, Phase 6.1), post-dating the abandonment of Structure 22 (B114, Phase 5), is not stratigraphically related to the construction of Structure 24 and the stone causeway and therefore does not provide a *terminus post quem* date for their construction.

Block 113: Post-abandonment deposits in Structure 22 (Illus 44, 65 & 66)

Block 113 constitutes a series of post-abandonment deposits which filled Structure 22 (B114, Phase 5). The basal deposit, filling the building to a depth of roughly 0.1 m, consisted of yellowish-brown loamy sand (F1102). Three sherds of heavily tempered pottery (V6), four carbonized grains of barley and the bones of two small passerines were present in the deposit. It is interpreted as a windblown sand which filled the abandoned building, its walls having become nesting sites for, possibly, sparrows.

The structure was then rapidly backfilled with small to medium, angular and subangular stones in a matrix of dark brown sandy loam with shells (F1097). Tip lines in the deposit clearly indicate that the building was filled from the south-east. The deposit was rich in pottery and included examples of flat- and flat inverted-rimmed vessels. A total of seventy-nine sherds (V21–27, V95, V128–129, V132, V176, V247–248, V 269 & V271), of Fabric Types 1.1, 1.2, 3.1 and 3.2, was recovered from this dump-layer.

A layer of very dark greyish-brown sandy loam with small to medium angular and subangular stones (F1081 & F1082) was subsequently deposited over the north wall of Structure 22 (B114, Phase 5), spilling away to the north. The deposit contained low concentrations of mammal bones (15 g/10 l), fish bones (2 g/10 l) and shells (30 g/10 l) and trace amounts of burnt peat, charcoal, charred barley and wild seeds. Five sherds (V16 & V17) of tempered coarse pottery, of Fabric Types 3.1 and 3.2, including two sherds from a flat-rimmed vessel, were also recovered from this deposit. It is interpreted as a dump deposit, enriched with midden material.

Over this, and extending over the south wall of Structure 22 (B114, Phase 5), was formed a mound of shells in a matrix of dark brown sandy loam (F1091), roughly 3 m across and 0.45 m high. A single sherd (V174) of tempered pottery, of Fabric Type 1, was recovered from this deposit. It is interpreted as a shell midden, mixed with windblown sand.

Radiocarbon dates on samples of winkles (340 cal BC–cal AD 75: GU-3275c) and limpets (235 cal BC–cal AD 115: GU-3061c) in the deposit provide *termini ante quo* dates for the occupation and abandonment of the building. The same deposit also provides a *terminus post quem* date for the cutting of the secondary enclosure ditch (B212, Phase 6.2) to the south. The construction of Structure 24 (B110, Phase 6.1) and a stone-laid path (B112, Phase 6.1) to the north also post-date Block 113 deposits (F1081 & F1082) but are stratigraphically unrelated to the dated *terminus post quem* horizon, the shell midden F1091.

Block 204: Drain (Illus 59 & 67)

Block 204 constitutes a linear stone-capped (F2041) feature. The sides (F2090) and base (F2091) of the feature were also lined with stones. It was cut into the upper edge of the primary ditch terminal (B214, Phase 6.1) and lay parallel to, and on a level with, the footings of Structure 18 (F2182: B210, Phase 6.1), immediately to the south-west. The feature, 0.4 m wide and 0.3 m deep, was exposed over a length of just over 2 m, extending beneath the Upper Section. It was filled with dark brown loam (F2045). Two sherds of tempered coarse pottery (V69 & V149), of Fabric Type 1.1, were recovered from the fill.

The feature is interpreted as a drain, falling from the south-east and emptying into the primary ditch (B214, Phase 6.1).

Block 206: Primary paving at entrance (Illus 68 & 69)

Block 206 is a single context block, comprising an area of paving (F2095) at the north-east entrance into the enclosure. It

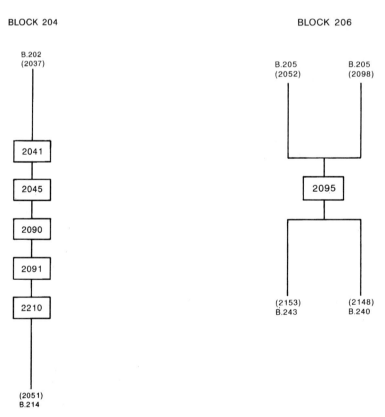

BLOCK 204

B.202
(2037)

2041

2045

2090

2091

2210

(2051)
B.214

BLOCK 206

B.205   B.205
(2052)   (2098)

2095

(2153)   (2148)
B.243   B.240

Illus 67   Block 204 stratigraphic matrix   Illus 68   Block 206 stratigraphic matrix

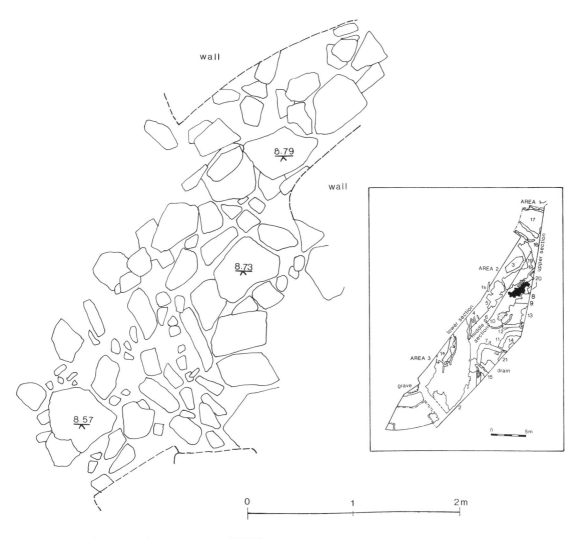

Illus 69   Primary paving at entrance (B206)

was formed of medium to large flat stones and extended beneath a kerb and higher level of paving (B205) which is associated with the remodelling of the entrance area in Phase 6.2. It was exposed over an area of roughly 5 m by 2 m, aligned north-east to south-west but eroded on its seaward side. A wall (Structure 8: B234, Phase 6.1), interpreted as part of the south side to the entrance façade, lay adjacent to the south-east. A pivot-stone (SF199) was incorporated into the paved surface next to the wall.

The enclosure of the site and the construction of an entrance across the enclosure ditch are interpreted as part of a fundamental reorganization of the settlement. The primary paving of the passage (F2124: B220, Phase 6.1) between Structure 2 (B249:304, Phase 5) and Structure 7 (B236, Phase 6.1), roughly 8 m to the south-west, is interpreted as a contemporary event, associated with this reorganization. Ordnance Datum levels on these two stratigraphically divorced segments of paving (F2095: 8.75–8.80 m OD and F2124: 8.90–9.01 m OD) would not contradict this interpretation.

Block 210: Structure 18, primary enclosure wall and north-west side of passage façade (Illus 70 & 71)

Structure 18 constitutes a series of floor deposits and two segments of drystone masonry (F2182 & F2183), over which

Structure 19 (B209, Phase 6.2) was later erected. Thus concealed by later masonry, only the outline of its walls can be shown on plan (Illus 71). Wall F2182 lay parallel and adjacent to the primary ditch enclosure (B214, Phase 6.1), its base on a level with an external drain (B204, Phase 6.1). Wall F2183 lay at right angles to the line of the primary ditch and approximately 2.5 m to the east of the ditch terminal.

Wall F2182 was roughly 3 m long, 1.2 m wide and up to 0.4 m high. It was constructed over Block 215 (Phase 5) deposits, which have been radiocarbon dated to the period 770–375 cal BC (GU-3273c). Wall F2183 was of similar dimensions but of unknown width. Wall F2183 was constructed over the infill (B244, Phase 4) of Structure 3 and, at its south-west end, overlay the north wall (F2155: B243, Phase 4) of Structure 5.

Walls F2182 and F2183 were not tied together at the corner, the area between them being filled with an ashy silt deposit similar to that recorded over the floor (see below). The north-east end of wall F2183 was constructed with a well-built, coursed face. The south-east end of wall F2182, opposite, was ragged.

A series of fragmentary deposits was preserved over a restricted area (c. 1.5 m by 1 m) within the angle formed by the wall fragments, the remainder having been removed through erosion of the sea-bank. The basal deposit, abutting both walls, comprised a layer of dark brown silty clay (F2208) with stones, shells and charcoal flecks. Possibly derived from the underlying deposits (B244, Phase 4) which post-date the abandonment of Structure 3, this material (F2208) is interpreted

BLOCK 210

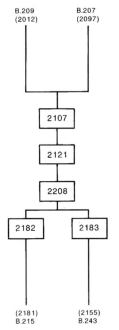

Illus 70   Block 210 stratigraphic matrix

as make-up for the overlying paved floor (F2121). On this surface lay a spread of ash and charcoal (F2107), rich in artefacts.

Twelve sherds of untempered or slightly tempered pottery (V151, V157 & V193), including pieces from a flat-rimmed and flat-based vessel, were recovered from this layer. A copper alloy bar or ingot (SF107), copper alloy fragments forming a ring (SF109), three clay moulds (SF178B), including one from a decorative boss, two tuyère fragments (SF108 & 137) and fragments of vitrified clay, interpreted as hearth or furnace lining, were also present in this deposit. X-ray fluorescence analysis (Part 5.4) of samples of the vitrified clay confirmed the presence of copper. The presence of lead, zinc, tin and a trace of copper was identified in two of the mould fragments (Part 5.4). The deposit was also relatively rich in fuel ash (10 g/10 l) and burnt peat (6 g/10 l). Fifteen grains of naked barley were also recovered from this deposit (F2107).

The walls of Structure 18 are interpreted as fragments of an enclosure wall (F2182) and a return wall (F2183) at the entrance into the primary enclosure. The space between the wall fragments may represent the site of a post-hole or socket for a post forming part of a gate or similar entrance feature. This possibility, however, could not be explored within the confines of the area available for excavation. The structure may, in view of the fact that it stands to the east of the primary ditch terminal, have formed the principal entrance façade. The nature and homogeneity of the cultural assemblage recovered from the restricted area behind the walls suggest strongly that metalworking activity was undertaken within a secondary building, now lost, which was constructed up against the enclosure wall.

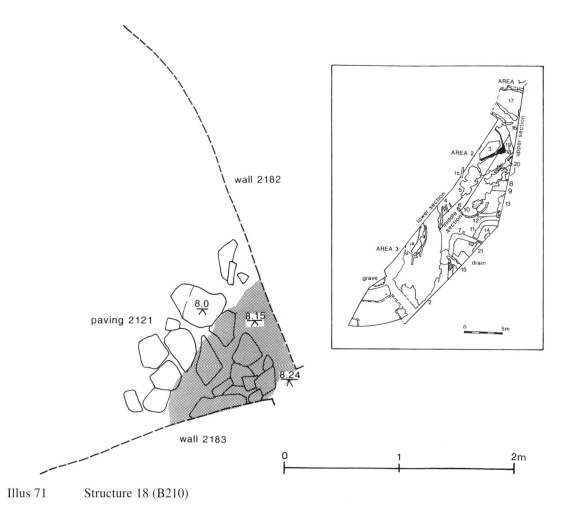

Illus 71   Structure 18 (B210)

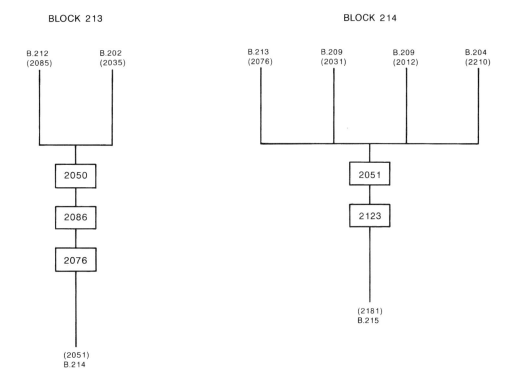

Illus 72   Block 213 stratigraphic matrix   Illus 73   Block 214 stratigraphic matrix

Block 213: Fills of primary ditch (Illus 72)

Block 213 comprises a series of deposits which filled the primary ditch (B214, Phase 6.1). The basal sediment comprised a thin layer of dark grey clayey silt (F2076), with small to medium stones and occasional shells. Occasional cattle and sheep/goat bones were also present. Twenty-four sherds of tempered coarse pottery (V31, V121–123, V156 & V190), of Fabric Types 1, 1.1 and 3.1, were also recovered from this deposit. The basal sediment is interpreted as a natural silting of the ditch, with midden material incorporated. The ditch was then backfilled with rubble (F2086) and shells (F2050). No stabilization horizons or layering were evident in these deposits and the backfilling is assumed to have been rapid.

Radiocarbon dating of both limpets (400–50 cal BC: GU-3274c) and winkles (405–100 cal BC: GU-3058c) from the infill (F2050) supports the interpretation that the ditch was rapidly backfilled. The dates also provide a *terminus post quem* for the secondary recutting of the ditch (B212, Phase 6.2). As *termini ante quo* dates, comparison of the radiocarbon dates from the primary backfill and the radiocarbon date from the earlier shell midden (B215, Phase 5: 770–375 cal BC: GU-3273c), which was cut by the primary ditch, potentially reflects the duration of the enclosure in its primary form. Statistical analysis (Part 4.1) indicates that there is a 69 per cent probability that the difference between these dates lies between 50 and 340 years. Minimal duration may also be reflected in the thinness of the primary sediment (F2076).

Block 214: Structure 16, primary enclosure ditch
(Illus 31, 73 & 74)

Structure 16, the primary enclosure ditch, was cut through earlier shell (F2181: B215, Phase 5) and sand deposits

(B250:305, Phase 3), its base cut into the underlying till. Only a 3 m length of the ditch survived in the exposed cliff-section. Its inner edge lay approximately 14.5 m from the roundhouse (Structure 2).

The ditch (F2123) was 1.2 m deep, with steep sides and a flat base. Only the south side and part of a terminal remained, the north side of the ditch having been truncated by a secondary recut (F2122: B212, Phase 6.2). The remaining side and terminal fragment, the latter roughly 1 m long, were revetted with a crudely coursed drystone wall formed of medium to large angular stones (F2051). Two large edge-set stones, oversailed by random coursed masonry, were set at the junction between the terminal and the side-fragment.

A stone-capped drain (B204, Phase 6.1), which emptied into the ditch, was set above the terminal junction, at the level of the contemporary ground surface. A substantial wall (F2182: B210, Structure 18), interpreted as part of the enclosure wall, lay just inside the line of the primary ditch.

Radiocarbon dating (770–375 cal BC: GU-3273c) of the earlier shell midden (B215, Phase 5) provides a *terminus post quem* date for the construction of the primary ditch and enclosure of the site. Statistical analysis (Part 4.1) of the radiocarbon dates from the shell midden (B215, Phase 5) which was cut by the primary enclosure and the shell midden (B237, Phase 5) which accumulated against the east wall of the roundhouse (Structure 2) indicates that there is a 68 per cent probability that Block 237 predates Block 215 and, therefore, that the cutting of the primary enclosure ditch post-dates the construction of the roundhouse.

The argument that these two shell middens may be broadly contemporary, and thus provide a basis upon which the construction of the roundhouse and the cutting of the primary enclosure ditch can be chronologically differentiated, may be strengthened by the fact that these were the only shell accumulations on the site where cockle shells were present in significant, albeit relatively low, numbers (Part 6.6).

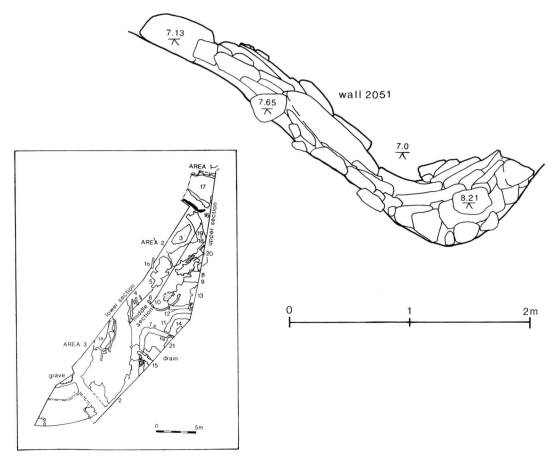

Illus 74   Structure 16: primary ditch (B214)

Block 220: Extra-mural roundhouse passage (Illus 75–77)

Block 220 constitutes a series of superimposed paved surfaces and associated deposits which were located in the deep sondage between Structure 2 (B249:304, Phase 5) and Structure 7 (B236, Phase 6.1). The surfaces were exposed over an area up to 1 m wide and 3 m long. The upper elements, although truncated to the north through erosion of the sea-bank, nonetheless clearly merged with a roughly level surface or stone platform (B221, Phase 6.1) which lay immediately to the north of Structure 7. To the south, the surfaces survive beneath the standing Upper Section. As a group of contexts which have been blocked together purely on locational criteria, the block is clearly of some chronological duration.

The primary passage level (F2124) was constructed of very large, flat angular stones, forming a smooth surface. Individual stones spanned the full width of the passage, their upper surfaces broken and crazed *in situ*, possibly the result of subsidence associated with the roundhouse. The paving was laid over an earlier, levelled rubble horizon (F2126: B237, Phase 5) and abutted the roundhouse wall to the west and the footings of Structure 7 to the east. Datum levels on the paving ranged from 8.90 m to 9.01 m. This primary passage level is directly linked to, and post-dates, the construction of Structure 7, and is indirectly linked, by interpretation and inference, to the laying of the primary paving (F2095: B206, Phase 6.1) at the entrance into the enclosure. It was overlain by a thin wash deposit of sterile brown silt with small stones (F2125).

The secondary passage level (F2109) was constructed of a mixture of large, flat angular stones and smaller stone cobbling, again forming a smooth surface throughout the passage. The larger, flat stones were similarly broken and crazed *in situ*. Datum levels on the paving ranged from 9.03 to 9.18 m. This secondary

BLOCK 220

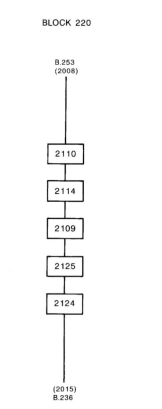

Illus 75   Block 220 stratigraphic matrix

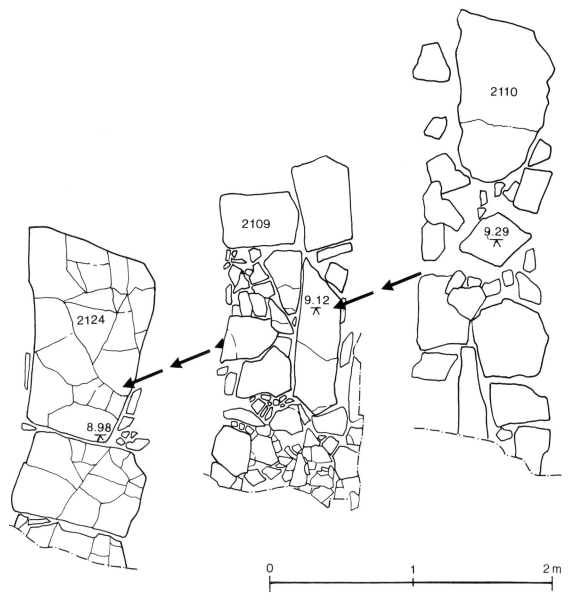

Illus 76   Superimposed floor levels in extra-mural passage (B220)

passage level, and/or its successor (F2110), is indirectly linked, by interpretation and inference, to the laying of the secondary paving (F2053: B205, Phase 6.2) at the entrance into the enclosure. It was overlain by a thick (0.15 m) layer of sterile brown silt with splintered shale fragments (F2114), the stone inclusions possibly representing a period of local stone robbing or dressing associated with reconstruction of the roundhouse wall, prior to the laying of the tertiary floor level (F2110).

The tertiary passage level (F2110), unlike its predecessors, was constructed of a mixture of angular and subrounded stones, its upper surface less regular and smooth and in places void of stones. The absence of any *in situ* crazing may indicate that the third relaying of the passage post-dates subsidence of the roundhouse wall. Nonetheless, it clearly predates the insertion of an external buttress (F2115: B219, Phase 6.2) against the roundhouse wall. Datum levels on the tertiary paving ranged from 9.22 to 9.30 m OD. It was overlain by a thick deposit of splintered shale fragments (F2008: B253, Phase 6.2).

Block 221: Stone platform (Illus 59 & 78)

Block 221 constitutes a stone-revetted (F2072) and levelled stone surface or platform (F2049), fragments of which were traced at the north end of the extra-mural roundhouse passage (B220, Phase 6.1). The upper surface of the platform extended around and abutted the footings of Structure 7 and overlay rubble deposits over which Structure 7 was also erected. The laid surface also sealed the truncated remains of Structure 6 (F2195: B239, Phase 6.1). The platform was only partially excavated, on its south side where it abutted the exterior of the roundhouse.

The platform is interpreted as an extensive, deep rubble horizon, its upper surface roughly laid to form a paved area between the extra-mural roundhouse passage and the enclosure entrance. The rubble deposits, of which the platform is composed, are interpreted as the structural remains of buildings associated with the occupation of the site in Phase 5 or earlier. Immediately to the

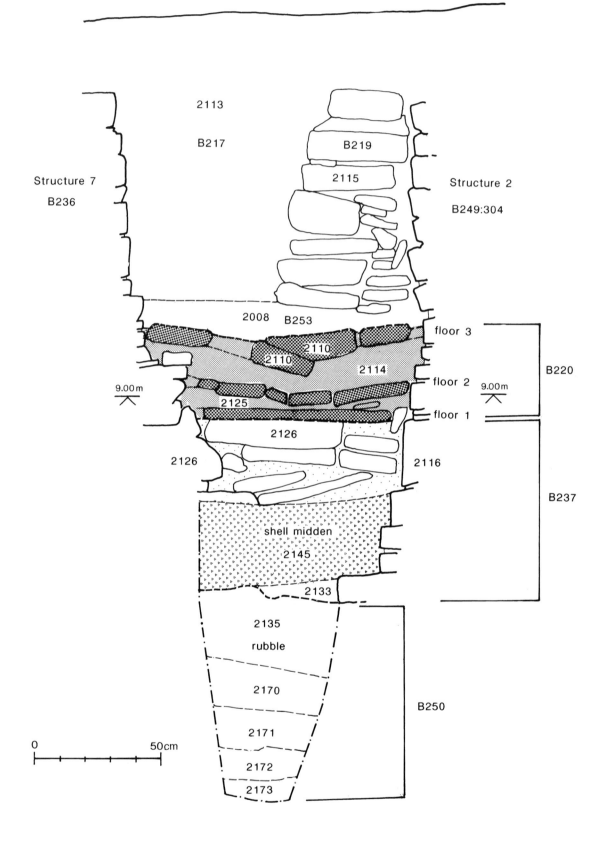

Illus 77   Section across passage between Structures 2 and 7

BLOCK 221

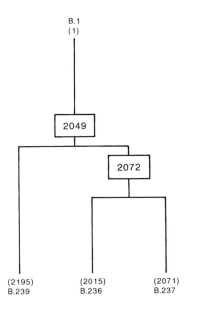

north of Structure 7, the laid surface of the Block 221 stone platform merged into a rubble spread (F2018: B235, Phase 6.1), indistinguishable from the rubble core of the Block 221 stone platform except insofar as it abutted Structure 7 (B236, Phase 6.1) and extended beneath the walls of an adjacent building, Structure 11 (B229, Phase 6.1).

Block 229: Structure 11 (Illus 79–81)

The walls (F2005) of a small, free-standing, subrectangular building, its north-west corner noticeably rounded, were butted against the north exterior face of Structure 7 (B236, Phase 6.1). Only a small part of the building or annexe, its longer axis aligned east–west, was located in the excavation area. It was roughly 1.8 m wide, and more along its longer axis, within walls up to 0.85 m thick and surviving to a height of 1.5 m. The north wall incorporated a low lintelled opening at its base, 0.7 m high and 0.75 m wide. No recognizable floor was located.

The walls were of solid stone construction. The masonry was composed predominantly of thin subangular stones, roughly laid in courses. Occasional larger stones, and subrounded slabs, were present in the west wall of the building. Stylistically, its masonry was similar in appearance and construction to that of Structure 7, immediately adjacent.

The building was filled with midden material (B224, Phase 6.3), radiocarbon dating of which provides a *terminus ante quem* date of cal AD 25–330 (GU-3282c) for its construction. Structures 12 (B227, Phase 6.2) and 13 (B225, Phase 6.2) were subsequently erected, respectively, against and over the walls of Structure 11.

Illus 78   Block 221 stratigraphic matrix

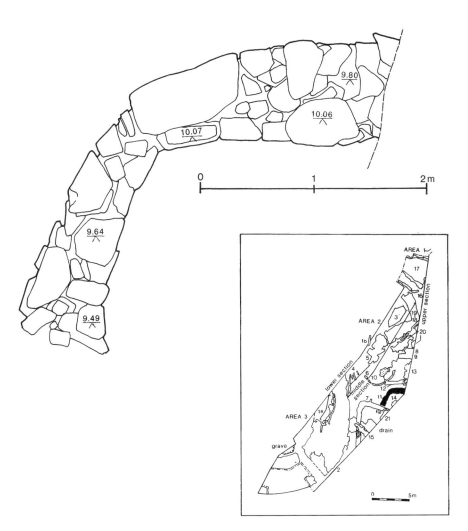

Illus 79   Structure 11 (B229)

Illus 80   Structure 11 (B229) from E, abutting Structure 7 (B236)

Illus 81   Interior elevation view of north wall of Structure 11 (B229)

Block 234: Structure 8, south side of primary entrance façade (Illus 82 & 83)

Structure 8 constitutes a fragmentary drystone wall, aligned roughly east to west, which protruded out of the Upper Section. It was overlain by the north wall of Structure 9 (B233, Phase 6.2) and abutted by paving (B205, Phase 6.2) associated with the secondary refurbishment of the entrance. The south face (F2187) and core (F2189) of the wall were visible only in elevation, the west end of the wall clearly ending with a built terminal. The north face (F2099), and part of the core, were visible on plan to the north of Structure 9. Overall, the masonry fragments describe a wall roughly 1.2 m wide and more than 1.3 m long, the wall disappearing beneath the Upper Section to the east.

A spread of medium subangular flat stones (F2175), possibly the remains of a paved surface, and a layer of brown silty clay (F2176) were exposed at the base of the section, adjacent to the south side of the wall, but were not investigated further. A layer of dark brown loam (F2188), with charcoal and clay flecks, which abutted the west side of the terminal, may represent a contemporary accumulation against the wall-fragment or levelling material associated with the construction of Structure 9 (B233, Phase 6.2).

The wall fragment is interpreted, on the basis of its stratigraphy and location, as the terminal to the south side of the primary entrance façade.

Block 235: Rubble (Illus 84)

Block 235 constitutes a rubble horizon (F2018), of medium to large angular and subangular stones, immediately north of Structure 7 (B236, Phase 6.1). To the west it merged with the laid surface of the Block 221 stone platform. While indistinguishable from the rubble core of the Block 221 stone platform, it was stratigraphically differentiated by its relationship to the walls of

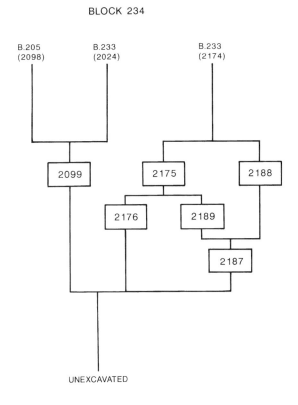

Illus 82   Block 234 stratigraphic matrix

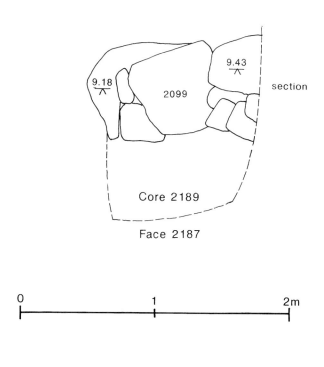

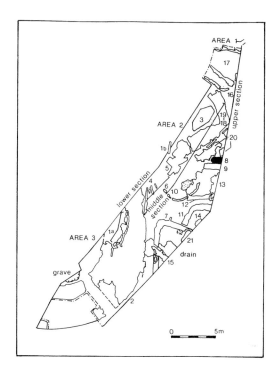

Illus 83   Structure 8, south side of entrance façade (B234)

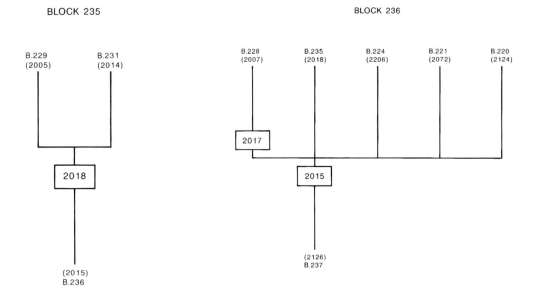

BLOCK 235

BLOCK 236

Illus 84   Block 235 stratigraphic matrix   Illus 85   Block 236 stratigraphic matrix

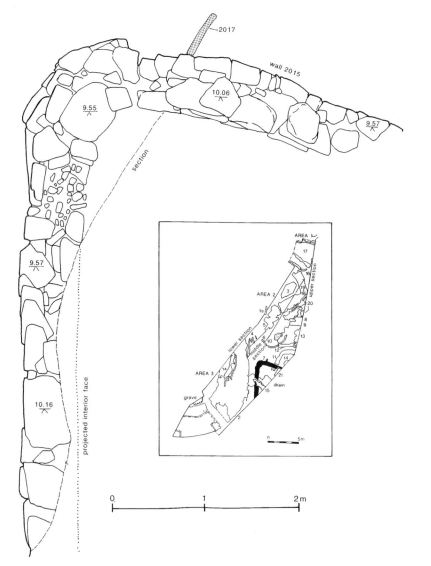

Illus 86   Structure 7 (B236)

Illus 87   Structure 7 (B236), from W, with Structure 15 (B218) over and exterior face of roundhouse (Structure 2) in foreground

Structure 7 (B236, Phase 6.1) and Structure 11 (B229, Phase 6.1), abutting the former and extending beneath the walls of the latter building. A single stone pounder/grinder (SF193) was recovered from this deposit.

Block 236: Structure 7 (Illus 85–87)

Structure 7, a large subrectangular free-standing building with rounded corners, was constructed over post-roundhouse rubble deposits (F2126: B237, Phase 5). The base of its wall lay 0.7 m above the base of the roundhouse and at the same level as the primary paved passage (F2124: B220, Phase 6.1) which extended between the two buildings. Structure 7 was aligned roughly north–south and lay roughly 1 m east of the roundhouse.

The building, only part of which was exposed in the excavated area, measured at least 4.5 m by 3 m inside walls 0.65 m wide and standing up to 1.2 m high. The walls (F2015) were faced internally and externally and comprised a solid-built stone core. The masonry consisted of close-fitting and coursed medium to large angular stones, albeit less substantial than the stonework found in the roundhouse. No trace of an entrance was located. The interior of the building, not excavated, was filled with rubble and charcoal-rich sandy soil (B224, Phase 6.3).

A thin orthostat (F2017), 0.5 m wide, 0.1 m thick and 1.3 m high, stood against the exterior north wall. To the east of the orthostat were appended the walls of Structure 11 (B229, Phase 6.1), a building whose masonry and mode of construction were of a similar style to that exhibited by Structure 7.

Radiocarbon dates from the post-roundhouse shell midden (F2145: B237, Phase 5) provide a *terminus post quem* date of 800–390 cal BC (GU-3059c & GU-3271c) for the construction of Structure 7. A *terminus ante quem* date of cal AD 25–330 (GU-3282c) is provided by the dating of shell deposits (F2004: B224, Phase 6.3) which post-date the abandonment of Structure 11.

Block 239: Structure 6 (Illus 31, 88, 89 & 109)

The fragmentary remains of Structure 6, traced at the south end of the Middle Section, were partially exposed in plan and in elevation, beneath the walls of Structure 10 (B231, Phase 6.2). The structure comprised a single-faced, drystone wall (F2195) which had been cut into underlying rubble infill deposits (B240, Phase 4). The wall stood up to 0.4 m high and contained both orthostatic and coursed masonry features. The wall-face, concave to the north-east, appeared to define the partial outline of a curvilinear building. The fragmentary remains of a paved floor (F2152), exposed over an area of roughly 2 m by 1 m, were traced inside the building.

The building was filled with rubble debris and shells (B238, Phase 6.2) and its wall was partially overlain by the laid stone surface forming the stone platform, Block 221. Radiocarbon dating of shells from the infill (B238, Phase 6.2), if contemporary with their deposition, indicates a *terminus ante quem* date of 50 cal BC–cal AD 235 (GU-3278c) for the construction of Structure 6.

BLOCK 239

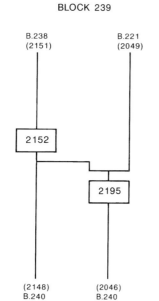

Illus 88   Block 239 stratigraphic matrix

3.2.7 Phase 6.2: Enclosed Roundhouse Settlement and Secondary Enclosure (Illus 90)

Summary

Phase 6.2 accommodates several structures and features which are either demonstrably associated with the secondary enclosure of the site, for stratigraphic or chronological reasons, or are likely to be so because of their spatial relationships with buildings and deposits whose stratigraphic position in the hierarchy is fixed.

The principal criteria which have governed the identification of Phase 6.2 blocks are the cutting of the secondary enclosure ditch (B212) and the construction of buildings and features relative to or in association with it. In very broad terms, Phase 6.2 spans the first quarter of the first millennium AD.

Order of composition

Block sequence: 212, 252, 209, 205, 233, 232, 238, 231, 230, 228, 227, 226, 225, 253 & 219

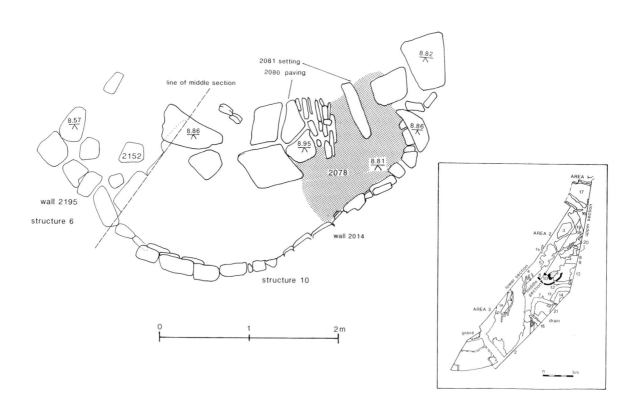

Illus 89   Structures 6 and 10 (B239 & B231)

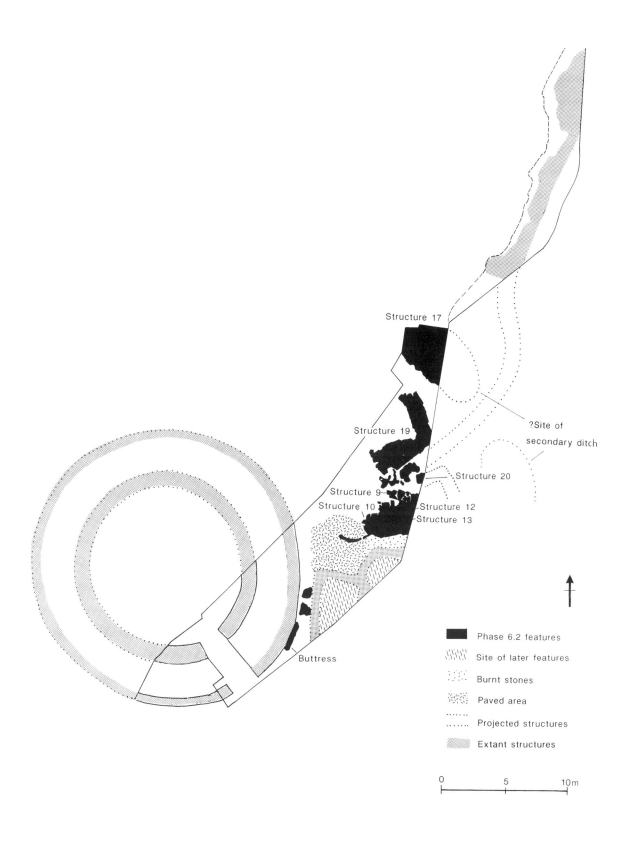

Structure 17

Structure 19

?Site of
secondary ditch

Structure 20

Structure 9

Structure 10

Structure 12

Structure 13

Buttress

■ Phase 6.2 features

Site of later features

Burnt stones

Paved area

Projected structures

Extant structures

0   5   10m

Illus 90   Phase 6.2 structures

Block 205: Structure 20, secondary paving at entrance and passage façade (Illus 91–93)

Block 205 constitutes a series of secondary levels of paving at the north-east entrance into the enclosure and the refashioning of the passage through the entrance façade.

The primary members of the block consist of a stone kerb or wall (F2052) and a wall fragment (F2098). These formed, respectively, the north-west and south-east sides of the refurbished entrance to the enclosure, and were set 1 m apart at their narrowest point. Both walls overlay the primary level of paving (B206, Phase 6.1). All subsequent paving levels were laid with respect to them. The alignment of the walls suggests that the entrance passage was splayed externally.

The kerb or wall (F2052) on the north-west side of the entrance was constructed of very large subrounded stones, set on edge and butted against the external face of Structure 19 (B209, Phase 6.2). The space between the wall-faces was filled with a brown loamy soil containing limpets (F2073). A single sherd of heavily tempered coarse pottery (V173), a cobble tool (SF78), two lumps of pumice (SF77a,b), and bones of cattle and sheep/goat were also present in this deposit. It is interpreted as midden material.

Only a short stub of the wall fragment (F2098) on the south-east side of the passageway was exposed within the excavated area. Its terminal was constructed of two large orthostats, 0.8 m high, with large boulders behind laid across the width of the wall. The wall fragment was 0.8 m long, of similar width, and continued beneath the Upper Section in a north-easterly direction. It was erected against the north side of Structure 8 (B234, Phase 6.1), part of the primary entrance façade.

The primary levels of secondary paving (F2065 & F2060) comprised medium to large, subangular and subrounded stones which formed a roughly level series of surfaces at, respectively, 8.98 m OD and 9.10 m OD. The upper surface of F2060 incorporated a pounder/grinder (SF67). It was subsequently covered with a brown loamy soil (F2059), the same deposit filling gaps in the surface of the earlier paving. Part of the skeleton of a large, arthritic cat (Part 6.2) was recovered from this deposit.

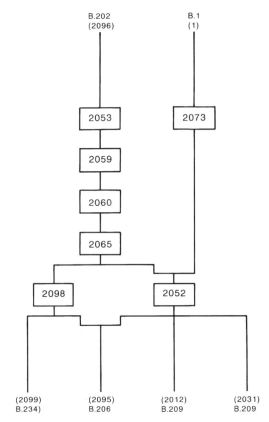

Illus 91   Block 205 stratigraphic matrix

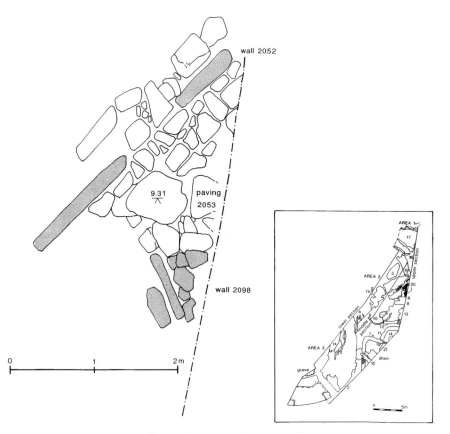

Illus 92   Structure 20, secondary paving and entrance façade (B205)

Illus 93   Secondary paving (F2060: B205) and orthostatic walls (F2052 & F2098: B205) at the
                enclosure entrance, from SW

Cattle and sheep/goat bones, the latter including neonates, were also present. Overlying and partially sealing this deposit was a laid surface of medium to large flat stones (F2053). Ordnance Datum levels on this upper paving (9.31 m OD) would correlate with either the secondary (F2109: 9.03–9.18 m OD) or tertiary (F2110: 9.22–9.30 m OD) paving levels in the extra-mural roundhouse passage (B220, Phase 6.1) to the south.

The soil deposit (F2059) may represent levelling material for the latest paved surface (F2053) in the entrance passage. The anthropogenic inclusions indicate that the material was probably derived from a site midden deposit. Deliberate burial on the threshold, however, may be indicated by the finding of a substantial part of a cat's skeleton.

Block 209: Structure 19, secondary enclosure wall and north-west side of passage façade (Illus 94–96)

Block 209 constitutes the inner (F2012) and outer (F2031) wall faces of Structure 19, a substantial L-shaped structure which was erected on the north-west side of the entrance threshold. It was constructed over the earlier wall fragments (F2182 & F2183: B210, Phase 6.1) which formed part of the primary enclosure wall and entrance façade and clipped the cut for the primary enclosure ditch (B214, Phase 6.1).

The wall lay parallel, and its return at right angles, to the external secondary ditch enclosure (B212, Phase 6.2). The enclosure wall lay roughly 1.4 m inside the line of the secondary enclosure ditch (B212, Phase 6.2). The position of the secondary ditch terminal, and thus its spatial relationship to the secondary enclosure wall, is not known but is assumed to have lain to the east of the primary ditch terminal.

The enclosure wall was roughly 4 m long, 1.2 m wide and up to 0.7 m high. The return section was roughly 3 m long and of

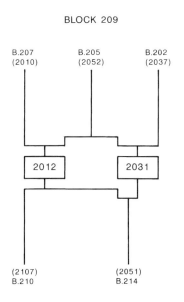

BLOCK 209

Illus 94   Block 209 stratigraphic matrix

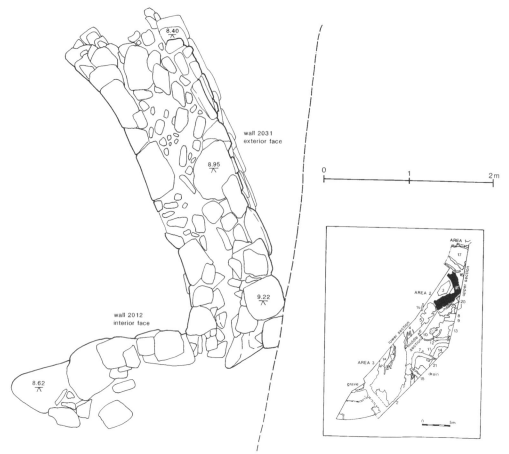

Illus 95   Structure 19 (B209), secondary enclosure wall and north-west side of entrance façade

Illus 96   Structure 19 (B209), secondary enclosure wall and north-west side of entrance façade, from E: with post-abandonment collapse and dump deposits (B207) to west

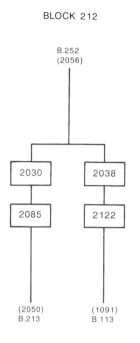

BLOCK 212

Illus 97   Block 212 stratigraphic matrix

similar width and height. It was abutted externally by the stone kerb and paving associated with the secondary entrance façade (B205, Phase 6.2). No trace of any floor surfaces, within the angle formed by the wall fragments, survived.

The walls of Structure 19 are interpreted as fragments of an enclosure wall and its return at the secondary entrance into the enclosure. Radiocarbon dating of mammal bones from midden material (B207, Phase 6.3) which was dumped behind its walls indicates that the secondary entrance façade was abandoned some time before cal AD 80–365 (AA-9564).

Block 212: Structure 17, secondary enclosure ditch (Illus 97–100)

Structure 17, the secondary enclosure ditch, lay roughly 1.5 m to the north of the earlier ditch. It was cut through the previously backfilled (B213, Phase 6.1) ditch, completely removing the north side of the earlier feature and removing all but a fragment of its terminal. The north side of the secondary ditch was cut through the shell midden (B113, Phase 6.1) which accumulated over the ruins of Structure 22, its base cut into the underlying till and exposing bedrock on its north side. Just over 3 m of the ditch was exposed in the excavated area. Its inner edge lay approximately 16 m from the roundhouse (Structure 2: B249:304, Phase 5) and 1.4 m outside the secondary enclosure wall (Structure 19: B209, Phase 6.2).

The ditch (F2122) was up to 1.7 m deep, with angled sides and a flat base. On the south side, where the ditch truncated the fill of the primary ditch, the cut was lined with yellow clay (F2085). The clay, presumably derived from the till, may have been used

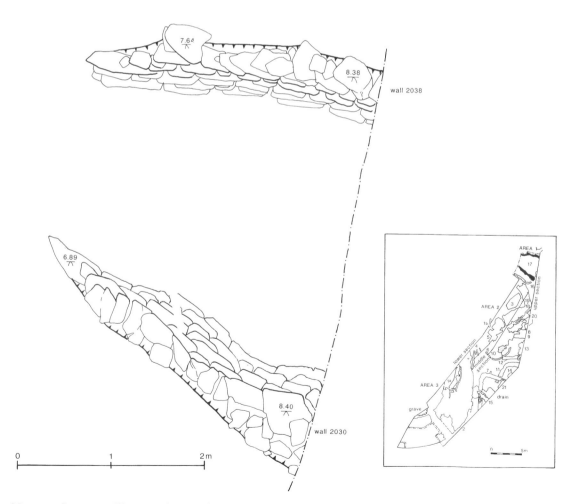

Illus 98   Structure 17, secondary enclosure ditch (B212)

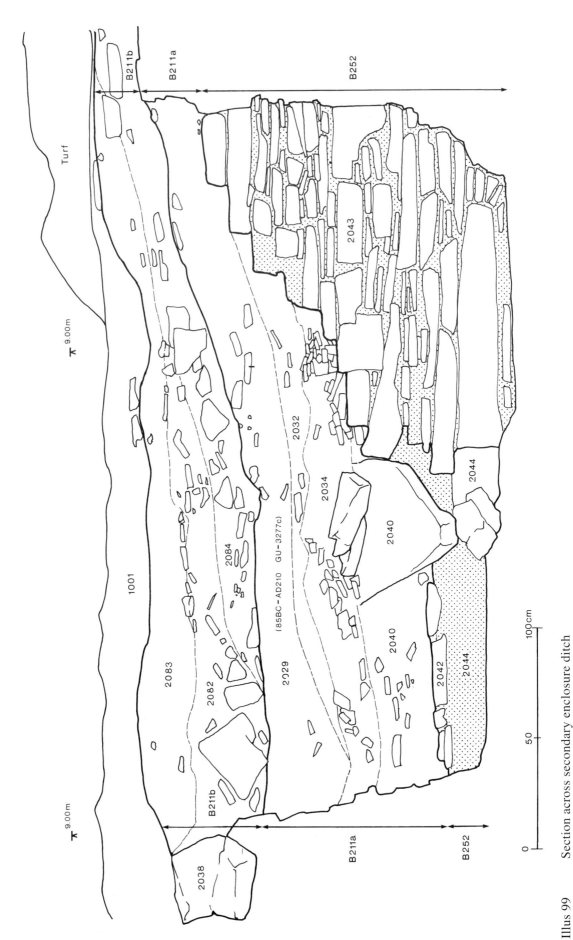

Illus 99   Section across secondary enclosure ditch

Illus 100   Secondary enclosure ditch (Structure 17: B212), from W, with primary fills and buttress (B252) overlain by B211 infill

temporarily to stabilize the exposed shell fill of the primary ditch. No other trace of the primary backfill deposits (B213), associated with the earlier ditch, were located within the excavated area.

The sides of the ditch were revetted with crudely coursed drystone walls (F2030 & F2038), formed of medium to large subangular and subrounded stones. The basal course, in places, incorporated very large rounded beach boulders. Just over 3 m wide at the standing section, the ditch narrowed markedly to the west where it was reduced to a width of just over 2 m. No evidence for a terminal was found. It is assumed, on the basis of the evidence for the refurbishment of the enclosure wall and entrance façade (Structures 19 & 20: B209 & B205), to lie to the east of the primary ditch terminal, behind the standing cliff-section.

Radiocarbon dating (235 cal BC–cal AD 115: GU-3061c) of the earlier shell midden (B113, Phase 6.1), cut by the north side of the secondary ditch, provides a *terminus post quem* date for its construction. Radiocarbon dating (400–50 cal BC: GU-3274c) of the infill material (B213, Phase 6.1) from the primary ditch, which was cut by the south side of the secondary enclosure, does not contradict this dating.

Block 219: Stone buttress and blocking of the extra-mural roundhouse passage (Illus 77, 101, 102 & 114)

Block 219 comprises a drystone wall (F2115) which was erected against the external face of Structure 2 (B249:304, Phase 5), and a second, blocking, wall (F2006) which was constructed across the passage between that building and Structure 7 (B236, Phase 6.1) to the east. Both walls were erected over a thick layer of splintered stone fragments (F2008: B253, Phase 6.2), a deposit which is interpreted as stone-robbing debris.

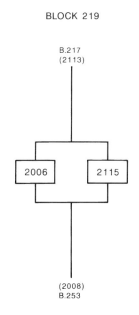

BLOCK 219

B.217
(2113)

2006	2115

(2008)
B.253

Illus 101   Block 219 stratigraphic matrix

Illus 102   Blocking (B219) of extra-mural passage, from S, with roundhouse (Structure 2) to west and
                 Structure 7 to east

The blocking wall (F2006) was constructed of large water-worn slabs and boulders, its south face roughly set in courses. The north side of the blocking wall consisted of thin but very large subangular stones, pitched on edge. The blocking wall, overall, was 1.25 m wide and stood up to 0.75 m high. The wall effectively blocked communication along the passage between the two buildings and marks its formal abandonment. The wall may also have functioned as a buttress, supporting one or other or both of the adjacent buildings.

A second wall (F2115) lay immediately south of the blocking wall. It, too, was constructed of large water-worn slabs, roughly coursed. It was erected against the external face of Structure 2 (B249:304, Phase 5) and is interpreted as a buttress. The feature coincides with a prominent outward lean in the east wall sector of Structure 2. The wall was 1.05 m wide at its base, reducing to a width of 0.6 m at its surviving upper surface, and stood 0.85 m high. Only a 1.3 m length of the wall was exposed within the excavated area. The feature, however, continues behind the standing Upper Section.

The presence of one or two buttressing walls against the exterior face of Structure 2, despite the earlier evidence for stone-robbing (B253, Phase 6.2) nearby and the clear evidence for the abandonment of the extra-mural passage, nonetheless, would seem to imply that occupation was still continuing inside the building at this time.

Block 225: Structure 13 (Illus 103 & 104)

Block 225 constitutes the walls, internal features and deposits associated with Structure 13. Only a small fragment of the

building lay within the excavated area. The upper elements of the building were recorded in plan and form a coherent structure. Although assigned to Phase 6.2, the building could be later.

One of the latest buildings on this part of the site, it lay across, at right angles to, and over the remains of Structures 11 (B229, Phase 6.1) and 12 (B227, Phase 6.2). Only a short fragment of coursed, drystone masonry (F2027), forming the south-west corner of a room or cell of a larger cellular building, survived. The single-faced wall fragment was 1 m long and 0.30 m high and, like that of Structure 12, it was revetted into the mound of rubble and burnt stones (B228, Phase 6.2).

The wall fragment delimited an area of paving (F2020 & F2101) which extended to the north and abutted wall F2024, an earlier wall originally associated with Structure 9 (B233, Phase 6.2) but one which had also been reused as the north side of Structure 12 (B227, Phase 6.2). The building was at least 5 m wide, along its north to south axis.

Against the north interior wall-face, and below the level of its paved floor, were the remains of a sunken stone-lined feature, 1.20 m long, 0.30 m deep and at least 0.60 m wide. The base of the feature was paved with medium subangular stones (F2021); its south and west sides were constructed of large stones (F2023), set on edge to form a lining. The feature is interpreted as a trough. Its base lay roughly 0.70 m above the floor of Structure 12 (F2022: B227, Phase 6.2).

The lower elements of the block were recorded only in section and are imperfectly understood. Re-examination of the evidence suggests that a series of superimposed stone (F2047 & F2011) and orange peat ash (F2033 & F2028) deposits, below the base of the trough (F2021), while conceivably associated with this building, as levelling material for its floor and trough, are more likely to represent dumped deposits inside the earlier building, Structure

BLOCK 225

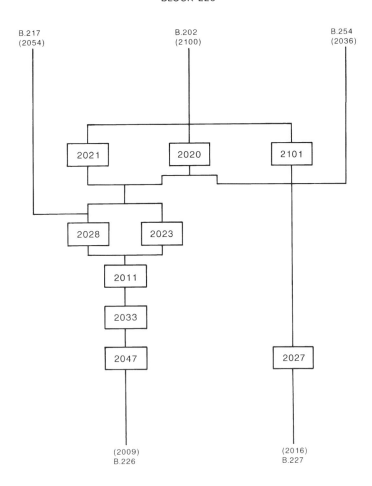

Illus 103   Block 225 stratigraphic matrix

12. These dumped stone and ash deposits, therefore, would be more appropriately correlated with Block 226 deposits (below). High concentrations of carbonized hulled barley grains were recorded from both the upper (F2028: 214/10 l) and lower (F2033: 372/10 l) ash deposits and these figures constitute the overall density for the block (288/10 l), the highest concentration recorded on the site. Some cattle and sheep/goat bones (79 g/10 l) and shells (23 g/10 l), and fuel ash and charcoal in trace quantities, were also present. Two fragments of a vessel with a rolled-rim (V197), of Middle Iron Age type (Part 5.1) and its fabric an untempered sandy clay, were also recovered from the lower ash deposit (F2033).

Block 226: Post-abandonment deposits in Structure 12

Block 226 comprises a deposit of soil and rubble (F2009) which filled Structure 12 (B227, Phase 6.2) after its abandonment. The deposit consisted of dark brown silty loam with small to medium subangular stones and occasional larger subangular and angular stones. The deposit extended throughout the building, overlying its floor, walls and internal fittings. Twenty sherds of tempered and untempered coarse pottery (V31, V109, V143, V163, V195, V203–205, V244 & V257), of Fabric Types 1, 1.1 and 3.1, were recovered from the deposit. The deposit also contained cattle, sheep/goat and cat bones (112 g/10 l) and carbonized barley (37/10 l). Trace amounts of fish bones, shells and charcoal were

also present. The deposit is interpreted as collapsed masonry from the wall-head, augmented with dumps of midden material. Refit sherds from Vessel 244 were also recovered from the infill (B211, Phase 6.3) of the secondary enclosure ditch.

Block 227: Structure 12 (Illus 105–107)

Block 227 constitutes the internal wall face (F2016) and stone floor (F2022) of Structure 12, together with a secondary internal masonry feature (F2019) which was constructed at the west end of the building. The building lay just inside the secondary enclosure wall.

The building was erected over and to the east of Structure 10, its floor overlying the infill deposits (B230, Phase 6.2) and wall (B231, Phase 6.2) of the earlier building. The internal single-faced wall (F2016) of Structure 12 was revetted into the deposits which formed a mound (B228, Phase 6.2) against Structure 7 (B236, Phase 6.1) and Structure 11 (B229, Phase 6.1) to the south. The construction of this building is the most likely cause for the truncation and levelling of earlier deposits (B228 & B230, Phase 6.2) on this part of the site.

The masonry of the single-faced drystone wall (F2016) consisted predominantly of orthostats, oversailed by medium to large subangular and angular stones laid in random courses. The wall-face was preserved to a height of 0.9 m. Prior to excavation, two of its stones protruded through the turf.

The wall-line was curvilinear on plan, concave to the north. Only the south and fragments of the east and west return walls

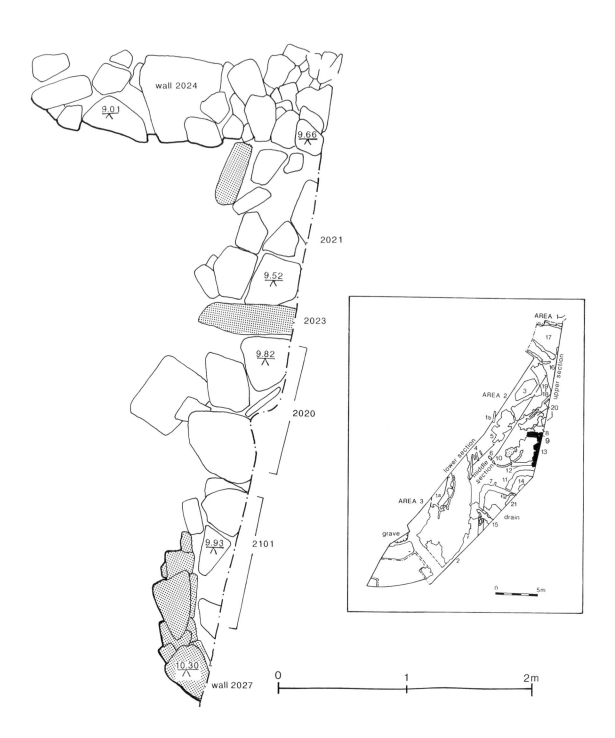

Illus 104   Structure 13 (B225)

survived. An earlier wall (F2024: B233, Phase 6.2), part of Structure 9 to the north, was reused as the north wall of Structure 12. The walls, together, like the earlier building to the west, Structure 10, define the outline of a subcircular or subsquare room or cell, roughly 3.5 m in diameter. No hearth was present inside the room and it is almost certainly part of a larger, cellular building. Although eroded to the west, the building continues beneath the standing Upper Section to the east.

The floor (F2022) of the building was neatly paved with medium to very large subangular stones. The floor abutted wall F2016 to the south and the earlier wall, F2024 (B233, Phase 6.2), to the north. Over the floor was built a short section of coursed drystone masonry (F2019), the stonework faced to the east. It was butted against the interior wall-face (F2016), close to its surviving south-west corner, and lay at 45° to it. The masonry fragment was 1.2 m long, 0.45 m wide and 0.35 m high. Unlikely to represent the remains of a radial dividing wall, because of its alignment, the feature is interpreted as the remains of a raised bench or platform which originally extended across the west side of the room.

No contemporary occupation deposits survived inside the building. Radiocarbon dating of earlier infill dumps (B230 & B238, Phase 6.2) provide *termini post quo* dates of 70 cal BC–cal AD 220 (GU-3279c) and 50 cal BC–cal AD 235 (GU-3278c), respectively, for the construction of Structure 12.

Block 228: Rubble and burnt stones

Block 228 constitutes a spread of medium subangular and subrounded stones, with occasional larger stones, many shells and fragments of splintered stone in a matrix of dark brown loam (F2007). Burnt stones, including heat-fractured beach pebbles, were also present.

The deposit formed a mound, up to 0.9 m high and roughly 3 m across but it had been levelled to the north where it merged with

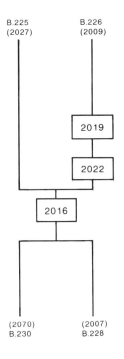

Illus 105   Block 227 stratigraphic matrix

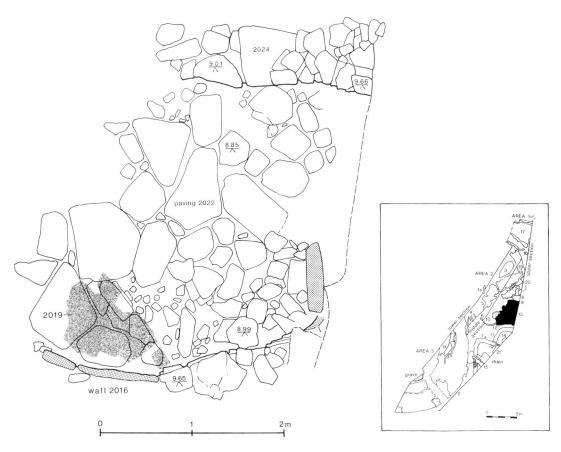

Illus 106   Structure 12 (B227)

Illus 107   Structure 12 (B227), from N

the post-abandonment deposits (B230, Phase 6.2) which filled the ruins of Structure 10. The mound abutted the north exterior faces of Structure 7 (B236, Phase 6.1) and Structure 11 (B229, Phase 6.1) to the south. It was subsequently truncated on the north by the construction of Structure 12 (B227, Phase 6.2).

Thirty-eight sherds of coarse pottery (V139, V144, V162, V189, V210–211, V214, V234, V236, V245, V251, V263 & V272), the majority of them untempered and burnished, were recovered from this deposit. The feature is interpreted as a mound of occupation debris, augmented with burnt-mound material.

The mound may have been associated with the occupation of Structure 10, immediately to the north; the occurrence of Block 228 mound-material over its ruins was possibly the result of post-depositional processes associated with its later levelling. The radiocarbon-dating evidence for the post-abandonment deposits (B230, Phase 6.2) from Structure 10, therefore, is irrelevant to the dating of the mound. The best dating evidence for the mound, like that for the construction of Structure 10 (B231, Phase 6.2) itself, comes from the infill deposits (B238, Phase 6.2) of Structure 6. This provides a *terminus post quem* date of 50 cal BC–cal AD 235 (GU-3278c) for the formation of the mound.

Block 230: Post-abandonment deposits in Structure 10

Block 230 comprises dump deposits of soil and rubble which filled Structure 10 (B231, Phase 6.2) after its abandonment. They are likely to represent midden material and were differentiated from the overlying rubble horizon (B228, Phase 6.2) only by the absence of burnt stones.

The deposits (F2013 & F2070) consisted of dark brown loam with shells, small to medium subangular stones and frequent small fragments of splintered stone. The deposits extended throughout

the building, overlying its floor, walls and internal surfaces and fittings. Twenty-nine sherds of tempered and untempered coarse pottery (V134, V146, V160, V185 & V265), of Fabric Types 1, 1.1 and 2, including one burnished example, were recovered from the deposits. The anthropogenic content of the block, compared to the underlying surface deposits (B231, Phase 6.2), is presented in Table 3 below.

Radiocarbon dating of shells from F2013 provides a *terminus post quem* date of 70 cal BC–cal AD 220 (GU-3279c) for the construction of Structure 12 (B227, Phase 6.2). The implications of the date as a *terminus ante quem* for the abandonment of Structure 10, statistical analysis of the building's potential duration and the problems of residuality are discussed below (see B231).

Block 231: Structure 10 (Illus 89, 108 & 109)

Block 231 constitutes the internal wall-face, stone fittings and primary occupation surfaces inside Structure 10. The building was erected over and to the east of Structure 6 (B239, Phase 6.1), its internal single-faced wall (F2014) revetted into the deposits (B238, Phase 6.2) which filled the earlier building. To the east its wall was cut into deposits (B232, Phase 6.2) post-dating the abandonment of Structure 9.

The masonry of the single-faced drystone wall (F2014) comprised a mixture of large angular stones, set on their sides, and medium to large subangular and angular stones laid in random courses. The wall-face formed a shallow arc on plan, concave to the north. Only the south and fragments of the east and west return walls survived. They appear, however, to define the outline of a subcircular or subsquare room or cell, just over 3 m across internally, and presumably part of a larger, cellular building. A spread of ashy silt (F2075: see below), below the

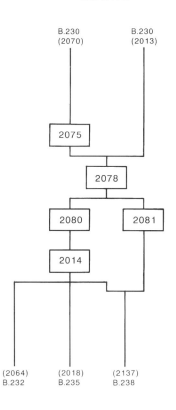

BLOCK 231

Illus 108   Block 231 stratigraphic matrix

floor of Structure 12 (B227, Phase 6.2), suggests that the building continued to the east, below the standing Upper Section.

Large, flat angular stones (F2080), within the arc of the wall-line and overlain by deposits (F2075 & F2078: see below) which abutted the interior wall-face, are interpreted as the remains of a paved floor inside the building. Adjacent to the surviving floor fragment, and possibly in the centre of the room or cell, was an arrangement of thin, angular, edge-set stones (F2081) forming a linear stone feature 0.75 m long and 0.3 m wide. The feature, together with the adjacent paving fragment, is interpreted as chocking stones for a stone-built feature, possibly a trough. It is unlikely to have been a hearth, given the absence of evidence for *in situ* burning on the paved surface.

A thin (50 mm), stone-free and shell-free spread of dark grey silt (F2078) with ash and charcoal inclusions extended across the eastern side of the building, partially overlying the paved floor (F2080) and abutting the linear stone feature (F2081) and interior wall-face. Two sherds (V153 & V180) of untempered pottery, charred barley grains (hulled and indeterminate) and burnt seeds and fragments of uncultivated plants, of heathers, sedges and docks, were recovered from this primary deposit. Burnt peat and charcoal were also present in low quantities (Table 3). The primary deposit is interpreted as an occupation surface which was formed from debris from an associated, but unlocated, hearth inside the building.

The primary deposit was overlain by a spread of brown, ashy and charcoal-flecked, sandy silt with fragments of shells (F2075). It extended beneath the floor of Structure 12 (B227, Phase 6.2) to the east. Although of a similar anthropogenic composition (Table 3) to the primary surface, the lower concentrations of cereal and other plant remains, and the substantially increased presence of pottery and shells provides some evidence to suggest that the deposits derive from different depositional processes.

Forty sherds (V70–71, V76–78, V115, V142, V160, V186, V187, V194 & V258–259) of slightly tempered (Fabric Type 1.1) and untempered (Fabric Type 1) coarse pottery, the latter including examples of burnished wares, were recovered from F2075. The deposit was also relatively rich in shells.

TABLE 3: COMPARISON OF ANTHROPOGENIC INPUTS TO SURFACE DEPOSITS (B231) AND POST-ABANDONMENT DEPOSITS (B230) IN STRUCTURE 10

Block	F no.	Pot	Mammal	Fish	Shell	Fuel ash	Burnt peat	Charcoal	Cereal	Seed
230		6g	22g	7g	539g	4g	1g	2g	1	4
231	2075	64g	37g	3g	240g	0	<1g	2g	4	3
231	2078	<1g	37g	2g	1g	<1g	2g	3g	15	15

Standardized as weight/frequency per 10 l sediment

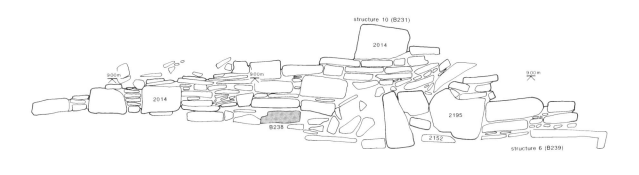

Illus 109   Elevation of Structures 10 and 6 (B231 & B239)

The secondary deposit (F2075) was initially interpreted as an upper, intact occupation horizon within Structure 10. Comparison of the anthropogenic inputs to the Structure 10 surface deposits, however, suggests that the upper deposit (F2075) may represent a levelled surface of dumped midden material inside the abandoned building or disturbed occupation material which has become mixed with what are clearly later infill deposits (B230, Phase 6.2).

Radiocarbon dating of the underlying deposits (B238), filling the earlier building, Structure 6, clearly indicates that Structure 10 was constructed after 50 cal BC–cal AD 235 (GU-3278c). Radiocarbon dating of shells from the overlying infill deposits (B230), if contemporary with the event, would provide a *terminus ante quem* date of 70 cal BC–cal AD 220 (GU-3279c) for the abandonment of Structure 10. Statistical analysis (Part 4.1) indicates that there is a 54 per cent probability that the lower date (B238) is younger than the upper date (B230). This strongly suggests that the dump deposits, with which Structure 10 was later filled, are residual and derive from an earlier midden on the site. On the assumption, however, that the dated samples are contemporary with the deposits, the chronological difference between the two dates can be calculated and some indication of the building's duration can thus be inferred. Statistical analysis indicates that there is a 68 per cent probability that the difference between the two dates is less than 100 years. There is, however, a strong possibility that Block 230 deposits, like those which in part comprise Block 228 (Phase 6.2), have been redeposited. The *terminus ante quem* value of Block 230, therefore, is weak.

Block 232: Post-abandonment deposits in Structure 9

A dump deposit of small to medium subangular and subrounded stones and fragments of splintered stone in a matrix of loose brown loam (F2064) overlay the floor of Structure 9 (B233, Phase 6.2). The deposit, first observed beneath the stone floor (F2022: B227, Phase 6.2) of Structure 12, was also cut by the wall fragment (F2014: B231, Phase 6.2) forming Structure 10.

Cattle, pig and sheep/goat bones (261 g/10 l), fish bones (10 g/10 l) and shells (1278 g/10 l) were present in high concentrations. Twenty sherds (V30, V75, V108, V114, V131, V141, V146, V159, V239 & V240) of untempered or slightly tempered coarse pottery, predominantly of Fabric Types 1 and 1.1, including three sherds of burnished pottery, were also recovered. The deposit is interpreted as rubble and midden material which was dumped inside the ruins of Structure 9 after its abandonment.

Block 233: Structure 9 (Illus 110 & 111)

Block 233 constitutes the fragmentary wall and floor deposits associated with Structure 9. The building lay just inside the secondary entrance façade (Structure 20: B205, Phase 6.2) and at roughly 45° to it. The building was truncated on the west through erosion of the sea-bank and its relationship to the projected course of any continuation of the entrance passage is unknown. Any substantial continuation of the building to the west, however, would have certainly intruded upon the entrance passage and have created a dog-leg in its course.

The north wall (F2024) of the building was erected over the remains of the southern fragment of the primary entrance façade wall (Structure 8: F2099 & F2187: B234, Phase 6.1). The wall stood up to 1 m high, 0.8 m wide and protruded 1.9 m from the standing Upper Section. It was aligned roughly east–west and appears to have formed part of a rectilinear building. The wall was free-standing and was constructed of large to very large subangular and subrounded stones. To the south and abutting the face of the wall was a spread of compacted yellow clay and occasional large flat, subangular stones (F2167). Over this lay a patchy layer of dark brown silty clay with charcoal flecks and peat ash (F2169). Over both was an oval spread, up to 0.7 m across, of greyish-white peat ash (F2168) and loose brown silt (F2166), rich in artefacts. The deposits were truncated to the south by the

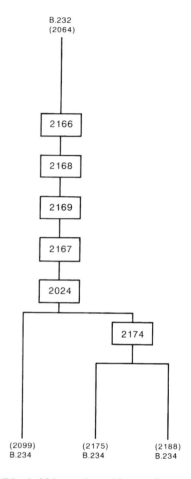

Illus 110   Block 233 stratigraphic matrix

construction of Structure 10 (B231, Phase 6.2) and, particularly, Structure 12 (B227, Phase 6.2), and no trace of the building's original south wall was located within the area investigated. The north wall (F2024) was subsequently reused in both Structures 12 (B227, Phase 6.2) and 13 (B225, Phase 6.2).

The floor deposits inside Structure 9, particularly the silt layer F2166, were extremely rich in artefacts. Over 900 sherds of coarse pottery, the majority burnished, were recovered from these deposits. Vessel forms included examples of small, flat-based, straight-sided or barrel-shaped vessels (Part 5.1). Six laminated sandstone discs (SF160a–f), the majority with diameters in the range 100–130 mm, were found with the pottery fragments. The upper stone of a rotary quern (SF205), a small stone weight (SF179), two stone pounders/grinders (SF165 & SF167) and one cobble tool (SF166) were also recovered from this deposit. Cattle bones (48 g/10 l), fish bones (3 g/10 l), shells (59 g/10 l) and trace amounts of burnt peat, charcoal, naked barley (from F2167) and wild seeds were also present in low concentration, by comparison with the later infill deposits (B232, Phase 6.2). The floor deposits and their associated artefacts are interpreted as occupation material which was left *in situ* at the time of the building's abandonment.

The *terminus ante quem* value of the radiocarbon date from the post-abandonment deposits (B230, Phase 6.2) filling an overlying building, Structure 10, is discussed elsewhere (B231, Phase 6.2). The spatial and stratigraphical relationships between Structure 9, the secondary entrance façade (B205, Phase 6.2) and ditch (B212, Phase 6.2), however, would indicate a broad date within the first quarter of the first millennium AD for the construction and occupation of Structure 9. The implications of this relatively early date for the dating of burnished wares in the Northern Isles are discussed elsewhere (Part 5.1).

Illus 111   Structure 9 (B233)

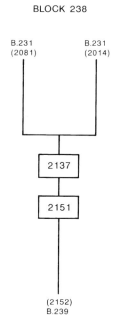

BLOCK 238

Illus 112   Block 238 stratigraphic matrix

Block 238: Post-abandonment deposits in Structure 6 (Illus 31 & 112)

Block 238 constitutes infill and dump deposits inside Structure 6. The floor (F2152: B239, Phase 6.1) was overlain with compact brown silt and medium subangular stones (F2151). This deposit formed, in section, a triangular wedge around the north part of the building. On the basis of its content and form and the presence of a tip line in its upper surface, this deposit is interpreted as collapsed wall fabric. It was overlain, and the building was filled, with rubble debris and shells (F2137). This deposit is interpreted as midden material. Its anthropogenic content (mammal bone 24 g/10 l: fish bone 17 g/10 l: shells 1908 g/10 l: cereals 1/10 l) is dominated by shells. No artefacts were recovered from this deposit.

Radiocarbon dating of this deposit, if contemporary with its deposition, indicates a *terminus ante quem* date of 50 cal BC–cal AD 235 (GU-3278c) for the construction of Structure 6. The same date provides a firm *terminus post quem* date for the later construction of Structure 10 (B231, Phase 6.2).

Block 252: Primary fills of secondary ditch and its refurbishment (Illus 99 & 113)

Block 252 constitutes the primary fills of the secondary ditch and the construction of a buttress against the south side of the ditch.

BLOCK 252

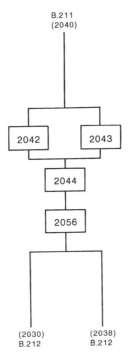

Illus 113   Block 252 stratigraphic matrix

The basal deposit, located only at the seaward side of the ditch, was a layer of dark grey, charcoal-flecked sandy silt (F2056). Nine sherds (V81, V82, V133, V147, V182 & V 191) of, mostly, untempered pottery, of Fabric Types 1 and 1.1, including an example of Middle Iron Age type (PTS7: Part 5.1), were recovered from this deposit. Cattle, sheep/goat, grey seal, gannet and fish bones were also present.

The basal deposit was sealed by a 0.25 m thick layer of dark brown sandy silt (F2044) with small stones and fragments of shell. Nine sherds (V31, V74, V94, V135, V136, V140 & V177) of untempered and tempered pottery, of Fabric Types 1 and 3.1, were recovered from this layer. Cattle, sheep/goat, raven, corvid and fish bones were also present.

The anthropogenic content (mammal bones 17 g/10 l: fish bones 15 g/10 l: shells 900 g/10 l: fuel ash 2 g/10 l: burnt peat 2 g/10 l: charred naked barley 7/10 l) of the primary fill deposits indicates a measure of some dumping of midden material into the ditch. Human skeletal material, recovered during samples processing, was also present in the bone assemblage from F2044. Comprising only the bones of the lower legs and feet, they have been identified as adult, robust and probably male (Part 6.1). The presence of a fairly complete suite of lower leg and foot bones indicates that the bones are likely to have been deposited in an articulated state.

The primary fill deposits are interpreted as silt-wash, enriched with sand and midden material.

A drystone wall (F2043) was subsequently erected over the primary silt deposits in the ditch. It was constructed against the south side of the ditch revetment and was set at right angles to it. The wall was up to 1.3 m long, 1.4 m high and, in elevation, appears to have had a staggered or stepped profile. Of unknown width, because it was located exactly in line with the standing section, subsequent erosion of the cliff-face over the winter of 1990 indicates that the wall is more than 0.3 m wide. The wall is interpreted as a buttress for the south side of the ditch revetment.

Overlying the primary fill deposits and abutting the buttress was an extensive spread of medium to large subangular and subrounded stones (F2042), forming a roughly level surface throughout the ditch. Initially interpreted as a crudely paved surface to the floor of the ditch, the stones are perhaps more likely to represent demolition debris, associated with the later abandonment (B211, Phase 6.3) of the ditch.

Block 253: Stone-robbing and abandonment of the extra-mural roundhouse passage (Illus 77 & 114)

Block 253 constitutes a 0.15 m thick deposit of splintered stone fragments (F2008) which extended throughout the passage between Structure 2 (B249:304, Phase 5) and Structure 7 (B236, Phase 6.1) and over which a stone buttress and cross-wall (B219, Phase 6.2) were subsequently built. Shells were common (249 g / 10 l). Other anthropogenic indicators were only present in trace quantities. No artefacts were recovered from this deposit.

The stone element in the deposit is interpreted as debris associated with the stone-robbing of adjacent buildings. The anthropogenic assemblage probably represents residual material, derived from displaced wall-core material and deposited during the course of the robbing activity.

Illus 114   Detail of section through extra-mural passage, from N: showing B253 debris overlying a series of superimposed floor surfaces (B220) and underlying external buttressing (F2115: B219) of the roundhouse to west

3.2.8 Phase 6.3: Abandonment of Enclosure

Summary

Phase 6.3 witnesses what appears to have been a major period of infilling of the secondary enclosure ditch (B211), the adjacent entrance façade (B207) and Structures 7 and 11 (B224) to the south. Each of these deposits is radiocarbon dated, roughly, to the first quarter of the first millennium AD, and, together, the phase is characterized as one of cessation of occupation on this part of the site (Area 2) at that time or shortly thereafter. Concentrations of fish bones (Part 6.3) of butterfish, sea scorpion, sandeels and small specimens of freshwater eels in the backfill (B211) of the ditch and the infill of the entrance façade (B207) probably point to the presence of natural predators, probably otters, on the site. Their presence, nesting and feeding in among the ruined buildings, reinforces the interpretation that the site was almost certainly deserted at this time.

It is possible that Block 238 (Phase 6.2), which is similarly dated, should also be assigned to this horizon. On this model, the stratigraphic chain above Block 238 (B225–228 & B230–231) would post-date the major abandonment phase, Phase 6.3. The presence, however, of refit material (V244) in the ditch fill (B211), almost certainly derived from post-abandonment deposits (B226) filling Structure 12, indicates that the bulk of the stratigraphic chain above Block 238 is likely to pre-date the backfilling of the secondary ditch, and thus may be assigned to Phase 6.2.

Order of composition

Block sequence: 211, 207 & 224

Block 207: Post-abandonment deposits in Structure 19 (Illus 31, 96 & 115)

Block 207 constitutes the infill deposits, 0.9 m deep, which filled Structure 19 after its abandonment. These directly overlay the floor and occupation deposits (B210, Phase 6.1) associated with Structure 18, no trace of a floor associated with Structure 19 (B209, Phase 6.2) having survived.

The basal deposit (F2097) comprised small subangular and subrounded stones, with occasional fragments of splintered stones, in a matrix of brown silt. Three sherds of untempered and slightly tempered pottery, one example (V218) burnished, another (V31) slipped, were recovered from this deposit. Cattle, sheep/goat, pig, grey seal, cetacean, red deer and bird bones were also present. This deposit is interpreted as midden material which was dumped behind the entrance façade. It was overlain by larger stones and splintered stone fragments, densely packed, and brown loam (F2010). Occasional cattle, sheep/goat and grey seal bones and three sherds of coarse pottery (V116 & V149) were also recovered. It is interpreted as stone robbing debris, mixed with midden material. The presence of otters is inferred on the basis of the discovery of concentrations of small, fragmented fish bones, referable to non-economic species (Part 6.3).

Radiocarbon dating of mammal bones and shells from the primary fill deposit (F2097) provides *termini post quo* dates, of cal AD 80–365 (AA-9564) and 190 cal BC–cal AD 120 (GU-3280c) respectively, for the dumping of the upper, rubble and midden, deposit (F2010) behind the entrance façade and an indicative date for its abandonment.

Block 211: Fill deposits of secondary enclosure ditch (Illus 99 & 116)

Block 211 constitutes a series of deposits which filled the secondary enclosure ditch upon its abandonment. Two principal subgroups can be recognized within these deposits. The lower group of deposits (F2029 and below, B211a), up to 1.2 m deep, dips towards the north side of the ditch and indicates that the material was dumped into the ditch from the south, or interior side of the enclosure. This deposit model is reinforced by the refit finds' assemblage. No soil stabilization horizons were evident among these fills and the deposits are interpreted as a deliberate and rapid backfilling of the ditch. An upper group of deposits (F2082–2084, B211b), up to 0.5 m deep and characterized as brown and grey silts with small to medium subangular stones and occasional shells and splintered stone fragments, was void of any artefactual or ecofactual material. It is interpreted as a predominantly natural silting of the top of the abandoned ditch.

The basal deposit comprised large to very large angular stones in a matrix of brown loam with some shells (F2040). Three sherds (V119 & V244) of untempered pottery, two of them burnished, and an assemblage of cattle, sheep/goat and pig bones, and bones from a raven, were recovered from this deposit. It is interpreted as collapsed masonry from the wall buttress (F2043: B252, Phase 6.2), mixed with midden material.

The immediately overlying deposits, in sequence F2034, F2032 and F2029, all similar, vary only in their relative proportions of splintered stone fragments, soil and shells; the former being concentrated towards the base of this sequence, soil and shells towards the top. Smoothed, slipped and burnished wares were all present in these deposits (Part 5.1). Refit sherds from Vessel 30, a flat-rimmed vessel with a smoothed exterior, and Vessel 244, a flat-rimmed burnished vessel, are common to each of them. Sherds of the latter vessel were also recovered from the basal deposit (F2040). Other finds from this lower group of contexts include a stone pounder/grinder (SF43) and a fragment of a tuyère (SF46b), the latter almost certainly derived from Structure 18 (B210, Phase 6.1) deposits. Cattle and sheep/goat bones were also present.

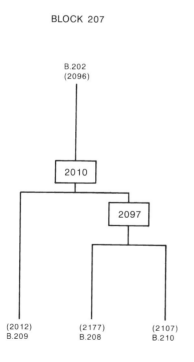

BLOCK 207

B.202
(2096)

2010

2097

(2012)
B.209

(2177)
B.208

(2107)
B.210

Illus 115   Block 207 stratigraphic matrix

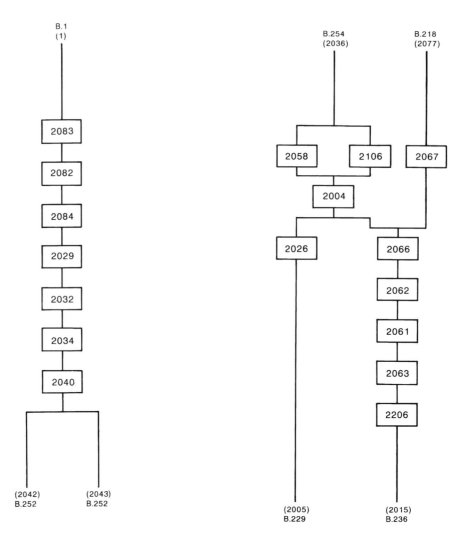

Illus 116   Block 211 stratigraphic matrix

Illus 117   Block 224 stratigraphic matrix

Fragmented fish bones (Part 6.3), of non-economic species, were recovered from F2029. Their presence almost certainly implies the presence of otters, or other natural predators, on the site at this time.

The lower group of deposits, each characterized by the presence of splintered stone fragments, is interpreted as stone robbing debris associated with the dismantling of adjacent buildings, intermixed with redeposited midden and occupation material. The artefact assemblage from the ditch fills suggests that this material derived, at least in part, from the clearing out of Structures 9, 12 and 18/19 to the south. Shells from F2029, the uppermost of the lower group of deposits, have been radiocarbon dated to the period 85 cal BC–cal AD 210 (GU-3277c). This provides a *terminus post quem* date for the final silting deposits (F2082-F2084) and an indicative date for the abandonment of this feature.

Block 224: Post-abandonment deposits in Structures 7 & 11 (Illus 117 & 118)

Block 224 constitutes a series of deposits which filled Structures 7 and 11 after their abandonment. Deposits filling Structure 11 were removed to the base of the walls. Those filling Structure 7 were only partially removed, excavation ceasing at a surface (F2206) roughly coincident with the top of the surviving wall-head.

The basal deposit inside Structure 11 (B229, Phase 6.1) comprised dark grey loam, heavily flecked with charcoal (F2026). Over this was dumped a 0.9 m thick deposit of dark brown loam, with occasional large stones and splintered stone fragments (F2004). Shells and cattle and sheep/goat bones were also present. This deposit is interpreted as midden material, dumped inside the ruins of the building and extending over its south wall into Structure 7 beyond. Cut into the north-east corner was a dump of shells (F2058).

Structure 7 was also filled with midden material (F2004). This overlay a deposit of large subangular stones and splintered stone fragments (F2066) which, in turn, sealed a series of charcoal-flecked sand lens deposits (F2061–F2063). At the base of the excavated section was further large rubble (F2206), interpreted as collapsed masonry from the wall-head. Smoothed and burnished wares were common in these deposits. Overlying all these deposits was a 0.8 m deep deposit of medium to large subangular stones, with frequent splintered stone fragments (F2067 & F2106).

Two radiocarbon dates were obtained from bulk samples of the midden deposit (F2004). One, on cattle and sheep/goat bones, produced a date of 360 cal BC–cal AD 15 (AA-9565). A second, on limpets, was dated to cal AD 25–330 (GU-3282c). The disparity in the dates would seem to imply that the deposit either accumulated over some considerable period of time or was derived from deposits of differing age.

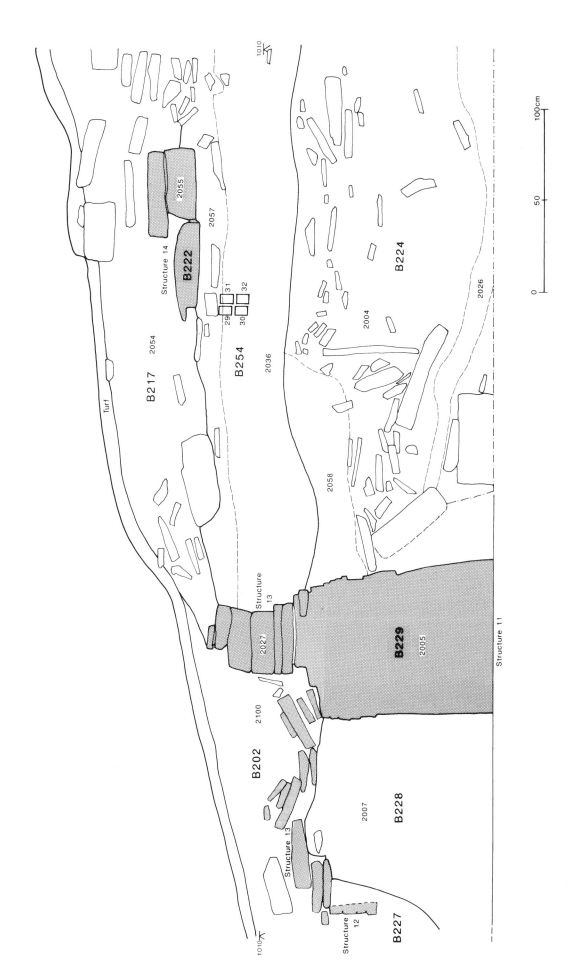

Illus 118   Upper section: Structures 11, 13 & 14

3.2.9 Phase 7: Late Iron Age Deposits

Summary

With the infilling of the enclosure ditch and the apparent cessation of occupation within the enclosure in Phase 6.3, the next clearly datable horizon of activity comes from Area 1. It is represented by the formation of a series of dump sediments, possibly laid down in connection with cultivation on the site. This activity is broadly dated, by radiocarbon, to the period AD 250–750. A ground surface subsequently developed in the top of these deposits.

Order of composition

Block sequence: 107, 106 & 105

Block 105: Late Iron Age ground surface (Illus 44)

Block 105 constitutes an extensive band of black sandy silt-loam (F1011), roughly 0.2 m thick. It was formed in the top of the underlying sediments (B107, Phase 7) and was sealed by 'farm mound' deposits (B104, Phase 8). The silt-loam band, in places lensed with peat ash, formed a continuous, more or less level and very distinct horizon throughout the Area 1 cliff-section. Its upper boundary abrupt, its lower boundary clear and smooth, it was interpreted in the field as a buried ground surface.

Like Block 107 sediments, from which it was derived, the anthropogenic content of F1011, with the exception of fuel ash inclusions (8 g/10 l), was generally low. The sediment contained occasional mammal bones (36 g/10 l), fish bones (10 g/10 l) and shells (32 g/10 l). Trace quantities of burnt peat, cereals and other seeds were also present. Flax (1/10 l), a feature of the overlying 'farm mound' deposits (B103 & B104, Phase 8), first appears at this level. A single flint flake (SF71) was also recovered.

Post-excavation analysis (Part 6.11) has confirmed the identification of the sediment as an *in situ* buried ground surface. Pollen analysis (Part 6.9) has indicated that the surface supported an acidic heath vegetation immediately prior to burial. Preservation of undisturbed humified plant remains at the interface between the ground surface and the overlying 'farm mound' deposits (B104, Phase 8) reflects the rapidity with which the surface was buried.

It is clear that the old ground surface developed over a considerable period of time. Statistical analysis of the radiocarbon dates (Part 4.1) from the top of the underlying Block 107 sediments (cal AD 520–870: GU-3065) and the base of the overlying Block 104 deposits (cal AD 990–1240: GU-3067) indicates that there is a 69 per cent probability that the ground surface existed for 310–525 years.

Block 106: Linear cut feature and possible post-hole (Illus 44 & 119)

Two negative features were cut into the upper surface of Block 107 deposits. Both are of unknown function and association. They clearly testify, however, to activity broadly contemporary with (F1114) or earlier than (F1068) the formation of the ground surface (F1011: B105, Phase 7) which developed in the upper surface of the Block 107 sediments.

The cut (F1068) for the smaller feature, possibly the remains of a post-hole, was U-shaped in section and was 0.15 m deep and 0.2–0.3 m across. It was filled with dark brown sandy silt and clay loam (F1066 & F1067).

The second, larger cut (F1114), probably the remains of a linear feature, was V-shaped in section, 0.35 m deep and 0.5 m wide. The fill of the cut was indistinguishable from the overlying buried soil horizon (F1011: B105, Phase 7).

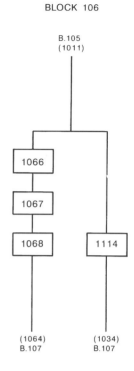

Illus 119   Block 106 stratigraphic matrix

The nature of the fill of the smaller feature, which is dissimilar from the ground surface horizon (F1011: B105, Phase 7), suggests that it was either cut prior to the formation of the ground surface or that its upper profile has been destroyed by bioturbation and soil formation processes. The larger feature, on the other hand, was almost certainly cut through the buried ground surface (F1011: B105, Phase 7) and backfilled with the same deposits.

Radiocarbon dating of Block 107 deposits indicates that the Block 106 features were cut after cal AD 620–880 (GU-3064c) or cal AD 520–870 (GU-3065). Radiocarbon dates from the base of the primary 'farm mound' sediments (B104, Phase 8), which were deposited over the buried ground surface (B105, Phase 7), indicate that the features were cut before the period cal AD 990–1240 (GU-3067).

Block 107: Late Iron Age ash deposits (Illus 44 & 120)

Block 107 constitutes a series of shallow, horizontally layered deposits, 0.50–0.90 m deep. The deposits extended throughout the Area 1 cliff-section, overlying the shell midden (B109, Phase 6.1) to the south, and the causeway (B112, Phase 6.1) and Structure 23 (B111, Phase 6.1) to the north. These deposits, in burying the causeway, mark a significant change in the use of the enclosed site to the south and their dating (below) reinforces the Phase 6.3 dates as *termini ante quo* dates for the abandonment of the enclosed roundhouse settlement.

The deposits were sealed, throughout the course of the exposed cliff-section, by the Block 105 (Phase 7) buried ground surface which developed in the top of the Block 107 sediments.

The deposits were predominantly sandy and silty loams and were brown, reddish-brown or black. Charcoal flecks and fragments of shells were common; cattle, sheep/goat and pig bones were rare. Occasional animal burrows, up to 100 mm in diameter, and frequent worm burrows, 5–20 mm in diameter, were also present. Fuel ash, ranging from <1 g to 58 g/10 l (F1069), was present in some quantity (7 g/10 l), above average for the site.

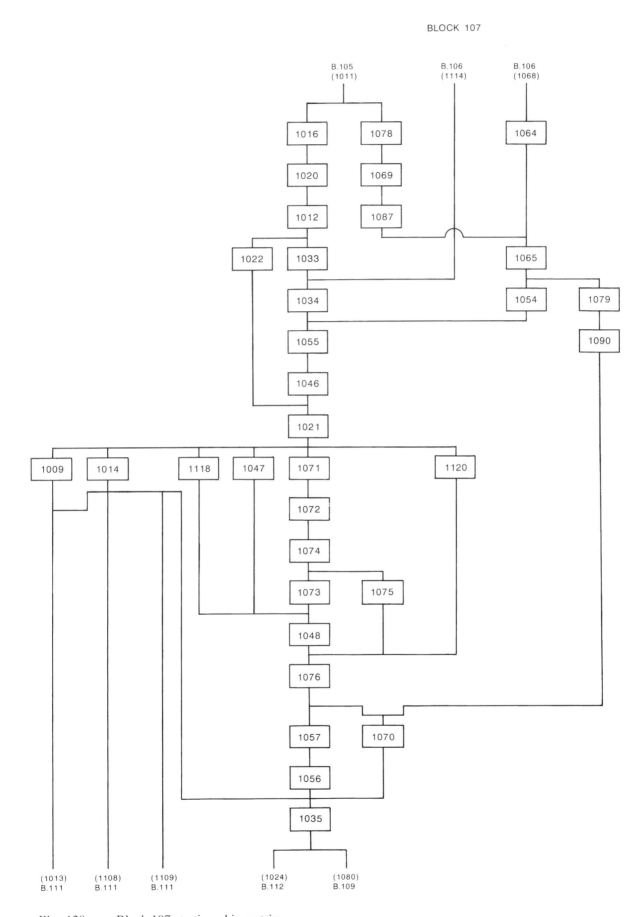

Illus 120   Block 107 stratigraphic matrix

However, the anthropogenic input to these deposits, generally, was low with rare mammal bones (22 g/10 l), fish bones (4 g/10 l) and shells (23 g/10 l) and trace quantities only of burnt peat, charcoal, cereals and other seeds. Artefacts were similarly rare. Six sherds of coarse untempered pottery, the majority smoothed or burnished, and a comb fragment (SF6), made from antler, were the only artefacts recovered as a result of excavation and an extensive wet-sieving programme of just under 600 l of deposits.

Interpreted on site as some form of specialized midden dump, post-excavation analysis (Part 6.11) of the composition, fabric and microstructure has identified the sediments as *in situ* ash dumps, deposited infrequently, with intervening periods of soil formation. Diatom analysis (Part 6.10) indicates burnt turves as the most likely source of the mineral residue. The original stratigraphy of the dumps, however, has been largely destroyed by soil formation and bioturbation. Cultivation has been proposed (Part 7.1) as a possible mechanism for the spreading of the deposits, thus providing an explanation for their considerable extent, but this cannot be confirmed on the basis of the evidence available.

Radiocarbon dates were obtained from both the base and top of the Block 107 sediments. Mammal bones in the basal deposit (F1035) were dated to the period cal AD 285–670 (GU-3063). Two dates, cal AD 620–880 (GU-3064c) and cal AD 520–870 (GU-3065), on shells and mammal bones respectively, were obtained from the top of the sediments (F1034). Statistical analysis of these dates (Part 4.1) indicates that there is a 69 per cent probability that

the sediments accumulated over a period of 45–270 years. Further analysis (Part 7.1) has suggested that the Block 107 sediments remained close to the ground surface for at least 400 years.

The difference in date between the underlying Block 109 (Phase 6.1) deposits (400–70 cal BC: GU-3062c) and the basal date (cal AD 285–670: GU-3063) from Block 107 sediments would appear to indicate a hiatus in the use of this part of the site during Phase 6.2 of the site's occupation.

3.2.10 Phase 8: The 'Farm Mound' and Final Structures on Area 2 (Illus 121)

Summary

Phase 8 accommodates a series of dated horizons on Area 1, represented by the 'farm mound' deposits, and an undated range of deposits and structures, clearly post-roundhouse in date, which lie at the top of the cliff-section on Area 2. All of this latter group, with the exception of Structure 15 (B218), are linked to the stratigraphic chain above a silty ash horizon (B254).

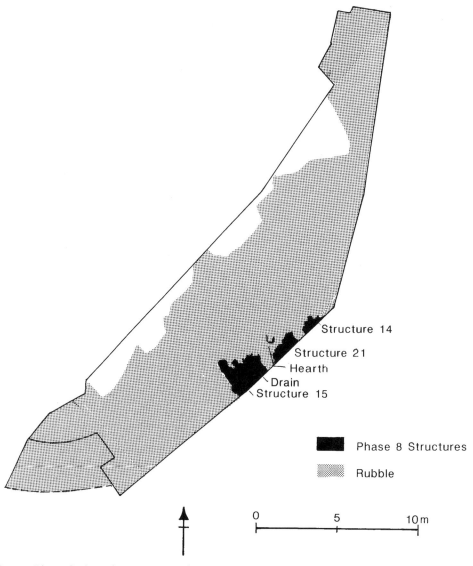

Illus 121   Phase 8: Area 2 structures only

The correlation of the ash deposits (B254) on Area 2 with the 'farm mound' levels (B103 & B104) on Area 1 forms the basis of the phasing scheme proposed here (Part 4.4). The results of the post-excavation tests of this correlation (Part 6.11), however, are ambiguous. The placement of the Area 2 stratigraphic chain of Block 254 and above in Phase 8, rather than Phase 7, therefore, is arbitrary.

The final structures on Area 2 are assumed to be medieval or late medieval in date, assignable to within the period AD 1100–1500. The 'farm mound' deposits are broadly dated to within the period AD 1100–1250.

Order of composition

Block sequence: 104, 103, 102, 218, 254, 222, 223, 217, 203 & 216

Block 102: Upper 'farm mound' deposits (Illus 44 & 122)

Block 102 constitutes the uppermost part of the 'farm mound', as represented by Blocks 103 and 104. The deposits comprise brown sandy loams and, in effect, represent the interface between the base of the modern turf and topsoil and the top of the Block 103 deposits. Frequent worm burrows testify to biological activity at this level. The anthropogenic inputs to the deposits were similar in type to the 'farm mound' deposits proper, albeit present in lower concentrations. No artefacts were recovered from these deposits.

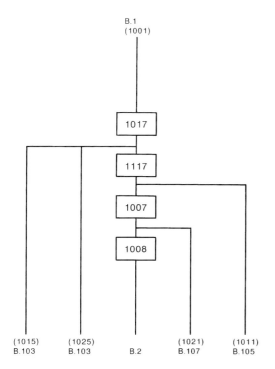

Illus 122   Block 102 stratigraphic matrix

Block 103: Secondary 'farm mound' deposits (Illus 44 & 123)

Block 103, like the primary mound (B104, Phase 8) below, constitutes a mound of thin but extensive layers and lenses of essentially brown and dark brown sandy silt loam deposits, similarly rich in fish bones. The deposits were of a similar character, disposition, depth and extent, albeit that the secondary mound deposits were shifted to the north of the primary mound. Accumulation, also, was rapid. Analyses of the composition, sources and mode of deposition and post-depositional changes to the deposits are discussed elsewhere (Part 7.1).

The secondary 'farm mound' deposits were similarly rich in the remains of fish bones (71 g/10 l), again principally saithe and cod. Relatively large quantities of fuel ash (8 g/10 l) were also present, ranging between <1 g to 17 g/10 l concentration at context level. There were also occasional mammal bones (24 g/10 l) and shells (68 g/10 l), as well as trace quantities of burnt peat (2 g/10 l, range <1 g–5 g/10 l) and charcoal (1 g/10 l, range <1 g–2 g/10 l). The deposits were also moderately rich in cereal grains (38/10 l); barley, oats and flax were present in the ratio of 50:44:6, a similar proportion to that observed in the earlier Block 104 deposits.

Again, few artefacts were recovered, despite the extensive sieving programme. Just under 350 l of sediments were sieved. A copper alloy ring (SF70) with two incised lines along one side and a piece of copper alloy sheet (Rt, F1010) were recovered from F1010, a deposit near the top of the secondary mound deposits. A curved iron blade (SF69), possibly a sickle, from F1030, and a fragment of a copper alloy strip (SF102), decorated on one side with a lozenge pattern, from F1018, both deposits lying in the upper part of the secondary mound, were also recovered. A copper alloy pin (SF101) and a strap handle of medieval type (SF5) may also be assigned to these or the primary mound deposits (see B104 below).

Shells from the upper part of the secondary mound (F1030) have been radiocarbon dated to cal AD 1010–1280 (GU-3069c). The date and the implications for the chronology and duration of the mound are discussed below (see B104, Phase 8).

Block 103 deposits, like those forming Block 104, have been identified as mineral residues, derived from the burning of turves and other organic sediments, mixed with fish-processing waste and occasional domestic debris (Part 7.1). The mound is interpreted as a mound of ash and ash residues, associated with the processing of fish.

Block 104: Primary 'farm mound' deposits (Illus 44 & 124)

Block 104 constitutes a mound of thin but extensive layers and lenses of greyish- and reddish-brown sandy silt loam deposits, rich in fish bones. The overall hue of the deposits was characterized as 'grey', in contradistinction to the essentially 'brown' colour of the secondary 'farm mound' deposits (B103, Phase 8). The deposits, up to 0.9 m deep, fall to the north-west and west and indicate a point of origin which lies behind the standing cliff-section. Although concentrated at the south end of Area 1, principally between Column Sampling Sites A–C, a spread of primary mound material extended to the north. In all, the primary mound deposits were exposed over a distance of roughly 18 m.

The mound accumulated directly over the Late Iron Age buried ground surface (B105, Phase 7). It was postulated, on the basis of the highly stratified nature of the deposits, the absence of evidence for trampling and the absence of a buried soil horizon within the mound, that accumulation must have been rapid. This was tested as part of the post-excavation programme and confirmed by the preservation of undisturbed humified plant remains at the interface between the Late Iron Age buried ground surface (B105, Phase 7) and the primary mound, and by the radiocarbon dating (see below) of the primary and secondary mound deposits. Analyses of the composition, sources and mode of deposition and post-depositional changes to the deposits are discussed elsewhere (Part 7.1).

The primary 'farm mound' deposits were extremely rich in the remains of fish bones (108 g/10 l), primarily saithe and cod. Rare mammal bones (42 g/10 l) and occasional shells (162 g/10 l) were also present. Fuel ash was rare (1 g/10 l, range <1 g–3 g/10 l); burnt peat rare to abundant (5 g/10 l, range 2 g–28 g/10 l); and

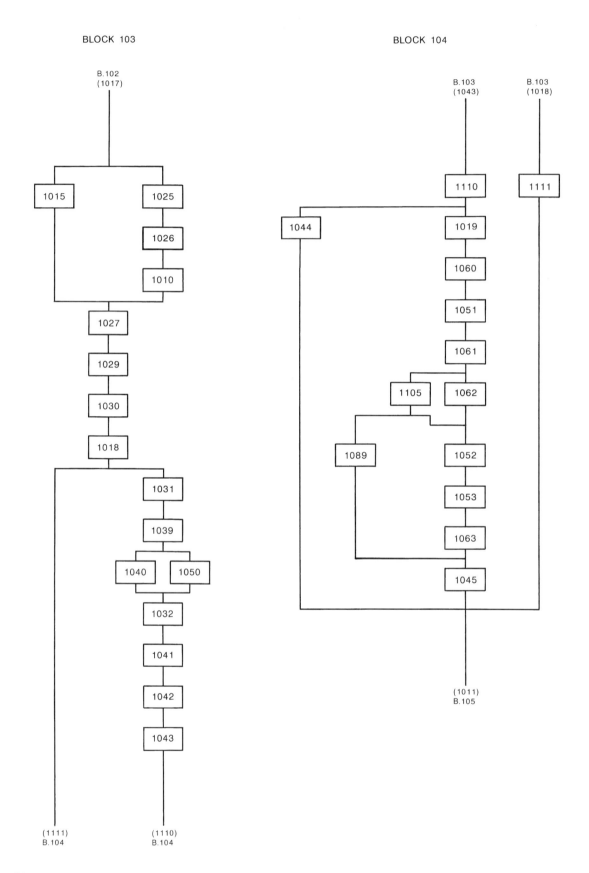

Illus 123   Block 103 stratigraphic matrix   Illus 124   Block 104 stratigraphic matrix

BLOCK 203

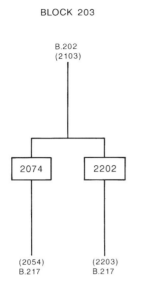

Illus 125   Block 203 stratigraphic matrix

F1110) and several copper alloy fragments (SF68 & Rt, F1110) were recovered from F1110, the top of the primary mound. An iron nail head (Rt, F1105), with a square shaft and subcircular head, was recovered from F1105. A copper alloy pin (SF101), possibly from a penannular brooch, and a strap handle of medieval type (SF5) were also recovered during the cutting back of the upper part of the Area 1 section. Although unstratified, both derive from either the primary or secondary 'farm mound' (B104 or B103).

From Sample Column B (Illus 44), near the base of the mound (F1063), were found several lumps of lime mortar, one of them impressed (Part 5.5). This was the only record of mortar from the site. Its presence implies the destruction or refurbishment of a mortared building in the vicinity at the very time of the mound's inception.

Cattle and sheep/goat bones and shells from the basal deposit (F1045) of the mound have been radiocarbon dated to cal AD 990–1240 (GU-3067) and cal AD 990–1255 (GU-3066c) respectively. These dates are statistically indistinguishable from that recorded (cal AD 1010–1280: GU-3069c) from an upper part of the secondary mound deposits (B103, Phase 8). An indication of the duration or formation period of the mound (B103 & B104) can be estimated. Statistical analysis of the primary and secondary mound dates indicates that there is a 69 per cent probability that the difference is less than 160 years.

Block 104 deposits have been identified as mineral residues derived from the burning of turves and other organic sediments, mixed with fish-processing waste and occasional domestic debris (Part 7.1). The mound is interpreted as a mound of ash and ash residues, associated with the processing of fish.

charcoal rare to frequent (2 g/10 l, range <1 g–4 g/10 l). The deposits were also moderately rich in cereal grains (31/10 l); barley, oats and flax were present in the ratio of 55:37:8. This is a similar proportion to that observed in the later Block 103 deposits.

Few artefacts were recovered, despite the extensive sieving programme. Over 400 l of sediments were sieved. A piece of copper alloy sheet (Rt, F1110), a possible copper alloy rivet (Rt,

Block 203: Structure 21 (Illus 125–127)

Block 203 constitutes the drystone wall (F2074) and paved floor (F2202) of a building which was erected over the rubble deposits (B217, Phase 8) associated with the collapse of Structure 2. The wall was also constructed over a stone-built hearth (B223, Phase 8).

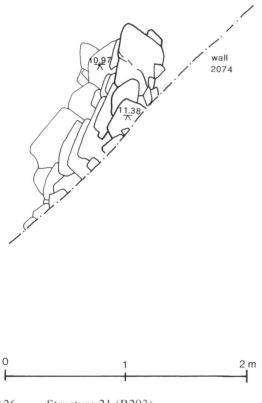

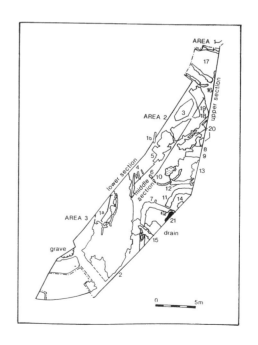

Illus 126   Structure 21 (B203)

Illus 127   Structure 21 (B203) from W, with Structure 14 (B222) in background

The wall, having slumped to the east, appears to have been free-standing. It was roughly 0.4 m wide, 0.7 m high and protruded 1 m from the face of the Upper Section. It was constructed of medium to large subrounded and subangular stones, laid in courses, and was aligned roughly north–south.

A line of thin, large, angular stones (F2202) was located in the Upper Section, immediately to the south-west of the wall fragment. These were traced over a distance of roughly 4 m and are interpreted as a floor surface associated with a building which has been all but removed through erosion of the sea-bank.

Block 216: Drain (Illus 128 & 129)

A stone-built feature (F2068), interpreted as a drain, was inserted against the standing wall of Structure 15 (B218, Phase 8) and cut into the underlying ash deposits (B254, Phase 8).

The feature was constructed inside a trench (F2105) which was roughly 1.25 m wide and 0.5 m deep. The drain comprised a stone base, coursed drystone sides and capstones. The interior of the drain was 0.4 m wide, 0.35 m deep and it protruded 1.3 m from the Upper Section. It was aligned north-west to south-east, falling to seaward.

The construction trench was filled with loose brown sandy silt with small to medium subrounded stones (F2104), not dissimilar from the Block 254 (F2057) deposits through which it had been cut. The drain was filled with brown silt (F2069). No artefactual or ecofactual material was recovered from these deposits. The feature may be associated with unlocated structures which lie to the east of the Upper Section.

BLOCK 216

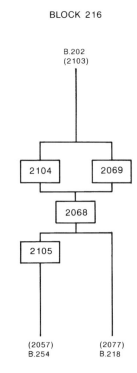

Illus 128   Block 216 stratigraphic matrix

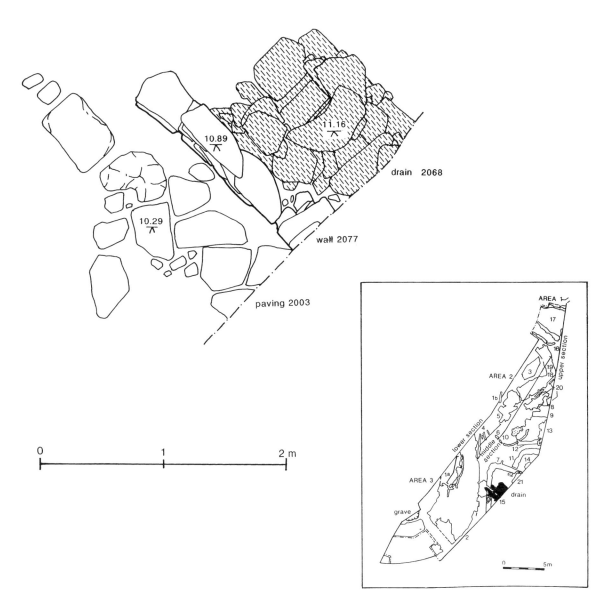

Illus 129   Structure 15 (B218) and drain (B216)

Block 217: Rubble, final collapse of Structure 2 (Illus 118)

Block 217 constitutes a mass of rubble, with voids, which accumulated over Structure 14 (B222, Phase 8) and Structure 15 (B218, Phase 8). The stones, which were predominantly subangular in form, varied from medium to very large. Fragments of splintered stones and a small assemblage of tempered pottery, mostly Fabric Type 3.2, and a stone disc (SF13) were also recovered from these deposits. This small assemblage of pottery from Block 217 represents the only record of coarse pottery from a Phase 8 context. It stands out in the analysis (Part 5.1: Table 23) of the phase distribution of fabric types as anomalous and almost certainly represents residual material.

A distinctive line of very large angular stones (F2201), located towards the south end of the exposed section and pitched to the south-east, almost certainly represents collapsed masonry from the wall-head of Structure 2 (B249:304, Phase 5). It is likely that much of this rubble horizon derives from the collapse of this building.

Block 218: Structure 15 (Illus 129–131)

Block 218 constitutes the drystone wall (F2077) and paved floor (F2003) of a building which was erected over the ruins of Structure 7 and cut into the post-abandonment rubble infill deposits (B224, Phase 6.3).

The sole surviving single-faced wall was 0.3 m wide, 0.6 m high and protruded 1.8 m from the face of the Upper Section. It was constructed of medium to large subangular and subrounded stones, roughly laid in courses, and was aligned north-west to south-east. A concentration of very large stones, located in section 1 m to the south-west of the wall and forming part of an overlying rubble horizon (B217, Phase 8), may represent the site of an associated wall.

The remains of a paved floor, formed of large, flat subrounded stones, was located at the base of the wall. It extended over an area of roughly 2.5 m by 1 m and overlay the earlier wall (F2006: B219, Phase 6.2) which blocked access around the extra-mural roundhouse passage. The floor and wall fall markedly to the west. Levels on the floor indicate that the building has been constructed on a gradient of roughly 1:8.

Illus 130   Structure 15 (B218), from W, with floor (F2003) extending over earlier blocking wall (B219) in foreground

The wall and floor fragment are interpreted as either an entrance area to a subrectangular building which has been all but destroyed through erosion of the sea-bank or a stone-revetted passage over the ruins of the earlier settlement.

Block 222: Structure 14 (Illus 118 & 132)

The fragmentary remains of a drystone wall (F2055), 0.7 m wide, 1 m long and 0.3 m high, protruded from the Upper Section. The wall was free-standing, aligned roughly north to south, and was erected over the mound of ash residues (B254, Phase 8).

The wall is of uncertain function and association. A stone-built hearth (B223, Phase 8), its longer axis aligned north–south, was located 1.5 m to the west at the same stratigraphic level. It may represent an internal feature to a building which has otherwise been completely removed through erosion of the sea-bank. The remaining wall (F2055), therefore, may represent a side wall of a subrectangular building, aligned north–south.

Block 223: Hearth (Illus 132)

A rectangular stone-built box (F2001), its longer axis aligned north–south, was located 1.5 m to the west of Structure 14 (B222, Phase 8). It too had been constructed over the earlier ash deposits (B254, Phase 8).

Three sides of the feature remained. It was constructed of thin angular stones which were set on edge and placed over and around a large, flat stone whose upper surface was burnt and heat-fractured. The feature was 0.45 m wide, 0.1 m deep and at least 0.7 m long.

BLOCK 218

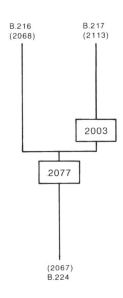

Illus 131   Block 218 stratigraphic matrix

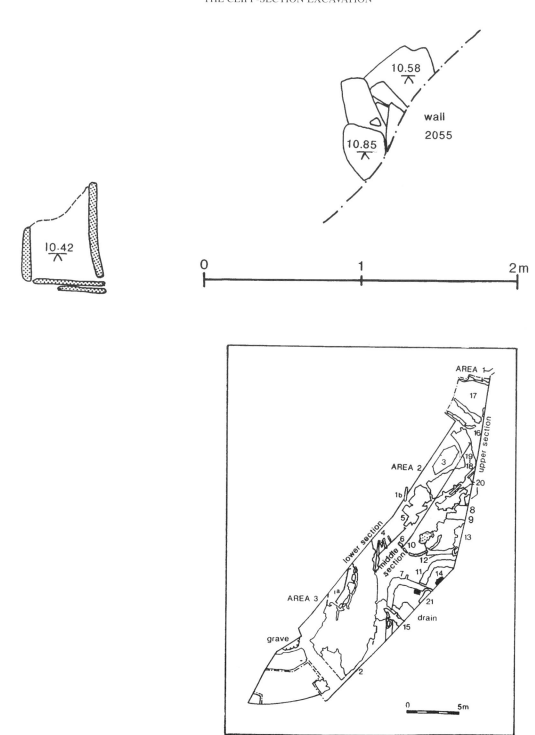

Illus 132   Structure 14 (B222) and hearth (B223)

A deposit of charcoal-flecked orange ashy silt (F2000) filled the feature and spread over its sides. The deposit contained charred grains of both barley (7/10 l) and oats (2/10 l). This is the only record of oats (*Avena* sp) from the deposits on Area 2. Oats, otherwise, are a characteristic of the Area 1 'farm mound' deposits (B103 & B104, Phase 8: Part 4.3.84).

The feature is interpreted as a hearth which possibly formed an internal feature inside Structure 14 (B222, Phase 8). The grain assemblage may have been introduced to the deposit through domestic grain-drying or through the use of straw as kindling.

Block 254: Mound of ash residues (Illus 118 & 133)

Block 254 constitutes a 0.5 m deep sandy silt deposit (F2002, F2036 & F2057). The deposit was lensed with brown, pale orange and bright orange layers of ash. It was virtually stone-free and contained occasional charcoal flecks, mammal bones and shells. A pounder/grinder (SF159) was recovered from F2036. The uppermost horizon, a greyish-brown sandy silt (F2057) which extended beneath the walls of Structure 14 (B222, Phase 8) and Structure 21 (B203, Phase 8), was interpreted in the field as a possible buried ground surface.

BLOCK 254

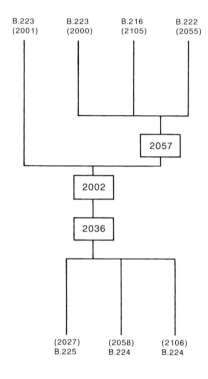

Illus 133   Block 254 stratigraphic matrix

The deposit overlay the infilled ruins of Structure 7 (B236, Phase 6.1) and Structure 11 (B229, Phase 6.1) and abutted the south wall of Structure 13 (B225, Phase 6.2). The sediments dipped to the north-west and indicate a point of origin behind the Upper Section. The mound to the west of the modern churchyard, identified during the course of the topographical survey (Part 2.2), is postulated as a possible source for this material. A correlation with the Area 1 'farm mound' deposits (B103 & B104, Phase 8) was proposed on the basis of the texture and colour of the deposits. This hypothesis was tested as part of the post-excavation programme.

Soil thin-section analysis (Part 6.11) of sediments F2057 and F2036 confirmed their identification as ash residues in which a soil had developed. The correlation of Block 254 deposits with the 'farm mound' sediments (B103 & B104, Phase 8), rather than the earlier Late Iron Age ash deposits (B107, Phase 7), cannot be established on the basis of the soil thin-section evidence (Part 6.11). The absence of flax, a characteristic of the 'farm mound' deposits (B103 & B104, Phase 8), might indicate a correlation with the earlier, Block 107 (Phase 7) deposits.

3.2.11 Phase 9: Modern Turf and Topsoil, Rubble and Erosion Horizon

Phase 9 comprises the modern turf and topsoil horizon (B1 & B301), a spread of rubble (B202) on Area 2, immediately below the turf, and the backfill deposits (B201) from the nineteenth-century excavations (Lowe 1994) which filled the roundhouse.

A channel (B101) at the north end of Area 1, cut into the underlying till and filled with brown sandy loam and frequent small to medium and occasional large subrounded and subangular stones, is interpreted as a modern erosion feature. A stone ard point (SF3) was recovered from this feature.

Chronology, Sequence and Phasing

4.0 Introduction

Christopher Lowe

This section attempts to bring together those elements of the cultural assemblage which are chronologically sensitive or have implications for the chronology, sequence or phasing of the site. The correlation table (Part 4.5) presents an interpretative overview of the distribution through time of the floruits of selected material types. The section concludes with a connected account of the stratigraphy and structural development of the site over time.

4.1 Radiocarbon Dating, Calibration and Statistical Analysis

Magnar Dalland

4.1.1 The Radiocarbon Dates

Twenty-seven radiocarbon dates were obtained from excavation material. These are distributed among twenty contexts and nineteen blocks. The taphonomy of the samples is considered in an archive report (Lowe 1992) and is discussed, where appropriate, in the presentation of the archaeological evidence for the excavated structures and deposits (Part 3.2).

TABLE 4: RADIOCARBON DATES & CALIBRATION TABLE

F no.	Block	Material	Phase	Sample	Date bp	SCR range	Prob	LCR Range	Prob
3056	312	cattle	1.0	AA-9561	4240±60	2920 BC–2785 BC	70.35	3020 BC–2700 BC	95.62
2170	250	cattle, pig	3.0	AA-9560	3175±60	1525 BC–1415 BC	70.39	1610 BC–1320 BC	96.09
2134	245	cattle, deer	4.0	AA-9562	3100±85	1515 BC–1320 BC	68.34	1535 BC–1115 BC	95.46
3022	302	limpets	5.0	AA-9563c	2675±65	870 BC–795 BC	68.77	970 BC–790 BC	95.46
2145	237	winkles	5.0	GU-3271c	2445±65	665 BC–390 BC	68.86	800 BC–390 BC	96.49
2145	237	limpets	5.0	GU-3059c	2425±65	610 BC–385 BC	68.45	800 BC–390 BC	96.71
2181	215	limpets	5.0	GU-3273c	2385±65	505 BC–385 BC	69.22	770 BC–375 BC	95.51
1100	117	limpets	5.0	GU-3268c	2335±65	465 BC–380 BC	68.85	625 BC–190 BC	95.47
1095	115	limpets	5.0	GU-3060c	2335±65	465 BC–380 BC	68.85	625 BC–190 BC	95.47
2050	213	limpets	6.1	GU-3058c	2215±65	400 BC–230 BC	68.49	405 BC–100 BC	95.61
1080	109	limpets	6.1	GU-3062c	2185±65	395 BC–185 BC	69.47	400 BC–70 BC	95.75
2050	213	winkles	6.1	GU-3274c	2165±65	350 BC–120 BC	68.95	400 BC–50 BC	95.79
1091	113	winkles	6.1	GU-3275c	2085±65	195 BC–25 BC	68.94	340 BC–AD 75	95.74
1091	113	limpets	6.1	GU-3061c	2055±65	150 BC–AD 20	68.44	235 BC–AD 115	95.70
2013	230	limpets	6.2	GU-3279c	1935±65	20 BC–AD 125	69.48	70 BC–AD 220	95.53
2137	238	limpets	6.2	GU-3278c	1925±65	20 BC–AD 130	69.11	50 BC–AD 235	95.55
2004	224	cattle, sheep	6.3	AA-9565	2115±60	200 BC–35 BC	68.49	360 BC–AD 15	95.80
2097	207	limpets	6.3	GU-3280c	2025±65	95 BC–AD 70	68.77	190 BC–AD 120	95.83
2029	211	limpets	6.3	GU-3277c	1945±65	15 BC–AD 125	68.71	85 BC–AD 210	95.76
2004	224	limpets	6.3	GU-3282c	1845±65	AD 100–AD 235	69.34	AD 25–AD 330	95.64
2097	207	cattle, pig, sheep, deer	6.3	AA-9564	1815±60	AD 110–AD 245	70.07	AD 80–AD 365	95.51
1035	107	cattle, pig, sheep	7.0	GU-3063	1570±90	AD 410–AD 610	68.44	AD 285–AD 670	95.50
1034	107	cattle, pig, sheep	7.0	GU-3065	1370±90	AD 600–AD 705	68.90	AD 520–AD 870	95.49
1034	107	limpets	7.0	GU-3064c	1295±65	AD 650–AD 775	69.34	AD 620–AD 880	95.67
1045	104	cattle, sheep	8.0	GU-3067	920±60	AD 1015–AD 1155	69.00	AD 990–AD 1240	95.48
1045	104	limpets	8.0	GU-3066c	925±65	AD 1010–AD 1155	69.25	AD 990–AD 1255	95.56
1030	103	limpets	8.0	GU-3069c	865±80	AD 1095–AD 1280	69.42	AD 1010–AD 1280	95.81

Sample code GU/AA ****c: date corrected for marine reservoir effect (−405±40)

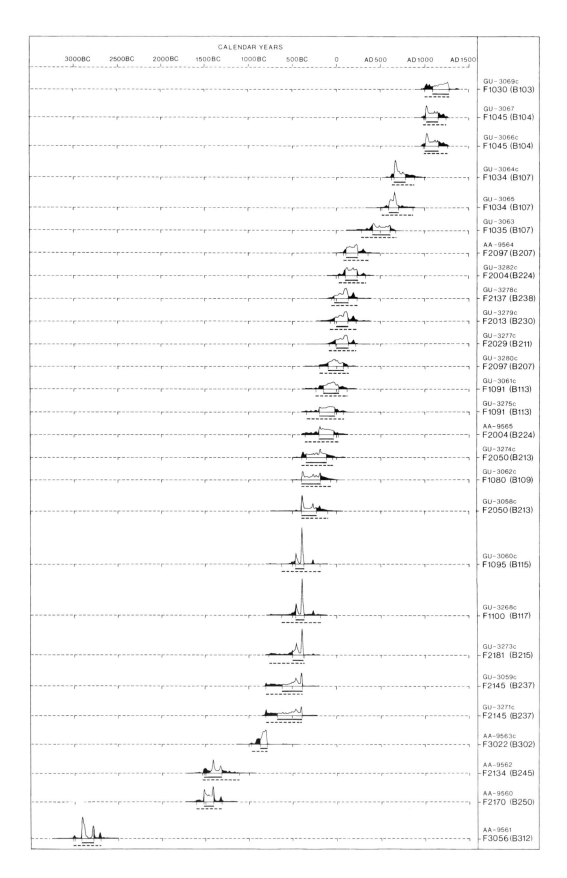

Illus 134   Probability distribution of the radiocarbon dates

There was insufficient material to date the human remains from the Phase 1 cist (B311: GU-3057) and the fish bones from the Phase 8 'farm mound' deposits (B104: GU-3068). The material dated derived from two sources: terrestrial animal bones and sea shells. The shell dates have been corrected by a factor of -405±40 years to take account of the marine reservoir effect. Samples thus corrected are suffixed GU/AA****c in Table 4 and elsewhere and only the corrected and calibrated LCR dates are used in this report.

The dates were calibrated using data from Pearson *et al* (1986), to produce a calibrated probability distribution (PD) for each date (Illus 134). The solid and dashed lines below each PD curve mark, respectively, the short (SCR) and long continuous range (LCR). These are the shortest continuous ranges for which the probability that the date lies within the stated range is greater than or equal to, respectively, 68.26 per cent (SCR) and 95.45 per cent (LCR). These values are equal to the probabilities of the one and two sigma ranges of a normal distribution.

The data which constitute the PD curves are summarized, at 100 years resolution, in Table 5. The data for each date are displayed in three columns. The left column shows the probability of the date to lie within a 100-year interval. The second and third columns present the probability for the date to be younger than, or older than, the lower limit of the 100-year period defined.

4.1.2 Statistical Analysis

4.1.21 Introduction

A series of statistical analyses were undertaken to determine the duration, contemporaneity and formation period of various structures and deposits on the site. The statistical evaluations are based on the calibrated Probability Distributions (PDs) of the radiocarbon dates which have been calculated on the basis of the Belfast calibration curve (Pearson *et al* 1986). Most evaluations are based on PDs of the age difference between two dates. In some cases the stratigraphical relationship between the samples has been used to limit the range within which the age difference could lie (Dalland 1993).

4.1.22 Method

The evaluations are based on two assumptions: that the true age of the samples used for dating lies within the formation period of the context; and that the dates of samples used in evaluating the duration of an event represent the beginning and end of that event.

The first point is the general presumption behind the use of radiocarbon dates. In those cases where the calibrated dates of samples contradict the stratigraphic relationship between the samples, the discrepancy is ascribed to statistical variations rather than contaminated samples.

The second assumption is inherently incorrect. Unless the formation period of the contexts above and below is short in relation to the precision of the dates, or the samples derive from the top of the lower context and the base of the upper context, the evaluation of the duration will be an overestimate. This would be further increased if there were any hiatus in the formation of the context sequence.

The radiocarbon samples derive from two sources; terrestrial animal bones and sea shells. Shell dates have been corrected by a factor of -405±40 years, to take account of the marine reservoir effect. Given the uncertainty about the validity of this global correction factor, comparison of dates of terrestrial material with dates of marine origin in the calculation of PDs of age difference has been avoided.

In some cases there were two dates of the same material from a context used in the calculation. In such cases, the dates were tested using the Student's t-test. If they passed the test, an average of the two age-difference PDs was used.

The PDs of the age differences are variously illustrated as graphs of probability distribution or cumulative probability. The probability distribution graph shows the probability for the difference to lie within 5 year intervals. This graph is particulary useful in those instances where the probability peaks at a difference greater than 0–5 years. The cumulative graph presents the cumulative probability showing the probability of the difference to be smaller or larger than any given number of years. A summary of the PDs is also presented in tables with the data condensed into 50- and 100-year intervals. The range column in the tables shows the probability of the difference to lie within the range shown in the left-hand column. The two right-hand columns show the probability of the difference to be more or less than the lower limit of the corresponding period.

4.1.221 The duration of Structure 22 (B114)

The evaluation of the maximum and minimum durations for the occupation of Structure 22 is based on three radiocarbon dates, in the following stratigraphical sequence:

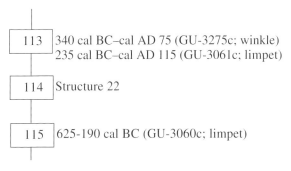

The evaluation of the time span between Blocks 115 and 113 is based on the average of the two difference distributions GU-3061c/GU-3060c and GU-3275c/GU-3060c. The dates reflect the stratigraphic relationships of the samples. The probability

TABLE 5: PROBABILITIES OF DATES TO FALL WITHIN CENTURIES

PERIOD	GU-3069c F 1030 865±80 BP	GU-3067 F 1045 920±60 BP	GU-3066c F 1045 925±65 BP	GU-3065 F 1034 1370±90 BP	GU-3064c F 1034 1295±65 BP	GU-3063 F 1035 1570±90 BP	AA-9564 F 2097 1815±60 BP	GU-3282c F 2004 1845±65 BP	GU-3278c F 2137 1925±65 BP	GU-3279c F 2013 1935±65 BP	GU-3277c F 2029 1945±65 BP	GU-3280c F 2097 2025±65 BP
AD1500–AD1600	0.0 0.0 100											
AD1400–AD1500	0.0 0.0 100											
AD1300–AD1400	1.0 1.0 99.0	0.0 0.0 100	0.0 0.0 100									
AD1200–AD1300	37.2 38.2 61.8	11.6 11.6 88.4	11.6 11.6 88.4									
AD1100–AD1200	31.9 70.0 30.0	36.8 48.4 51.6	34.4 46.0 54.0	0.0 0.0 100	0.0 0.0 100							
AD1000–AD1100	28.1 98.1 1.9	48.1 96.5 3.5	48.6 94.6 5.4	0.0 0.0 100	0.0 0.0 100							
AD900–AD1000	1.9 100 0.0	3.5 100 0.0	5.3 99.9 0.1	0.4 0.4 99.6	0.8 0.8 99.2							
AD800–AD900	0.0 100 0.0	0.0 100 0.0	0.1 100 0.0	5.6 6.0 94.0	15.2 16.0 84.0	0.0 0.0 100						
AD700–AD800				13.9 19.9 80.1	32.3 48.3 51.7	0.0 0.0 100						
AD600–AD700				67.6 87.5 12.5	51.4 99.7 0.3	15.1 15.2 84.8						
AD500–AD600				10.4 97.9 2.1	0.3 100 0.0	29.1 44.3 55.7	0.0 0.0 100	0.0 0.0 100	0.0 0.0 100			
AD400–AD500				2.1 100 0.0		39.2 83.4 16.6	0.4 0.4 99.6	0.1 0.1 99.9	0.5 0.5 99.5	0.0 0.0 100	0.0 0.0 100	
AD300–AD400				0.0 100 0.0		11.7 95.1 4.9	12.6 13.1 86.9	7.0 7.2 92.8	4.9 5.4 94.6	0.3 0.3 99.7	0.2 0.2 99.8	0.0 0.0 100
AD200–AD300						4.6 99.6 0.4	35.0 48.0 52.0	24.7 31.8 68.2	37.6 42.9 57.1	3.7 4.0 96.0	2.7 2.9 97.1	0.1 0.1 99.9
AD100–AD200						0.4 100 0.0	45.9 93.9 6.1	52.3 84.1 15.9	43.9 86.8 13.2	33.3 37.2 62.8	29.0 31.8 68.2	4.8 4.9 95.1
AD0–AD100							5.9 99.9 0.1	14.9 98.9 1.1	12.6 99.4 0.6	46.2 83.4 16.6	47.7 79.5 20.5	31.9 36.7 63.3
100BC–AD0							0.1 100 0.0	1.1 100 0.0	0.6 100 0.0	15.6 99.0 1.0	19.0 98.5 1.5	46.0 82.8 17.2
200BC–100BC								0.0 100 0.0	0.0 100 0.0	1.0 100 0.0	1.5 100 0.0	15.4 98.2 1.8
300BC–200BC										0.0 100 0.0	0.0 100 0.0	1.2 99.4 0.6
400BC–300BC											0.0 100 0.0	0.6 100 0.0
500BC–400BC												0.0 100 0.0

Top table (probability distributions, %):

PERIOD	GU-3061c F 1091 2055±65 BP			GU-3275c F 1091 2085±65 BP			AA-9565 F 2004 21115±60 BP			GU-3274c F 2050 2165±65 BP			GU-3062c F 1080 2185±65 BP			GU-3058c F 2050 2215±65 BP			GU-3060c F 1095 2335±65 BP			GU-3268c F 1100 2335±65 BP			GU-3273c F2181 2385±65 BP			GU-3059c F 2145 2425±65 BP			GU-3271c F 2145 2445±65 BP			AA-9563c F 3022 2675±65 BP		
AD300–AD400	0.0	0.0	100																																	
AD200–AD300	0.0	0.0	100																																	
AD100–AD200	1.7	1.7	98.3	0.0	0.0	100																														
AD0–AD100	20.2	21.9	78.1	0.4	0.4	99.6	0.0	0.0	100	0.0	0.0	100	0.0	0.0	100	0.0	0.0	100																		
100BC–AD0	46.9	68.8	31.2	10.7	11.2	88.8	3.7	3.7	96.3	0.7	0.7	99.3	0.3	0.3	99.7	2.6	2.6	97.4	0.0	0.0	100	0.0	0.0	100	0.0	0.0	100	0.0	0.0	100						
200BC–100BC	26.0	94.8	5.2	40.3	51.5	48.5	28.9	32.6	67.4	11.3	12.0	88.0	6.7	6.9	93.1	18.6	21.1	78.9	0.3	0.3	99.7	0.3	0.3	99.7	0.0	0.0	100	0.0	0.0	100	0.0	0.0	100			
300BC–200BC	3.3	98.1	1.9	36.4	87.8	12.2	45.3	77.9	22.1	36.2	48.2	51.8	29.4	36.4	63.6	32.4	53.6	46.4	8.4	8.7	91.3	8.4	8.7	91.3	2.1	2.1	97.9	0.4	0.4	99.6	0.1	0.1	99.9			
400BC–300BC	1.9	100	0.0	7.4	95.2	4.8	13.1	91.0	9.0	26.5	74.7	25.3	30.3	66.7	33.3	44.0	97.6	2.4	47.8	56.6	43.4	47.8	56.6	43.4	25.9	28.0	72.0	11.5	11.9	88.1	6.8	6.9	93.1	0.0	0.0	100
500BC–400BC				4.8	100	0.0	9.0	100	0.0	25.1	99.8	0.2	32.6	99.3	0.7	2.3	99.9	0.1	33.8	90.4	9.6	33.8	90.4	9.6	44.1	72.1	27.9	38.6	50.5	49.5	32.3	39.2	60.8	0.0	0.0	100
600BC–500BC				0.0	100	0.0	0.0	100	0.0	0.2	100	0.0	0.7	100	0.0	0.1	100	0.0	5.0	95.4	4.6	5.0	95.4	4.6	11.8	83.9	16.1	17.5	68.0	32.0	19.4	58.7	41.3	0.6	0.6	99.4
700BC–600BC										0.0	100	0.0	0.0	100	0.0	0.0	100	0.0	1.5	96.9	3.1	1.5	96.9	3.1	6.2	90.1	9.9	13.2	81.2	18.8	16.9	75.6	24.4	0.9	1.5	98.5
800BC–700BC																0.0	100	0.0	3.1	100	0.0	3.1	100	0.0	9.7	99.9	0.1	17.6	98.8	1.2	21.8	97.4	2.6	5.2	6.7	93.3
900BC–800BC																			0.0	100	0.0	0.0	100	0.0	0.1	100	0.0	1.2	100	0.0	2.6	100	0.0	78.7	85.5	14.5
1000BC–900BC																																		14.0	99.5	0.5
1100BC–1000BC																																		0.4	99.9	0.1
1200BC–1100BC																																		0.1	100	0.0

Bottom table (probability distributions, %):

PERIOD	AA-9562 F 2134 3100±85 BP			AA-9560 F 2170 3175±60 BP			AA-9561 F 3056 4240±60 BP		
1000BC–900BC	0.0	0.0	100	0.0	0.0	100			
1100BC–1000BC	1.1	1.1	98.9	0.0	0.0	100			
1200BC–1100BC	4.8	5.9	94.1	0.8	0.8	99.2			
1300BC–1200BC	13.6	19.6	80.4	10.6	11.4	88.6			
1400BC–1300BC	29.6	49.2	50.8	57.6	69.0	31.0			
1500BC–1400BC	37.8	87.0	13.0	27.8	96.8	3.2			
1600BC–1500BC	11.8	98.8	1.2	3.2	100	0.0			
1700BC–1600BC	1.2	100	0.0	0.0	100	0.0			
1800BC–1700BC	0.0	100	0.0						
1900BC–1800BC									
2000BC–1900BC									
2100BC–2000BC									
2200BC–2100BC									
2300BC–2200BC									
2400BC–2300BC							0.0	0.0	100
2500BC–2400BC							0.1	0.1	99.9
2600BC–2500BC							3.6	3.7	96.3
2700BC–2600BC							30.3	34.0	66.0
2800BC–2700BC							26.7	60.7	39.3
2900BC–2800BC							34.9	95.6	4.4
3000BC–2900BC							4.4	100	0.0
3100BC–3000BC							0.0	100	0.0
3200BC–3100BC							0.0	100	0.0
3300BC–3200BC									

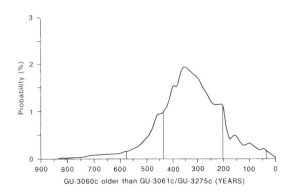

Illus 135   PD diagram of Blocks 113 & 115

distribution of the average age difference between
GU-3061c/GU-3275c and GU-3060c shows that
there is a 99.5 per cent probability that the difference
is positive. The effect of imposing the stratigraphical
information on this distribution is therefore minimal
(Illus 135). The probabilities quoted below (Table 6)
are based on the re-normalized distribution.

According to these calculations, there is a 68 per
cent probability that the age difference between the
dates from Blocks 113 and 115 is between 205 and 435
years, and it is 95 per cent probable that the difference
is between 35 and 575 years. As shown in Table 6, it is
only 3.7 per cent probable that the difference is less
than 100 years, and there is only a 3.1 per cent chance
that the difference is more than 600 years.

4.1.222 Contemporaneity of Structure 2 (B249:304) and the primary enclosure ditch (B214)

The probability that Structure 2, the roundhouse, and
the primary enclosure ditch are contemporary can
only be partially evaluated. In considering the
chronological relationship of the two structures, there
are three possibilities: (a) that the roundhouse predates the primary enclosure; (b) that the roundhouse
and primary enclosure are contemporary; or (c) that
the roundhouse post-dates the primary enclosure.

It is possible to calculate the probability that
Statement (a) is true by comparing the dates from a
shell midden (B237) which accumulated against the
roundhouse, and the date from another shell midden
(B215) which was truncated by the cutting of the
primary enclosure ditch.

There are two identical dates, undertaken
separately on limpet and winkle shells, from Block
237, of 800–390 cal BC (GU-3059c & GU-3271c).
There is one date from Block 215: 770–375 cal BC
(GU-3273c: limpet).

Analysis of the dates from Blocks 237 and 215,
using the average of the difference PDs between the
two dates from Block 237 and the one date from Block
215, indicates that there is a 68 per cent probability
that Block 237 is earlier than Block 215, and therefore
that the roundhouse predates the primary enclosure.

TABLE 6: SUMMARY OF THE PROBABILITY DISTRIBUTION OF THE AGE DIFFERENCE BETWEEN BLOCKS 113 AND 115.

50 years summary
Probabilities

Period (years)	Range	More than	Less than
900–950	0.0	0.0	100.0
850–900	0.0	0.0	100.0
800–850	0.1	0.2	99.8
750–800	0.3	0.4	99.6
700–750	0.6	1.1	98.9
650–700	0.9	2.0	98.0
600–650	1.1	3.1	96.9
550–600	1.7	4.8	95.2
500–550	3.2	8.0	92.0
450–500	7.2	15.2	84.8
400–450	11.7	26.9	73.1
350–400	17.3	44.1	55.9
300–350	18.1	62.2	37.8
250–300	14.2	76.4	23.6
200–250	11.3	87.7	12.3
150–200	5.3	93.0	7.0
100–150	3.3	96.3	3.7
50–100	2.4	98.7	1.3
0–50	1.3	100.0	0.0

100 years summary
Probabilities

Period (years)	Range	More than	Less than
900–1000	0.0	0.0	100.0
800–900	0.1	0.2	99.8
700–800	0.9	1.1	98.9
600–700	2.0	3.1	96.9
500–600	4.9	8.0	92.0
400–500	18.9	26.9	73.1
300–400	35.4	62.2	37.8
200–300	25.5	87.7	12.3
100–200	8.6	96.3	3.7
0–100	3.7	100.0	0.0

4.1.223 The duration of the primary enclosure ditch (B214)

The evaluation of the maximum and minimum
durations for the primary enclosure ditch is based on
three radiocarbon dates, in the following
stratigraphical sequence:

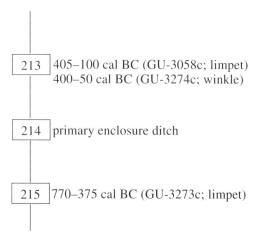

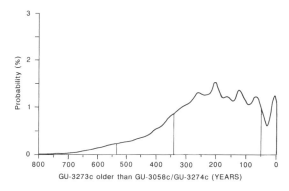

Illus 136   PD diagram of Blocks 215 & 213

The evaluation of the time span between Blocks 213 and 215 is based on the average of the two difference distributions GU-3273c/GU-3058c and GU-3273c/GU-3274c. The PDs of the upper two dates and the lower date have a very slight overlap; there is a 96 per cent probability that GU-3273c is older than GU-3058c, and a 99 per cent chance that GU-3273c is older than GU-3274c. The average of the probability of the two dates being younger than GU-3273c is about 97 per cent.

The effect of imposing the stratigraphical information on this distribution is therefore minimal (Illus 136). Table 7 lists the probabilities, based on the re-normalized distribution. There is a 69 per cent probability that the difference between the dates from Blocks 213 and 215 is between 50 and 340 years, and it is 96 per cent probable that the difference is less than 535 years. As shown in Table 7, it is only 8.6 per cent probable that the difference is less than 50 years, and there is a 6.2 per cent chance that it is more than 500 years.

4.1.224 The duration of the secondary enclosure ditch (B212)

The evaluation of the maximum and minimum durations for the secondary enclosure ditch is based on five radiocarbon dates, in the following stratigraphical sequence:

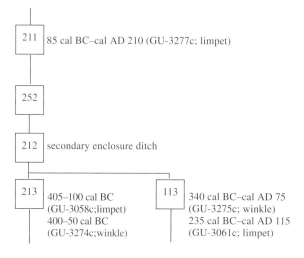

TABLE 7: SUMMARY OF THE PROBABILITY DISTRIBUTION OF THE AGE DIFFERENCE BETWEEN BLOCKS 215 AND 213, ADJUSTED FOR STRATIGRAPHY.

50 years summary
Probabilities

Period (years)	Range	More than	Less than
750–800	0.0	0.0	100.0
700–750	0.2	0.2	99.8
650–700	0.5	0.8	99.2
600–650	1.1	1.8	98.2
550–600	1.9	3.7	96.3
500–550	2.5	6.2	93.8
450–500	3.2	9.4	90.6
400–450	4.4	13.8	86.2
350–400	6.8	20.6	79.4
300–350	9.6	30.2	69.8
250–300	12.1	42.3	57.7
200–250	13.4	55.8	44.2
150–200	12.4	68.1	31.9
100–150	12.2	80.3	19.7
50–100	11.1	91.4	8.6
0–50	8.6	100.0	0.0

100 years summary
Probabilities

Period (years)	Range	More than	Less than
700–800	0.2	0.2	99.8
600–700	1.6	1.8	98.2
500–600	4.4	6.2	93.8
400–500	7.6	13.8	86.2
300–400	16.4	30.2	69.8
200–300	25.5	55.8	44.2
100–200	24.6	80.3	19.7
0–100	19.7	100.0	0.0

The secondary enclosure ditch (B212) was cut into the infill (B213) of the primary ditch to the south and an earlier shell midden (B113), filling Structure 22 to the north. Each of these blocks is dated by two radiocarbon dates. Since the two dates from Block 113 are later than those from Block 213, it is likely that the Block 113 dates represent the better estimate of a *terminus post quem* date for the construction of the secondary enclosure ditch. A *terminus ante quem* date is provided by shells (B211), which were deposited in the secondary ditch at its abandonment. The evaluation, therefore, is based on the radiocarbon dates from Block 211, above, and Block 113 below.

The evaluation of the time span between Blocks 211 and 113 is based on the average of the two difference distributions GU-3061c/GU-3277c and GU-3275c/GU-3277c. Based on the dates alone, there is a 92 per cent probability that GU-3275c is older than GU-3277c, and a 87 per cent chance that GU-3061c is older than GU-3277c. The average of the probability of the two dates being older than GU-3277c is about 90 per cent.

Since the two stratigraphically lower dates are assumed to be older than GU-3277c, the age difference must lie in the positive region of the distribution. The

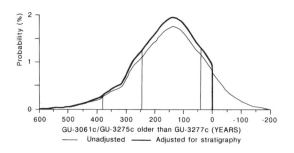

Illus 137   PD diagram of Blocks 113 & 211

4.1.225 The duration of Structure 10 (B231)

The evaluation of the maximum and minimum durations for the occupation of Structure 10 is based on two radiocarbon dates, in the following stratigraphical sequence:

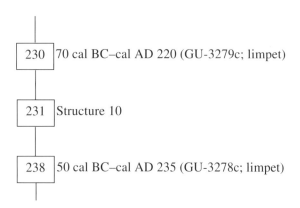

positive part was therefore re-normalized, creating an adjusted difference distribution based on the stratigraphical sequence (Illus 137). Table 8 lists the probabilities, based on the adjusted distribution. There is a 68 per cent probability that the age difference between the dates from Block 113 and Block 211 is between 40 and 245 years, and it is 95 per cent probable that the difference is less than 380 years. As shown in Table 8, it is only 11.3 per cent probable that the difference is less than 50 years, and there is only a 3 per cent chance that the difference is more than 400 years.

The probability distribution of the age difference shows that there is a 54 per cent probability that the lower date is younger than the stratigraphically more recent sample GU-3279c. Since the stratigraphically lower date GU-3278c is assumed to be older than GU-3279c, the age difference must lie in the positive region of the distribution. As the probability of the age difference being negative is nil, the positive part can be re-normalized, creating a difference distribution based on the stratigraphical sequence (Illus 138). Table 9 lists the probabilities, based on this re-normalized distribution.

According to these calculations, there is a 68 per cent probability that the difference is less than 100 years, and a 95 per cent probability that it is less than 205 years. Given the assumptions inherent in the methodology (Part 4.1.22), this is likely to represent an overestimate for the duration of the occupation of Structure 10.

TABLE 8: SUMMARY OF THE PROBABILITY DISTRIBUTION OF THE AGE DIFFERENCE BETWEEN BLOCKS 113 AND 211, ADJUSTED FOR STRATIGRAPHY.

50 years summary
Probabilities

Period (years)	Range	More than	Less than
650–700	0.0	0.0	100.0
600–650	0.0	0.0	100.0
550–600	0.1	0.1	99.9
500–550	0.4	0.5	99.5
450–500	0.8	1.3	98.7
400–450	1.7	3.0	97.0
350–400	3.3	6.3	93.7
300–350	5.3	11.6	88.4
250–300	10.2	21.8	78.2
200–250	14.3	36.0	64.0
150–200	18.0	54.0	46.0
100–150	19.0	73.1	26.9
50–100	15.6	88.7	11.3
0–50	11.3	100.0	0.0

100 years summary
Probabilities

Period (years)	Range	More than	Less than
600–700	0.0	0.0	100.0
500–600	0.5	0.5	99.5
400–500	2.6	3.0	97.0
300–400	8.6	11.6	88.4
200–300	24.4	36.0	64.0
100–200	37.0	73.1	26.9
0–100	26.9	100.0	0.0

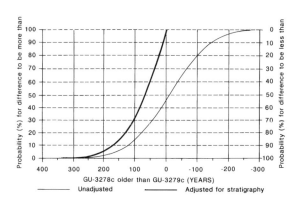

Illus 138   Cumulative PD diagram of Blocks 230 & 238

TABLE 9: SUMMARY OF THE PROBABILITY DISTRIBUTION OF THE AGE DIFFERENCE BETWEEN BLOCKS 230 AND 238, ADJUSTED FOR STRATIGRAPHY.

50 years summary
Probabilities

Period (years)	Range	More than	Less than
400–450	0.0	0.0	100.0
350–400	0.1	0.1	99.9
300–350	0.3	0.3	99.7
250–300	1.1	1.4	98.6
200–250	3.6	5.0	95.0
150–200	8.6	13.5	86.5
100–150	18.2	31.7	68.3
50–100	29.6	61.3	38.7
0–50	38.7	100.0	0.0

100 years summary
Probabilities

Period (years)	Range	More than	Less than
400–500	0.0	0.0	100.0
300–400	0.3	0.3	99.7
200–300	4.6	5.0	95.0
100–200	26.7	31.7	68.3
0–100	68.3	100.0	0.0

4.1.226 The duration of the Late Iron Age ash mound (B107)

The evaluation of the maximum and minimum durations for the formation of the Late Iron Age ash mound is based on three radiocarbon dates, in the following stratigraphical sequence, at context level:

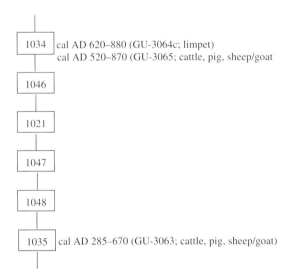

Four contexts were stratified between the dated horizons. The upper context (F1046) is sealed by F1034 and is dated by GU-3064c (limpet) and GU-3065 (cattle, pig, sheep/goat bones). The lower context (F1048) overlies F1035 and is dated by GU-3063 (cattle, pig, sheep/goat bones). GU-3065 and GU-3063 were selected as the basis for the evaluation of the formation period, as both contain the same type of dating material.

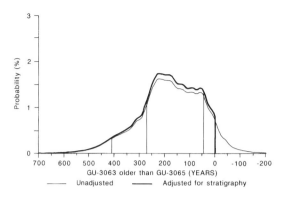

Illus 139   PD diagram of GU-3063 & GU-3065

The PDs of the two dates have a very slight overlap; there is a 6 per cent probability that GU-3065 is older than GU-3063. The effect of imposing the stratigraphical information on this distribution is therefore small (Illus 139). Table 10 lists the probabilities, based on the re-normalized distribution.

There is a 69 per cent probability that the age difference between the date GU-3063 from F1035 and GU-3065 from F1034 is between 45 and 270 years, and it is 96 per cent probable that the difference is less than 410 years. As shown in Table 10, it is 10.3 per cent probable that the difference is less than 50 years, and there is only a 5.2 per cent chance that the difference is more than 400 years.

TABLE 10: SUMMARY OF THE PROBABILITY DISTRIBUTION OF THE AGE DIFFERENCE BETWEEN GU-3063 AND GU-3065, ADJUSTED FOR STRATIGRAPHY.

50 years summary
Probabilities

Period (years)	Range	More than	Less than
650–700	0.0	0.1	99.9
600–650	0.1	0.2	99.8
550–600	0.2	0.4	99.6
500–550	0.6	1.1	98.9
450–500	1.3	2.3	97.7
400–450	2.9	5.2	94.8
350–400	4.5	9.8	90.2
300–350	6.7	16.5	83.5
250–300	11.3	27.8	72.2
200–250	17.0	44.8	55.2
150–200	16.3	61.1	38.9
100–150	14.6	75.7	24.3
50–100	14.0	89.7	10.3
0–50	10.3	100.0	0.0

100 years summary
Probabilities

Period (years)	Range	More than	Less than
600–700	0.2	0.2	99.8
500–600	0.9	1.1	98.9
400–500	4.2	5.2	94.8
300–400	11.3	16.5	83.5
200–300	28.3	44.8	55.2
100–200	30.9	75.7	24.3
0–100	24.3	100.0	0.0

4.1.227 The duration for the formation of the Late Iron Age buried ground surface (B105)

The evaluation of the maximum and minimum durations for the formation of the Late Iron Age buried ground surface is based on four radiocarbon dates which form its upper and lower chronological limits. Two radiocarbon dates were recovered from F1045, a basal deposit in the 'farm mound' (B104), overlying the buried ground surface (B105). The radiocarbon dates have been calibrated to:

cal AD 990–1255 (GU-3066c; limpet)
cal AD 990–1240 (GU-3067; cattle, sheep/goat)

The lower limit of the formation period is defined by two dates from F1034, the uppermost deposit in the underlying mound of ash deposits (B107):

cal AD 520–870 (GU-3065; cattle, pig, sheep/goat)
cal AD 620–880 (GU-3064c; limpet)

In order to avoid having to compare terrestrial with marine dates, the PD of the age difference between contexts F1034 and F1045 is derived from the average of the difference PD of the two marine

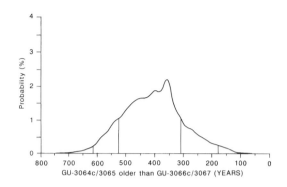

Illus 140   PD diagram of Blocks 107 & 104

samples (GU-3064c & GU-3066c) and the two terrestrial samples (GU-3065 & GU-3067). The difference PDs of the two pairs of dates lie entirely in the positive region. There was therefore no need for stratigraphical adjustment (Illus 140).

There is a 69 per cent probability that the age difference between Blocks 107 and 104 is between 310 and 525 years, and it is 96 per cent probable that the difference is between 180 and 615 years. As shown in Table 11, it is only 3.5 per cent probable that the difference is less than 200 years, and there is only a 3 per cent chance that the difference is more than 600 years.

4.1.228 The duration for the formation of the 'farm mound'

Two radiocarbon dates were recovered from F1045, a basal deposit in the 'farm mound' (B104). The dates are calibrated to:

cal AD 990–1255 (GU-3066c: limpet)
cal AD 990–1240 (GU-3067: cattle, sheep/goat)

TABLE 11: SUMMARY OF THE PROBABILITY DISTRIBUTION OF THE AGE DIFFERENCE BETWEEN BLOCKS 107 AND 104.

	50 years summary		
	Probabilities		
Period (years)	Range	More than	Less than
750–800	0.1	0.1	99.9
700–750	0.2	0.3	99.7
650–700	0.6	0.9	99.1
600–650	2.1	3.0	97.0
550–600	6.2	9.1	90.9
500–550	10.8	20.0	80.0
450–500	15.2	35.2	64.8
400–450	17.3	52.5	47.5
350–400	19.9	72.4	27.6
300–350	12.8	85.2	14.8
250–300	7.1	92.2	7.8
200–250	4.2	96.5	3.5
150–200	2.4	98.9	1.1
100–150	0.9	99.8	0.2
50–100	0.2	100.0	0.0
0–50	0.0	100.0	0.0

	100 years summary		
	Probabilities		
Period (years)	Range	More than	Less than
700–800	0.3	0.3	99.7
600–700	2.7	3.0	97.0
500–600	17.0	20.0	80.0
400–500	32.5	52.5	47.5
300–400	32.7	85.2	14.8
200–300	11.3	96.5	3.5
100–200	3.3	99.8	0.2
0–100	0.2	100.0	0.0

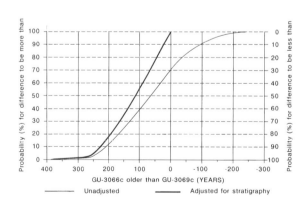

Illus 141   Cumulative PD diagram of Blocks 103 & 104

TABLE 12: SUMMARY OF THE PROBABILITY DISTRIBUTION OF THE AGE DIFFERENCE BETWEEN BLOCKS 103 AND 104, ADJUSTED FOR STRATIGRAPHY.

50 years summary
Probabilities

Period (years)	Range	More than	Less than
400–450	0.0	0.0	100.0
350–400	0.2	0.2	99.8
300–350	0.7	0.9	99.1
250–300	3.1	4.0	96.0
200–250	13.1	17.1	82.9
150–200	17.4	34.5	65.5
100–150	20.5	55.1	44.9
50–100	21.8	76.9	23.1
0–50	23.1	100.0	0.0

100 years summary
Probabilities

Period (years)	Range	More than	Less than
400–500	0.0	0.0	100.0
300–400	0.9	0.9	99.1
200–300	16.2	17.1	82.9
100–200	37.9	55.1	44.9
0–100	44.9	100.0	0.0

An upper part of the 'farm mound' F1030 (B103) has produced one radiocarbon date, calibrated to :

cal AD 1010–1280 (GU-3069c: limpet)

An evaluation of the formation period can be calculated on the basis of the dates from GU-3066c and GU-3069c, as both consist of the same type of dating material.

The probability distribution of the age difference indicates that there is a 30 per cent probability that the lower date (GU-3066c) is younger than the stratigraphically more recent sample GU-3069c. Since the stratigraphically lower date GU-3066c is assumed to be older than GU-3069c, the age difference must lie in the positive region of the distribution. As the probability of the age difference being negative is nil, the positive part can be re-normalized, creating a difference distribution based on the stratigraphical sequence (Illus 141). Table 12 lists the probabilities, based on this re-normalized distribution.

According to these calculations, there is a 69 per cent probability that the difference is less than 160 years, and a 96 per cent probability that it is less than 250 years. As indicated in Table 12, the probability for the difference to be less than 50 years is 23 per cent, and the probability for it to be less than 100 years is 45 per cent. The probability for the difference to be more than 200 years is 17.1 per cent and the probability for it to be more than 300 years is less than 1 per cent.

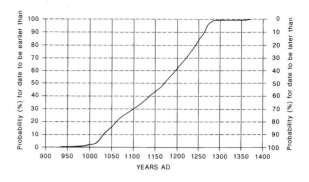

Illus 142   Cumulative PD diagram of GU-3069c

4.1.229 The terminal date for the accumulation of deposits in the 'farm mound' (B103)

The terminal date for the accumulation of deposits in the 'farm mound' (B103) can be calculated on the basis of the date GU-3069c (cal AD 1010–1280) from Block 103, on the assumption that the sample dated is contemporary with final accumulation in the 'farm mound'. Illus 142 shows the cumulative probability distribution for GU-3069c. The data are tabulated in Table 13.

TABLE 13: CUMULATIVE PROBABILITY DISTRIBUTION FOR THE AGE OF GU-3069c

50 years summary
Probabilities

Year cal AD	Older than	Later than
900	0.0	100.0
950	0.2	99.8
1000	1.9	98.1
1050	15.7	84.3
1100	30.0	70.0
1150	43.4	56.6
1200	61.8	38.2
1250	83.9	16.1
1300	99.0	1.0
1350	99.1	0.9
1400	100.0	0.0

100 years summary
Probabilities

Year cal AD	Older than	Later than
900	0.0	100.0
1000	1.9	98.1
1100	30.0	70.0
1200	61.8	38.2
1300	99.0	1.0
1400	100.0	0.0

If this date represents the termination of 'farm mound' accumulation, it is 98 per cent probable that this happened before cal AD 1280. As Table 13 shows, there is only a 16 per cent chance for a cessation of accumulation after cal AD 1250. The probability for the accumulation to have ceased before cal AD 1020 is less than 5 per cent.

4.2 The Artefactual Sequence

Christopher Lowe

4.2.1 Introduction

The majority of artefacts was recovered by hand, a few as a result of the environmental samples processing programme. Only pottery, the querns and the metal artefacts appear to be chronologically sensitive. No steatite or soapstone vessels or artefacts, often indicative of Viking or Norse occupation, were recovered from the site.

4.2.2 Pottery

Full analysis of the coarse pottery assemblage, and its morphology, are presented elsewhere (Part 5.1). A summary of the trends is presented here.

4.2.21 Aceramic phases

Phase 1 was totally aceramic, while Phase 7 and Phase 8 deposits were virtually so. Six sherds were recovered from Phase 7 deposits and only one (a strap handle) from the overlying 'farm mound' deposits of Phase 8, despite the intensive samples-processing programme. All the pottery from Phase 8, otherwise, was recovered from a late rubble spread (B217) and almost certainly represents residual material. The nineteenth-century excavations on the site may be considered the most likely source of this contamination.

4.2.22 Tempered and untempered wares

Although the assemblage for Phases 2 to 5 is small (94 sherds), 95 per cent of the sherds are either heavily or moderately tempered. Less tempered and untempered wares dominate the larger assemblage (1463 sherds) of Phases 6.1 to 6.3. Heavily tempered fabrics appear to be an early feature of the ceramic assemblage, with untempered and less tempered fabrics a feature of the later assemblage (Table 14).

TABLE 14: SUMMARY OF PHASE DISTRIBUTION OF POTTERY FABRIC TYPES

Phases	Untempered	Moderately tempered (10–50%)	Heavily tempered (>50%)	Total sherds
2–5	5%	26%	69%	(94)
6.1–6.3	22%	75%	3%	(1463)

4.2.23 Surface treatment

The ways in which the surfaces of the vessels were treated, with but two exceptions, appear not to be chronologically sensitive. Polished surfaces are unique to Phase 6.2. Burnished wares, although first appearing in Phase 6.1 (3 sherds), become common in Phases 6.2 and 6.3, with 98 per cent of the burnished wares associated with these two phases. Radiocarbon dates from the site would indicate a floruit for burnished and polished wares in the first quarter of the first millennium AD.

4.2.3 Querns

Only three querns, two dish and one rotary, were recovered during the course of the excavation. Both dish querns (SF123 & SF124) were found, together with their grinders, in Phase 4 contexts. One (SF123) had been reused as packing material inside a post-hole associated with Structure 5 (B243, Phase 4). The second (SF124) was set into the floor of Structure 3 (B246, Phase 4), adjacent to a possible hearth. An abundance of charred grain (363/10 l), naked barley where identifiable, and lumps of burnt peat (34 g/10 l) were recovered from the area adjacent to the quern and hearth. Structure 3, like the radiocarbon-dated building, Structure 4, with which it is stratigraphically associated, may be broadly assigned to the latter half of the second millennium BC. The presence of dish-querns would not be inconsistent with this dating.

The upper stone of a rotary quern (SF205) was recovered from the floor of Structure 9 (F2166: B233, Phase 6.2), in association with a group of six pot-lids and a large assemblage of mostly burnished wares. Although not directly dated, Structure 9 and its associated deposits and finds has been broadly assigned to the first quarter of the first millennium AD (Part 3.2). The presence of a rotary quern in these deposits would not be inconsistent with this dating. No evidence for 'quern replacement', *sensu* Caulfield (1978), was found within the small and chronologically discrete assemblage recovered from this site.

4.2.4 Metal

Only fourteen metal artefacts, or multiple fragments thereof, were found, despite the generally favourable circumstances for their survival. Half of these, small fragments of mainly copper alloy sheet, were recovered from the environmental sampling programme. The majority of the metal finds from the site were of copper alloy. Ten of the finds, including an iron nail head (Rt, F1105) and a possible iron sickle (SF69), were associated with the 'farm mound' (B103 & B104, Phase 8). Two copper alloy objects, including a possible ingot (SF107), were found in association with metalworking activity behind Structure 18 (B210, Phase 6.1). Of the remaining two items, one (Rt, F1001) was found in topsoil, the other (Rt, F2157) from the processing of a sample of the deposits forming the wall-core of Structure 4 (F2157: B245, Phase 4). Their presence here, although not impossible chronologically, may represent later contamination of the exposed section, either prior to or during the excavation.

Metal artefacts at St Boniface are associated with Phase 6.1 and, predominantly, with Phase 8 deposits.

4.3 Anthropogenic Content and the Ecofactual Sequence

Christopher Lowe

4.3.1 Introduction

An intensive programme of environmental sampling was conducted as part of the excavation (Part 2.1). Over 3400 l of sediment were processed. The extent to which each phase was sampled, and thus an indication of the degree to which different phases are either under- or over-represented, is listed in Table 15.

TABLE 15: VOLUME OF SAMPLES PROCESSED BY PHASE

Phase	Blocks	Litres
1	10	333
2	2	15
3	4	52
4	7	195
5	11	393
6.1	17	212
6.2	15	356
6.3	3	190
7	3	749
8	10	815*
9	5	104
Sum	**87**	**3414**

*Area 1 'farm mound' = 788l

The results of this programme were subsequently standardized and expressed as weight (g) or, in the case of cereal grains and other seeds, frequency concentration per 10 l of sediment (Table 16). This allows some assessment to be made of the anthropogenic content of each block and differences between them. The standardization of the original data at context level was undertaken independently to create the summaries at both block and phase level.

A summary of these data, totalled and ordered by phase, is presented as Table 17.

A five-point scale of relative abundance of the different environmental inputs is listed in Table 18. This provides the basis for the qualitative statements which are made in the account of the excavated structures and deposits (Part 3.2).

Detailed discussion of the environmental material is contained in the various specialist reports (Part 6). Only a summary, insofar as the different material types contribute as inputs to the excavated blocks, is

presented here, together with an overview, where appropriate, of the implications, if any, for the sequence or chronology of the site.

4.3.2 Mammal Bone

The excavation produced only a small sample of animal bone (Part 6.2), despite the generally favourable soil conditions for its preservation (Part 6.11). Only five blocks produced animal bone, principally cattle, sheep and some pig, in concentrations in excess of 100 g/10 l. In absolute terms, such quantities are low. With the exception of Block 202 (Phase 9), a late rubble spread, the material typically derived from the infilling of buildings abandoned in Phase 6.2 or 6.3 (B207, B226 & B232). A relatively high concentration (120 g/10 l) was also recorded from Block 312, part of the Phase 1 windblown sand horizon.

The generally rare occurrence of animal bone on the site suggests that primary middens lay outwith the excavated area. The rare use of antler on the site appears to be associated with Phase 4 deposits. A red deer metacarpal was recovered from an upper floor surface inside Structure 4 (B245, Phase 4), a perforated handle (SF134) was recovered from a lower floor level and two tine fragments (SF144a,b) were found in the backfill of an associated robber trench. A further tine fragment (SF116), recovered during the cutting back of the Middle Section over Structures 3 to 5 (all Phase 4), although unstratified, almost certainly also belongs to Phase 4. Two antler tines were recovered from Block 202 deposits (Phase 9), a redeposited rubble spread which was almost certainly derived from the nineteenth-century excavation of the roundhouse (Structure 2, Phase 5) or Structure 1a (B307, Phase 2). Another tine was found in Block 116 (Phase 5) and a comb fragment from Block 107 (Phase 7), the Late Iron Age ash mound, was also formed of antler.

4.3.3 Fish Bone

The presence of fish bones on the site (Part 6.3) was typically a feature of the 'farm mound' (Phase 8) and topsoil sediments on Area 1. These (B1, B102-B104) were the only blocks to record concentrations in excess of 20 g/10 l. Blocks 103 and 104 recorded densities, respectively, of 71 g and 108 g per 10 l sediment. Occasional (10 g–19 g/10 l) fish bones were recorded from the primary windblown sand horizon (B312, Phase 1), from the ash spread (F2143: B246, Phase 4) inside Structure 3, from the infilling of structures abandoned in Phase 6.2 or 6.3 (B207, B211, B232, B238 & B252), including the secondary enclosure ditch, and from the Late Iron Age buried ground surface (B105, Phase 7).

The overall sequence in the utilization of this resource reflects rare to occasional use in Phases 1 to 7, with intensive exploitation, on what is interpreted as a semi-industrial scale, a feature of Phase 8.

TABLE 16: ANTHROPOGENIC INPUTS TO BLOCKS, ORDERED BY PHASE

Data standardized as weight (g) or frequency concentration per 10 l sediment

Block	Phase	Vol (1)	Mammal bone	Fish bone	Marine shell	Fuel ash	Burnt peat	Charcoal	Cereal	Other seed
108	1	21	1	9	0	0	0	0	5	0
118	1	76	0	0	0	0	0	0	0	0
119	1	141	11	2	0	1	0	0	1	3
308	1	20	13	1	14	0	0	0	1	0
309	1	19	86	0	1	3	2	1	3	0
311	1	46	4	1	9	2	1	1	7	9
312	1	10	120	12	0	1	0	0	0	0
307	2	15	33	2	15	0	0	1	10	1
248	3	42	12	0	4	1	3	2	13	0
250	3	8	73	2	15	0	5	7	9	75
305	3	2	23	2	19	1	8	4	60	0
240	4	9	36	2	106	0	17	1	6	13
243	4	65	19	2	15	0	0	0	5	0
245	4	83	65	4	98	1	10	3	13	3
246	4	38	47	12	14	1	3	4	32	0
114	5	16	34	1	59	1	1	1	1	0
115	5	12	62	4	1782	0	0	1	0	0
116	5	57	10	2	63	0	0	3	4	2
117	5	8	7	0	546	0	0	0	0	0
208	5	21	1	0	4960	0	0	0	0	0
215	5	19	17	0	4766	0	0	0	2	0
237	5	111	51	3	1496	0	0	1	1	0
302	5	88	18	8	23	17	0	1	4	1
304	5	61	66	6	235	0	1	2	64	2
109	6.1	40	12	1	340	0	0	0	2	2
113	6.1	76	25	5	1165	0	1	0	3	1
204	6.1	11	12	4	447	7	1	2	0	0
210	6.1	50	33	6	35	10	6	3	8	3
213	6.1	35	16	6	2745	0	0	0	3	0
205	6.2	50	10	1	1323	0	0	0	2	0
225	6.2	38	79	0	23	1	0	1	288	0
226	6.2	32	112	1	7	0	0	1	37	1
230	6.2	42	22	7	539	4	1	2	1	4
231	6.2	48	37	2	140	0	1	2	8	8
232	6.2	15	261	10	1278	0	0	1	0	0
233	6.2	57	48	3	59	0	1	2	4	10
238	6.2	10	24	17	1908	0	0	0	1	0
252	6.2	40	17	15	900	2	2	0	7	0
253	6.2	24	8	4	249	0	0	1	5	0
207	6.3	75	146	14	228	4	0	0	7	2
211	6.3	26	66	12	1084	0	0	1	0	2
224	6.3	89	80	2	514	2	4	4	26	12
105	7	167	36	10	32	8	1	0	5	5
107	7	582	22	4	23	7	1	1	6	2
102	8	61	28	21	2	1	0	0	17	2
103	8	320	24	71	68	8	2	1	38	7
104	8	407	42	108	162	1	5	2	31	6
223	8	21	0	0	0	0	1	1	10	0
254	8	6	40	1	1	0	0	1	53	0
1	9	59	8	44	28	4	0	1	8	3
202	9	25	113	17	3209	0	0	0	0	0
301	9	20	66	0	33	6	0	1	12	0

4.3.4 Shell

Shells, predominantly limpets with some winkles, were common on the site. Sixteen blocks recorded concentrations in excess of 400 g/10 l. These were typically midden dumps and pit fills associated with Phase 5 features (B115, B117, B208, B215 & B237) or deposits dumped inside structures abandoned in Phases 6.1–6.3 (B113, B204, B205, B211, B213, B224, B230, B232, B238 & B252), including both the primary and the secondary enclosure ditches. A high density was also recorded from the Phase 9 rubble spread (B202), although this is probably

attributable to the nineteenth-century excavations on the site.

Low concentrations were recorded from Phase 1 (2 g/10 l: max 14 g/10 l), Phase 2 (15 g/10 l: max 15 g/10 l), Phase 3 (6 g/10 l: max 19 g/10 l) and Phase 4 (54 g/10 l: max 106 g/10 l) deposits. Similarly, little shell was present in the Late Iron Age ash deposits (B107, Phase 7) or the overlying 'farm mound' (B104, Phase 8), with 25 g/10 l and 108 g/10 l respectively. The overall impression is that utilization of this marine resource was essentially a feature of Phases 5 and 6 of the site's occupation. Furthermore, the presence of cockle

TABLE 17: PHASE SUMMARY OF ANTHROPOGENIC INPUTS

Data standardized as weight (g) or frequency concentration per 10 l sediment

Phase	Vol (1)	Mammal bone	Fish bone	Marine shell	Fuel ash	Burnt peat	Charcoal	Cereal	Other seed
1	333	14	2	2	1	0	0	2	2
2	15	33	2	15	0	0	1	10	1
3	52	22	1	6	0	3	3	14	12
4	195	45	5	54	1	6	2	14	2
5	393	35	4	1037	4	0	1	12	1
6.1	212	22	5	966	3	2	1	4	1
6.2	356	49	5	506	1	1	1	37	3
6.3	190	104	8	479	3	2	2	15	6
7	749	25	5	25	7	1	1	6	2
8	815	33	83	108	4	3	2	32	6
9	104	44	29	794	3	0	1	7	2

TABLE 18: FIVE POINT SCALE OF RELATIVE ABUNDANCE PER 10 l SEDIMENT

Material	Blocks Present	Absent	Rare	Occasional	Frequent	Common	Abundant	Maximum	Mean*1	Mean*2	Median	Mode
Mammal bone	50	37	<50g	50–99g	100–149g	150–199g	>200g	261g	25g	44g	28g	10–19g
Fish bone	43	44	<10g	10–19g	20–29g	30–39g	>40g	108g	5g	11g	4g	1–9g
Shell	47	40	<100g	100–199g	200–299g	300–399g	>400g	4960g	354g	655g	98g	1–100g
Fuel ash	24	63	<5g	5–9g	10–14g	15–19g	>20g	17g	1g	4g	2g	1g
Burnt peat	23	64	<5g	5–9g	10–14g	15–19g	>20g	17g	1g	3g	2g	1g
Charcoal	33	54	<2g	2–3g	4–5g	6–7g	>8g	7g	1g	2g	1g	1g
Cereal	43	44	<10	10–19	20–29	30–39	>40	288	10	19	7	1–9
Other seed	25	62	<10	10–19	20–29	30–39	>40	13	1	4	3	1–5

Mean *1: average of all blocks
Mean *2: average of constituent blocks only

shells in two Phase 5 shell midden accumulations (B215 & B237) may also be chronologically significant. These were the only blocks where cockle shells were present in significant, albeit relatively low, numbers (Part 6.6). Their presence in these blocks provides some support to the argument that the construction of the roundhouse and the cutting of the primary enclosure ditch represent asynchronous events (see B214, Phase 6.1: Part 3.2.6). The relative absence of shells from post-Phase 6 deposits might also indicate that there was little, if any, disturbance to the Iron Age site (Phases 5 & 6) prior to the excavations around the middle of the last century.

The hypothesis that different species of marine shells take up carbon from the sea at a different rate, and thus generate a differential marine effect when dated by the radiocarbon method, was tested as part of this project. This hypothesis was developed as a result of preliminary observations of the radiocarbon dates on limpet and winkle samples from excavations in the Western Isles (J. Barber, pers comm). Three contexts had sufficient material with which to explore this hypothesis. Radiocarbon dates (Part 4.1) were obtained from the following samples of limpets and winkles (Table 19).

The results of this analysis provide no support to the hypothesis that there is a differential marine effect according to the species tested.

4.3.5 Fuel Ash

Vesicular fuel ash, the material derived from the heating of a fuel source rich in silica, such as turves, was present in just over a quarter of all excavated blocks. Concentrations ranged from 1 g to 2 g/10 l on average.

The highest levels were recorded from the foundation or make-up deposits for the secondary walling (B302, Phase 5) which was inserted inside the roundhouse. Concentrations here reached 70 g/10 l for one of the block members (F3022), or 17 g/10 l for the block as a whole. The deposit was interpreted as reworked midden material. A high value (10 g/10 l) was also recorded from the surface deposits (B210, Phase 6.1) behind Structure 18, the primary enclosure wall and entrance façade; an area where metalworking activity appears to have been undertaken.

Relatively high values were also recorded, not surprisingly, from the ash deposits on Area 1 (Table 20).

There is, however, a marked difference between the values recorded for Phase 7, including the ground surface (B105) which developed in the top of the underlying sediments (B107), and the primary 'farm mound' (B104) of Phase 8. The secondary 'farm mound' (B103, Phase 8), on the other hand, presents a similar signature to that of the earlier deposits. The

TABLE 19: COMPARISON OF RADIOCARBON-DATED SAMPLES OF LIMPETS AND WINKLES

F no.	Block	Phase	Type	Uncal (bp)	Calibrated *	GU
2145	237	5	Limpets	2830±50	800–390 BC	3059c
2145	237	5	Winkles	2850±50	800–390 BC	3271c
2050	213	6.1	Limpets	2620±50	405–100 BC	3058c
2050	213	6.1	Winkles	2570±50	400–50 BC	3274c
1091	113	6.1	Limpets	2460±50	235 BC–AD 115	3061c
1091	113	6.1	Winkles	2490±50	340 BC–AD 75	3275c

* calibrated (LCR) and corrected for marine reservoir effect (–405±40)

composition and source of the Area 1 ash deposits is discussed further in Part 7.1.

The occurrence of vesicular fuel ash appears to have been predominantly a feature of the later phases of the site's occupation and reflects the use of a mineral-rich source of fuel. Its presence in a Phase 5 (B302) context, as a reworked deposit, suggests some earlier use. Its relative absence from Phase 4 and earlier deposits, however, suggests that a different fuel source was then being exploited (Parts 4.3.6 & 4.3.7).

TABLE 20: VESICULAR FUEL ASH CONTENT OF AREA 1 ASH DEPOSITS

Block	Phase	Block summary	Context range
103	8	8 g/10 l	<1 g–17 g/10 l
104	8	1 g/10 l	<1 g–3 g/10 l
105	7	8 g/10 l	8 g/10 l
107	7	7 g/10 l	<1 g–58 g/10 l

4.3.6 Burnt Peat

Small lumps of burnt peat were present in just over a quarter of all excavated blocks in concentrations of 1 g to 2 g/10 l on average.

The highest levels were recorded from the post-abandonment deposits (B240, Phase 4: 17 g/10 l) over Structures 4 and 5 and from Structure 4 (B245, Phase 4) itself. Here the block record of 10 g/10 l concentration varied from 4 g/10 l to 24 g/10 l for individual occupation horizons within the building. A contemporary building, Structure 3 (B246, Phase 4), also recorded extremely high levels (34 g/10 l) from an occupation surface, although overall the block density registered only 3 g/10 l.

Relatively high counts were also recorded from the Phase 3 sand horizon (B250:305: 6 g/10 l, range 5 g–8 g/10 l), Phase 6.1 deposits associated with metalworking activity behind Structure 18 (B210: 6 g/10 l, range 5 g–8 g/10 l) and the primary 'farm mound' deposits (B104: 5 g/10 l, range 2 g–28 g/10 l) of Phase 8. Relatively low counts were recorded from the secondary 'farm mound' deposits (B103, Phase 8: 2 g/10 l, range <1 g–5 g/10 l).

The burning of peat, although undertaken throughout the site's history, appears to pre-date the extensive use of a mineral-rich fuel source. Burnt peat is most prevalent in Phase 4 and earlier deposits, and, interestingly, in view of the relative absence of a vesicular fuel ash (Part 4.3.5), in the primary 'farm mound' deposits (B104) of Phase 8.

4.3.7 Charcoal

Charcoal was present in just under a third of all excavated blocks in concentrations of 1 g/10 l on average. Only material with sides greater than 4 mm was identified (Part 6.8). The phase distribution of the material identified, therefore, is uneven. Heather was present in the majority of samples identified; conifers (spruce, pine and larch) were present in about half. Small quantities of oak were identified in Phase 7 and later deposits. Occasional fragments of willow, birch and ash were identified in Phase 3 and Phase 4 deposits. Willow was also present in Phase 6.1 and Phase 8, birch and hazel in Phase 9.

The highest levels were recorded from the Phase 3 sand horizon (B250:305: 7 g/10 l, range 4 g–8 g/10 l), from occupation surfaces inside Structure 3 (B246, Phase 4: 4 g/10 l, range 1 g–5 g/10 l) and Structure 4 (B245, Phase 4: 3 g/10 l, range 1 g–16 g/10 l), and from the metal-working activity associated with Structure 18 (B210, Phase 6.1: 3 g/10 l, range 2 g–5 g/10 l). A high concentration was also recorded from the post-abandonment deposits filling Structures 7 and 11 (B224, Phase 6.3: 4 g/10 l, range 1 g–7 g/10 l).

Charcoal, although present in all phases of the site's occupation, has a similar phase distribution to burnt peat, although this, in part, reflects the dominance of burnt heather in the charcoal assemblage. Nonetheless, the appearance of charcoal on the site, in concentration, whether derived from the burning of peaty turves, driftwood or the local tree-cover, like the use of peat, appears to pre-date the extensive use of a mineral-rich fuel source. It is most prevalent in Phase 4 and earlier deposits. Like the burnt peat distribution, although less pronounced, charcoal also contributes more to the primary 'farm mound' deposits (B104, Phase 8: 2 g/10 l, range <1 g–4 g/10 l) than it does to the succeeding secondary 'farm mound' (B103, Phase 8: 1 g/10 l, range <1 g–2 g/10 l).

4.3.8 Cereals

4.3.81 Introduction

Charred cereal grain was present in half of all excavated blocks, in concentrations of roughly 10 grains per 10 l sediment, on average. Differing phase distributions and chronologies are reflected in the different crops used.

4.3.82 Hulled barley

The highest cereal grain concentration, at block level, was associated with ash deposits below Structure 13 (B225, Phase 6.2: 288/10 l). The grain, where sufficiently well preserved, was hulled barley. High counts of hulled barley were also recorded from the post-abandonment deposits (B226, Phase 6.2: 32/10 l) filling Structure 12 and the Phase 8 ash deposits on Area 2 (B254: 53/10 l).

Four grains of hulled barley were recovered from the sand horizon (B248, Phase 3) below Structure 4 (B245, Phase 4), suggesting perhaps an overlap with the cultivation of naked barley, discussed below. Only naked barley was identified in the Phase 3 sand horizon (B250:304), outwith the limits of Structure 4 (B245, Phase 4). The presence, therefore, of hulled barley in that part of the sand horizon which was sealed by a later building is anomalous. The few grains of hulled barley may represent derived material, from higher up the section. It is noticeable, for example, overall, that the phase distribution of hulled barley is essentially associated with Phases 6.2 and later.

4.3.83 Naked barley

High grain-density counts were also recorded from deposits within the walls of Structure 2 (B249:304, Phase 5: 64/10 l), the underlying sand horizon (B250:305, Phase 3: 74/10 l and 60/10 l) and the floor and associated deposits inside Structure 3 (B246, Phase 4: 32/10 l). This latter figure, however, masks considerable variability at context level. The fill of the stone feature, possibly a hearth or flue in the floor of Structure 3, for example, recorded a cereal density of 363/10 l. In all three cases, the grain, where identifiable, was naked barley. Naked barley, although recovered from occasional Phase 5 and Phase 6.1 and Phase 6.2 contexts, essentially appears to have been associated with Phases 1–4 of the site's occupation.

The appearance of naked barley in Phase 5, where it accompanied deposits which were used as core (F3020: B249:304) and levelling (F3029: B302) material in the construction of the roundhouse (Structure 2), is clearly residual. Its occurrence in the primary levels (F2044: B252, Phase 6.2) of the secondary enclosure ditch may also be residual, reflecting perhaps the dumping of old material in the ditch. However, the presence of naked barley in the

floor deposits associated with metalworking behind Structure 18 (F2107: B210, Phase 6.1) and the floor of Structure 9 (F2167: B233, Phase 6.2) seems less likely to represent residual material, given the otherwise cultural homogeneity of the relevant deposits. In these cases it would seem to reflect a late survival of this cereal type.

4.3.84 Oats and flax

Relatively high cereal counts were recorded from the 'farm mound', 31/10 l and 38/10 l from Blocks 104 and 103 (Phase 8) respectively. Here the grain assemblage of hulled barley, oats and flax was in the ratio of 55:37:8 and 50:44:6 for the primary (B104) and secondary (B103) mounds respectively. With the exception of five grains of flax which were recovered from the buried ground surface (F1011: B105, Phase 7) at Sampling Column B, representing a concentration here of just over 1/10 l, grains of flax were only recovered from the 'farm mound' (B103 & B104, Phase 8) deposits; together with a few from the erosion feature (B101) and modern topsoil (B1), both Phase 9. Flax clearly forms a small but significant part of the 'farm mound' assemblage and its arrival on site post-dates, roughly, AD 1100.

Oats, too, appear to be essentially a feature of the 'farm mound' deposits. A total of 883 identifications of oats was made. Cultivated or black oats (*Avena strigosa* Schreb.), including chaff, were identified positively in only twelve cases: in two instances in Block 103 deposits, with ten cases found in Block 104 contexts. Only two examples of wild oat (*Avena fatua* L), including chaff, were identified positively, both from Block 104 deposits. The remaining 869 identifications of oats were only to genus level (*Avena* sp or cf *Avena* sp).

Four grains were recovered from topsoil (Phase 9), another four were associated with a late hearth on Area 2 (B223, Phase 8) and nine were recovered from the Late Iron Age ash deposits (B107, Phase 7). The remainder, 866 identifications, were recovered from the 'farm mound' (B103 & B104, Phase 8). The cultivation of oats on the site, not present before Phase 7 (B107), and even then in only extremely low concentrations and without identification to species, appears to be associated with the formation of the 'farm mound'.

4.4 The Architectural Sequence

Christopher Lowe

Fifteen of the twenty-five structures recorded in the excavation have been interpreted as habitable buildings (Table 21).

Data with regard to the structural form, masonry type and style are fairly complete for all but Structure 3, a building which was indicated only by an area of paving and a hearth. Of the rest, essentially three types of structure form were distinguished:

TABLE 21: SUMMARY OF EXCAVATED STRUCTURE TYPES

Phase	Block	no.	Structure type	Structure form	Masonry type	Masonry style	wall width
2	307	1a	building	curvilinear	freestanding, dump	coursed	>0.60
4	246	3	building				
4	245	4	building	cellular	freestanding, faced	coursed	1.70
4	243	5	building	rectilinear	single-faced	coursed & orthostatic	
5	249:304	2	building	curvilinear	freestanding, faced	coursed	3.80
5	114	22	building	cellular	single-faced	coursed & orthostatic	
6.1	239	6	building	curvilinear	single-faced	coursed & orthostatic	
6.1	236	7	building	rectilinear	freestanding, faced	coursed	0.65
6.1	229	11	building	rectilinear	freestanding, faced	coursed	0.85
6.2	233	9	building	rectilinear	freestanding, faced	coursed	0.80
6.2	231	10	bulding	curvilinear	single-faced	coursed & orthostatic	
6.2	227	12	building	curvilinear	single-faced	coursed & orthostatic	
6.2	225	13	building	?curvilinear	single-faced	coursed	
8	222	14	building	rectilinear	freestanding, faced	coursed	0.70
8	203	21	building	rectilinear	freestanding, faced	coursed	0.40
2	255	1b	kerb				
6.1	234	8	entrance façade		freestanding, faced	coursed	1.20
6.1	214	16	primary ditch				
6.1	210	18	entrance façade		freestanding, faced	coursed	1.20
6.1	111	23	kerb				
6.1	110	24	wall		freestanding, dump	coursed	1.50
6.2	212	17	secondary ditch				
6.2	209	19	entrance façade		freestanding, faced	coursed	1.20
6.2	205	20	entrance façade		freestanding, faced	coursed & orthostatic	0.80
8	218	15	?passage		single-faced	coursed	

curvilinear, rectilinear and cellular or lobate. The walls of the buildings were either free-standing with a faced interior and an exterior of dump construction, free-standing and faced inside and out, or single-faced only, the walls having been cut into and revetted by earlier deposits. Their masonry was either coursed or of coursed and orthostatic construction. Variation in the widths of the walls of free-standing buildings was also apparent.

Free-standing structures are a feature of the buildings throughout all structural phases of the site. Single-faced structures, on the other hand, have a somewhat limited phase distribution (Phases 4–6.2). Clearly, these phases are precisely those where the appropriate conditions prevailed to allow the construction of buildings of this type. Their absence in Phase 8, on the other hand, may indicate that this type of construction was not then used. The use of orthostatic construction (Phases 4–6.2) is also absent from buildings assigned to Phase 8.

Curvilinear buildings have a similar phase distribution (Phases 2 & 5–6.2) to the single-faced structures. Indeed, with the exception of the roundhouse (Structure 2) and Structure 1a, which are both free-standing structures, all the curvilinear buildings on the site were single-faced. Conversely, all the single-faced buildings, with the probable exception of Structure 5, were curvilinear. Rectilinear buildings, on the other hand, again with the probable exception of Structure 5, were all free-standing structures and have a wide phase distribution (Phases 4, 6.1, 6.2 & 8). As basic building types, neither curvilinear nor rectilinear building forms appear to be chronologically sensitive.

Only two positive chronological factors appear to emerge. Cellular or lobate buildings (Structures 4 &

22) appear to be restricted to Phases 4 and 5. Thick-walled (>1 m) structures (Structures 2, 4 & possibly 1a), meanwhile, tend to be relatively early (Phase 5 and earlier). Thin-walled (<1 m) buildings (Structures 7, 9, 11, 14 & 21), on the other hand, tend to be relatively late (Phase 6.1 and later).

4.5 Correlation of Dating Evidence

Christopher Lowe

This section presents a tabular summary (Illus 143) of the chronological or sequential significance of the artefactual, ecofactual and architectural attributes considered above in Sections 4.2–4.4. It is an interpretative overview which attempts to periodize and depict the floruits, rather than simply the presence or absence, of the various attributes previously examined.

4.6 Phasing and Connected Account

Christopher Lowe

4.6.1 Introduction

The phasing scheme adopted has been defined, principally, on the basis of the site stratigraphy and the radiocarbon-dating programme: in all, eleven phases of activity on the site have been identified. The phasing scheme attempts to provide a coherent and interpretable order to the data. The sequences which can be perceived in the artefactual and ecofactual records for the site are not incompatible

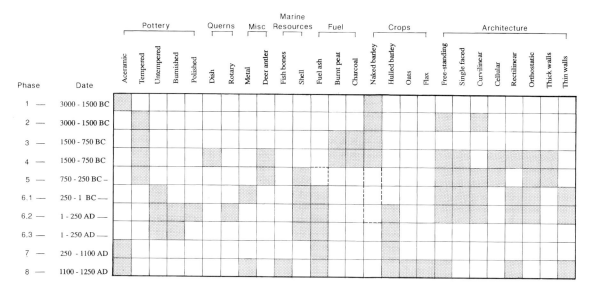

Illus 143　　　Correlation table of various attributes to phase

with the phasing scheme proposed here. These records, however, have not been used to define the phasing, but are, rather, a reflection upon it. The phasing scheme and its nomenclature are as follows:

Phase 1:　　early funerary activity
Phase 2:　　the earliest settlement
Phase 3:　　windblown sand
Phase 4:　　the settlement of the late second millennium bc
Phase 5:　　unenclosed roundhouse settlement
Phase 6.1　enclosed roundhouse settlement
Phase 6.2:　enclosed roundhouse settlement and secondary enclosure
Phase 6.3:　abandonment of enclosure
Phase 7:　　Late Iron Age deposits
Phase 8:　　the 'farm mound' and final structures on Area 2
Phase 9:　　modern turf and topsoil, rubble and erosion horizon

The adopted nomenclature attempts to reflect the principal theme of each phase. Both descriptive and chronological terms are used in these phase titles, where appropriate. Each phase, in turn, attempts to encompass and define those elements of the site stratigraphy where fundamental changes occur in the way in which the site was used, its spatial arrangements were defined or the 'architecture' of the place was expressed.

Perhaps unconventionally, certain phases identified also have duration. This is most clearly seen in Phase 6.2 where, clearly, there is continuing structural development on the site, leading to the superimposition of buildings. To have subdivided the phase groups into subphases would have led to a fragmentation of the record, creating a plethora of small subgroups which would be chronologically unrelated except within the larger phase grouping.

This has been resisted wherever possible as it would lend a spurious, and arguably unnecessary, level of detail to the proposed phasing scheme. For the same reasons, the chronologies which have been assigned to the phase groups have been expressed, at best, as mostly periods of not less than quarter millennia.

4.6.2 Connected Account: The Stratigraphic and Chronological Sequence (Illus 144–148)

The earliest deposits on the site consisted of sandy loam soils and relic sand-blow deposits, the latter surviving only in those places where sealed beneath later buildings. Cattle bone from the primary sandy surface itself has been radiocarbon dated to the early third millennium cal BC (3020–2700 cal BC: AA-9561) and presumably reflects the presence of Neolithic settlement in the area.

The earliest use of the site appears to have been funerary. This activity clearly pre-dates the deposition of windblown sand in Phase 3 and it is assumed that it also pre-dates the structures of the earliest settlement of Phase 2. Radiocarbon dates from above (1610–1320 cal BC: AA-9560, B250:305, Phase 3) and below (3020–2700 cal BC: AA-9561, B312, Phase 1) the funerary features would indicate a second or late third millennium date for their construction.

The funerary assemblage comprised three stone-lined cut features, possibly cists, and a small cairn. Two of the cut features, aligned roughly north-east to south-west, were cut into the sand and till, and lay adjacent to one another. One, forming a stone-lined chamber roughly 1.5 m by 0.7 m, contained the skull of an adult male (Part 6.1). The absence of other bones and, in particular, the absence of tooth enamel may indicate that the skull alone was transferred to the chamber some time after death. A third stone-

Illus 144   General view across the LBA and IA settlement (Area 2), from NW

lined pit, similarly aligned, lay nearby. It may represent a further grave.

A small cairn, set upon a broad stone *annulus*, lay immediately to the south of this group of cut features where it had been preserved within the thickness of the wall of the later roundhouse (Structure 2). A cut for a rectangular pit, beneath the cairn, is interpreted as a probable burial chamber. It has been reconstructed as a small monument, roughly 2 m in diameter and set upon an *annulus* roughly twice as wide. The cairn stood roughly 0.5 m above its contemporary land surface and was ultimately inundated with windblown sand.

The funerary assemblage forms a spatially discrete group of features, concentrated in the area of the later roundhouse (Structure 2). This, however, was the only area on the site where primary levels were excavated in plan to any great extent. The extent of the cemetery which is implied by these structures, therefore, is unknown.

The earliest settlement remains on the site share the same lower stratigraphy as the funerary structures of Phase 1. For the purposes of recording and interpretation, the earliest buildings have been assigned, albeit arbitrarily, to Phase 2. The structural remains of this phase, however, were fragmentary and sparse, and have differing upper stratigraphies (Part 3.2). One (Structure 1b) comprised no more than a stone kerb or wall-footing, sealed beneath rubble and windblown sand deposits of Phase 3. The second building (Structure 1a), in part preserved beneath the wall of the later roundhouse, appears to have been a curvilinear structure, constructed with free-standing walls, probably of dump construction externally. A sherd of heavily tempered pottery (V1), of Late Bronze Age or Early Iron Age type, from a hearth deposit inside the building may suggest the correlation of Structure 1a with the settlement of the late second millennium BC (Phase 4). However, the presence of heavily tempered wares among the fill deposits of the later roundhouse wall may represent a possible source of contamination.

The funerary and structural remains of Phases 1 and 2 are the earliest known features on the site. They can be dated not later than the mid-second millennium BC and, as indicated by the radiocarbon dates from contexts at and near the base of the section, could be considerably earlier.

Windblown sand and rubble deposits subsequently accumulated over the remains of Structure 1b and were, themselves, in turn sealed by the construction of Phase 4 buildings (Structures 3 & 4) and the later roundhouse (Structure 2) of Phase 5.

No upstanding remains of buildings were identified from Phase 3 although a single post-hole, like the rubble deposits which permeate this horizon, is presumably testament to some degree of building activity at this time. This rubble horizon is interpreted as demolition debris associated with buildings which were constructed in or after Phase 2 but prior to Phases 4 or 5. The stability of this horizon is unclear. Certainly, deflation can be positively identified in Phase 4 by comparing the anthropogenic inputs of the sand under and outwith the walls of Structure 4. An earlier, Phase 3, deflated sand horizon may be postulated. Radiocarbon dates, from cattle and pig bones in the Phase 3 sand and rubble horizon and from cattle and deer bones from an occupation horizon inside Structure 4 (Phase 4), indicate that the deposits sealed beneath Structure 4 accumulated within the period 1610–1320 cal BC (AA-9560) to 1535–1115 cal BC (AA-9562).

The upstanding remains of the Late Bronze Age settlement of the late second millennium cal BC (Phase 4) were located in the area immediately to the north of the later roundhouse (Structure 2). Rubble deposits beneath the roundhouse may represent further remains of buildings of either this or the Phase 3 settlement. It appears to have been unenclosed but, insofar as can be seen, the buildings did not extend outwith the area that was later enclosed (Phase 6.1).

Three buildings (Structures 3–5) have been assigned to Phase 4. Structure 4, part of a free-standing, cellular or lobate building, was constructed with thick rubble- and earth-filled walls, faced on both sides. A series of well-stratified floor surfaces was preserved inside this building, one of which, containing cattle and red deer bone, was radiocarbon dated to 1535–1115 cal BC (AA-9562). Structures 3 and 5 derive their dating solely on the basis of their relationship to Structure 4. The pottery, bone and cereal assemblage which is associated with these buildings, however, appears to be typical of the early phases of the site's occupation.

Structure 3 lay roughly 8 m to the north of Structure 4, at the same stratigraphic level. It was marked only by an area of paving. The presence of a possible hearth or flue, an adjacent quern, and a dense concentration of charred naked barley grains, abundant fragments of burnt peat and relatively high levels of charcoal, together suggest that the building was associated with the drying of grain. Structure 5 was subsequently built over and between Structures 3 and 4 after their abandonment. It was a large rectilinear drystone building which was later partitioned at its northern end. Upon its abandonment, it was filled with soil and rubble, into

Illus 145   Structure 4 in foreground, from W, with roundhouse (Structure 2) to south and Structures 6 and 7 higher up the section

and over which buildings of Phase 6.1 were later constructed. The rubble is interpreted as demolition debris associated with the construction, occupation, abandonment and reconstruction of buildings on the site over some considerable period of time. It is most likely to derive from the demolition of buildings of Phase 4 or the primary extra-mural roundhouse settlement of Phase 5. No *in situ* structural remains were, however, apparent within this horizon.

No stratigraphic relationships were defined between the buildings of Phase 4 and those of Phase 5, principally the roundhouse (Structure 2). Their differentiation, therefore, depends largely upon the radiocarbon date from a floor deposit inside Structure 4. With the exception of the dominant fuel type, which appears to change around Phases 4 and 5 (Illus 143), both phases display similar cultural attributes. A prima-facie case for the priority of Structure 4 over the roundhouse could be advanced on the basis of the projected alignment of the exterior wall-face, its juxtaposition with the roundhouse wall more easily explained as an earlier feature which was partially dismantled, rather than as a later feature which was built up against it. This notwithstanding, it is clear that Structure 4 remained partially standing after the construction of the roundhouse. The fact that this building was not completely levelled, as those beneath the roundhouse clearly were, would indicate a measure of continuity between the settlements of Phases 4 and 5. This may be reflected in the homogeneity of the Phase 4/5 cultural assemblage.

Phase 5 is marked by the construction on the site of a substantial thick-walled roundhouse or broch (Structure 2). The interior and exterior wall faces were erected on sand to the west and over rubble to the east. Structure 1a was sealed beneath the north wall sector of the roundhouse. The remains of a cairn, part of the Phase 1 funerary assemblage, were incorporated into the south wall sector. At least part of the earlier settlement (Structure 4) was left standing.

Few buildings of the Phase 4 settlement, and none of those postulated for Phase 3, were exposed during the course of the excavation. Nonetheless, the construction of the roundhouse and its insertion into an existing settlement appear to mark a significant change in the nature of that settlement (Part 7.2).

The walls of the roundhouse were constructed with a solid soil and rubble core. The building was entered from the south-east and the exterior face, in this sector, stood nearly 3 m high. The entrance was checked at the line of the primary interior wall-face by two large orthostats and the remains of a bar-hole were traced on the left (south), behind the check. A 'guard-cell' lay outwith the checks, on the north side of the passage. Only part of the south and east sectors of the roundhouse survived but sufficient to demonstrate that the building measured roughly 17.6 m externally. At least two phases of construction were apparent. In its primary phase the walls were 3.2–3.8 m wide, providing an internal space 10.6 m across (*c.* 90 sq m). A series of additional internal wall-skins was added, apparently for stability after

what appears to have been an early collapse or possibly in connection with the construction of a secondary roundhouse inside the building. This thickening of the wall-base effectively reduced the internal area by half.

Radiocarbon dating of a shell midden which accumulated against the exterior of the roundhouse, indicates that the building was constructed in or around the second quarter of the first millennium cal BC (800–390 cal BC: GU-3059c & GU-3271c). Other buildings of the Phase 5 settlement, however, are poorly represented in the archaeological record for the site. In the main, the extra-mural settlement of Phase 5 is represented by the rubble deposits which were incorporated into the 'rubble raft' (B221, B235 & B240), on which buildings of Phase 6.1 and later were subsequently erected, and presumably also by earlier buildings of Phase 4, such as Structures 4 and 5, which at least overlap with the beginnings of the Phase 5 settlement. The roundhouse dominated the settlement through to its abandonment in Phase 6.3. The final collapse of the building, represented by the large rubble slabs of Block 217, is placed in Phase 8.

Statistical analysis (Part 4.1) of the radiocarbon dates from the shell midden which was cut by the primary enclosure and the shell midden which accumulated against the east wall of the roundhouse indicates that there is a 68 per cent probability that the cutting of the primary enclosure ditch post-dates the construction of the roundhouse. It seems probable, therefore, that the primary roundhouse settlement was unenclosed. Phase 5, therefore, has been defined as an unenclosed roundhouse settlement of the period, roughly, 750–250 BC.

One further building (Structure 22) may belong to the Phase 5 settlement, albeit relatively late in the sequence. It lay outwith the (later) primary roundhouse enclosure of Phase 6.1 and, on this basis, is interpreted as an outlying member of the unenclosed roundhouse settlement of the late first millennium cal BC. Part of a small cellular building, Structure 22 was cut into earlier rubble deposits (B117) which are interpreted as structural remains of buildings, of Phase 5 or earlier, which lay in the vicinity of the later enclosure ditch. The remaining Phase 5 deposits largely comprise shell midden dumps and pits filled with shells. Radiocarbon dates from these deposits span the second and third quarters of the first millennium cal BC (Table 4).

The subsequent enclosure of the site in Phase 6.1 represents a fundamental change in the nature of the settlement. The primary enclosure of the settlement is dated, in very broad terms, to the last quarter of the first millennium BC or slightly earlier. To this phase, principally, belong the cutting of the primary enclosure ditch, the construction of a stone-built enclosure wall and entrance façade, represented by Structure 18, on the north side of the entrance, and Structure 8 to the south, and the creation of a stone-built causeway or path, extending across the dunes to the north of the site. A drystone wall (Structure 24), outwith the ditched enclosure, may be associated with the causeway, either as an outer boundary wall to the enclosure or as a retaining wall for the mound of deposits which formed over and around the abandoned remains of Structure 22 to the south.

The primary enclosure ditch was cut through earlier shell and sand deposits, into the underlying till, and had been truncated on the north by the cut for the secondary enclosure ditch. It was 1.2 m deep and 3 m long, its east end forming a constructed terminal. The sides of the ditch were revetted with a coursed drystone wall. The inner edge of the primary ditch lay approximately 14.5 m from the roundhouse or roughly 23.3 m from its projected centre. A stone-capped drain emptied into the ditch from the south-east. Structure 18, part of the primary enclosure wall and entrance façade, lay just inside the line of the primary ditch. The south-east side of the primary entrance façade is represented by the wall fragment (Structure 8) and the paving on the threshold.

A major reorganization of the settlement, now within the enclosure, also appears to have been undertaken. The earlier extra-mural settlement was levelled to form a 'rubble raft' or stone terrace on which Structures 7 and 11, and possibly Structure 6 as well, were subsequently erected.

The fragmentary remains of Structure 6 were only partially exposed in plan and in elevation, beneath the walls of a later building, Structure 10. Structure 6 comprised a single-faced, curvilinear drystone wall which had been cut into and was partially overlain by rubble deposits (Part 3.2) which formed the 'rubble raft' on which all the later buildings were erected. Structure 6, if part of Phase 6.1 rather than Phase 5, lay directly opposite the entrance into the enclosure.

Structure 7 lay to the south of Structure 6 and roughly 1 m east of the roundhouse. It was constructed over post-roundhouse rubble deposits, interpreted as the levelled remains of the Phase 5 extra-mural roundhouse settlement, and the base of its wall lay 0.7 m above the base of the roundhouse. It was a large subrectangular free-standing building with rounded corners, and measured at least 4.5 m by 3 m inside walls 0.65 m wide and standing up to 1.2 m high. The walls were faced internally and externally and comprised a solid-built stone core. A thin orthostat stood against the exterior north wall. To the east of the orthostat were appended the walls of Structure 11, a building whose masonry and mode of construction were of a similar style to that exhibited by Structure 7.

The stone passage around the roundhouse, between it and Structure 7 to the east, was also created at this time, presumably allowing access between the enclosure entrance to the north-east and the entrance to the roundhouse to the south-east. Although evidence has been obscured or removed by the later construction of buildings of Phase 6.2, to the north of Structure 11, and erosion of the sea-bank to the west, it seems likely that the enclosed settlement of Phase 6.1 was formally laid out along radial lines. The position of Structure 6, however, appears to interrupt direct access between the enclosure entrance and the passage around the roundhouse. It may, however, form part of the Phase 5 settlement. Metalworking activity was carried out in an area behind the primary enclosure wall.

Phase 6.2 is marked by the infilling of the primary ditch, its recut to the north and the refurbishment of the enclosure wall and entrance façade, represented by Structure 19 to the north of the entrance and Structure 20 to the south. On the basis of the radiocarbon dates and the stratigraphic evidence, the Middle Iron Age settlement of Phase 6.2 is broadly assigned to the first quarter of the first millennium AD (Table 4).

The primary enclosure ditch was rapidly backfilled with shells and subsequently recut. Radiocarbon dating (235 cal BC–cal AD 115: GU-3061c) of an earlier shell midden, which was cut by the north side of the secondary ditch, provides a *terminus post quem* date for its construction. Radiocarbon dates (400–50 cal BC: GU-3274c & 405–100 cal BC: GU-3058c) from fill deposits in the primary ditch, which was cut by the south side of the secondary enclosure, do not contradict this dating.

The secondary enclosure ditch lay roughly 1.5 m to the north of its predecessor. It was up to 1.7 m deep and 3 m wide. Its sides were revetted with coursed drystone masonry and the south side was subsequently buttressed by a drystone wall. The inner edge of the ditch lay approximately 16 m from the roundhouse or roughly 24.8 m from its projected centre.

No trace of a terminal was found. It is assumed, on the basis of the evidence for the refurbishment of the enclosure wall and entrance façade, to lie to the east of the primary ditch terminal, behind the standing cliff-section. It is assumed, therefore, to have lain closer to the external causeway than its predecessor. The causeway, although partially covered with midden material which has been radiocarbon dated to 400–70 cal BC (GU-3062c), presumably continued in use throughout Phase 6.2. It was finally sealed by the Phase 7 Late Iron Age ash mound, the base of which is radiocarbon dated to cal AD 285–670 (GU-3063).

The entrance façade was also remodelled at this time. Structure 19, on the north-west side of the entrance, was constructed over its predecessor, Structure 18, to form a single L-shaped structure. Structure 20, comprising a stone kerb, threshold and wall-fragment, formed the south-east side of the entrance. It abutted the primary entrance façade on this side (Structure 8) and overlay the primary paving at the threshold. The wall alignments suggest that the secondary entrance was narrower than its predecessor and externally splayed.

The recovery of a substantial part of a cat's skeleton from a make-up deposit below the latest paving in the entrance may represent deliberate burial on the threshold into the enclosure. The presence of human skeletal material in the primary levels of the secondary enclosure ditch, in an area close to the entrance, may also reflect ritual activity on this part of the site at this time.

Structures 9, 10, 12 and 13, which were erected in the area between Structure 11 and the enclosure entrance, have been identified as elements of the

Illus 146   General view, from N, across Area 2, with Structure 10 in foreground

secondary enclosed settlement. They may represent, in part, rebuildings of earlier structures. Structure 10, for example, appears to occupy the same stance as that of the earlier building, Structure 6. Structure 12, in turn, occupies part of the stance of Structure 10, and Structure 13 was ultimately built over Structure 12. The sequence of the Phase 6.2 buildings, therefore, is sequential, with only one building ever occupying the ground between Structures 7/11 and the entrance at any one time. Structures 7 and 11, like the roundhouse, are assumed to have continued in use throughout this phase.

The earliest building in this sequence was Structure 9. It lay just inside the secondary entrance façade and had been erected over the remains of the southern fragment of the primary entrance façade wall (Structure 8). Disturbed by later construction on the site, Structure 9 appears to have been a rectilinear, free-standing building and of a similar construction to Structures 7 and 11, of Phase 6.1, to the south. Only its north wall survived, to be reused subsequently in the construction of both Structures 12 and 13.

The floor deposits inside Structure 9 were extremely rich in artefacts and included the upper stone of a rotary quern, several stone pot-lids and a large assemblage of burnished pottery, including examples of small flat-based, straight-sided or barrel-shaped vessels.

Structure 10 was constructed over the remains of Structure 6 to the west and Structure 9 to the north. It was a single-faced, curvilinear structure, just over 3 m across internally, and presumably part of a larger, cellular building. A stone-built feature, set into the paved floor, is interpreted as the remains of a trough. An adjacent dump of midden material and stones, many of them burnt, is interpreted as a mound of occupation debris including burnt-mound material. The occurrence of burnt stones and the presence of the trough inside Structure 10, adjacent, may suggest that the building and the formation of the mound are associated. Burnished wares were recovered from the mound. Radiocarbon dates from fill deposits of Structure 6 clearly indicate that Structure 10 was constructed after 50 cal BC–cal AD 235 (GU-3278c).

Structure 12 was erected over and to the east of Structure 10 and its internal single-faced wall was revetted into the mound of rubble and burnt stones which had accumulated against Structure 7 and Structure 11 to the south. The construction of Structure 12 is the most likely cause for the truncation and levelling of earlier deposits on this part of the site.

The south internal face of the building consisted predominantly of orthostats, oversailed by coursed drystone masonry. An earlier wall, part of Structure 9, was reused as the north side of the room or cell.

Illus 147   View, from SW, towards the enclosure entrance façade

Together, the walls define the outline of a subcircular or subsquare room or cell, roughly 3.5 m in diameter. It is, however, almost certainly part of a larger, cellular building, preserved below the Upper Section to the east. The remains of a raised bench or platform were traced on the west side of the room. Radiocarbon dating of earlier infill dumps provide *termini post quo* dates of 70 cal BC–cal AD 220 (GU-3279c) and 50 cal BC–cal AD 235 (GU-3278c) for the construction of Structure 12.

Structure 13 was the latest building on this part of the site and, although assigned to Phase 6.2, could be later. The building lay across, at right angles to, and over the remains of Structures 11 and 12. Only a short fragment of coursed, drystone masonry, forming the south-west corner of a room or cell of a larger cellular building, survived. The single-faced wall fragment, like that of Structure 12, was revetted into the mound of rubble and burnt stones. To the north, the structure reused an earlier wall, originally associated with Structure 9. Against the north interior wall-face, and below the level of its paved floor, were the remains of a sunken stone-lined trough, 1.2 m long, 0.3 m deep and at least 0.6 m wide.

Construction activity in Phase 6.2 was not only undertaken in the area around the entrance. The extra-mural roundhouse passage, for example, was relaid on at least two occasions and these have been

correlated with the refurbishment of the enclosure entrance. Extensive stone-robbing of buildings close to the passage, probably the roundhouse, subsequently occurred, filling the passage with a 0.15 m deep deposit of splintered stone fragments and shells. Access around the extra-mural roundhouse passage may have continued for some time after this but was subsequently blocked off with the construction of a wall across the passage. An external buttress was also erected against the roundhouse wall at the same time. Although there may have been some lowering of the roundhouse wall-head, as represented by the accumulation of stone debris in the passage, nonetheless, the construction of an external buttress strongly suggests that occupation was still continuing inside the roundhouse at this time.

Construction activity during Phase 6.2 appears to have been associated solely with features within the enclosure: none has been identified outwith the enclosure. This is in contrast to the situation seen in Phases 5 (Structure 22) and 6.1 (Structure 24, the causeway & ?Structure 23) and may reflect a decline in the status and prestige of the Phase 6.2 settlement. A hiatus in the use of the external northern fringe of the site (Area 1) may also be reflected in the disparity between the radiocarbon dates for the initiation of the Late Iron Age ash mound deposits of Phase 7 (cal

AD 285–670: GU-3063) and the underlying shell midden dumps of Phase 6.1 (400–70 cal BC: GU-3062c).

The abandonment (Phase 6.3) of the Middle Iron Age enclosed settlement is represented by the rapid infilling of the secondary enclosure ditch, the adjacent entrance façade and Structures 7 and 11 to the south. Each of these deposits is radiocarbon dated, roughly, to the first quarter of the first millennium AD (Table 4), and, together, the phase is characterized as one of cessation of occupation on this part of the site at that time or shortly thereafter. The structures were filled with midden material, rubble and shells. Burnished wares were common in these deposits. Concentrations of fish bones (Part 6.3) of butterfish, sea scorpion, sandeels and small specimens of freshwater eels in the backfill of the ditch and the infill of the entrance façade probably point to the presence of natural predators, probably otters, on the site. Their presence, nesting and feeding in among the ruined buildings, reinforces the interpretation that this part of the site was almost certainly deserted at this time.

With the infilling of the enclosure ditch and the apparent cessation of occupation within the enclosure in Phase 6.3, the next clearly datable horizon of activity (Phase 7) comes from outwith the enclosure, to the north. It is represented by the formation of a series of dump sediments. Anthropogenic indicators, with the exception of fuel ash, were rare. Artefacts were similarly rare. Six sherds of coarse untempered pottery, the majority smoothed or burnished, and a comb fragment (SF6), formed from antler, were the only artefacts recovered as a result of excavation and an extensive wet-sieving programme of just under 600 l of deposits.

The Phase 7 sediments have been identified as *in situ* ash dumps, deposited infrequently, with intervening periods of soil formation. Diatom analysis (Part 6.10) indicates burnt turves as the most likely source of the mineral residue. This activity is broadly dated, by radiocarbon, to the period cal AD 250–750 (Table 4).

The ash dumps comprised a series of shallow, horizontally layered deposits, up to 0.9 m deep. Cultivation has been proposed (Part 7.1) as a possible mechanism for the spreading of the deposits. The deposits extended throughout the Area 1 cliff-section, overlying the shell midden to the south, and the causeway and Structure 23 to the north. These deposits, in burying the causeway, mark a significant change in the use of the enclosed site to the south. Radiocarbon dates were obtained from both the base and top of the sediments. Mammal bones in the basal deposit were dated to the period cal AD 285–670 (GU-3063). Two dates, cal AD 620–880 (GU-3064c) and cal AD 520–870 (GU-3065), on shells and mammal bones respectively, were obtained from the top of the sediments. Statistical analysis of these dates (Part 4.1) indicates that there is a 69 per cent probability that the sediments accumulated over a period of 45–270 years. Further analysis (Part 7.1) has suggested that the deposits remained close to the

ground surface for at least 400 years. The primary date reinforces the Phase 6.3 dates as *termini ante quo* dates for the abandonment of the enclosed roundhouse settlement to the south.

Two negative features were subsequently cut into the upper surface of the ash deposits. Although of unknown function and association, they clearly testify to activity which was either broadly contemporary with or earlier than the formation of the ground surface which developed in the upper surface of the underlying sediments. By extrapolating from the latest radiocarbon dates in the ash dump deposits, the earliest radiocarbon dates from the overlying 'farm mound' and statistical analysis (Part 4.1) for the duration of the buried ground surface, it seems likely that the cut features, and the ground surface itself, should be assigned roughly to the last quarter of the first millennium AD.

The buried ground surface developed in and sealed the earlier deposits throughout the length of the exposed cliff-section on Area 1. Like the earlier sediments, from which it was derived, the anthropogenic content of the ground surface, with the exception of fuel ash inclusions, was generally low. A single flint flake (Part 5.2) was the only artefact recovered. Trace quantities of cereals and flax, the latter a feature of the overlying 'farm mound' deposits, were also present.

The fact that the ground surface was preserved intact and the identification, from pollen analysis (Part 6.9), that the surface supported an acidic heath vegetation immediately prior to burial, strongly suggest that there was little or no human interference on the site during the period of its formation. If the possible cultivation regime, which can be inferred for the spreading of the underlying mineral ash deposits, can be dated broadly to the period cal AD 250–750, and 'farm mound' formation (see below) can be assigned to *c*. cal AD 1100, this suggests a second period of abandonment at the interface between Phases 7 and 8, or roughly the period cal AD 750–1100.

The 'farm mound' deposits accumulated directly over the Late Iron Age buried ground surface. The mound was traced for roughly 18 m in section. The results of an auger survey suggest that the sediments were deposited on a slope to the north of the Iron Age settlement mound, extending over an area roughly 60 m north to south and 90 m transversely. Roughly 1 m deep at the exposed cliff-section and in excess of 3 m at the summit, the overall volume of the mound is estimated at 6000 cu m. This represents the residue from the burning of 60,000–120,000 cu m of dried peat or roughly 12,000 cu m of dried peaty alluvium (Part 6.11).

The mound comprised thin but extensive layers and lenses of greyish- and reddish-brown sandy silt loam deposits, up to 1 m deep and extremely rich in fish bones. Grains of barley, oats and flax were also present. Few artefacts, however, were recovered, despite the extensive sieving programme. Over 750 l of sediments were sieved. Several copper alloy artefacts, including a ring, a decorated strip, a

Illus 148   The Area 1 'farm mound' section, from N, together with the IA causeway and settlement beyond. The prominent dark band of the LIA ground surface (B105) is clearly visible in section

possible rivet, a pin, possibly from a penannular brooch, and several fragments and pieces of copper alloy sheet, an iron nail head, a possible iron sickle, and a strap handle from a jug of medieval type were the only artefacts found. From the base of the mound were recovered several lumps of lime mortar. This was the only record of mortar from the site. Its presence implies the demolition or refurbishment of a mortared building on the site, possibly a church or other high-status building, at the very time of the mound's inception, c. cal AD 1100.

Accumulation was rapid, given the highly stratified nature of the deposits, the absence of evidence for trampling, the absence of buried soil horizons within the mound, and the preservation of undisturbed humified plant remains at the interface between the buried ground surface and the overlying mound. Rapid formation is also reflected in the radiocarbon dates from the base (cal AD 990–1240: GU-3067 and cal AD 990–1255: GU-3066c) and upper part of the mound (cal AD 1010–1280: GU-3069c). Statistical analysis of the lower and upper dates indicates that there is a 69 per cent probability that the difference is less than 160 years and this provides an indication of the duration or formation period of the mound.

The 'farm mound' deposits have been identified as mineral residues derived from the burning of turves

and other organic sediments, mixed with fish processing waste and occasional domestic debris. Although only the periphery of the monument was explored, this activity seems, on the basis of the radiocarbon dates and the volumes of material deposited, to have been intensive but of a relatively short duration. Radiocarbon dating of the upper mound deposit indicates that the present-day ground surface, overlying the mound, has developed over the past 700 years.

A series of relatively late buildings (Structures 14, 15 & 21) and deposits on Area 2, post-dating the abandonment of the Middle Iron Age settlement, have also been assigned to Phase 8, although no stratigraphic relationship with the 'farm mound' deposits on Area 1 could be demonstrated. Overlying a mound of ash residues, in the top of which a soil had developed, the final structures on Area 2 were represented by a series of rectilinear walls or buildings, one of them associated with a rectangular stone-built hearth. The buildings are assumed, on the basis of their rectilinear form, their thin walls, and position at the top of the cliff-section, to be medieval in date. A subrectangular building, on a mound to the south-east of the cliff-section, possibly the Binnas Kirk of the local oral tradition (Part 2.2.4), may represent part of this later settlement. These buildings may be associated with the fish-processing site or could post-date it. This settlement, if not the same as that associated with the fish-processing site, however, was almost certainly abandoned before *c.* AD 1500, the date of the earliest surviving rental documents from the island. An abandonment in the medieval period may also be reflected in the absence of settlement toponymy at the site.

4.6.3 Summary

Structural activity on the site, in the form of funerary structures and the fragmentary remains of two buildings (Structures 1a & 1b,) can be first recognized in the second or late third millennium BC. A period of sand-blow (Phase 3) may mark the abandonment of the early site. Rubble deposits within the sand, if not part of the earlier structures, however, may represent continuing structural activity on the site. Nonetheless, certainly from the foundation of the Late Bronze Age settlement in Phase 4, the unenclosed roundhouse settlement of the Early Iron Age (Phase 5), through to its subsequent enclosure in Phase 6.1 and its refurbishment in the Middle Iron Age (Phase 6.2), settlement on the site appears to have continued unbroken. This encompasses, broadly, the period 1250 cal BC–cal AD 250 or a little later. During this time, buildings were constructed, repaired, robbed, levelled, rebuilt, reused and ultimately abandoned.

With the subsequent abandonment of the enclosed settlement, activity was shifted to the north. This period (Phase 7), roughly AD 250–750, possibly starting late within this range, witnessed the formation of an extensive accumulation of ash residues which were subsequently levelled, possibly through cultivation. The formation of a deep plaggen-soil is interpreted as the result of Late Iron Age and possibly Early Christian ecclesiastical activity on the site (Part 7.2). At the end of this period, this area was likewise abandoned and a ground surface, supporting an acidic heathland vegetation, developed in the top of the earlier sediments. This period of abandonment is assigned, broadly, to the period AD 750–1100 and, historically, would coincide with the period of the Viking settlement of the islands. Reuse of the site, over the period *c.* AD 1100–1200, or a little later, is marked by the formation of the 'farm mound' to the north. The final, post-roundhouse structures to the south may be broadly contemporary with this activity or a little later.

PART 5

Material Culture

5.1 The Coarse Pottery

Ann MacSween, with catalogue with Jenny Shiels and geological identifications and comment by Dianne Dixon

5.1.1 Introduction

The pottery assemblage comprises 1,719 sherds, representing an estimated 270 vessels. The nature of the excavation has meant that there is a relatively high proportion (7 per cent) of uncontexted sherds (Table 22). The majority of sherds are from Phase 6, with lesser numbers from Phases 3, 4 and 5. The assemblages from Phases 7 and 8 are similar to the Phase 3 assemblage, and may be residual. For this reason, the pottery from these phases has been omitted from this discussion. Pottery from Phase 9 (post-medieval and modern) is grouped with the uncontexted finds. The high sherd to vessel ratio in the assemblage results from the presence of large numbers of sherds from four vessels in Structure 9 (B233, Phase 6.2).

A complete catalogue is contained in the project archive and only illustrated sherds are described fully in the report. The catalogue entries are given in the following form: vessel number (V), finds number (SF), context (F), area (A) and block (B).

The majority of sherds are body sherds, with only 44 vessels being represented by rim sherds and 34 by basal sherds. Only 3 sherds (V12, Illus 160; V55, Illus 152 & V262, Illus 154) are decorated. The majority of vessels have not had any surface treatment, but burnishing was noted on 50 vessels, and slipping, usually a wet-hand finish in the same clay, was recorded on 33 vessels.

TABLE 22: SHERDS AND VESSEL NUMBERS

	No. of sherds	No. of vessels
Phase 2	1	1
Phase 3	10	4
Phase 4	30	15
Phase 5	53	15
Phase 6	1463	165
Phase 7	5	4
Phase 8	13	3
Phase 9	31	9
u/s	113	54
Total	**1719**	**270**

TABLE 23: SUMMARY OF FABRIC BY PHASE (CONTEXTED SHERDS)

	Untempered	10–50%	>50%
Phase 2	0	1	0
Phase 3	0	0	4
Phase 4	3	4	8
Phase 5	0	5	8
Phase 6	87	65	13
Phase 7	2	2	0
Phase 8	0	0	3
Phase 9	4	4	1

TABLE 24: SUMMARY OF SURFACE FINISH BY PHASE (CONTEXTED SHERDS)

	Untreated	Smoothed	Burnished	Polished	Slipped
Phase 2	0	0	0	0	1
Phase 3	2	0	0	0	2
Phase 4	9	4	0	0	2
Phase 5	4	4	0	0	7
Phase 6	90	27	32	2	14
Phase 7	1	1	2	0	0
Phase 8	0	2	0	0	1
Phase 9	4	1	1	0	3

5.1.2 Technology

A summary of the data for fabric and surface finish is presented in Tables 23 and 24. Certain contrasts in surface finishing and fabric were noted between the sherds from Phases 4 and 5 and those from Phase 6. All the burnished sherds in the sequence were recovered from Phase 6, or later, contexts. Again with fabric, there is a marked division between tempered and untempered sherds, the majority of sherds from contexts in Phases 4 and 5 being tempered with rock fragments, compared with the assemblage from contexts in Phase 6, which has over 50 per cent of untempered vessels.

5.1.3 Morphology

The morphology of the pottery assemblage is considered in three categories: Late Bronze Age/Early

Iron Age, Middle Iron Age (first to fourth centuries AD) and Medieval, with diagnostic uncontexted finds included where appropriate.

5.1.31 Late Bronze Age/Early Iron Age

The sherds from Phases 3 and 4 are in general morphologically undiagnostic but in technological terms the majority are heavily tempered and often slipped. The earliest diagnostic pottery in the assemblage is Vessel 61 (Illus 149), a heavily tempered vessel with a splayed rim, which was recovered from a series of post-roundhouse midden deposits (F2071: B237, Phase 5). The deposit has been radiocarbon dated to the period 800–390 cal BC (GU-3059c & GU-3271c). Three similar rims (V85, Illus 150; V103, Illus 151; & V86) were recovered from unstratified contexts.

In both form and fabric these sherds are similar to pottery recovered at Tofts Ness on Sanday, from deposits contemporary with Structure 5, the Late Bronze Age/Early Iron Age roundhouse (MacSween, forthcoming a). The Tofts Ness pottery was tempered with igneous rock identified as olivine dolerite, possible sources being the Hoy basalt or one of the small outcrops of igneous rock within the Eday Flags at Deerness, Shapinsay and Copinsay (Dixon forthcoming). Basalt fragments deriving from one of these sources were identified in V103, one of the heavily splayed rims in the St Boniface assemblage, and in V100, a basal sherd. The other splayed rim sectioned (V85) was found to be tempered with muddy siltstone.

Splayed rims are characteristic of other Later Bronze Age and Early Iron Age sites in the north of Scotland. At Jarlshof, for example, the earliest examples are associated with contexts of the Bronze Age Village II (Hamilton 1956, 37, fig. 18). Again at Kilphedir, Sutherland, first occupied in the fifth century BC (Fairhurst & Taylor 1971) pottery with similar rims was recovered.

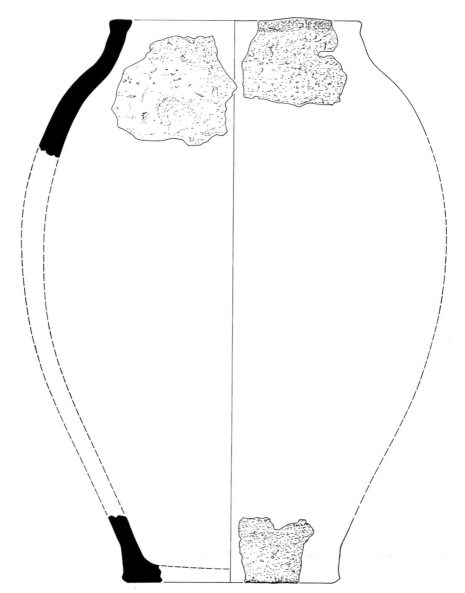

Illus 149   V61, SF87A, F2071, A2, B 237, Phase 5 (1:2)

Illus 150   V85, SF11A, 0, A1, u/s (1:2)

Illus 151   V103, SF25A, 0, A2, u/s (1:4)

5.1.311 Catalogue of illustrated pottery

V61, SF87A, F2071, A2, B237, Phase 5 (Illus 149)
Twelve sherds from a flat-based, necked vessel with a shoulder.
The rim is slightly splayed with a flat lip. Red. Fabric – fine clay
tempered with 40 per cent angular rock fragments. Hard-fired.
T 13 mm; Dia 180 mm.

V85, SF11A, 0, A1, u/s (Illus 150)
Heavily splayed rim. 30 mm below the lip the walls slope out
sharply to a shoulder. Grey with red surfaces. Fabric – fine clay
tempered with 60 per cent angular rock fragments. Hard-fired.
T 10 mm.

V103, SF25A, 0, A2, u/s (Illus 151)
Four body and three rim sherds, from a shouldered vessel. The lip
is splayed. Red. Fabric – fine clay tempered with 50 per cent
angular rock fragments. Hard-fired.
T 9 mm.

5.1.312 Pottery thin-sections

PTS2, V1, SF191, F3033, A3, B307, Phase 2
The groundmass quartz grains are <0.5 mm with a preponderance
of smaller particles. The temper fragments are variants of silty
mudstone and muddy siltstone, some micaceous, some finely
layered, others grading into one another. Size ranges from 3 × 2
mm to 2 × 1 mm, with some disintegrating into smaller
fragments. All appear to have been fairly rotten and soft when
added.
Source: a local origin is most probable, derived from a mudstone
horizon within the Rousay Flags.

PTS3, V103 (illustrated)
The groundmass grains are few, consisting of quartz and
individual basaltic minerals. The clay matrix is fine-grained, pure
clay, with a low content of ultrafine quartz.
The temper comprises basalt fragments, both fresh and altered,
possibly the weathered outer skin and fresh inside of a basalt
cobble. The basalt has a distinctive texture, the often idiomorphic
olivine phenocrysts fresh with only a little serpentine formed
along cracks, commonly with magnetic crystals adhering to and
partially enclosed by them, set in the network of elongate, almost
acicular, plagioclase laths which are grouped and aligned in bands.
The pyroxenes have crystallized in aggregates of small stubby

prisms, between the plagioclase laths. Most mesostases are zoned
feldspar – one or two may be glassy but are somewhat altered.
There are a few rounded fragments (< 1 mm) of quartz-mica low-
grade metamorphic rock, and a single 1 mm grain of quartz.
Sources: Hoy, Shapinsay, Copinsay or Deerness are possible, with
Hoy perhaps more likely as the basalts are extensively exposed at
the coast. Basalt was noted in pottery from Tofts Ness, although
the basalts used are sufficiently different to indicate that they
come from different flows.

PTS4, V85 (illustrated)
The groundmass particles are very fine fragments of muddy
siltstone plus angular quartz, < 0.2 mm, in moderate amounts. The
temper fragments are very irregular in size and shape, subangular,
often laminated, muddy siltstone with siltstone layers and lenses.
Sources: muddy siltstone, which is locally plentiful, was added to
sandy clay, which was not derived from silt-grade rock.

PTS5, V100, SF38A, F2039, A2, B249, Phase 5
The groundmass particles are basaltic minerals and ultrafine (<0.1
mm) quartz. The temper is essentially basalt, some fresh, but more
weathered fragments, similar but not identical to that in PTS3.
Though coarse, the fragments are, overall, smaller and not so
sharply outlined as in PTS3, because of differences in the raw
material, not to the preservation environment of the sherd. There
are occasional small rounded siltstone fragments, and a few
angular, c. 0.5 mm quartz.
Source: source of the basalt temper is close to that used for PTS3.

5.1.32 Middle Iron Age

Three decorated sherds may date to the Middle Iron
Age (first to fourth centuries AD). One (V55, Illus
152) is a rim sherd decorated on the exterior with
incised lines, and probably from a small straight-
sided or barrel-shaped vessel. It was found in context
F2166, a floor deposit in Structure 9 which contained
the majority of the burnished pottery. The second
sherd (V262, Illus 154) is decorated with oblique
ridges and grooves, and is decorated in a similar
manner to a vessel from the latest broch levels at
Upper Scalloway in Shetland (Context 229, Block
6.7: Sharples, forthcoming).

The only sherd decorated with applied decoration is an everted rim with a thickened lip adorned with a pinched band (V12, Illus 160). It was made from an untempered sandy clay, probably local in origin (PTS6). Pinched decorated bands are commonly found on broch and other settlement sites in the Northern Isles, for example at Clickhimin (Hamilton 1968, 122, fig. 53), Jarlshof (Hamilton 1956, 46, fig. 25) and Howe (Ross 1994) where the pinched band is usually applied at the point of inflection of an everted rim with the body of the vessel. In the case of the St Boniface sherd the band was applied just below the lip of the vessel, a practice noted on pottery from St Ninian's Isle (Small *et al*, 1973, fig. 3).

In the St Boniface assemblage, much of the pottery from Phase 6 is made of untempered clay, and burnishing is common. The typical vessel has round shoulders and a short neck (e.g. V32, V35 & V36: Illus 155, 158 & 159), although there are also examples of more straight-sided vessels (e.g. V34, Illus 156) and barrel-shaped vessels (eg. V52, Illus 157). One example of a rolled rim (V197, Illus 153) was recovered. It is possible that Vessels 80 and 28 (Illus 161 & 162) also date to this period. Vessel 80 is an undecorated vessel with a short neck, while Vessel 28 is a flat-based vessel with a rounded shoulder and a short neck, similar in form to vessels from the Iron Age roundhouse settlement at Clickhimin (Hamilton 1968, 57, fig. 32).

Undecorated, burnished pottery has been recovered from sites dating to the Late Iron Age in the Northern Isles, with assemblages having been recovered from sites including Pool (MacSween 1990; MacSween forthcoming b), Howe (Ross 1994) and Kebister (Dalland & MacSween forthcoming). At Pool, the Late Iron Age deposits dated to the fifth to early seventh century AD. The St Boniface assemblage indicates that these sites may represent the later end of a tradition beginning in the early first millennium AD.

5.1.321 Catalogue of illustrated pottery

V55, SF162Y, F2166, A2, B233, Phase 6.2 (Illus 152)
Flat rim, probably from a small straight-sided or barrel-shaped vessel. The exterior is decorated with incised, roughly parallel, oblique lines which were incised with a fine-pointed implement when the vessel was almost dry. Exterior burnished. Coil constructed – diagonal coil junctions. Red with a grey core. Fabric – untempered sandy clay.
T 7 mm; Dia 120 mm.
V197, SF42, F2033, A2, B225, Phase 6.2 (Illus 153)
Rolled rim which has been formed by turning the top coil of the vessel to the exterior. The exterior of the rim has spalled off. The

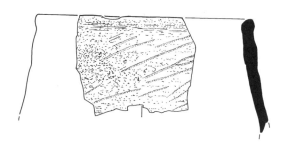

Illus 152   V55, SF162Y, F2166, A2, B 233,
                 Phase 6.2 (1:2)

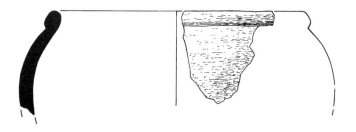

Illus 153   V197, SF42, F2033, A2, B 225, Phase 6.2 (1:2)

Illus 154   V262, SF20A, 0, A2, u/s (1:2)

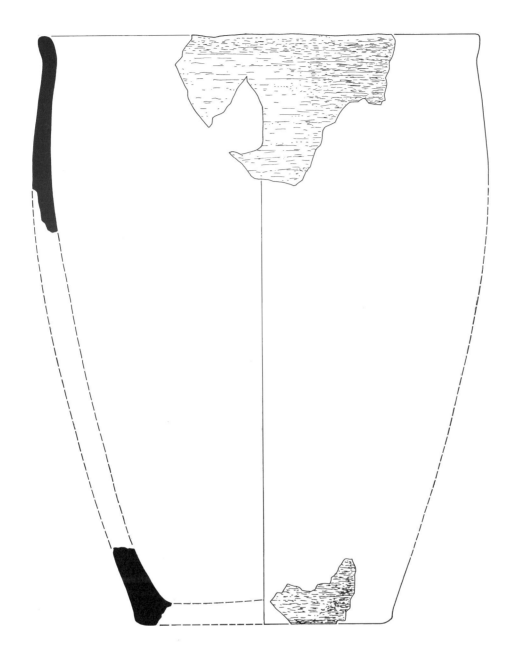

Illus 155   V32, SF162A, F2166, A2, B 233, Phase 6.2 (1:2)

sherd is probably from a vessel with a rounded shoulder. Grey with brown surfaces. Fabric – untempered sandy clay. Hard-fired.
T 8 mm; Dia 150 mm.

V262, SF20A, 0, A2, u/s (Illus 154)
Decorated rim sherd. The top coil has broken off at the point of inflection, but it appears that the sherd is from a vessel with an everted rim. The exterior is burnished and decorated with oblique ridges and grooves. Buff exterior, grey interior. Fabric – untempered sandy clay.
T 6 mm.

V32, SF162A, F2166, A2, B233, Phase 6.2 (Illus 155)
A total of 128 sherds from a flat-based vessel with slightly angled sides. The rim is plain with an internal bevel and the vessel has a short neck below which the walls slope out gradually to a shoulder. Exterior smoothed. Red with a grey core. Fabric – sandy clay with around 5 per cent of rock inclusions, probably natural to the clay.
T 10 mm; Dia 240 mm.

V34, SF162C, F2166, A2, B233, Phase 6.2 (Illus 156)
A total of 156 sherds from a flat-based vessel with slightly angled sides and a plain rim. Exterior burnished. Coil-constucted with N-shaped junctions, apart from the top coil which is U-shaped and has detached at some points around the rim. The interior of the vessel towards the base has been thinned by scraping. Red with a grey core. Fabric – sandy clay with around 5 per cent of rock inclusions, probably natural to the clay.
T 13 mm; Dia 280 mm.

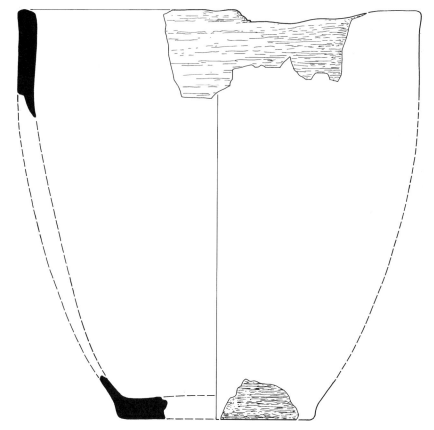

Illus 156   V34, SF162C, F2166, A2, B 233, Phase 6.2 (1:2)

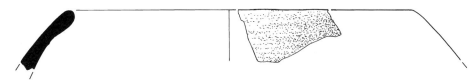

Illus 157   V52, SF162V, F2166, A2, B 233, Phase 6.2 (1:2)

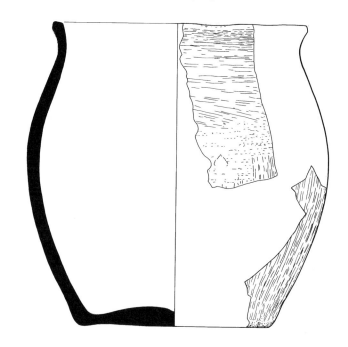

Illus 158   V36, SF162E, F2166, A2, B 233, Phase 6.2 (1:2)

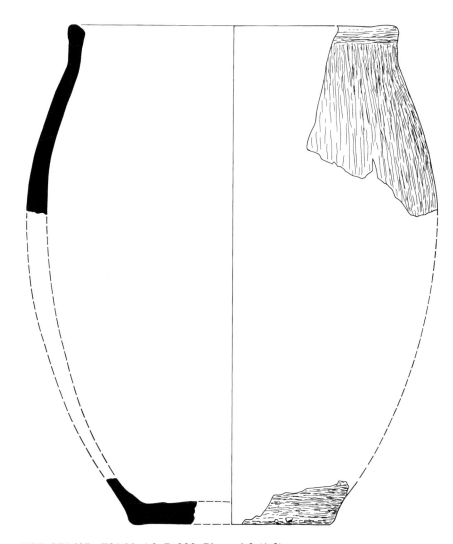

Illus 159   V35, SF162D, F2166, A2, B 233, Phase 6.2 (1:2)

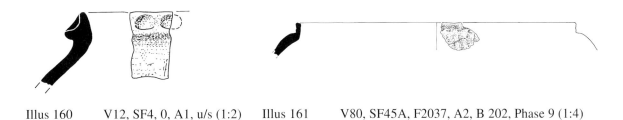

Illus 160   V12, SF4, 0, A1, u/s (1:2)   Illus 161   V80, SF45A, F2037, A2, B 202, Phase 9 (1:4)

V52, SF162V, F2166, A2, B233, Phase 6.2 (Illus 157)
Rim sherd and two body sherds from a vessel with an inverted rim. Exterior burnished. Scraping marks on the interior where the walls have been thinned. Brown with a grey core. Fabric – untempered sandy clay.
T 8 mm; Dia 220 mm.

V36, SF162E, F2166, A2, B233, Phase 6.2 (Illus 158)
Sixty-one sherds from a flat-based vessel with a short neck and a rounded shoulder. The rim is slightly everted. The base has been strengthened by the addition of an extra coil in the angle of the base. The exterior of the vessel is completely burnished, and the interior is burnished on the bevel of the rim. Grey with red surfaces. Fabric – untempered sandy clay. Hard-fired.
T 9 mm; Rim Dia 140 mm; Basal Dia 110 mm.

V35, SF162D, F2166, A2, B233, Phase 6.2 (Illus 159)
A total of 123 sherds from a flat-based vessel with a neck and a rounded shoulder. The rim is slightly everted with an internal bevel and a flattened lip. The upper part of the vessel is burnished, and the surface of the lower part is well-smoothed. The upper 30 mm of the interior is also burnished. Red with a grey core. Fabric – sandy clay with 5 per cent of rock inclusions, probably natural to the clay. Hard-fired.
T 11 mm; Dia 200 mm.

V12, SF4, 0, A1, u/s (Illus 160)
Everted rim with finger-impressed band just below the lip. Grey with red margins. Fabric – fine untempered clay. Hard-fired.
T 6 mm.

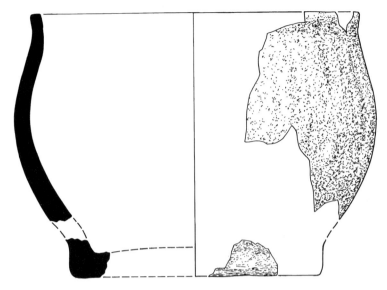

Illus 162   V28, SF8A, F1080, A1, B 109, Phase 6.1 (1:2)

V80, SF45A, F2037, A2, B202, Phase 9 (Illus 161)
Rim with a short neck, probably from a globular or shouldered
vessel. Grey. Fabric – fine clay tempered with 10 per cent angular
rock fragments. Hard-fired.
T 11 mm.

V28, SF8A, F1080, A1, B109, Phase 6.1 (Illus 162)
Fifty sherds from a flat-based vessel with a rounded shoulder and
short neck. The rim is flat. Slipped. Coil constructed with diagonal
junctions. Grey with red margins. Fabric – sandy clay tempered
with 20 per cent angular rock fragments. Hard-fired.
T 12 mm, Dia 210 mm.

5.1.322 Pottery Thin-sections

PTS6, V12 (illustrated)
The sherd comprises a pure clay with no added temper. The
groundmass particles are quartz, a few 0.4 mm, the majority 0.2
mm and smaller, with subordinate feldspar.
Source: no mineralogical evidence to indicate the source.

PTS7, V81, SF66E, F2056, A2, B252, Phase 6.2
The clay matrix has a high concentration of ultrafine quartz. The
fragments in the section are rounded/roughly rectangular, of variable
size, the coarsest 5 × 1 mm. No two are the same lithologically, with
mudstones, silty limestone and siltstone, with scattered quartz. The
assortment of rotten, softish fragments suggests that they were
present in a natural deposit of clay rather than deliberately added.
Source: local origin most likely: probably derived from Rousay Flags.

PTS1, V160, SF81A, F2070, A2, B230, Phase 6.2
The groundmass minerals are essentially quartz (angular, equi-
dimensional grains less than 0.2 mm) with very subordinate feldspar
(microcline), rare mica flakes and opaques, probably magnetite.
The temper fragments are of three distinct lithologies. The very
coarse (up to 7 × 4 mm) angular fragments are limestone, virtually
100 per cent carbonate, fine-grained calcite with some dolo-
mitization. The carbonate-cemented siltstone fragments are more
rounded, up to 2 mm in size. There are a few fragments of siltstone.
Source: the bedrock on Papa Westray is the Rousay Flags, which
consist largely of flagstones, i.e. rhythmic sequences of thinnly
bedded, carbonate-rich siltstones and silty mudstones alternating
with fine-grained sandstones. These are the obvious source for the
temper incorporated in this pottery.

PTS8, V36 (illustrated)
A fine clay with no added temper. The groundmass particles are

very fine grade (0.4 mm and less) with a greater concentration of
smaller grains. Quartz predominates, with subordinate feldspar,
most of the few being microcline, one or two cloudy orthoclases,
and the occasional mica flake.
Source: no mineralogical evidence to indicate source.

PTS9, V38, SF162G, F2166, A2, B233, Phase 6.2
The clay contains a few fragments, perhaps accidentally
incorporated rather than deliberately added as temper – a single 5
mm grain of quartz and two particles of quartz-feldspar-mica-
chlorite greenschist facies metamorphic rock. The groundmass
particles are essentially quartz evenly distributed through the range
1.5 mm to ultrafine with c. 10 percent feldspar (microcline,
plagioclase and cloudy orthoclase, and a few scattered mica flakes).
Source: no mineralogical evidence to indicate the source of the clay.

PTS10, V252, SF29B, A2, u/s
The fine clay has no added temper. The groundmass particles are
0.5 mm and finer, with a noticeably high proportion of larger
grains, generally angular. Quartz predominates, with some feldspar
(fresh microcline and plagioclase, variably altered orthoclase).
Source: no mineralogical evidence to indicate the source of the clay.

5.1.33 Medieval

The only sherd of coarse pottery which could date to
the medieval period is part of a handle, uncontexted,
but from the upper part of the 'farm mound'.

5.1.331 Catalogue of illustrated pottery

V13, SF5, A1, u/s (B103 / B104: 'farm mound' deposits) (Illus 163)
Section of handle from a medieval vessel. Exterior decorated with at
least one groove. Red with a grey core. Fabric – untempered sandy clay.
W 27.

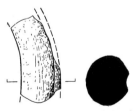

Illus 163   V13, SF5, A1, u/s (B 103 / 104: 'farm
                 mound' deposits) (1:2)

5.1.4 Conclusions

Owing to the nature of the excavation, most vessels in the assemblage were represented by only one or two sherds, and their dimensions and shape could not be determined. However, a study of the surface finishing and fabrics allowed the division of the assemblage into two major components, the earlier representing the Late Bronze Age and Early Iron Age, and the later representing the Middle Iron Age.

In establishing a coarse pottery sequence for the Northern Isles, the assemblage is important in that untempered, burnished pottery which has been noted at sites dating to the later part of the Iron Age, for example at Pool (MacSween 1990; MacSween forthcoming b) and Howe (Ross 1994) can be shown to have earlier origins. From the thin-sections, there is no reason to suppose that it is anything but locally produced.

The St Boniface assemblage has also provided more dating evidence for the very distinctive vessel type with a splayed rim, angular shoulder and heavily rock-tempered fabric, already noted in the Late Bronze Age/Early Iron Age levels at Tofts Ness (MacSween forthcoming a). The most likely source of the basalt temper is Hoy, where the outcrops are most extensive, and the possibility of a distribution source for temper or vessels in that area is suggested as a possibility. Although the rocks were not from the same source, it is possible that they were from the same outcrop.

5.2 The Coarse Stone, Flint and Pumice

Ann Clark

5.2.1 Coarse Stone Artefacts

There are forty-eight objects of coarse stone, the majority comprising cobble tools. There are seven stone discs, two dish querns, one rotary quern, two pivot stones, two perforated objects and one ard point (Part 5.2.4).

Most of the cobble tools are typical pounder/grinders which exhibit broad areas of faceting on the ends of the tool (e.g. SF159: Illus 164). All are made on the hard, fine-grained sandstone local to the island and they vary in form from cylindrical to flat-oval in section. The majority of the tools have been used on both ends but the amount of faceting which is present varies according to the amount of use and the origin and morphology of the cobble. Most of the facets are smoothly ground but on some pieces heavy battering and flaking are also present. About half of these pounder/grinders have additional wear on parts of the faces in the form of a slight flattening and smoothing.

The rest of the cobble tools are of a variety of shapes and sizes and all but one, which is a quartzite pebble (SF78), are of sandstone. The wear on these tools includes light faceting, flaking and polish. Two of the cobbles (SF166, Illus 165: & SF170) appear to have been flaked bifacially on one end to form an angled edge which was subsequently lightly faceted through use.

One cobble tool (SF34, Illus 166) is of interest. It is subrectangular in shape and has a band of faceting on one end and a large flake removed from the opposite end. Towards the faceted end there are discrete areas of high polish on the sides with visible striations running perpendicular to the length. Associated with the polish is a smoothly worn indentation on one side. Both types of wear would appear to have been formed by friction. It is unlikely to have formed during hafting as the side indentation must have been formed by high-speed friction, more usually associated with machinery. This piece is unstratified and so may have been used or accidentally worn in more modern times.

The stone discs range in diameter from 70 mm to 145 mm and are within the standard size range of such objects from Iron Age contexts. They are mostly subcircular in plan and one is burnt (SF160e). Six of the discs (SF160a-f) were found together and were associated with a large assemblage of pottery, much of it burnished (Part 5.1.32).

The two perforated objects are undistinguished. One (SF32) is simply a flat pebble with a natural perforation and this piece may have been selected intentionally from the beach gravels. The other (SF179) is a rather blocky piece of burnt sandstone with a central perforation.

One rotary quern (SF205) was found, in association with the stone discs and pottery assemblage. The two dish querns (SF123 & SF124) were found together with their grinders (Illus 167). They are made of boulders of sandstone and volcanic rock and have similar dimensions. The basins are deep and steep-sided although one, which was worked from one side of the boulder, is asymmetrical in cross-section and presents a shallow base (SF123, Illus 168). They are unlike the standard saddle querns which are commonly found on Iron Age sites, although varieties of hollowed stones have been identified from sites of this period.

The ard point (SF3) is a fine example of its type with a flat-oval cross-section and a pointed tip. It retains the characteristic U-shaped wear on one face although it appears to be a little abraded. Ard points are usually found in Bronze Age contexts in Orkney,

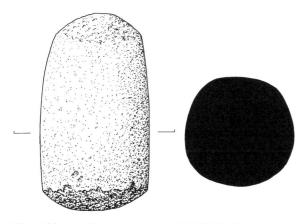

Illus 164   Pounder/grinder SF159 (1:2)

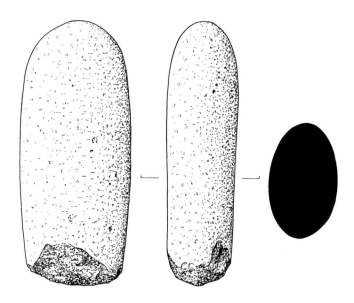

Illus 165   Cobble tool SF166 (1:2)

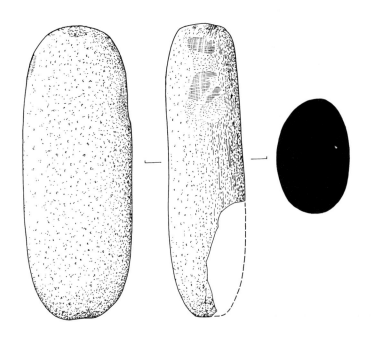

Illus 166   Cobble tool SF34 (1:2)

and it is uncertain how far into the Iron Age their use extended. An example from the Broch of Burrian, on North Ronaldsay, although essentially unstratified (MacGregor 1974), was nonetheless recovered in association with a standard Iron Age assemblage. The St Boniface ard point was recovered from an erosion horizon (B101) on the north side of the 'farm mound'.

One pivot stone (SF197) was associated with the roundhouse, where it had been reused in the construction of the drain below the floor. The second (SF199) was incorporated into the paving (B206) associated with the primary enclosure of the site in Phase 6.1.

With the exception of the group of artefacts from the floor of Structure 9 (SF160a–f, SF165–167, SF179 & SF205) and the single pounder/grinder (SF136) from the floor of Structure 4, the remaining stone artefacts were recovered from fill, make-up or construction deposits.

There does not appear to be any chronological differentiation within or between the artefact types

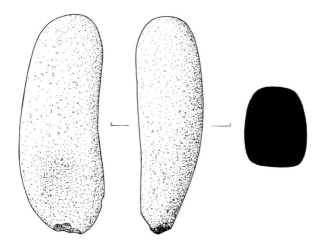

Illus 167   Grinder with quern SF123 (1:2)

found. Of note are the group of six stone discs found in Structure 9, in association with a number of pottery vessels and a rotary quern, and the two dish querns which were found together with their grinders, one from a post-hole associated with Structure 5 (B243, Phase 4), the other from the floor of Structure 3 (B246, Phase 4) where it was associated with a large quantity of charred naked barley (Part 3.2).

The assemblage has standard Iron Age elements, with the exceptions of the ard point (SF3) and the polished cobble tool (SF34), both of which may be considered as external elements.

5.2.2 Flint

There are six pieces of flint, of which two (SF120 & SF149) are flaked pebbles and the rest are chunks and broken flakes. The pebbles are small in size with flakes removed from the cortical surface. On one (SF120) there is sequential flaking along part of the edge from a natural flat face to form a steep, denticulate edge. The other flaked pebble (SF149) and a chunk (SF164) were recovered from the floors of Structure 4 (Phase 4) and Structure 9 (Phase 6.2) respectively. A flake (SF71) was recovered from the Late Iron Age ground surface (B105, Phase 7). A small chunk (SF161) was recovered from the primary soil horizon (B119, Phase 1) on Area 1. This small assemblage is not distinguished by specific tool types.

5.2.3 Pumice

There are twenty-two pieces of pumice, of which over a third are simple rounded lumps or fragments up to 50 mm in length. Most of the rest exhibit distinctive worn faces which are either flat or concave in section. On many of these pieces only one face has been utilized but two pieces (SF35 &

SF148) are multi-faceted and these are among the largest of the objects. Five pieces exhibit single grooves which, in all but one case, are quite shallow and on three examples these grooves are located in the same place, on the end of the lump.

Worn pumice is a common find on prehistoric and later sites in Orkney and Shetland. Little or no research, however, has been carried out on pumice to determine whether particular wear characteristics may be separated temporally.

Only one shaped object of pumice, a large probable fishing float, unstratified, was recovered. It has been worked to a regular ovoid shape and has been perforated through its long axis.

With the exception of one fragment (Rt, F3000) from the backfill deposits associated with the nineteenth-century excavations (B201, Phase 9) on the site, and another (Rt, F3046) from the primary sand horizon (B308, Phase 1), the fifteen stratified examples were associated with deposits of Phases 4 to 6.2. None was recovered from Late Iron Age (Phase 7) or medieval (Phase 8) deposits.

5.2.4 Coarse Stone, Pumice and Flint Catalogue

The entries are ordered by catalogue number. Measurements (in millimetres) at the end of each entry refer to maximum length; maximum width; maximum thickness; and other specified dimensions. The weight is given in grammes.

5.2.41 Coarse stone

5.2.411 Cobble tools

SF78, F2073, B205, Phase 6.2
Cobble tool. Quartz, flat oval. Two narrow facets formed on one sides and spread of light pecking around the ends. 72 × 60 × 27; 175 g.

Illus 168   Dish quern SF123 (1:2)

SF166, F2166, B233, Phase 6.2
Cobble tool. Sandstone, elongated oval. One end has been bifacially flaked with a narrow band of superimposed faceting. One worn face. 140 × 61 × 39; 550 g. (Illus 165)

SF169, F3022, B302, Phase 5
Cobble tool. Sandstone, subrectangular. Unifacial flaking from both ends through use. 135 × 51 × 33; 355 g.

SF170, F3022, B302, Phase 5
Cobble tool. Sandstone, flat oval. One end has been bifacially flaked with a narrow band of superimposed faceting. One worn face. 157 × 85 × 50; 1032 g.

SF172, F3022, B302, Phase 5
Cobble tool. Sandstone, flat oval. Small, light facet on narrow end. 133 × 76 × 28; 458 g.

SF173, F3022, B302, Phase 5
Cobble tool. Sandstone, oval. Small, light facet on narrow end. 78 × 34 × 31; 138 g.

SF174, F2017, B210, Phase 6.1
Cobble tool. Sandstone, narrow rectangular. Small facet on one end. The opposite end has been heavily unifacially flaked through use. 260 × 73 × 59; 1833 g.

Rt, F2145, B237, Phase 5
Cobble tool. Sandstone, flat oval. Parts of some faces used for polishing/burnishing. 97 × 49 × 26.

5.2.412 Pounders/grinders

SF2, U/S, Area 1
Pounder/grinder. Sandstone, burnt, subrectangular. Single rounded facet on both ends, one of which is truncated by breakage. 144 × 51 × 48; 533 g.

SF30, U/S, Area 2
Pounder/grinder. Sandstone, elongated oval. One roughly pecked, rounded facet on one end. The other end is lightly pecked. 135 × 55 × 47; 537 g.

SF33, U/S, Area 2: Pounder/grinder. Sandstone, cylindrical. One small, flattish facet on both ends. 153 × 53 × 48; 612 g.

SF43, F2034, B211, Phase 6.3: Pounder/grinder. Sandstone, subrectangular. Heavily worked single facets on both ends. On one end there is heavy unifacial flaking which truncates the facet. Localized areas of linear pecking on faces. 190 × 68 × 65; 1245 g.

SF67, F2060, B205, Phase 6.2
Pounder/grinder. Sandstone, flat oval. On one end there is a broad double facet with slight ridge. This is heavily worn with a great deal of flaking. There is some pecking on the opposite end and on one side and face. One worn face. 140 × 86 × 59; 1065 g.

SF104, F2079, B202, Phase 9
Pounder/grinder. Sandstone, subcylindrical. Broad double facets on both ends forming worn ridges. Facets smooth. Some flaking from broad end. One worn face. 113 × 82 × 73; 999 g.

SF105, F2079, B202, Phase 9
Pounder/grinder. Sandstone, burnt, subcylindrical. One broad, rounded facet on either end. Facets smooth. 109 × 66 × 56; 620 g.

SF136, F2132, B245, Phase 4
Pounder/grinder. Sandstone, flat oval. Broad double facet on one end with ridge and small facet on other. One worn face. 152 × 93 × 59; 1285 g.

SF159, F2036, B254, Phase 8
Pounder/grinder. Sandstone, subcylindrical. Broad, rounded facets on both ends. Some flaking from one end. Worn faces. 106 × 61 × 61; 629 g. (Illus 164)

SF163, F2121, B210, Phase 6.1
Pounder/grinder. Sandstone, subrectangular. Broad, rounded facet on both ends. On one end there is heavy flaking from the facet. One worn face. 147 × 68 × 56; 1025 g.

SF165, F2166, B233, Phase 6.2
Pounder/grinder. Sandstone, flat oval. On one end there are three facets with formed ridges. Some light flaking from the facets. One worn face. 188 × 100 × 50; 1375 g.

SF167, F2166, B233, Phase 6.2
Pounder/grinder. Sandstone, elongated oval. One small, flat fact formed on one end. Another facet on opposite end which is truncated by breakage. 170 × 74 × 45; 938 g.

SF171, F3022, B302, Phase 5
Pounder/grinder. Sandstone, flat oval. One end has a broad, rounded facet. The opposite end is heavily flaked and has a band of rounded faceting superimposed on the flaking. Heavily pecked down one side. 131 × 73 × 44; 753 g.

SF193, F2018, B235, Phase 6.1
Pounder/grinder. Sandstone, subrectangular. Broad, rounded facet on one end. The other end has been heavily bifacially flaked to form an angled edge. Some pecking down the sides. 183 × 87 × 57; 1552 g.

SF195, F3022, B302, Phase 5
Pounder/grinder. Sandstone, subcylindrical. Broad, rounded facets on both ends. One worn face. 104 × 76 × 73; 899 g.

SF196, F3022, B302, Phase 5
Pounder/grinder. Sandstone, elongated oval. Small, flat facet on either end. 163 × 81 × 51; 1102 g.

5.2.413 Stone discs

SF13, F2113, B217, Phase 8
Stone disc. Laminated sandstone. Bifacially flaked, circular in plan. 69 × 65 × 7.

SF160, F2166, B233, Phase 6.2
A group of six stone discs found together and associated with pots. All are made on laminated sandstone and have been either bifacially flaked (BF) or roughly flaked (RF) to shape.
a. BF/RF, subcircular, fragment missing, diameter 106; thickness 11.
b. BF, circular, broken lengthways, diameter 105; thickness 10.
c. BF, subcircular, 117 × 102 × 8.
d. RF, rough polygonal form, 129 × 127 × 14.
e. RF, subcircular, fragment missing, burnt on both faces, diameter 145; thickness 13.
f. RF, subcircular, fragment missing, 100 × 88 × 12.

5.2.414 Querns

SF123, F2119, B243, Phase 4
Quern and grinder. The quern is formed from a large sandstone boulder with a flat base. The dish has been worked from one side of the boulder and is asymmetrical in cross-section with a steep side and a shallow base in which the grinder rests. The grinder is a small, narrow cobble of sandstone. One face has been worn flat at one end which allows it to rest in the dish. There is some flaking from this end. Mortar: 290 × 200 × 170, dish 150 × 130 and 80 maximum and 20 minimum depth. Grinder: 114 × 43 × 36. (Illus 167 & 168)

SF124, F2131, B246, Phase 4
Quern and grinder. The quern is formed from a large boulder of volcanic rock which is very weathered and highly fragmented. The

base of the quern is flat and the dish is oval in plan with steep sides and a rounded base which is worn very smooth. The grinder is a narrow, oval sandstone cobble which has a round facet formed at one end while the opposite end is faceted and heavily flaked. One face has been worn smooth. Quern: *c.* 320 × 240 × 200, dish 180 × 140 × 65. Grinder: 160 × 80 × 62.

SF205, F2166, B233, Phase 6.2
Rotary quern. Subcircular sandstone slab, broken down length. Central hole is roughly biconical and the base is concave and worn smooth. Diameter *c.* 420 mm; thickness 85 mm; diameter of hole 71 mm maximum, 30 mm minimum.

5.2.415 Pivot stones

SF197, F3058, B304, Phase 5
Pivot stone. Large, rectangular block of sandstone. A circular depression has been formed on one face towards one end. The depression is regular in section and very smooth and worn. 375 × 200 × 140; depression 100 mm diameter, 25 mm deep.

SF199, F2095, B206, Phase 6.1
Pivot stone. Large sandstone boulder with a round base. The upper face is very flat and smooth and a depression has been formed towards one end. The depression is circular in plan and is very smooth and worn with high polish in places. 370 × 220 × 150; depression 65 mm diameter, 10 mm deep.

5.2.416 Perforated stones

SF32, F2025, B242, Phase 4
?Weight. Flat sandstone cobble with three natural perforations present on one end. Possibly selected for use as a weight. 107 × 84 × 23; 306 g.

SF179, F2166, B233, Phase 6.2
Weight. Subcircular piece of black micaceous sandstone. Heavily burnt/abraded. Central perforation made at slight angle from both faces. 54 × 50 × 20; diameter of hole 5; 47 g.

5.2.417 Ard point

SF3, F1004, B101, Phase 9
Ard point. Sandstone, broken across width. Oval in section and very finely pointed. One face is completely smooth, possibly abraded, and the opposite face has the characteristic U-shaped smoothing wear on the tip. 145 × 73 × 50.

5.2.418 Miscellaneous

SF34, U/S, Area 2
Subrectangular sandstone cobble. Single rounded facet on both ends, one of which is truncated by the removal of a single large flake. Towards the complete end there are patches of high polish on the sides with visible striations. Associated with the polish on one side is a worn indentation. Both the polish and the indentation may have been produced by high-speed friction. 154 × 59 × 40; 565 g. (Illus 166)

5.2.42 Flint

SF10, U/S, Area 2
Inner flake of mottled orange and white flint, broken. 20 × 17 × 16.

SF71, F1011, B105, Phase 7
Inner flake of grey flint, broken. 18 × 11 × 3.

SF120, U/S, Area 2
?Scraper/core. Pebble of mottled orange and white flint. Small amount of sequential flaking from a natural flat face to form a steep, denticulate edge. 35 × 28 × 20.

SF149, F2144, B245, Phase 4
Randomly flaked pebble of grey flint. 31 × 28 × 21.

SF161, F1077, B119, Phase 1
Small inner chunk of orange flint. 10 × 4 × 3.

SF164, F2166, B233, Phase 6.2
Inner chunk of orange flint. 28 × 17 × 16.

5.2.43 Pumice

Measurements in brackets refer to size of worn area where relevant.

SF24, F1080, B109, Phase 6.1
Fragment. Squared and angled with the remnant of a deep U-shaped groove. 47 × 44 × 40; groove 10 mm wide.

SF35, U/S, Area 2
Whole. Multi-faceted with distinctively worn flat and concave faces. 57 × 57 × 50.

SF40, F2039, B249, Phase 5
Whole. One flat face worn out to edges. 44 × 38 × 21; (30 × 30).

SF77a, F2073, B205, Phase 6.2
Whole. Rounded lump. 52 × 35 × 26.

SF77b, F2073, B205, Phase 6.2
Whole. One irregular concave face worn out to edges. 43 × 38 × 33.

SF121a, U/S, Area 2
Whole. One flat face worn out to edges. 52 × 33 × 29; (47 × 28).

SF121b, U/S, Area 2
Whole. One slightly concave face worn out to edges and one narrow V-shaped groove made on end. 64 × 39 × 31; (51 × 26); groove 2 mm deep.

SF148a, F2142, B245, Phase 4
Whole. Multi-faceted, concave faces. 63 × 55 × 45.

SF148b, F2142, B245, Phase 4
Whole. Rounded lump. 51 × 41 × 35.

SF150, F2138, B245, Phase 4
Whole. One concave face worn out to edges and a short V-shaped groove on one end. 30 × 30 × 21; (24 × 24); groove 5 mm wide and 2 mm deep.

SF194, F3022, B302, Phase 5
Fragment. 33 × 27 × 14.

Rt, F1080, B109, Phase 6.1
Fragment. 40 × 31 × 25.

Rt, F1083, B116, Phase 5
Whole. Possible short, narrow, U-shaped groove made on one side. 49 × 31 × 30; groove 4 mm wide, 2 mm deep.

Rt, F1098, B114, Phase 5
Whole. One slightly concave face and a U-shaped groove made on one end. 48 × 39 × 22: (33 × 33); groove 10 mm wide and 4 mm deep.

Rt, F2093, B243, Phase 4
Whole. Rounded lump. 48 × 46 × 20.

Rt, F2167, B233, Phase 6.2
Whole. Slightly concave face worn out to edges. 42 × 30 × 25; (36 × 19).

Rt, F2167, B235, Phase 6.2
Whole. Slightly concave face worn out to edges. 52 × 39 × 36; (49 × 32).

Rt, F3000, B201, Phase 9
Whole. Rounded lump. 36 × 32 × 20.

Rt, F3020, B304, Phase 5
Fragment. 20 × 20 × 13.

Rt, F3046, B308, Phase 1
Fragment. 20 × 20 × 11.

U/S, Area 1
Whole. One concave face. 47 × 40 × 35.

U/S, Area 1
Float. Regular elongated oval shape with perforation made through the middle down the long axis. 101 × 63 × 52; perforation *c*. 20 mm in diameter, 114 g.

5.3 The Worked Bone and Antler

Graeme Wilson

5.3.1 Introduction

There are twelve pieces of worked bone from this site. These comprise two points, a handle, a perforated pin, a comb fragment, two weaving batons, a tool fragment, a utilized long bone, and three fragments of waste or raw material. The items all appear to utilize bone already present on site for food (Part 6.2), with the possible exception of the whalebone objects, which may represent scavenging of carcasses. It is a small assemblage and it is not possible to draw many conclusions concerning on-site activities. None of the objects can be precisely dated by themselves but all fit within the site stratigraphy.

5.3.2 Bone Points

There are two pointed tools, one of antler (SF96), the other of bone (SF135). The antler point was recovered from F1084, a possible buried ground surface in Phase 5; the bone point from F2144, the primary floor level in Structure 4 (Phase 4).

The bone point has been made from the distal end of a metapodial, the unaltered, articulated condyles forming the end of the handle. Use-wear suggests a thrusting, twisting motion at the point. The other point is made from an antler tine, the tip modified to form a point, the base unfinished. As with the bone example, the point is relatively short and thus would have been very strong.

These pieces are part of a large group of objects probably associated with craftworking. Roes (1963, 36–7) and MacGregor (1985, 174–5) suggest leather working, or basketmaking. They are found in a wide variety of places, such as the Broch of Burrian (MacGregor 1974), on the Continent (Roes 1963) and

in Ireland (Hodkinson 1987). MacGregor (1985, fig. 93) illustrates examples from York. Although details of form vary, for example the proximal end of a metapodial is often used instead of, in this case, the distal end, the function is probably the same.

5.3.3 Handle

One item is identified as a handle (SF134), a curving section of antler tine from F2138, a secondary floor level in Structure 4 (Phase 4). This has a hole at both ends, the one at the smaller end is circular in plan, that at the other rectangular, and it seems likely that both ends have been used as sockets but it is difficult to say for what. The traces of use-wear at the small end of this handle suggest a twisting motion which would seem to fit with a bradawl-type tool. This handle is of a simple form and cannot be ascribed too exact a date. There is quite a large group of similar objects from the Broch of Burrian (MacGregor 1974), as well as wooden examples such as one from Viking Dublin (Lang 1988, fig. 28).

5.3.4 Perforated Pin (Illus 169)

This piece (SF198) was recovered from F3041, a make-up or levelling deposit for the floor within the roundhouse (Phase 5). It is made of a pig fibula, the head has been little altered and a hole has been bored through, probably from one side as one end has a wider diameter than the other. The shank is highly polished, but this polish does not extend to the head, which suggests that this was used as a pin rather than a needle. Wilson (1983) suggests that these should be interpreted as dress pins, the perforation being used to secure a piece of string which could then be tied around the end of the pin to stop it slipping out.

Similar pins are known from many sites in Scotland, and they have a wide date range, from the pre-Roman Iron Age to the Viking period. Examples are known from the Broch of Burrian (MacGregor 1974), Dun Cuier (unperforated) (Young 1956), Tuquoy (Smith forthcoming), Birsay (Curle 1982) and elsewhere in Britain and on the Continent (MacGregor 1985).

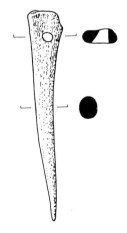

Illus 169   Bone pin SF198 (1:1)

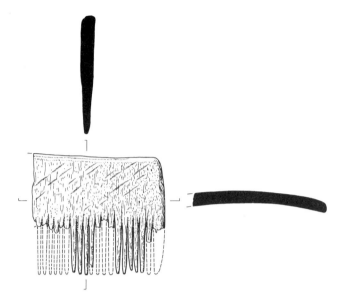

Illus 170   Comb fragment SF6 (1:1)

5.3.5 Comb Fragment (Illus 170)

A fragment of an antler comb (SF6) was recovered from Block 107 (Phase 7). This block represents deposits overlying the causeway (Block 112). It is difficult to say much about the comb, other than that it was single-sided with a slightly curved back. This piece has been broken at one end and is plain at the other. It is difficult to date this fragment exactly as it is incomplete. The block from which it came has been dated to cal AD 285–670 (GU-3063) at its base and cal AD 620–880 (GU-3064c) at the top. It is comparable to a comb fragment from Howe (Ballin Smith 1994,177, illus 100) and, like it, may be of Middle Iron Age date.

5.3.6 Weaving Swords

Two cetacean bone implements are interpreted as weaving swords. One is complete (SF122), the other fragmentary and without its handle (SF183). Weaving swords or batons are usually associated with warp-weighted looms, they are a specialized tool used to beat down the weft threads during weaving. The presence of these implements is therefore an indication of textile production at St Boniface.

The fragmentary weaving sword (SF183) was recovered from F2170, windblown sand in Block 250 (Phase 3). Although identified as a weaving sword, this is not certain – an alternative interpretation as a digging tool is possible, but the smoothness of its surface does not make this likely.

The complete sword (SF122, Illus 171) still has two rows of small parallel grooves worn upon the edge of the blade by the warp threads. The polish on this sword is in the area of the grooves and was probably made by the same actions – beating down the weft threads – that made the grooves. The careful carving of this tool contrasts with the execution of the notches, which have been cut quite roughly and appear to have been made as an afterthought. The freshness of the carving on this sword, lack of wear on the notches, and the localized polish suggest that it was lost soon after manufacture. It was recovered from F2133 (B237, Phase 5), a dump of splintered stone fragments abutting the plinth of the roundhouse, and therefore representing primary post-roundhouse activity. This was overlain by a shell midden dated to 800–390 cal BC (GU-3059c & GU-3271c).

The worn notches on the edges of the fragmentary blade and the fresh ones on the edges of the complete sword were probably used to wind wool or string, and there are similar notches on other tools associated with textiles, for example, whalebone tools from Foshigarry (Beveridge 1931).

Whalebone weaving swords are found in Viking Age north Norway (Sjovold 1974; Graham-Campbell 1980), however these are of a different shape, being much longer and thinner (up to 1 m in length) than ones such as those from St Boniface, which are wider and stronger. The variation in size may reflect the loom being used or the textile produced.

There are better parallels for the St Boniface swords with wooden weaving swords from Viking Dublin (Lang 1988). Among those illustrated by Lang are two similar in size and with straight or slightly curving blades. One of these, WD22, is

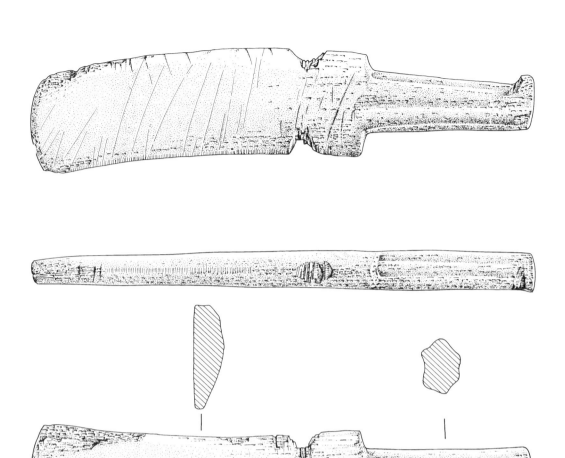

Illus 171   Weaving baton SF122 (1:2)

dated to the eleventh century. There are others from Viking Dublin that are of a similar size, with semicircular blades (e.g. WD79,80), and Lang illustrates one from Littleton Bog (Ireland) with a semicircular blade. There are also wooden examples from the Frisian Terp mounds (A. Smith, pers comm).

The two found at St Boniface are much earlier than the examples given above. Analysis of the large assemblage of weaving swords from Norway suggests that there is little development in this group of weaving swords over a period spanning the seventh to tenth centuries (Sjovold 1974). These tools have a long history, there being little need for change in form, and this is demonstrated by the close parallels between SF122 and those from Viking Dublin.

5.3.7 Tool Fragment

This small piece of a cetacean bone tool (SF144) was found in F2139, a robber trench fill (B245, Phase 4). Surface polish is visible, and it appears to be part of the useful end, but not enough is left to discuss it in any detail.

5.3.8 Utilized Long Bone

This (SF55) was found in F2040, the primary fill of the secondary enclosure ditch (B211, Phase 6.3). It is part of a bone which has been split along its length; the broken edges have been worn smooth, with many longitudinal scratches, some running for most of its length. It is provisionally identified as a runner, a fitting for the base of a sledge, but it is difficult to be certain. Runners have been identified from many sites (MacGregor 1985, 144–5), usually made from only slightly modified metapodials.

5.3.9 Waste or Raw Material

This category comprises three items (SF39, SF133 & SF141), all fragments of whalebone. Two pieces can fit into a general waste category; they are small and appear to be offcuts, the waste from the production of some other object. One (SF133) is from F2128 (B243, Phase 4), the primary occupation layer over the floor of Structure 5 or make-up associated with a secondary paved floor. The other (SF141) was found in wind-blown sand F2141 (B248, Phase 3). The remaining piece (SF39) is larger. It has been severed using either an axe or possibly an adze, but otherwise does not exhibit any signs of working. It may represent raw material, or possibly unused fuel (Clark 1947).

5.3.10 Catalogue of Worked Bone

Bone points

SF96, F1084, B116, Phase 5
This is a fragment of tine cut roughly at the base. The tip has been shaped to come to a point and there are smoothly worn surfaces here. The point is now broken. Knife marks 30 mm from the base encircle the tine and narrow it slightly. There are also many transverse knife marks all over. Length: 101 mm.

SF135, F2144, B245, Phase 4
This is a worked cattle bone. The distal end is damaged but otherwise the piece is in good condition. One end has been shaped to make a strong point. Almost the entire surface is highly polished, there are many knife marks transverse to the axis of the bone, and small scratches around the point, parallel to the axis or slightly curving. Overall Length: 112 mm. Length of point: 34 mm.

Handle

SF134, F2138, B245, Phase 4
A curving length of antler tine with polish on the convex side and worn smooth elsewhere. At the small end there are scratches cutting across the long axis. The small end has been cut flat and there is a round hole here. The larger end is also flat and there is a rectangular hole here. Length: 90 mm, diameter of round hole: 4 mm, depth: *c*. 18 mm, rectangular hole: 6 × 3 mm, depth: *c*. 2 mm.

Perforated pin (Illus 169)

SF198, F3041, B304, Phase 5
A perforated bone pin. The head is rectangular in plan and pierced by a small circular hole, which has a larger diameter on one side than the other. The head size decreases gradually to the shank, which is highly polished. Length: 56 mm, diameter of perforation: 5 mm/3 mm, dimensions of head: 4 × 9 mm.

Comb fragment (Illus 170)

SF6, B107, Phase 7
Fragment of an antler comb. Only 5 teeth are complete, none show signs of wear. One end is broken. Length: 37 mm, thickness: 3 mm, width: 31 mm, average length of teeth: 12 mm.

Weaving swords

SF122, F2133, B237, Phase 5 (Illus 171)
Cetacean bone weaving baton. The blade has a slight curve, away from the handle; it does not come to a point but has a flat end. One side of the blade is curved, the other flat, the lower edge is sharp, while the upper is blunt. Two notches are cut into the edges, opposite each other and near to the handle. The handle is ribbed in section and has a lug extending downwards from the end. Use wear is of two sorts. There are small parallel grooves along two of the edges, the sharp edge (the bottom) and on the top on the flat side. The surface of the bone is also polished, along the length of these grooves, on both sides of the blade. Overall length: 275 mm, length of handle: 92 mm, width of blade: 54 mm, thickness of blade: 18 mm, thickness of handle: 29 mm, length of lug on handle: 6 mm.

SF183, F2170, B250, Phase 3
Fragments of a cetacean bone weaving baton. The fragments join to make most of the blade, but the handle is missing. The end of the blade is flat, and the edges are rounded. There are four worn notches cut into the edges of the blade near the handle, two on each side, opposite each other, and one other notch further up the blade. The surface of the bone is worn smooth, almost polished. Length: 229 mm, width: 66 mm, thickness: 22 mm.

Tool fragment

SF144, F2139, B245, Phase 4
Tip fragment of cetacean bone object. The surface appears polished. Length: 47 mm.

Utilized long bone

SF55, F2040, B211, Phase 6.3
Fragment of a long bone, split lengthwise along the bone. There are no signs of working but many longitudinal scratches are on the broken surface of the bone and it has been worn smooth here. Length: 160 mm.

Waste or raw material

SF133, F2128, B243, Phase 4
Subtriangular fragment of cetacean bone. Length: 86 mm, width: 46 mm, thickness: 19 mm.

SF141, F2141, B248, Phase 3
Thick subtriangular fragment of cetacean bone. Length: 101 mm, width: 50 mm, thickness: 31 mm.

SF39, F2039, B249, Phase 5
Large fragment of cetacean bone. One end is broken along a series of axe or possibly adze cuts that reduced the thickness from *c*. 38 mm to *c*. 14 mm. The edges have been roughly smoothed with a knife. Length: 140 mm, thickness: 38 mm, width: 82 mm.

5.4 Metal Artefacts and Metalworking

5.4.1 Metal Artefacts

Ann MacSween

5.4.11 Copper alloy artefacts

The majority of copper alloy finds from the excavations were corroded fragments of copper alloy

Illus 172   Copper alloy strip decorated with
                 lozenge motifs SF102 (1:1)

sheet (SF68, F1110, B104, Phase 8 & Table 25). The
remainder comprised a fragment of a strip decorated
with lozenge motifs (SF102, F1018, B103, Phase 8:
Illus 172), a ring (SF70, F1010, B103, Phase 8), a
ring fragment (SF109, F2107, B210, Phase 6.1) and a
broken pin (SF101, B103/104, Area 1).

In addition, a small copper alloy bar with a
rectangular cross-section (SF107, F2107, B210,
Phase 6.1), possibly an ingot, was recovered from the
area within the angle formed by the primary entrance
façade (Structure 18). There is evidence that this area
was used for small-scale metalworking (see below).

The decorated strip, broken at both ends, and the
ring were both recovered from the secondary 'farm
mound' deposits (B103). The ring was shaped from a
band of copper alloy, tapering at one end. Similar
rings were recovered from the Viking settlement at
Freswick, Caithness (Curle 1939, 102; pl. L, no. 9).
The pin, although unstratified, was also recovered
from the 'farm mound' (B103/104). Although thick
in section, its dimensions suggest that it may be the
pin from a penannular brooch, with the head missing.

5.4.12 Iron artefacts

Only two iron artefacts were recovered during the
excavations. Both were recovered from the 'farm
mound'. One (Rt 1, Table 25) is an iron nail with a
square-sectioned shaft and a domed head. The other
(SF69) is a small sickle blade, of a type in use in the
Northern Isles from the Norse period until relatively
recently (Graham-Campbell 1980, 9; Fenton 1978, 337).

5.4.2 Metalworking

Gerry McDonnell

5.4.21 Fired and vitrified clay

Apart from one fragment of vitrified clay (SF46b,
F2034, B211, Phase 6.3) from the primary fill deposits
of the secondary enclosure ditch, evidence for
metalworking was from the floor deposit (F2107:
B210, Phase 6.1) associated with the area behind the
primary entrance façade (Structure 18). The fragments
of fired and vitrified clay (SF108 & SF137), including
the example (SF46b) from the fill of the ditch, are all
pieces of vitrified hearth or furnace lining. Two pieces
(SF108 & SF137) are tuyère mouth fragments, the
hole through which the air entered the hearth or
furnace. The diameters of the tuyère mouths are
c. 20 mm, which is the average diameter of tuyère

mouths recovered from archaeological excavations,
irrespective of period or location.

The vitrified face of two of the samples were
qualitatively analysed by X-ray fluorescence. Besides
the usual range of elements (Si, Ca, Fe) one sample had
a high copper peak. Since very little research of hearth
and furnace lining has been undertaken, not too much
significance should be placed on this result. However,
from other evidence available, it would be possible to
propose that the vitrified lining derived from a hearth
used to melt copper alloy. It should be noted that any
hearth would be suitable for copper alloy working. The
safest conclusion is that the lining derived from a
metalworker's hearth and was probably used at some
time for melting copper alloys. The deposit (F2107,
B210: Part 3.2), in which the vitrified clay and mould
fragments (below) were recovered, was also relatively
rich in fuel ash (10g/10l) and burnt peat (6g/10l).

5.4.22 Mould fragments

Three possible mould fragments were recovered (SF178,
F2107, B210, Phase 6.1). Two of the mould fragments
were too small and abraded to allow determination of
their original form, but the third may have been the
mould for a decorative boss (Illus 173). The three
fragments were fired red and two examples have dark
inner surfaces, indicating that they had been used.

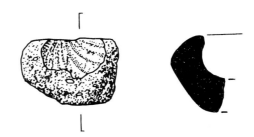

Illus 173   Mould for a decorative boss SF178 (1:1)

The inner surface of all three samples was analysed
by X-ray fluorescence. No copper alloy-based elements
were detected on one of the small fragments, but lead
and zinc with a trace of tin were found on the other two
fragments. A trace of copper was also detected in
addition on the smaller of the two fragments.

The presence of zinc cannot be used as an indicator
of the casting of brass alloys since it is extremely
volatile and will rapidly pass into the clay fragment of
the mould. The presence of the lead would indicate that
the alloy being used was essentially lead-based, but it
too is relatively volatile. It is probable that the moulds
were used for the casting of either lead or pewter.

5.4.3 Catalogue

Ann MacSween

SF108, F2107, B210, Phase 6.1
Five fragments of quartz-rich red/orange clay containing some,
probably natural, inclusions of siltstone. All the fragments are

TABLE 25: METAL FRAGMENTS RECOVERED FROM SAMPLES SORTING

Rt	F No	Block	Phase	Wt	
52	2157	245	4	0.1	2 copper alloy fragments
70	1010	103	8	0.4	copper alloy sheet
26	1110	104	8	0.1	2 copper alloy fragments
21	1110	104	8	0.7	copper alloy sheet, possibly part of a hafted object
21	1110	104	8	0.1	possible copper alloy rivet
1	1105	104	8	7.4	iron nail head, with the shaft broken off 5 mm below the head: shaft, square section; head, sub-circular.
4	1001	1	9	0.1	copper alloy fragment

vitrified to a depth of *c.* 13 mm on one surface; the other surface is missing. The vitrified portion of each fragment is grey and porous, and the surface of each has a 'glazed' appearance, and is black with patches of red.
T (max) 17; Wt 79.4.

SF137, F2107, B210, Phase 6.1
One fragment, as SF108.
T 14; Wt 18.8.

SF46, F2034, B211, Phase 6.3
One fragment, as SF108, but with a matt surface.
T 13; Wt 11.9.

SF178, F2107, B210, Phase 6.1
Three fragments of heat-hardened clay, probably moulds. All are made of a red quartz-rich clay with small rounded siltstone inclusions, probably natural to the clay. One of the fragments is abraded (23 × 26 mm) and has three hollows, one possibly segmented.
Wt 5.

The other two fragments may be parts of one mould. The larger fragment (Illus 173) has the impression of perhaps a pin-head or a decorative boss with a mushroom-head section. The surface of the object which made the impression had ridges which radiated out from the centre of its 'flat' side.
Combined Wt 6.9.

SF68, F1110, B104, Phase 8
Copper alloy fragments.
Wt 0.1.

SF69, F1030, B103, Phase 8
Curved iron blade, possibly a sickle blade, sharpened along the interior edge.
L 16.7; W 2.5; T (max) 5; Wt 30.2.

SF70, F1010, B103, Phase 8
Band of copper alloy, 7 mm at one end and tapering to 3 mm, which has been shaped to form a ring. There are traces of two fine incised lines along one side.
Dia (max) 10; W 3–7; T 1; Wt 1.0.

SF101, B103/104, Phase 8
Copper alloy rod with a square cross-section. Pointed at both ends and slightly curved. Possibly a pin from a penannular brooch.
L 105; W 5; Wt 13.1.

SF102, F1018, B103, Phase 8
Broken fragment of a copper alloy strip (Illus 172) decorated on one side with a lozenge pattern. Rectangular in cross-section. There are traces of what may be casting ridges along its length (A. Thompson, pers comm).
L 18; W 4; T 1; Wt 0.5.

SF107, F2107, B210, Phase 6.1
Copper alloy bar with a rectangular cross-section. Possible ingot.
L 98; T 4; W 7; Wt 13.

SF109, F2107, B210, Phase 6.1
Copper alloy fragments, forming approximately 50 per cent of a narrow ring.
Dia 15; Wt 0.1.

5.5 Lime Mortar

Christopher Lowe

An impressed lump of lime mortar (Illus 174) and several smaller fragments were recovered during the excavation of Sample Column B. The pieces were recovered from F1063, a deposit near the base of the primary 'farm mound' (B104, Phase 8).

One face of the larger, impressed piece (58 × 44 mm) is smooth and flat. The reverse is irregular and there is a ridge, up to 13 mm high, at one end, which preserves the impression of the masonry around or over which the mortar was applied. The fabric is hard. Occasional small shell fragments and grains of quartz are visible in the aggregate. Carbonized organic material is also present. The impressed lump and another fragment are 11–21 mm thick. The other fragments are 10–12 mm thick.

While the flat face of the larger, impressed lump would not exclude its use as a bonding mortar, it is, perhaps, more likely that the fragment represents a plaster render. No mortared buildings were traced during the course of the excavation.

Context F1063 represents the second of eight layers which were identified in the primary mound at Sample Column B. The basal deposit (F1045) has been radiocarbon dated to cal AD 990–1240 (GU-3067) and cal AD 990–1255 (GU-3066c) and this provides a *terminus post quem* date for the deposition of the mortar in the mound. The presence of this material implies the demolition or refurbishment of a mortared building on the site at the time of the mound's inception. A date of *c.* AD 1100 for the beginning of mound formation is proposed elsewhere (Part 7.1).

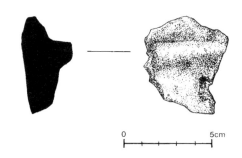

Illus 174   Impressed mortar from F1063, B104 primary 'farm mound'

PART 6

The Palaeoenvironmental Evidence

6.1 Human Bone

Daphne Home Lorimer

6.1.1 Summary

The human bones belonged to two individuals. Skeleton 1 was an adult male which was found in a small stone-lined grave (B311, Phase 1) below the floor of the roundhouse. The grave had been cut into the primary sand surface and was sealed by the sand and rubble deposits of Phase 3. The human remains consisted, principally, of the frontal and right parietal bones of a skull. The frontal bones were broken, stained with mould and cracked; due, possibly, to soaking and subsequent drying out.

Skeleton 2 was adult, probably male. It was recovered from the primary silt deposits (F2044: B252, Phase 6.2) which filled the base of the secondary enclosure ditch. The skeletal remains were deposited prior to the construction of a buttress wall against the south side of the ditch. The skeletal remains were represented by the bones of the lower legs and feet only.

Few non-metrical variations were recognized in either skeleton. Of pathological conditions, an osteoma was seen on the inner table of the frontal bone of Skeleton 1 and the posterior calcaneal spurs in Skeleton 2. Gray (1977) and Bass (1987) were used for general anatomical reference and estimation of age and sex.

6.1.2 Skeleton 1 (F3051, B311, Phase 1)

6.1.21 Inventory

Cranium

Frontal bone: part of the horizontal portion and almost the entire vertical portion of the frontal bone were present, although the vertical portion was in a fragmented state. All but two small fragments could be fitted together and consisted of:

one large fragment of the vertical plate with both supraorbital margins, superciliary ridges and glabella on the outer table and a large part of the frontal crest on the inner together with adjacent part of horizontal portion;
one large fragment with the left coronal suture and upper portion of the upper temporal ridge and frontal crest on the inner table;
one small fragment with the lower part of the upper temporal ridge;
one fragment with the left side of the coronal suture and the lower part of the upper temporal ridge;
two small fragments joining with this piece;
one fragment with coronal suture at bregma;
one fragment with bregma and left side of part of sagittal suture;
two small fragments with part of the coronal suture.

Petrous-temporal: right side: petrous portion and mastoid process slightly damaged; the squamous portion had its articular surface, styloid and zygomatic processes broken.

Sphenoid: one small fragment of right greater wing.

Facial bones: Malar: right side with zygomatic process missing.

and twenty-five very small fragments of tabular bone.

6.1.22 Sex

The sex was considered possibly male as the supraorbital margins were rounded and the superciliary ridges and mastoid process marked. The posterior root of the zygomatic process extended over the external auditory mearus on to the temporal ridge.

6.1.23 Non-metrical variations

A supraorbital foramen was seen on the left side of the frontal bone and there were possibly some small coronal ossicles.

6.1.24 Pathology

A small osteoma was noted on the left side of the inner table of the vertical portion of the frontal bone. It was situated 15 mm from the frontal crest and 26 mm above the orbital process. An osteoma is a protruding mass of abnormally dense, but otherwise normal, bone formed in the periosteum. It is normally asymptomatic unless in a site, such as the sinuses, where it can exert pressure (Ortner & Putschar 1987).

6.1.3 Skeleton 2 (F2044, B252, Phase 6.2)

Skeleton 2 was only represented by the bones of the lower legs and feet. They were adult, robust, probably male, but sex determination from measurements of the tibia, talus and calcaneus as given by Krogman & Iscan (1986) was conflicting and is not usually considered a very reliable indicator.

6.1.31 Inventory

Tibia: Right side: lower end and half shaft (cortex and part of cellular bone missing from lower anterior quarter).
Left side: complete except for post-mortem damage to internal surface in the region of the nutrient foramen.

Measurements

Maximum length	345 mm
Mid-shaft circumference	92 mm
Proximal breadth	82 mm
Distal breadth	55 mm

Fibula: Right side: lower end and four-fifths shaft, reconstructed from two parts. The point of attachment for the interosseous membrane was very marked.
Left side: head and shaft, reconstructed from two parts. Post-mortem damage to anterior surface of lower third.

Tarsal bones: Right side: Talus, calcaneus, cuboid, 1st cuneiform. 3rd cuneiform and navicular.
Left side: Talus, 1st cuneiform, 2nd cuneiform, 3rd cuneiform.

Metatarsals: Right side: 1st, 2nd, 3rd, 4th, 5th.
Left side: 1st, 2nd, 3rd, —, —.

Phalanges: Right side: 1st row: 1st, 2nd, —, 4th, —.

6.1.32 Sex

Possibly male. The tibial length lay within the male range but below the demarking point. The mid-shaft circumference and the diameters of the proximal and distal ends were above the male sectioning point, which, according to Krogman & Iscan (1986, 230–43), is supposed to have a 100 per cent accuracy. A discriminant function analysis of the talus and calcaneus, however, indicated the female sex.

6.1.33 Non-metrical variations

A medial squatting facet was seen on the left tibia but lateral facets appeared on both sides; lateral talar extensions occurred on both sides and a double anterior facet and a Peroneal tubercle appeared on the right calcaneus.

6.1.34 Pathology

Posterior calcaneal spurs, or enthesophytes of the Achilles tendon were noted on the right calcaneus. These are due to repeated or acute trauma causing bleeding and inflammation to the Achilles tendon (Mann & Murphy 1990). There were also possible degenerative changes to the inferior surface of the left 1st phalanx.

6.2 Mammal Bone

Finbar McCormick

6.2.1 Introduction

The excavation produced a very small sample of animal bone. It was derived from nearly ninety separate contexts belonging to nine broad phases of occupation. The small size of the samples, coupled with their dispersed distribution, greatly reduces the value of the material for quantitative analysis. In only one case, Phase 6.2, did sample size warrant the estimation of minimum numbers of individuals (MNI) values. In that instance there were estimated MNI values of three cattle, six sheep, two pig and one each of cat and grey seal.

6.2.2 General Results (Table 26)

The samples were generally too small to provide useful quantitative data. In general, however, pigs and cattle seem to have been more numerous during the early prehistoric period while sheep tended to dominate during the later phases. There were no definite incidences of goat being present and it is assumed that all the caprovine remains are of sheep. In terms of actual meat consumed, however, cattle were the most important food provider. Even during Phase 6.2 sheep would only have contributed 7 per cent of the carcass weight compared with 78 per cent in the case of cattle and 15 per cent in the case of pig on the basis of figures outlined in McCormick (forthcoming a). The food provided by wild animals would also have played an important role in the diet.

TABLE 26: PERCENTAGE DISTRIBUTION OF BONE FRAGMENTS BY PHASE (N = SAMPLE SIZE)

Phase	Approx. dates	Cattle	Sheep	Pig	Cat	Grey Seal	Red Deer	Cetacean	N
1	3000–1500 BC	66.6	7.4	25.9	–	–	–	–	27
3	1500–1250 BC	90.0	10.0	–	–	–	–	–	10
4	1250–750 BC	56.7	19.6	15.2	–	2.2	2.2	4.3	46
5	750–250 BC	20.5	71.8	7.7	–	–	–	–	39
6.1	250–0 BC	12.2	71.4	16.3	–	–	–	–	49
6.2	AD 0–250	16.5	60.4	9.4	12.9	0.6	–	–	170
6.3	c. AD 250	36.8	47.1	11.8	–	2.9	1.5	–	68
7	AD 250–750	31.6	52.6	15.8	–	–	–	–	19
8	AD 1000–1250	33.3	51.5	15.2	–	–	–	–	33

A dressed carcass of a red deer would have weighed about 53 kg compared with 10 kg in the case of sheep (after Clutton-Brock & Albon 1989, 60). Semimature grey seals could weigh between about 60 and 86 kg of which 70 per cent would be usable meat (McCormick 1981, 317).

6.2.3 Domesticates

Excavations at a Neolithic house at Knap of Howar indicate that sheep were dominant on Papa Westray during this period (Noddle 1979; 1983). The Knap of Howar material constituted a large sample so the data from the small Neolithic sample from St Boniface should not be regarded as contradicting this. At St Boniface, sheep, in terms of fragment totals, tended to dominate from the Early Iron Age onwards. No other Early Iron Age to Medieval period sites have been excavated on Papa Westray so one must look elsewhere in Orkney for comparative material for the later St Boniface material. Early Iron Age bone material from Orkney is exceedingly rare and, as in the case of St Boniface, is generally present in rather limited quantities. A small sample from Early Iron Age contexts (Phase 3) at the Howe, Mainland Orkney, produced MNI values of two cattle, two sheep, one pig and one red deer (Smith 1994, 140). Again, in an Early Iron Age context at Pierowall Quarry, Westray, a small sample produced MNI values of four cattle, four sheep and one pig along with remains of red deer, dog and cetacean (McCormick 1984, fiche 2.E9). Samples of this size, however, are too small to provide reliable data.

Much larger comparative samples are present from the pre-Norse or Pictish period, and from the Norse period in Orkney. The low incidence of pig noted at St Boniface is attested on all other Orcadian sites of the period but the relative importance of cattle and sheep varies. Table 27 compares the MNI percentage values of the three main domesticates from Pictish and Norse sites on Orkney. The methods used for estimating the MNIs from the different sites may not be consistent.

No dog or horse bones were found at St Boniface but it seems likely that this is due to sampling bias. Dog, for instance, was noted at the Neolithic Knap of Howar on Papa Westray (Noddle 1983, 94). Horse,

while not present on any pre-Iron Age Orcadian site, is well represented throughout later periods. Part of the skeleton of a very large cat was present in Phase 6.2 which dates approximately to AD 1–250. Conclusive differentiation between wild and domesticated cat is possible only in the skull but unfortunately this was missing. The measurements of the cat are listed in Table 30 and indicate that the cat was of a rather large size. The robustness of the bone indicates that the cat was most likely to be a large male domesticated cat rather than a small wild cat. The animal was also quite old at time of death and displayed arthritic features on its distal humerus. Although the Romans introduced the domesticated cat to England, until recently there has been no definite evidence for their presence in Scotland during the Roman Iron Age. In addition to St Boniface, cat has also been noted in the Phase 7 broch levels at Howe, mainland Orkney, which straddled the Roman period (Smith 1994, 139–40). Cat bones from earlier levels on the same site are probably intrusive.

TABLE 27: RELATIVE PERCENTAGES OF PRINCIPAL SPECIES FROM PRE-NORSE AND NORSE PERIOD ORCADIAN SITES (NODDLE 1979, 289; RACKHAM FORTHCOMING)

Site	Date	Cattle	Sheep	Pig	N
Skaill	Pre-Norse	45	40	15	40
Buckquoy	Pre-Norse	42	28	30	123
St Boniface	Pre-Norse	27	55	18	11
Skaill	Norse	32	49	19	77
Buckquoy	Norse	46	34	20	110
Tuquoy (Ph 12)	Norse	37	44	19	48

6.2.4 Ageing Data

The ageing data from St Boniface were extremely limited and preclude quantitative analysis. Some qualitative remarks, however, can be made. In the case of cattle there is evidence for a high incidence of juvenile animals present in all levels. Most of the cattle humeri, for instance, are unfused. According to Silver (1969, 285) this bone fuses at 12–18 months. The high incidence of juveniles is supported by the even more limited tooth eruption with the occasional neonate mandible being present.

Noddle (1979, 289), too, has noted a high incidence of juvenile cattle on Pictish and Norse sites on Orkney, some including many new-born, but with large numbers of older animals also present. Evidence from the Knap of Howar and Skara Brae suggest that the incidence of juvenile cattle present is even greater in earlier periods in Orkney. It seems likely that the high incidence of juvenile mortality is due to fodder shortage (McCormick forthcoming b).

The ageing data for sheep were also extremely limited. In the earlier prehistoric levels (Phases 1–5) most of those slaughtered seem to be semi-mature with few very young and very old animals being slaughtered. During the later phases there is, however, a growing number of juvenile and neonate individuals present. In the Phase 8 levels some of these neonate bones were found together and clearly represented the same individual. It is difficult to explain this phenomenon but the fact that semi-complete skeletons of neonates were also found in the topsoil might imply that these are simply naturally occurring phenomenon representing lambs dying in a sheltered spot after the site was abandoned by humans.

The ageing data for pigs are too limited to warrant discussion. The bones of rodents (voles and mice) were noted in many of the contexts but these cannot be shown to be contemporary with the deposits in which they were found. Sheep bones gnawed by rodents were also occasionally encountered.

6.2.5 Butchery/Pathology

With the exception of the juvenile animals, most bones were broken and some displayed chop or knife marks, clearly indicating that for the most part the material represented discarded food refuse. The semi-complete cat skeleton was an obvious exception and displayed no butchering marks. The sheep neonates from later levels also displayed no such marks and, for reasons outlined above, may not represent food refuse.

The samples of butchered bones are again too small to allow detailed analysis. Knife marks on the sheep bones were generally confined to the immediate vicinity of the articular areas of the long bones. Chop marks tended to be more frequently observed on cattle bones than knife marks, and appeared most commonly on the vertebrae. Some faint knife marks were noted on a red deer phalanx from Phase 6.3.

Few of the bones displayed pathological anomalies. A grey seal phalanx 1 from Phase 4 contained an abscess while a sheep metacarpal from Phase 4 had been broken and re-healed. Arthritis on the cat bones has already been noted.

6.2.6 Metrical Data

The measurements of the bones are recorded in Tables 28–30. The sheep bones are similar to those noted at Pre-Norse and Norse Buckquoy (Noddle

TABLE 28: CATTLE MEASUREMENTS (mm) AFTER VON DEN DRIESCH (1976)

Bone	Phase	GL	Bp	Bd	SD	BT	GLl
Calcaneus	1	104.1					
Astralagus	1			30.6			49.9
Metacarpal	6.3	164.8	51.1	51.9	28.2		
Calcaneus	4	117.5					
Radius	5		74.1				
Metatarsal	6.3	202.5	40.2	47.2	23.1		

TABLE 29: SHEEP MEASUREMENTS (mm) AFTER VON DEN DRIESCH (1976) * = Dp

Bone	Phase	GL	Bp	Bd	SD	BT	GLl
Humerus	6.3	119.1	36.5*	24.9	11.9	24.1	
Femur	6.3	156.8	37.9	31.7	11.8		
Tibia	6.3			22.9			
Tibia	6.2		58.2				
Metacarpal	8	120.5	22.2	25.1	14.8		
Calcaneus	8	47.9					
Metacarpal	5	120.1	22.3	25.7	13.0		
Metacarpal	5	119.8	20.1	23.1	12.7		

TABLE 30: CAT MEASUREMENTS (mm) AFTER VON DEN DRIESCH (1976) * = Dp

Bone	Phase	GL	Bp	Bd	SD	BT	LAR
Pelvis	6.2						11.9
Pelvis	6.2						11.9
Humerus	6.2	103.1	23.1*	20.9	7.3		
Femur	6.2	116.3	23.1	20.2	10.1		
Femur	6.2	116.8	22.8	20.4	9.2		
Tibia	6.2	119.0	21.6	15.1	8.5		
Tibia	6.2		21.5				

1977, 207). Cattle measurements for the same site are not published so direct comparison is not possible but the cattle seem to be larger than the diminutive cattle found in Iron Age Lewis, Outer Hebrides (McCormick forthcoming a).

6.2.7 Red Deer

One complete, red deer metacarpal was found in a Phase 4 context (F2134). Its measurements were as follows: GL 238.2 mm, Bp 35.1 mm, Bd 29.6 mm. A second deer bone, a phalanx 2, was found in a Phase 6.3 context (F2097). The question of deer in prehistoric Orkney is a vexed one and has been discussed extensively and summarized by Morris *et al* (1989, 105–6). Red deer were almost certainly introduced to Orkney by man and while they were not present at Neolithic Knap of Howar in Papa Westray they were noted at Neolithic Links of Noltland on neighbouring Westray (Clarke & Sharples 1985, 77).

6.2.8 Area 1: Intra-Site Variation

Samples of bone were collected from four columns (A–D) in the 'farm mound' on Area 1. In some

TABLE 31: AVERAGE FRAGMENT WEIGHT (g) FROM BULK SAMPLE RESIDUES, BY SAMPLE COLUMN (A–D)

F no	A	B	C	D
1001	0.18	0.44		1.25
1011		0.79	0.15	0.36
1030		0.39	0.18	0.09
1034		0.42		0.10
1035	0.04	0.06		
1037			0.38	0.70
1045	0.26	1.10	0.08	
1065	0.35	0.78		

instances contexts were represented in two or more of these columns and the material was considered to see if there was any consistent pattern in the fragment size across the section examined. In this way it was hoped that it would be possible to establish the relationship of the section examined to the centre of the 'farm mound', the location of which is unknown. It was also hoped that it could be discerned if the groups of animal bone from the same features in the different columns were of the same size.

In order to avoid bias due to differential hand retrieval, it was decided that only the sieved material from the bulk samples should be considered. The fragment size in each of the samples taken from Sample Columns A–D was calculated. Any features that spanned two or more columns were included in Table 31. The results show that there is no consistent trend in fragment size across the columns so the exercise did not help in establishing the location of the centre of the 'farm mound'.

6.2.9 Conclusion

The material from this excavation produced samples that were too small to provide much useful information. Although there has been a relatively large number of Orcadian excavations which have provided bones from the period between about 1000 BC and AD 1000 none has provided large enough samples to allow investigation of detailed questions concerning the animal husbandry of the period. Larger samples from this site would therefore be of great interest.

6.3 Fish Bone

Ruby Cerón-Carrasco

6.3.1 Methods

The fish remains were recovered from bulk samples after careful sieving through 1 mm mesh.

No deliberate hand-retrieval was undertaken. Identification of species was made using the comparative modern fish bone reference collection at the bone laboratory of AOC (Scotland) Ltd. Vertebrae identification was also based on a recent study done by the Department of Zoology of Aberdeen University (Boyle *et al* 1992). All remains were identified, where possible, to skeletal element and to species level. When this was not possible, they were assigned to the family group. Species were identified by examining mainly head elements such as the dentary, premaxilla, articular, maxilla, quadrate, otolith and vomer. In most samples vertebrae were identified to supplement the species list already identified by head elements. Although a large number of vertebrae were present in the assemblage, these were quite eroded and most had not enough diagnostic features to allow for accurate identification; their morphology, however, indicates that they belong to the Gadidae. It is not always possible to distinguish species from every skeletal element (Colley 1982; Wheeler & Jones 1989). In the case of the St Boniface fish assemblage, although every bone fragment was examined, elements such as branchiostegals, spines and fin rays were identified only to family level.

The size of the Gadoid species has been calculated by giving an approximate size range. This was done by matching the archaeological material to modern fish skeletons of known size based on 'total body' length. Therefore, the elements were categorized as 'very small' (<15 cm), 'small' (15–30 cm), 'medium' (30–60 cm), 'large' (60–120 cm) and 'very large' (>120 cm).

Where appropriate, the major paired elements were assigned to the left or right side of the skeleton. All elements were examined for signs of butchery and gnawing, and burning was also noted. The condition of the bone was also noted in all cases, where eroded and/or friable. The recording of preservation of these remains was based on two characters: texture on a scale of 1 to 5 (fresh to extremely friable) and erosion on a scale of 1 to 5 (none to extreme). The sum of both was used as an indication of bone condition; fresh to extremely poorly preserved on a scale of 1 to 10 (after Nicholson 1991).

6.3.2 Results

A full catalogue of results may be consulted in the site archive. Table 32 summarizes the numbers of bone elements representing all identified taxa in each phase of the site. The concentration of these bones in the sediment samples is also given. Tables 33–35 provide element size classifications of the three commonest taxa (Gadidae family, cod and saithe) in each phase, while Tables 36 and 37 further divide the Phase 8 element size data into Blocks 103 and 104.

TABLE 32: FISH BONE ELEMENTS BY PHASE

PHASE	1	3	4	5	6.1	6.2	6.3	7	8	9	Total
LATIN NAME/COMMON NAME											
Gadidae/Cod family	182	8	64	75	748	793	439	1171	8163	1007	12650
Gadus morhua/Cod			1	1	70	15	37	30	342	19	515
Gadus cf *morhua*/?Cod					5	8	1	5	20	1	40
Pollachius virens/Saithe	17	8	34		147	361	109	86	380	311	1453
Pollachius cf *virens*/?Saithe	7	3			3	63	3	1	68		148
Pollachius pollachius/Pollack					16	24		18	151	13	222
Pollachius cf *pollachius*/?Pollack			1	5			1	3	10	2	22
Cf *Merlangius merlangus*/Whiting									6		6
Cf *Molva molva*/Ling									1		1
Gaidropsarus cf *mediterraneus*/Shore rockling	2	3	4	5	5	5	40	1	3	1	69
Elasmobranchii/Skate/ray, dogfishes					1				4	2	7
Cf *Scyliorhinus canicula*/Dogfish										2	2
Raja clavata/Rocker									1		1
Pleuronectidae/Right-eyed flatfishes			3						7		10
Limanda limanda/Dab					2						2
Lepidorhombus whiffiagonis/Megrim			1				1				2
Anguilla anguilla/Eel		1	3	5	2	67			1		79
Cf *Conger conger*/Conger eel					1				12		13
Scomber scombrus/Mackerel									1		1
Salmonidae/Trout and salmon							1				1
Clupea harengus/Herring									35		35
Myoxocephalus scorpius/Bull-rout			6		3	4	34	4	7		58
Taurulus bubalis/Sea-scorpion		8	7	6	4	6	43	2	3	1	80
Cf *Agonus cataphractus*/Hooked nose							6			1	7
Cf *Labrus bergylta*/Ballan Wrasse		7		2	2	2					13
Cf *Belone belone*/Garfish			1			1	2				4
Pholis gunnelus/Butterfish		3	9	6	4	7	171		11	2	213
Ammodytidae/Sandeels				1	2	1	3	3	22	4	36
Unidentified	281	40	213	238	862	795	1222	1327	15642	2070	22690
Total	**489**	**81**	**347**	**344**	**1875**	**2153**	**2114**	**2651**	**24890**	**3436**	**38380**
Total volume sorted (litres)	333	52	195	393	212	356	190	749	815	104	3399
Concentration (identified elements/litre)	0.6	0.8	0.7	0.3	4.8	3.8	4.7	1.8	11.3	13.1	

6.3.3 Comment and Phase Distribution

In all phases, the dominant species are those from the Gadidae family. The main species represented are cod (*Gadus morhua*), saithe (*Pollachius virens*) and pollack (*Pollachius pollachius*). Other rarer Gadidae are whiting (*Merlangius merlangus*), a possible ling (cf *Molva molva*) and a few vertebrae assigned to shore rockling (*Gaidropsaurus mediterraneous*).

Species from other family groups are present in very small numbers compared to the Gadidae. Only a few cartilagenous fish remains were recovered; these are a few dermal denticles and vertebrae which have been calcified in the soil. Their identification to species was not possible but they may be referred to skate, ray or dogfish. Some flatfish bones were assigned to the right-eyed Pleuronectidae family group. A few vertebrae were tentatively assigned to the conger eel (cf *Conger conger*), and also present in a few contexts are vertebrae from the fresh-water eel (*Anguilla anguilla*). The general rarity of both cartilagenous fish and flatfish may, at least in part, reflect the poor preservation of their bones in archaeological contexts but this does not reduce the overwhelming dominance of the Gadidae.

6.3.31 Phases 1–5

Very few fish bones were recovered from contexts assigned to Phases 1 to 5 and the bone present was in the lowest concentration of any of the other site phases. Most of the bone came from the smaller size categories of Gadidae, of which saithe was the most abundant species identified.

6.3.32 Phase 6.1

Phase 6.1 produced a large amount of fish remains which belong to the smaller categories of Gadidae, mainly to young saithe.

6.3.33 Phase 6.2

Although there is a decrease in the concentration of fish remains as compared to the earlier phase, there is no difference either in species representation or size.

6.3.34 Phase 6.3

There is an increase of quantified elements in this phase. Species and size representation do not vary, by

TABLE 33: TOTAL GADIDAE ELEMENT REPRESENTATION BY SIZE AND PHASE

Size distribution

SIZE	VS	S	M	L	VL	UN	Total	% of phase assemblage
PHASE								
1	41	114	49	3		1	208	42.5
3	7	15					22	27.2
4	47	24	28	1	3		103	30.0
5	41	32	5	3	1	4	86	25.0
6.1	469	360	140	1	8	15	993	53.0
6.2	779	319	124	11	12		1245	57.8
6.3	274	230	143	1	3	3	654	30.9
7	99	373	289	120	4	430	1315	49.6
8	164	1345	1397	1036	398	4798	9138	36.7
9	432	350	133	76	12	351	1354	39.4
Total	**2353**	**3162**	**2308**	**1252**	**441**	**5602**	**15118**	

Size distribution (per cent)

SIZE	VS	S	M	L	VL	Number of elements
PHASE						
1	19.9	54.9	23.8	1.4		207
3	31.8	68.2				22
4	45.5	23.4	27.2	1.0	2.9	103
5	50.3	39.3	5.8	3.4	1.2	82
6.1	47.9	36.8	14.3	0.1	0.8	978
6.2	62.6	25.6	9.9	0.9	0.9	1245
6.3	42.1	35.3	22.0	0.2	0.5	651
7	11.2	42.2	32.6	13.5	0.5	885
8	3.8	31.0	32.2	23.9	9.2	4340
9	43.0	34.9	13.3	7.6	1.2	1003

TABLE 34: COD ELEMENT REPRESENTATION BY SIZE AND PHASE

SIZE	VS	S	M	L	VL	UN	Total	% of phase assemblage
PHASE								
4					1		1	0.3
5					1		1	0.3
6.1	37	30	6		2		75	4.0
6.2	19	2			2		23	1.1
6.3	21	15	2		1		39	1.8
7	4	12	12	8			36	1.3
8	8	60	101	99	91	1	360	1.4
9	10	3	1		6		20	0.6
Total	**99**	**122**	**122**	**107**	**104**	**1**	**555**	

TABLE 35: SAITHE ELEMENT REPRESENTATION BY SIZE AND PHASE

SIZE	VS	S	M	L	VL	Total	% of phase assemblage
PHASE							
1	11	7	6	1		25	4.9
3	1	10				11	13.6
4	30	4				34	9.8
6.1	86	38	25			149	8.0
6.2	255	112	56	1		424	19.7
6.3	61	43	7		1	112	5.3
7	21	35	26	4	2	88	3.3
8	40	106	137	150	16	449	1.8
9	186	101	5	20		312	9.1
Total	**691**	**456**	**262**	**176**	**19**	**1604**	

TABLE 36: BLOCK 103 (PHASE 8), GADIDAE ELEMENT FREQUENCY

SIZE	VS	S	M	L	VL	UN	Total	% of block sum
SPECIES								
Gadidae	50	452	347	241	104	1532	2726	89.5
Cod	1	11	19	38	20	1	90	2.9
Saithe	7	34	52	26	11	0	130	4.2
Pollack	2	9	8	9	9	0	37	1.2

TABLE 37: BLOCK 104 (PHASE 8), GADIDAE ELEMENT FREQUENCY

SIZE	VS	S	M	L	VL	UN	Total	% of block sum
SPECIES								
Gadidae	50	651	774	505	162	2892	5034	76.8
Cod	20	42	71	70	53	0	256	3.9
Saithe	29	133	68	130	4	0	364	5.5
Pollack	8	12	28	16	3	0	67	1.0

comparison with the material from Phases 6.1 and 6.2. There is, however, evidence to suggest that fish bone from specific contexts is a product of animal, and not human, activity. Deposits which post-date the abandonment of the secondary entrance façade, context F2097 (B207), in particular, contained a great amount of fish remains belonging to small species of freshwater eel (*Anguilla anguilla*), hooked-nose (*Agonus cataphractus*), sea-scorpion (*Taurulus bubalis*) and very small Gadidae. A large amount of this material was distorted and flattened which would indicate that these elements had gone through the process of digestion. The species and size representation of this context would indicate that a large proportion of the material derived from otter spraints.

6.3.35 Phase 7

There is a distinctive drop in the concentration of fish remains, by comparison with the assemblage of Phase 6. The assemblage is dominated by 'very small' and 'small' Gadidae, in particular saithe, but larger specimens are present, making up a quarter of the total catch.

6.3.36 Phase 8

Phase 8 contexts produced by far the largest fish bone assemblage (approximately 10,000 identified elements) and these sediments also contained the highest concentration of fish bone (11.3 elements per litre). Although the Gadidae still dominate the assemblage there is a clear shift to a high proportion of 'large' and 'very large' fish. There is also a change in the relative numbers of cod and saithe with similar numbers of the two species instead of dominant numbers of saithe, as is seen in the earlier phases.

Within Phase 8, there are sufficient bones to allow the comparison of results from the two main deposit groups (B103 & B104: Tables 36 & 37). No significant changes can be observed in either species composition or size between the earlier Block 104 and the later Block 103.

6.3.37 Phase 9

The total number of elements identified from Phase 9 is similar to Phases 6 to 7 but concentration in the sediments is similar to the high level seen in Phase 8. The size representation in the Gadidae is again dominated by 'very small' to 'medium' fish, as in the early phases but with rather more 'large fish' present. In those elements identified to species, the more abundant saithe is clearly dominated by only 'very small' and 'small' fish while the much less frequent cod is represented by all sizes in similar numbers.

6.3.4 Exploitation of Fish Resources

6.3.41 Origins of the fish bone

Fish bone may be introduced to a site by a variety of natural and human activities and it is important that these are clearly separated. There is no reason to doubt that the majority of the bone, comprising the abundant Gadidae, cod, saithe and pollack, is the product of fishing by man. Similarly, the rare larger specimens of other human food species, such as whiting, ling, conger eel, mackerel and herring, probably represent accidental human catches.

Some of the other species may have been introduced by predators like the otter (*Lutra lutra*) or even in the stomach contents of larger fish, caught by man. These processes probably explain the presence of the tiny butterfish, sea scorpion, sandeels and the small specimens of freshwater eel. Bones from these fish tend to be concentrated in a few contexts (F2010 & F2097: B207, Phase 6.3; F2029: B211, Phase 6.3 and part of the material recovered from F1097: B113, Phase 6.1) and may indicate the presence of otters. A proportion of the very small Gadidae may also have been introduced by natural predators and in particular the exclusive abundance of very small saithe in F2035 (B202, Phase 9) probably reflects such activity.

6.3.42 Fishing

Throughout the use of the site, the majority of the fish bones are interpreted as the product of fishing by man. In the early to later prehistoric phases (Phases 1–6), fishing involved the catching of small Gadidae, predominantly saithe. This is interpreted as a small-scale subsistance technique carried out from the shore which is recorded up to the present day in the Northern Isles where it is known as 'craig fishing' (Fenton 1973; 1978). In 'craig fishing', with the aid of rod and line, fish were taken close to the shore from rocky locations known as 'craig seats'. This Scots term has its roots in the Old Norse words *bersit* or *bergset* meaning 'berg', rock, and 'saet', seat. This points to a long tradition of use of this fishing technique. It was employed chiefly for the catching of young saithe but other species such as young pollack and cod could also be caught.

In Phase 7 (Late Iron Age), although the catching of young saithe continues to be the main fishing practice, there is also an addition in technology for the catching of 'medium' and 'large' Gadid specimens. Although the catch for these made up only a quarter of the entire catch, there is a clear shift from this phase to deep-water fishing technology, a feature which is further developed and widely exploited in the following phase.

In Phase 8 (Norse), there is a clear change in the catch with a shift to larger Gadidae and a greater emphasis on cod. In addition, the high concentration of fish bone is interpreted as evidence for a more intensive exploitation of fish resources, by comparison with the earlier phases. Smaller Gadidae still make up a significant portion of the catch so this change is interpreted as the product of the diversification of fishing techniques out from the shore into deeper water. Ethnographic accounts from the Northern Isles indicate two possible fishing methods. The first method employed from the craig seats was that of the 'steepa-dorro', probably derived from the Norwegian *stup*, meaning steep edge or cliff and *dorg*, a trolling line, meaning a trailing fishing line. This consisted of a line several fathoms in length with a cork float attached. At the end of the line there would be a hook with a large limpet used as a bait. At the shore end, the line was anchored to a stone and when the float gave signs of disturbance, the tackle was pulled in. The specimens caught in this way were mainly mature saithe and cod which

live further offshore than the younger fish. Occasional pollack and mackerel could also be taken in this way. Another fishing strategy could have been the use of small boats like those of traditional Norse design (*yål* or *fouraerings*) and long fishing lines with multiple hooks. The boats would have stayed close to the shore but in deep water, taking large cod, saithe, whiting, pollack, mackerel, conger eel, dogfish and rays.

Exploitation of fish in Phase 6 is unclear and this reflects the mixture of contexts assigned to the phase. Phase 9 sediments in Area 1 form the upper part of the Phase 8 'farm mound' and have a similar fish bone assemblage of small to large Gadidae. Phase 9 sediments in Area 2 are dominated by very small Gadidae which have been interpreted as the product of natural predators. The resulting total assemblage for Phase 9, therefore, is mixed.

6.3.43 Fish processing

Evidence for fish processing comes from cut-marks on individual elements and from the variable proportions of the different skeletal elements in the bone assemblage. Only the large assemblage from Phase 8 contains sufficient bone to allow a study of element proportions. In addition, all cut-marks (only twenty elements in total) were recorded on Gadoid bones from Phase 8. Therefore this discussion of fish processing relates only to Phase 8.

6.3.431 Cut-marks

Cut-marks on the supraclavicle and the posttemporal bones could have been created by chopping off the head of the fish (Colley 1983). A posttemporal bone from a 'large' Gadid displayed three horizontal deeply incised marks and it has been observed that such marks are inflicted by a badly sharpened blade. There were also dentaries, maxillae and a vomer bone with distinct cut-marks, as well as a few vertebrae which must have been assymetrically cut. These could be interpreted as an indication that some of the fish were being split axially (Colley 1989, 255). A fragment of a large branchiostegal was also recovered with cut-marks which could have been incurred during gutting (Colley 1989). A fragment of cleithra from a 'very large' Gadid was found to have been deliberately pierced, possibly for hanging up the fish for easy transportation.

One further example of a recorded cut is interpreted as having occurred during the life of the fish. A vomer bone from a 'large' cod showed distinctive evidence of pathological growth at the proximal end. This seems to have occured during the healing of an early injury, perhaps a wound caused by a hook while escaping from capture. The malformation was quite clearly inflicted by trauma and there is a clear indication that an object was inserted through the bone and then withdrawn.

6.3.432 Element representation

Relative over- or under-representation of any element in the fish bone assemblage can be explained either in terms of taphonomic bias or fish processing so it is important that the effects of these two are distinguished. In Table 38 the actual numbers of Gadid elements, including those identified to species, recovered from Phase 8 are compared with the total numbers of elements found in 100 complete fish (after Colley 1989, 254).

All elements of the skeleton have been recovered from Phase 8 indicating that fish were brought whole onto the site for processing. The overall pattern of representation reflects robustness of each element, so vertebrae are the most over-represented element and scales the most under-represented. Teeth are generally too small to have been retrieved during sieving. Among the head bones, there is a wide variation in representation. Robust elements such as the dentary, maxilla and quadrate are predictably well represented and the delicate palatine and pterytgoid are relatively rare. The otolith, although a physically robust element, is under-represented. Unlike all other elements, the otolith is calcium carbonate and it is assumed that it has experienced chemical dissolution in the sediments.

Surprisingly few cleithra were recovered. The cleithra is one of the large paired elements from the pectoral girdle of the fish skeleton. It is one of the most robust elements and would survive well in the archaeological deposits. This under-representation

TABLE 38: PHASE 8, GADIDAE COMMONEST ELEMENT REPRESENTATION

Anatomical part	Standard 100 fish	Phase 8
Scale	50000	439
Tooth	50000	59
Fin ray	7000	2494
Spine	5000	923
Branchiostegal	1400	417
Vertebrae	5300	2687
Otolith	200	13
Dentary	200	58
Premaxilla	200	39
Articular	200	34
Maxilla	200	45
Quadrate	200	52
Posttemporal	200	24
Supraclavicle	200	38
Cleithrum	200	7
Symplectic	200	17
Pterytgoid	200	12
Palatine	200	4
Hyomandibular	200	46
Ceratohyal	200	41
Epihyal	200	44
Opercular	200	17
Preopercular	200	25
Vomer	100	23
Parasphenoid	100	26
Basioccipital	100	15

could be caused by the fish-processing techniques employed. In Orkney the most likely form of processing of fish for preserving was that of drying; the windy weather can allow fish to dry quite rapidly. Fish would have been laid out, already filleted, on rocks or racks to dry. The absence of cleithra from assemblages is caused by the cleithra being left *in situ* to create some rigidity in the fillet (J. H. Barrett, pers comm). The dry-salted cod (bacalao) eaten at present in Spain, Italy and Portugal, display whole cleithra and parts of the vertebrae still attached to the fillet. The same occurs with dried fish from Scotland and other Continental products such as the salted whiting (*Merlangius merlangus*) from Belgium.

It is notable that the processed fish from the site were Gadidae, fish with white meat. This type of fish is most suitable for wind drying. For example a beheaded cod could have been hung in the open air to dry; the low temperatures in Orkney would preserve the fish and gradually dry it over a period of about six weeks to a water content of approximately 15 per cent. This product can have a 'shelf-life' of several years if stored correctly and is generally known as 'stock-fish' (Clucas & Sutcliffe 1981: Anderson Smith 1883).

6.3.433 Other processes

The association of the ash-rich deposits, which form the 'farm mound' (Part 6.11), and fish debris may indicate that other processes were undertaken on the site. There is no evidence for smoking of white fish at this time but the rendering of fish liver oil would have required fuel. It is likely that such processing would produce ash deposits. Although there is no artefactual evidence for this activity at St Boniface, it should be noted that cod and ling have been traditionally used for this purpose in Scotland and that the most important species used for the extraction of fish liver oil was young saithe (Smith 1984) which was particularly common at St Boniface.

6.3.434 Conclusion

It is concluded that the evidence from the Phase 8 assemblage is consistent with the processing of whole fish to produce dried fillets (stock fish) which were removed from the site for consumption elsewhere and for the possible extraction of fish liver oil.

6.3.5 Comparison with other Iron Age and Norse Fish Bone Assemblages in the North of Scotland

Freswick Links in Caithness produced fish remains from Pictish and Norse and Late Norse levels (Jones 1991). The general pattern of species and their size representation was similar, comprising immature saithe and medium to large saithe, cod and ling. Although concentration was higher in the Norse levels, there is clear evidence that in the Pictish period exploitation of fish resources was the same as in the Norse and Late Norse periods.

Tuquoy, on the neighbouring island of Westray, produced fish remains from Norse deposits with a species representation which pointed to a fishing practice based on the catch of immature saithe and medium to large saithe, cod, haddock and ling (Colley 1982).

Brough Road, Birsay Bay, Orkney produced Late Iron Age and Norse fish assemblages based primarily on the fishing for immature saithe (Colley 1989). As at Freswick Links, concentration of fish remains was greater in the Norse deposits.

The general pattern of Late Iron Age and Norse period fish bone assemblages in Northern Scotland tends to favour the view that fishing practices were the same but that expansion and intensification of fishing occurs during the Norse period.

The St Boniface fish bone assemblage presents us with an exceptional example of a specialized fishing industry in the Northern Isles of Scotland. There are comparisons with Pictish levels at Freswick Links and Brough Road and Phase 6.3 (Middle Iron Age) at St Boniface. However, Phase 7 (Late Iron Age) shows a definite decline in fishing practices, contrasted markedly by the assemblage from Phase 8 which displays an outstanding example of a specialized fishing industry during the Norse period.

6.4 Bird Bone

Sheila Hamilton-Dyer

6.4.1 Methods

The methods used for identification and recording were based on the FRU (Faunal Remains Unit, Southampton) Method 86 system, with some modifications. Identifications, after Cramp *et al* (1985), were made using the author's modern comparative collections and that at the FRU. Measurements follow von den Driesch (1976). Archive material includes metrical and other data.

6.4.2 Results

Sixty bird bones and fragments were available for examination. All identified species were present in small quantities only, usually one or two fragments. The fragment counts are biased by the presence of seventeen bones of raven from the primary and secondary fills of the secondary enclosure ditch. These are almost certainly from one individual, but are from two adjoining blocks: B252, Phase 6.2 and B211, Phase 6.3. There are additionally five corvid bones in B252 which are probably also from this bird.

Apart from the corvid bones there were fragments of several different seabirds, goose, grouse, domestic fowl, pigeon and blackbird-sized passerines. Three fragments of eagle, probably white-tailed eagle, were recovered from the late spread of ash deposits on Area 2 (B254, Phase 8). This species has been reported from archaeological assemblages all round Britain and bred in Orkney until the mid-nineteenth century.

Carnivore gnawing was present on a goose skull from the primary 'farm mound' deposits (B104, Phase 8). The marks are comparable with those of cat.

The small assemblage from St Boniface is insufficient to analyse the bird exploitation at this site. There are, however, a number of observations which can be made. Papa Westray currently has a large seabird colony at the north end of the island and seabirds have probably always been here in great numbers. It is difficult, however, to determine whether these seabird remains are natural or were deposited as a result of human activities. Butchery marks are present only on three goose fragments from Phases 8 and 9. Seabird exploitation, however, has been extensive in Orkney (Brothwell *et al* 1981; Hamilton-Dyer forthcoming; Serjeantson 1988; Serjeantson forthcoming) and it is interesting to note the presence of gannet, now available in Orkney only from Sule Stack. It seems likely that the sea birds were utilized by the site inhabitants. The passerines may also have been caught but are perhaps more likely to be natural mortalities. The raven is ambiguous. It is still a common cliff breeder and this may be a casual death, yet the raven also had a significant role in northern mythology.

The only positive identification of domestic fowl is from the uppermost deposits in the 'farm mound' (B102, Phase 8). Other galliforms are almost certainly grouse. This is in accordance with evidence from other sites: fowl probably arrived in southern England during the Iron Age (Maltby 1981) and are usually the most frequent bird remains found at post-Romano-British sites. They appear to have arrived late in Orkney. Even on most late Norse sites they remain few in number in comparison with sea birds (Serjeantson 1988).

6.5 The Crustacean Remains

Sheila Hamilton-Dyer

Crustacean remains were recovered from many contexts but very little was noted from Area 3. Relatively large concentrations were recovered from the post-abandonment deposits (B242, Phase 4) over Structure 5, a shell-filled pit on Area 1 (B115, Phase 5), the shell-midden (B113, Phase 6.1) which accumulated over Structure 22, the fill (B213, Phase 6.1) of the primary ditch and from the wall revetment of the secondary enclosure ditch (B212, Phase 6.2). The remains were mostly very small fragments and are difficult to assign to species. Several fragments had been burnt. All of the identified fragments are of *Cancer pagurus*, the edible crab. The size of the claw fragments indicates animals with a carapace of 160–200 mm breadth, a good size for eating.

6.6 Mollusc Shell

Stephen Carter

6.6.1 Methods

Mollusc shells were recovered from sediment samples processed on site. No hand collections were made during the excavation. The samples were processed in a water separation machine using 1 mm and 300 µm mesh sieves for the flot and a 500 µm mesh sieve for the retent.

For shells of marine species, both apical and non-apical shell fragments were sorted from the sample residues. The apical fragments were identified to species or genus using standard keys and guides (Graham 1971; Tebble 1976). Frequency was estimated by counting shell apices for gastropods and valve umbos for bivalve species.

For shells of non-marine species, apical shell fragments were sorted from the sample residues and identified to species or genus using the author's reference collection and standard keys and guides (Kerney & Cameron 1979; Macan 1977).

6.6.2 Marine Shells

6.6.21 Results

The results are summarized by phase in Table 39. No shells were recovered from Phase 2 deposits and, although this may be an artefact of the volume of deposits sampled, the total numbers of shells in Phase 1 and Phase 3 deposits, where larger sediment volumes were processed, are, nonetheless, negligible. With the exception of Phase 2, marine shells were recovered from deposits in all phases of site activity.

The assemblages in all phases are dominated by only two taxa. *Patella* spp. constitute at least 88 per

cent and, together with *Littorina littorea*, they total at least 97 per cent. The only other taxon that contributes more than 1 per cent of the total in any phase is *Cerastoderma edule* in Phase 5 (2 per cent). This is the result of significant numbers of *Cerastoderma edule* in only two contexts: the shell midden (F2145: B237) which accumulated against the exterior of the roundhouse, and a second shell midden (F2181: B215), to the north, which was cut by the primary ditch.

6.6.22 Discussion

The shell assemblages all derive from sieved samples. Therefore, although the numbers of shells may reflect sample size rather than actual abundance, the proportions of the various species in the assemblage are accurate, unlike those derived from hand collections. There are no significant changes in assemblage composition from Phase 4 to Phase 9 and the results suggest that only *Patella* spp. (limpets), *Littorina littorea* (winkle) and *Cerastoderma edule* (cockle) were deliberately collected, the latter only very rarely. All other species arrived as the result of accidental or exceptional collection. Shells of *Littorina littoralis* and *Lacuna vincta* are very small and were probably brought from the shore accidentally on other materials, such as driftwood or seaweed.

The dominance of *Patella* spp. and *Littorina littorea* indicates that a rocky shore, not unlike the modern shoreline, was being exploited. The extreme rarity in these assemblages of another rocky shore species, the common edible mussel (*Mytilus edulis*), suggests that it was absent from this particular coast. *Cerastoderma edule* is a sand-burrowing species and the closest modern populations are in the sandy shore on the east side of the island.

The Iron Age and Norse assemblages from St Boniface may be compared with Neolithic shell

TABLE 39: MARINE SHELL. FREQUENCY OF EACH TAXA BY PHASE

	1	3	4	5	6.1	6.2	6.3	7	8	9
Patella spp.. Various species of limpet	3	1	81	4541	2309	1488	844	120	671	953
Gibbula spp.. Various species of topshell				1						13
Gibbula magus (Linnaeus). Topshell									1	
Gibbula cineraria (Linnaeus). Grey topshell				2						
Calliostoma zizyphinum (Linnaeus). Common topshell										1
Lacuna vincta (Montagu). Banded chink shell					8				1	3
Littorina littoralis (Linnaeus). Flat periwinkle				8	13	3	1		1	8
Littorina littorea (Linnaeus). Winkle	1		5	40	182	126	31	7	87	74
Trivia monacha (da Costa). Cowrie					1					
Nucella lapillus (Linnaeus). Dogwhelk					2				1	
Buccinum undatum (Linnaeus). Common whelk									1	
Mytilus edulis (Linnaeus). Common mussel					2					
Ostrea edulis (Linaeus). Oyster			1							
Cerastoderma edule (Linnaeus). Cockle	3		1	114		8			1	1
Dosinia exolata (Linnaeus).					1					
Venus spp.. Various species of venus						1				
Venus casina (Linnaeus).				1						
Venerupis rhomboides (Pennant). Banded carpet shell.									1	
Ensis spp. Various species of razor shell.				3	4	1				1

assemblages from the Knap of Howar, only 1 km to the south along the coast (Evans & Vaughan 1983). The overall species' list is very similar and *Patella* spp. is again the dominant taxon. The only substantial difference is the higher proportion of *Ostrea edulis* (oyster) shells at the Knap of Howar. Only one shell was recovered at St Boniface, from the uppermost floor level in Structure 4 (B245, Phase 4), but this species constitutes roughly 7 per cent of the total assemblage at the Knap of Howar. It is possible that, although the two sites are close together, the oyster beds were not available to the inhabitants of the St Boniface settlement. However an alternative suggestion is that, as a result of the shoreline and sea floor changes that are known to have occurred here, the local oyster population died out before the Iron Age.

6.6.3 Non-Marine Shells

6.6.31 Results

Non-marine shells have been divided into three habitat categories: terrestrial, fresh water (including marshes) and brackish water.

6.6.32 Discussion

6.6.321 Terrestrial

Low-diversity assemblages of terrestrial snail shells were recovered from thirty-four samples. The limited range of species identified are all part of the modern fauna of Orkney (Kerney 1976) and were all present on Papa Westray in the Neolithic period at the Knap of Howar (Evans & Vaughan 1983). Most of the assemblages contain modern shells of *Vitrea contracta* and *Oxychilus* spp., presumably as a result of these species entering the vacuous rubble sediments from the cliff-face. It may be noted that only one sample from the relatively stone-free 'farm mound' sediments (F1035D: B107, Phase 7) contains any terrestrial shells. The presence of modern shells makes it impossible to interpret these assemblages in terms of prehistoric environment with any confidence. The relative abundance of modern shells indicates that prehistoric shells were not present or have not been preserved in most contexts.

6.6.322 Fresh water

Only seven shells from freshwater species were identified but their presence is interesting and requires some explanation. It is not possible to distinguish between the shells of *Succinea putris* and *Oxyloma pfeifferi* in all cases but given their current geographical distributions (Kerney 1976), the single shell from the uppermost backfill deposits (F2050: B213, Phase 6.1) of the primary enclosure ditch, is probably *O. pfeifferi*. Both species inhabit marshes or

wet grassland and are not truly aquatic. This is also the habitat of *Lymnaea truncatula*, which is present in the 'farm mound' deposits (F1032C & F1042C: B103, Phase 8). *Anisus leucostoma* occurs in a wide range of habitats including marshes, temporary ponds and permanent lakes. All three have been classified by Boycott (1936) as soft water species, capable of living in a wide range of water types and they are all recorded in present-day Orkney (Kerney 1976). None of these species could have lived in the sediments in which they were found. Their presence, therefore, must represent accidental incorporation with other materials. Three freshwater/marsh resources may have been exploited: water, vegetation and peat. The fact that some of the shells of *Lymnaea truncatula* were burnt could suggest that they were brought on to the site in peat for fuel but the evidence is clearly extremely limited.

6.6.323 Brackish water

Only one brackish water species has been identified, *Hydrobia ulvae*. This is found in a wide range of brackish water habitats including estuaries, salt marshes and coastal lagoons. The precise source of these shells is not apparent but their presence on site clearly results from accidental transport with other materials from the shore. As in the case of the small marine shells, driftwood and seaweed are possible vehicles for *Hydrobia ulvae*.

6.7 The Charred Plant Remains

Sheila Boardman

6.7.1 Introduction

One hundred and eighty-four samples (*c*. 2–70 l), representing 144 soil contexts, were processed for the recovery of ecofactual and artefactual remains. Samples were processed using a water separation machine (Kenward *et al* 1980). The light fractions (flots) were collected in sieves with mesh sizes of 1 mm and 300 microns, and the heavy residue (retent), in a 1 mm mesh. All fractions were allowed to dry slowly before being sorted.

The greater than 1 mm flots were sorted completely, by eye or using a low power light microscope. Normally 50 per cent of each retent was sorted. Retents from dating samples were totally sorted. No 300 micron flots were sorted. Macroplant identifications were carried out using a modern seed reference collection and various reference keys and texts. Particular use was made of Nilsson & Hjelmqvist's (1967) *Carex* key, as well as photographs and descriptions of *Carex* nutlets, which were supplied by Camilla Dickson, Department of Botany, University of Glasgow. In general, the retents produced few plant macrofossils. Excepting the mineralized seeds, there were few plant remains or species which were not represented in the flots. It is possible, however, that some rarer classes of plant material were missed altogether.

More than 140 samples, representing 128 soil contexts, produced charred plant remains. Mineralized seeds were present in a few samples. Nomenclature follows Clapham *et al* (1987).

6.7.2 Species Represented

6.7.21 Cultivated plants

Barley was the most frequent cereal found throughout the site. It is represented by hulled and naked grains and a few six-row barley (*Hordeum vulgare* L.) rachis internodes. Asymmetric grains also indicate the presence of six-row barley, in hulled and naked grain (*H. vulgare* L. var. *nudum*) forms.

Oat (*Avena* sp.) grains cannot be reliably identified to species without their accompanying chaff (floret bases). Where oat chaff was present in the deposits, the fragments tended to be poorly preserved and indeterminate to species. Two oat species were identified in samples from the Phase 8 'farm mound' deposits (B103 & 104): black, bristle, or pointed oat (*A. strigosa* Schreb.), and wild oat (*A. fatua* L.). Black oat was widely cultivated in Scotland in the past.

The other cultivated species was flax (*Linum usitatissimum* L.). Flax seeds were also common in samples from the 'farm mound'. Many seeds were not well preserved and occasionally fusing had occurred. Flax may have been utilized for fibres, or its seeds pressed for oil. The protein-rich seeds may also have been used to supplement the diet of humans and animals (Bond & Hunter 1987; Jensen 1979; Bell & Dickson 1989).

6.7.22 Wild species

Edible species included crowberry (*Empetrum nigrum* L.), although this is not very palatable, wild radish (*Raphanus raphanistrum* L.) and the brassicas (*Brassica*). Black mustard (*Brassica* cf *nigra* (L.) Koch) is another plant with oil-yielding seeds. Charlock (*Sinapis*), however, the frequent alternative to the brassicas, is a very common field weed. A number of wild species are known for their use historically, to make a crude flour or gruel in times of poor harvest, e.g. fat hen (*Chenopodium album* type), knotgrass (*Polygonum aviculare* type) and corn spurrey (*Spergula arvensis* L.). These are also very common field weeds.

Another useful plant is ling (*Calluna vulgaris* (L.) Hull). This is fairly abundant on the cliffs and moors of modern Westray, and may have been collected for thatching, bedding, furnishings or a variety of other purposes (Edlin 1973). Crowberry (*Empetrum nigrum* L.) is typical of the drier parts of bogs and moors, on hillslopes and at higher altitudes where *Calluna-Erica cinerea* plant communities are found. Crowberry stems have many similar uses to those of

ling. The frequency of small twigs, including ling, in the St Boniface deposits, however, may be more a reflection of fuel usage, in particular the utilization of peat and heathland turves (Parts 6.8, 7.1 & below).

Other possible weeds of cultivation were orache (*Atriplex*), brome/chess (*Bromus*), bindweed (*Fallopia*), hemp-nettle (*Galeopsis*), cleavers (*Galium*), chickweed (*Stellaria*) and penny-cress (*Thlaspi*). More typical of grassy locations are sedge (*Carex*), heath grass (*Danthonia*), plantain (*Plantago*), cinquefoil (*Potentilla*), buttercup (*Ranunculus*), yellow-rattle (*Rhinanthus*), dock (*Rumex*) and clover (*Trifolium*). Most of these are also found in archaeological crop assemblages (Greig 1991) and many of the taxa above can occur naturally in coastal locations. Other possible habitats include damp ground (*Carex, Polygonum persicaria* L.), and scrub (*Galeopsis*).

Species with a preference for more acidic soils include wild radish, ling, crowberry, heath grass and sheep's sorrel (*Rumex acetosella* L.). Heath grass is common in moorland today but the frequency of its seeds in some archaeological grain deposits has suggested that it is a former cornfield weed (van der Veen 1987; Greig 1991). The sedges from the site, tentatively identified to species level, are all capable of growth in neutral to basic soils. Many sedges have a preference for damp, acidic soils. Corn spurrey (*Spergula arvensis* L.) is found predominantly today on light, well-drained soils. The other wild species are generally tolerant of a wide range of habitats and soils.

6.7.3 Discussion

6.7.31 Distribution and composition of the charred plant samples

Cereal grains, chaff and straw, and the seeds of wild species were recovered. Also present were stems, rhizomes and tuberous material. However, only fourteen samples had more than 100 charred plant components. These came from F2136 (B246, Phase 4), F2028 and F2033 (B225, Phase 6.2), F2004 (B224, Phase 6.3), F1048C (B107, Phase 7), F1062B, F1052B, F1051B, F1105A and F1110C (B104, Phase 8), and F1039C, F1030C, F1039D and F1032D (B103, Phase 8). Most of these samples were dominated by cereal grains.

6.7.311 Areas 2 and 3

Cultivated plant remains from these areas comprised almost exclusively barley grains. Area 3 had very few identifiable plant remains. A single Area 2 sample (F2000: B223, Phase 8), associated with a late hearth deposit, produced four indeterminate oat grains. The principal find in the earlier phases for all areas of the site seems to be naked six-row barley, although many grains could not be identified beyond genus (*H.* sp.). Hulled barley grains were also present in the earlier deposits.

Two Area 2 samples (F2028 & F2033: B225, Phase 6.2) were particularly cereal rich, with approximately 340 and 820 cereal grains respectively. Both are derived from dump deposits below Structure 13. These are deposits of almost pure barley, suggestive of fully processed crops (Hillman 1981; 1984). Only hulled grains were securely identified, but the material was poorly preserved. Both samples also contained many 'heat-blasted' cereal fragments. None of the grains showed signs of germination or insect attack. These crop products may have become accidentally charred during storage or grain drying.

Of the well-stratified deposits from Area 2, seventeen samples produced charred plant remains. Context F2145 (B237, Phase 5), from a shell midden which accumulated against the exterior wall of the roundhouse, had a few badly preserved cereals, including naked six-row barley. The floor surfaces inside Structure 4 (B245, Phase 4) had five productive samples. These produced small amounts of naked and indeterminate barley grains and/or a few wild species. The latter included brassica/charlock, sedge, heath grass, dock and clover. Context F2144 had eight cereal straw nodes. The mineralized seeds in context F2139 may not be contemporary with the charred material. Mineralization is a natural process and this may have occurred long after the deposits were created or used.

No plant remains were recovered from the post-roundhouse ash mound (F2036) or the soil (F2057) which developed in its upper surface (both B254, Phase 8). The rubble and midden fills (B224, Phase 6.3) associated with the abandonment of Structures 7 and 11 produced small amounts of hulled and indeterminate barley, and a range of wild species not dissimilar from those recovered from the Area 1 'farm mound' (see below). These included brassica/charlock, ling, and many sedges, including common sedge (*Carex* cf *nigra* (L.) Reichard); also heath grass, ribwort plantain, knotgrass, cinquefoil, dock, chickweed and clover. These reflect a variety of possible habitats, including cultivated fields, lowland grassland or dune vegetation, hillsides, cliffs or heath, and some damper ground. One sample (F2062: B224, Phase 6.3) produced two straw nodes.

Naked and indeterminate barley grains were recovered from the floor deposits associated with the primary entrance façade (F2107: B210, Phase 6.1). The wild species included ling, sedge, goosefoot/orache, heath grass and bindweed. Five indeterminate barley grains were recovered from the fill of the primary enclosure ditch (F2050: B213, Phase 6.1). A handful of barley grains were recovered from the post-abandonment deposits (F2097: B207, Phase 6.3) of the secondary entrance façade. No plant material was recovered from the fill of the secondary enclosure ditch (B211, Phase 6.3).

In summary, of the well-stratified deposits from Area 2, only two samples produced more than fifty plant remains (F2004 & F2058: B224, Phase 6.3). Cereal chaff was absent throughout and cereal straw nodes were scarce. The samples were generally dominated by barley grains. The Block 224 (Phase 6.3) deposits produced a wider range of wild plant species. Some of these may have grown in cultivated fields (see above), although most can be found today in grassland ranging from the seashore and dunes (e.g. orache, chickweed and clover) to the clifftops (ling). Ling would not have grown as a weed of barley but the situation is less clear for the other acid-loving species present, as these may reflect simply the collection of heather, peat and turves as fuel, or the cultivation of more acidic soils.

6.7.312 Area 1

The earlier deposits on Area 1 (B118, Phase 1, and B116, Phase 5) are characterized by indeterminate barley grains. Hulled barley, oat and flax were present in the later 'farm mound' (B103 & B104, Phase 8) deposits. A handful of flax grains were also recovered from the buried ground surface (B105, Phase 7).

Samples from the buried ground surface (B105, Phase 7) and the 'farm mound' above (B102, B103, & B104, Phase 8) produced a similar range of cultivated plants, but these samples also differed in many respects. The oat grains from B103 and B104 (Phase 8) include black oat and wild oat. Oat grains were present in much greater numbers here than in the underlying Late Iron Age ash dumps (B107, Phase 7). They dominate a number of samples in the upper part of the 'farm mound' (B103, Phase 8). Meanwhile, flax seeds were more numerous in the lower part of the 'farm mound' (B104, Phase 8). Both major 'farm mound' deposits produced generally greater quantities of plant remains than the earlier midden (B107, Phase 7), and also a wider range of wild plant species.

Many of the wild plant species have been noted elsewhere at St Boniface. Ling was present only in three Area 1 samples. Meanwhile, crowberry seeds were more frequent than in other parts of the site. The other wild species in the Area 1 samples, particularly those from B103 and B104 (Phase 8), again indicate a variety of possible habitats and sources of material.

Two other factors have a bearing on the origins of the plant material in the 'farm mound'. First, samples here contained much rhizomatous and tuberous material. This might suggest that cereals, together with associated weeds, were harvested by uprooting (cf. Hillman 1981). Alternatively, this material may be derived from turves/peat burnt as fuel. Both activities may have taken place, with the refuse from each becoming mixed on the 'farm mound'. In view of the general absence of cereal chaff and straw, however, and the large numbers of ling stems (Part 6.8), the latter hypothesis would seem to be the more likely.

Secondly, many cereal grains in samples from the 'farm mound' showed signs of sprouting and/or insect attack. This implies some deliberate destruction of cultivated plants. Elsewhere at St Boniface, small-scale crop cleaning operations and accidents associated with cooking or grain drying, may account for the bulk of the plant remains.

6.7.32 Origins of the crops

The general lack of cereal chaff and straw may be a reflection of only limited crop processing at St Boniface, because crops were imported to the site already processed. However, this situation may also reflect the many conditions under which such fragile plant remains can be destroyed, such as fierce household fires, disturbance and reworking of deposits, or moisture fluctuations due to freely draining soils.

The low numbers of plant remains per litre of soil, and poor preservation in general, hint at losses of fragile material. Meanwhile, it was only rarely possible to distinguish between crop products that may have been destroyed accidentally and crop-processing refuse. Different types of refuse also seem to have been mixed, in hearths and/or middens, particularly crop-processing debris and fuel waste. These are demonstrated, on the one hand, by the small numbers of cereal grains throughout the deposits. Losses of the valuable crop product (as suggested for two Area 2 samples above) should be rare occurrences. Meanwhile, burnt amorphous material and certain plant species, e.g. ling, attest to the use of peat/turves as fuel.

Three general conclusions can therefore be drawn. First, on-site crop-processing activities could not be identified clearly from the charred plant remains. Secondly, variations in crop-related activities, between different structures and through time, were difficult to discern. Thirdly, local cultivation of the crops present, although likely, could not be demonstrated. Also uncertain, therefore, is whether Iron Age and Norse cultivation was concentrated in the dune or machair zone, as in recent times, or whether it was spread more widely onto the acid soils. It was also impossible to identify, further, the areas which may have been used for turf cutting.

6.7.33 Other sites

Six-row barley is the principal cereal species recovered from Iron Age sites in Scotland. At Dun Mor Vaul on the Hebridean island of Tiree, hulled and naked six-row barley grains were present (Renfrew 1974). Naked barley grains and small quantities of possible emmer wheat (*Triticum dicoccum* Schubl.) were recovered from Bu Broch, Orkney (Dickson 1987, 137–42). At Crosskirk Broch in Caithness, hulled barley grains and a single seed of flax were found (Dickson & Dickson 1984, 147–55). Meanwhile, at Warebeth Broch, Stromness, Orkney, a rare find of human coprolites revealed the probable remains of a meaty broth to which barley grains and flax seeds had been added (Bell & Dickson 1989). On the Scottish mainland, hulled six-row barley, some wheat (where identifiable, emmer), and oat (including *A. strigosa* Schreb.), seem to be the norm (Boyd 1988; Greig 1991).

Cultivated plants in the earlier Iron Age levels at St Boniface are confined to barley. Flax and oats are predominantly associated with the 'farm mound' deposits. Wheat was not present in any of the samples examined from the site.

Norse sites in the Birsay Bay area on mainland Orkney, have produced hulled six-row barley, cultivated oat (*Avena sativa* L.) and wild oat, plus a range of wild species reflecting the local environment (Donaldson *et al* 1981; Donaldson 1986). Nearby, at Saevar Howe, hulled six-row barley, oat and flax were recovered from Norse house floors. Similar remains, in quantity, are cited from Barvas Machair, Lewis, in the Western Isles (Dickson 1983, 114).

At the multi-period settlement of Pool, Sanday, flax appears to be a Viking introduction. It was not apparently present in late Iron Age or Pictish levels (Bond & Hunter 1987). Closer to St Boniface, at Tuquoy on neighbouring Westray, pre-Norse deposits were not encountered but the now familiar Norse crops were present: hulled six-row barley, oats and flax (Nye & Boardman forthcoming). The wild species present at Tuquoy and St Boniface are also very similar, not surprisingly given their proximity. A narrower range of wild plant species was present at St Boniface, however, reflecting possibly the less extensive deposits at the latter site, as well as poorer preservation conditions and more impoverished local flora. Meanwhile, at the majority of the Iron Age and Norse sites discussed above, crowberry, ling and other plant species which represent blanket bog or grassland heath communities were recovered. This demonstrates the importance of these plant communities in the largely treeless environment which existed in Orkney by the mid-Flandrian period (Donaldson 1986).

Little is known about Medieval agriculture in the Northern Isles. Activity apparently continues at some Norse sites, although this is greatly reduced in scale or intermittent and related largely to the kelp burning industry. At Tuquoy, barley and oats continue to be present in post-Norse deposits although this may be due, in part, to the reworking of old material (Nye & Boardman forthcoming). Elsewhere in Scotland, the evidence for medieval agriculture is heavily biased towards the large urban centres, where a mosaic of regional differences seem to be reflected in the plant material (Boyd 1988).

6.7.4 Conclusions

The charred plant evidence from Iron Age and later deposits at St Boniface fits well with the general picture that is emerging for agriculture in Northern Scotland. This picture currently reveals quite a high degree of uniformity, at least in the major crops present. Variations are also beginning to emerge, with the uptake of different crop species possibly a reflection of differing local conditions and also of differing crop husbandry practices. Details of the latter were difficult to extract from the St Boniface assemblage because of the mixed nature of the samples.

Rubble layers, middens and redeposited 'farm mound' deposits are not the most promising contexts for archaeobotanical investigation. These are likely to contain the most mixed plant remains reflecting a wide variety of activities and possible sources, e.g. from barns and byres, construction and furnishing materials, hearth debris, crop-processing waste, food debris and so on. Meanwhile, more discrete deposits such as floors, ditches and pits, which may have been associated with particular crop-related activities, are likely to have been regularly cleaned. This appears to be reflected in samples from floor deposits and other well-stratified layers in Areas 2 and 3 at St Boniface.

Fortunately, the very detailed sampling programme has enabled a broad level of temporal resolution to be achieved, even in the complex Area 1 deposits. This, and the results gained from the current study, may be further enhanced by experimental soil micro-morphological work (Part 6.11), and the development of new techniques for the identification of difficult groups of charred plant macrofossils, particularly root and stem tissues.

6.8 Carbonized Wood

Anne Crone

6.8.1 Introduction

Selected samples of charcoal were examined to determine what kinds of materials were burnt on the site, whether these were available locally and whether any changes could be detected in the fuel resource over time.

Samples from twenty-four contexts were examined. The only criterion for selection was the presence of identifiable fragments, defined as those greater than 4 mm along at least one axis. The samples that could be identified are unevenly distributed throughout the stratigraphy of the site. For example, eight of the twenty-four samples were derived from the 'farm mound' deposits of Phase 8, while only one sample of identified material was associated with Phase 5 deposits.

Heather (Calluna vulgaris) can be identified macroscopically by the twisted and pitted nature of its stems and it is therefore possible to recognize, at a glance, whether a sample is composed entirely of heather or whether other species are present. Conifers can also be rapidly identified as to order (i.e. Coniferae) by examination of their transverse- or cross-section but can be identified as to genus or species only if the fragments are large enough for other sections to be prepared. Thus, in Table 40, heather and conifers are quantified as proportions of the whole sample while other identified species are quantified in terms of numbers of identified fragments.

6.8.2 Results

Heather was present in all but four of the twenty-four contexts examined. Samples from nine contexts were composed entirely of heather and in another four examples heather formed 99 per cent of the total sample. Heather would not have been used as a fuel itself but would form the residue after burning peat. Conifers were found in fourteen samples. Spruce (cf. Picea), pine (Pinus sylvestris) and one tentative identification of larch (cf. Larix) were identified among the conifers. Fragments of willow (Salix sp.), birch (Betula sp.), hazel (Corylus avellana), oak (Quercus sp.) and ash (Fraxinus excelsior) were also identified in very small amounts.

TABLE 40: CARBONIZED WOOD

F no.	Block	Phase	Species/Order	Quantity
2140	248	3	Coniferae	99%
			Pinus sylvestris	(2)
2146	248	3	Picea	(4)
			Corylus avellana	(1)
2170	250	3	Betula sp.	(1)
			Calluna vulgaris	99%
2155	243	4	Fraxinus excelsior	(1)
			Pinus sylvestris	(5)
			Calluna vulgaris	(*)
			Coniferae	99%
2144	245	4	Pinus sylvestris	(2)
			Picea	(2)
			Coniferae	99%
			Calluna vulgaris	(*)
2143	246	4	Calluna vulgaris	99%
			Salix sp.	(1)
3020	304	5	Calluna vulgaris	100%
2045	204	6.1	Picea	(5)
2107	210	6.1	cf Larix	(1)
			Salix sp.	(1)
			Calluna vulgaris	99%
2033	225	6.2	Calluna vulgaris	100%
2062	224	6.3	Calluna vulgaris	100%
1011	105	7	Picea	(2)
			Coniferae	99%
1021	107	7	Coniferae	50%
			Calluna vulgaris	50%
			Pinus sylvestris	(2)
1034	107	7	Pinus sylvestris	(2)
			Coniferae	75%
			Calluna vulgaris	(*)
1065	107	7	Calluna vulgaris	(*)
			Pinus sylvestris	(2)
			Quercus sp.	(3)
1030	103	8	Pinus sylvestris	(1)
			Corylus avellana	(1)
			Picea	(1)
			Calluna vulgaris	(*)
1039	103	8	Calluna vulgaris	(*)
			Salix sp.	(1)
			Coniferae	(*)
			Pinus sylvestris	(1)
1045	104	8	Calluna vulgaris	100%
1051	104	8	Calluna vulgaris	100%
1052	104	8	Calluna vulgaris	100%
1063	104	8	Calluna vulgaris	99%
			Coniferae	(*)
1105	104	8	Pinus sylvestris	(7)
			Calluna vulgaris	50%
			Coniferae	50%
1110	104	8	Calluna vulgaris	100%
3000	201	9	Betula sp.	(9)
			Calluna vulgaris	(*)
			Corylus avellana	(1)
			Quercus sp.	(1)

(*) present

6.8.3 Discussion

There are, as yet, no pollen data available from Papa Westray but the general picture from pollen profiles on mainland Orkney and neighbouring Westray is one of a virtually treeless environment from the mid-Holocene onwards (Bunting 1993). Birch, willow and hazel are present in small quantities in the pollen spectra throughout the Flandrian and today these species can still be found in small patches of scrub woodland in sheltered positions (Berry 1985, 71). It is therefore possible that the birch, hazel and willow found in the St Boniface assemblage formed part of the local tree-cover of the island but the minute amounts retrieved indicate their rarity.

All other species in the assemblage must have been brought onto the island, either arriving as driftwood or by direct importation. Without the presence of marine molluscan boreholes in the wood it is impossible to state categorically that the timbers burnt were driftwood. However, prior to the appearance of the Norse in the Northern Isles, it is unlikely that there would have been an active timber trade in the North Atlantic and it seems most reasonable to assume that, prior to Phase 8, the wood used at St Boniface was driftwood. The use of driftwood for fuel and for building is well attested in the Northern and Western Isles from the Neolithic onwards (Dickson 1992). Graham (1952) has demonstrated, on the basis of North Atlantic currents, that the source of spruce driftwood is almost certainly America, while pine could have come from either America or Scotland, depending on species.

6.8.4 Conclusion

The occupants of the site at St Boniface clearly used whatever was available as fuel. Throughout the 2500 years or more that the site was occupied there was a heavy reliance on peat or turf (Part 7.1), with driftwood and local scrub woodland being exploited whenever available. This pattern of fuel usage did not change throughout the occupation of the site. Peat resources on the smaller islands were seriously depleted by the eighteenth century and the movement of fuels from one island to another is well documented (Berry 1985, 176).

6.9 Pollen Analysis of the Late Iron Age Buried Soil

Richard Tipping

6.9.1 Introduction

The buried soil (F1011: B105, Phase 7) exposed at St Boniface satisfies all criteria devised following work on similar deposits at Biggar Common, Lanarkshire (Tipping *et al* 1994). The profile was well preserved, intact with a turf-layer present, was well sealed by overlying deposits from post-depositional processes,

and the relationship between all likely contaminants and the soil profile can be examined. The profile is also well understood from soil micromorphological analysis (Part 6.11).

The sediments were pollen-analysed at a sampling resolution not normally adopted for such deposits (Tipping *et al* 1994), and results are compatible with soil micromorphological interpretation. When combined with measures of pollen concentration and preservation, this approach can allow the isolation of a 'valid' pollen assemblage, one that can be closely linked to the vegetation and land-use practices existing immediately prior to burial, from ones dominated by deteriorated or reworked pollen.

6.9.2 Methods

The buried soil and overlying sediments were contained within Monolith 16, adjacent to Sample Column C (Illus 175). A Kubiena tin (length 8.0 cm) was inserted, encompassing both the sediment of F1045 (B104, Phase 8) (the uppermost 3.0 cm of the Kubiena tin) and the buried soil (3.0–8.0 cm). The Kubiena tin was levered out and saturated with distilled water before being sealed and placed in a freezer.

When the sample had frozen, the soil block was extracted from the Kubiena tin and thin slices of sediment shaved off with a scalpel. Twenty-three slices were obtained, with a mean thickness of 0.34 ± 0.07 cm. From these slices, subsamples of volume 0.6 cc were taken for pollen analyses, and the remainder used for the determination of percentage dry weight, percentage carbon (by l-o-i at 550 °C for 4 hours) and percentage free carbonate (by l-o-i at 925 °C for 4 hours).

The palynological subsamples were treated by standard chemical techniques (cf. Moore *et al* 1991), including rigorous hydrofluoric acid digestion, and separation of coarse and fine mineral particles through 150 μm and 10 μm sieves respectively. *Lycopodium* tablets (Stockmarr 1971) were added for pollen concentration determination at the earliest stage. The residue was stained, embedded in silicon oil, and slides analysed on a Prior microscope at magnification ×400, and magnification ×1000 for difficult grains and all size measurements.

In addition to conventional percentage and concentration counts, the preservation state of each grain was assessed on the dominance of one of six categories: well preserved, slightly or heavily crumpled (differentiation was generally made on whether one or both axes of the grain were folded), broken, corroded or amorphous. Grains rendered indeterminable were also recorded and similarly categorized.

Microscopic charcoal was extremely abundant. Because of this, charcoal had necessarily to be counted on only a small proportion of the area covered for pollen counts, and the results multiplied to approximate totals corresponding to full pollen counts.

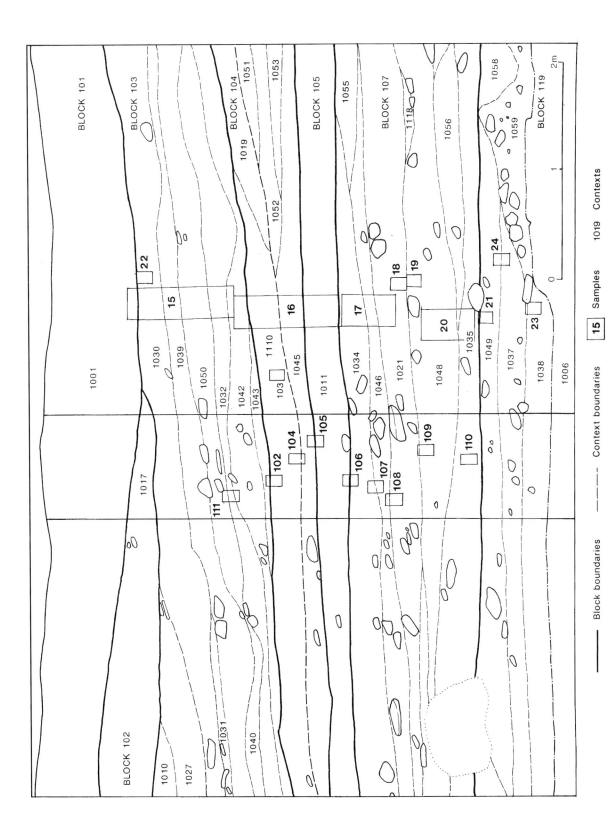

Illus 175　　Area 1 section at Sample Column C

6.9.3 Results

Illus 176 shows the rather generalized stratigraphy obtained from description of the Kubiena tin, supplemented by the more detailed description available from thin-section analysis (Part 6.11), and the sedimentological data from the twenty-three sediment slices. The micro-stratigraphy is also generalized, in that it was obtained from thin-section description of a profile sampled some 50–60 cm from Monolith 16, and need not correspond precisely with the stratigraphy analysed here. In particular, the lenses of reworked soil profile material (F1011) within F1045 do not correspond with any of the samples analysed in this report.

Illus 177 and 178 contain the data for the twelve pollen spectra analysed. Samples 6–8 are from F1045, the sediment sealing the buried soil. Since the concern in examining this sediment was to recognize grains potentially contaminating the soil surface, only the lowermost 1 cm of F1045 was analysed. Sample 9 (2.9–3.2 cm) is predominantly from the uppermost part of the turf-line, but may in part contain material from overlying sediment. Contiguous samples were then counted until Sample 16, below which it was decided on various lines of evidence (Part 6.9.4 below) that pollen spectra were of increasingly uncertain value. Illus 177 contains determinations of pollen concentrations for total dryland pollen (t.l.p.; those taxa in Illus 178 from *Alnus* to Umbelliferae inclusive), total pollen (t.p.: all pollen and spore types) and for t.p. plus all indeterminable grains. Also plotted are ratios derived from these values, and the preservation states for determinable and indeterminable grains. Illus 178 presents the percentages of total pollen for all pollen taxa, with concentration values for the major taxa, *Calluna*, Gramineae < 8 μm anl-D and Compositae Liguliflorae, the pollen sum attained, numbers of t.p. taxa per spectrum and charcoal counts.

6.9.4 Interpretation

6.9.41 Sedimentological data

Illus 176 shows that all analysed sediments have very similar sedimentological properties. The boundaries between them cannot be distinguished on these data. The overlying sediment is characterized by more erratic carbon values, but mean values for samples 1–8 are closely comparable with the turf-line. Sample 9 contained a noticeable amount of bone, which has induced an anomalous value for free carbonate.

Slight but more distinct changes occur within the soil profile, where below sample 12, percentage dry weight rises consistently. This is probably related to increased packing density in the lower horizon. Carbon percentages are also slightly lower below sample 13. These differences suggest that the horizons detected in thin-section (Part 6.11) can be

recognized in these samples, but with the turf-line having a thickness of only 1.6 cm here, covering samples 9 to 14.

6.9.42 Soil pollen data

The soil micromorphological interpretation (Part 6.11) indicates that in all respects other than abundance and form of organic matter, the turf-line is comparable to the lower soil horizon (B107), and is in effect an overlay on a pre-existing deposit. F1011 appears to be an anthropogenic deposit, modified by pedogenic processes. It is polleniferous, first, through subaerial deposition of pollen onto the ground surface and, secondly, through possibly containing an 'original' pollen assemblage derived from the existing sediment.

With the exception of sample 13, pollen concentrations consistently decline down-profile. If it is assumed that addition of new material to the soil surface is greater than removal of pre-existing material through pollen translocation and decay, and given uniform rates of pollen translocation below the soil surface, a profile of declining concentrations will result from the fact that greater concentrations of pollen can be downwashed from the soil surface through time.

Pollen translocation is, however, unlikely to have proceeded at a uniform rate. Soil micromorphological analysis (Part 6.11) notes increases of fine sediment in the lower parts of F1011, and the sedimentological data suggest a higher packing density lower in the profile. Losses through pollen translocation should therefore be reduced, leading to increased pollen concentrations at depth. However, pollen concentrations continue to decline. It is necessary to invoke further losses, through processes of deterioration. Thus, on *a priori* grounds, the pollen assemblages in horizons below the top of the soil will be distorted to an extent by differential preservation, and this can be inferred for the lower soil horizon (below). There is, however, evidence of a sharp discontinuity at the boundary between the turf-line and the lower soil horizon; sample 13 has anomalously high pollen concentrations (Illus 177), and the boundary is characterized in Illus 178 by a sharp change in proportions of Gramineae and Compositae Liguliflorae. It is necessary to assume some impediment to pollen translocation at this boundary, although it is not seen in the sedimentological data.

Pollen spectra within the turf-line can be expected to retain a small proportion of the original pollen assemblage, and addition of some recycled pollen, virtually identical to the original assemblage, but will predominantly comprise 'fresher' material which accumulated during the formation of the turf-line. The pseudo-stratification apparent in the turf-line as a result of the survival of organic laminae (observed in thin-section) might imply some confidence in the interpretation of pollen spectra as a stratigraphic sequence.

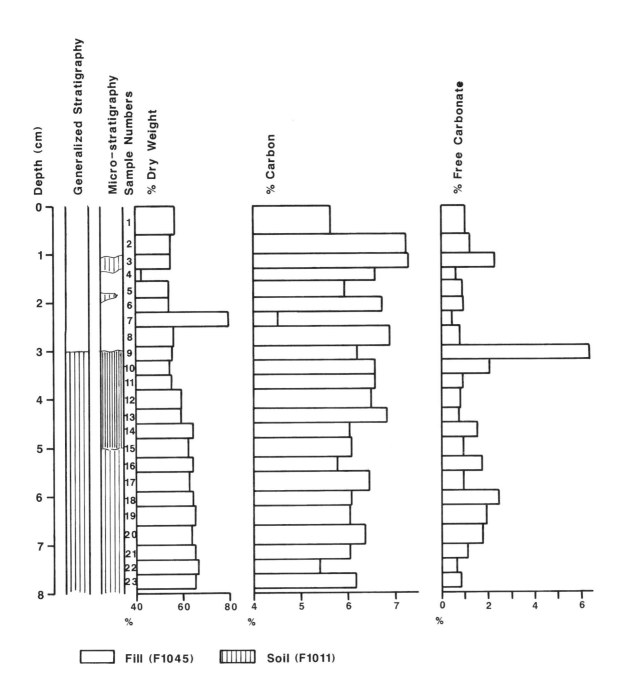

Illus 176   Sediment stratigraphy, soil micromorphological stratigraphy, sample numbers and thicknesses
                 and sedimentological data

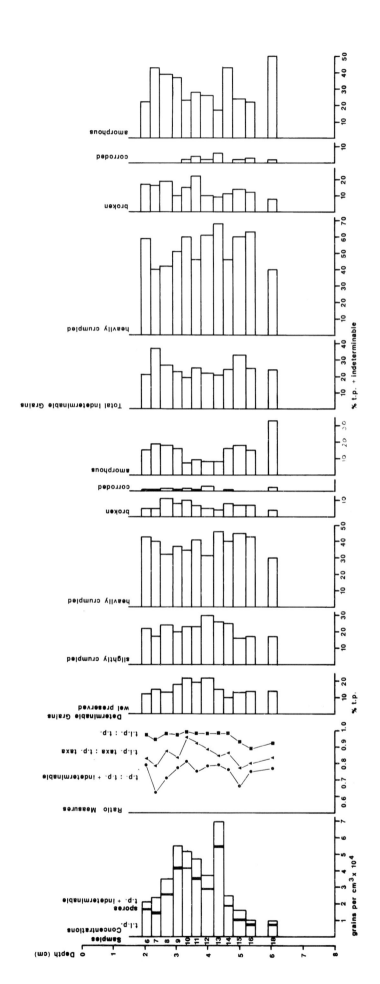

Illus 177   Pollen concentration data, concentration and taxonomic ratios, and preservation data for determinable and indeterminable pollen grains

6.9.43 Reliability of pollen spectra for palaeoecological interpretation

The interpretative value of spectra at St Boniface is much harder to assess than at Biggar Common (Tipping *et al* 1994) because fern spores (Filicales) were virtually absent from the samples. The intensity of pollen deterioration (Illus 177) is the only remaining approach and all spectra are poorly preserved. Crumpling is the dominant deterioration type and the severity of deterioration is clear from the far greater percentages of grains heavily, rather than slightly, crumpled. Consistently more than 20 per cent of all grains are rendered indeterminable, and of these the overwhelming majority are again heavily crumpled. It is almost certain that these indeterminable grains included taxa not recorded as determinable grains, and so there must be some loss of information in these assemblages. How serious this is cannot be determined. Although losses are suspected, it cannot be established whether these losses render the diagram uninterpretable. For example, numbers of taxa recorded per spectrum are consistently high (Illus 178), as high as commonly encountered from well-preserved organic sediments, and this suggests that losses of taxa are relatively few.

Intense levels of crumpling can be expected to preserve preferentially robust, thick-walled pollen grains. There is evidence in the lower soil horizon that this has occurred. Compositae Liguliflorae is a robust grain and, in addition, through its distinctive appearance, is recognisable when represented by only fragments; *Pinus* is not robust, but is similarly very distinctive even if only fragments are represented. Both these types show increases in the lower soil horizon. These increases are interpreted as indicating preferential loss of weaker-walled pollen types in the lower soil horizon, and this is reflected also in the increased numbers of microscopic charcoal fragments relative to the abundance of pollen (e.g. as fragments per 100 t.p. in Illus 178) in the lower soil horizon.

6.9.44 Possible contributing sources to the turf-line pollen assemblages

Illus 177 and 178 show that samples 6–8, from F1045, are polleniferous, and clearly a potential source of contamination to the turf-line. More problematic still is the observation that there are few differences, either in taxa represented or preservation states, between these sediments. Mixing of components within the turf-line is seen in the organic laminae, presumed buried by surface-casting earthworms, but burial beneath an overlying sediment would greatly limit or halt any such process. In addition, F1045 contains, in its lowermost 2 cm, lenses of material comparable to the soil profile (Part 6.11). The mode of emplacement is unclear, but as well as discrete lenses, smaller fragments might be expected to be more intimately

and uniformly mixed. This suggests that the soil profile is more likely to have been the source of pollen to the sediment rather than *vice versa*.

Their proximity to the turf-line might lead to the assumption that these lenses were derived from this unit. However, there are indications that the pollen assemblages within F1045 bear a stronger resemblance to those in the lower part of F1011 than to the turf-line. For example, *Huperzia selago*, *Sphagnum* and *Potentilla* type are found only in the sediment and lower soil horizon (allowing for mixed pollen assemblages in both samples 9 and 13), and there are notably higher proportions of *Pteridium* in these two sediments also.

Although the representation of spores (*Huperzia*, *Sphagnum*, *Pteridium*) is enhanced in poorly preserved pollen assemblages, processes of post-depositional deterioration which affected the pollen assemblage of F1045 but not those of the immediately underlying turf-line are difficult to accept, given their generally close comparability, and it is considered that the counts from F1045 are representative of a pollen assemblage which has always been different from that in the turf-line. The simplest interpretation is that F1045 derived from the lower soil horizon of F1011, or material of comparable origin.

6.9.45 Palaeoecological interpretation of the turf-line

In reconstructing the vegetation that formed during accumulation of the turf-line, caution must be exercised on two counts: first, because part of the assemblages in these spectra probably derive from the original pollen content of F1011 and, secondly, because it is suspected that some losses of taxa have occurred even within the turf-line as a result of post-depositional deterioration (above).

The processes of soil accumulation and pollen translocation discussed above lead to the suggestion that pollen spectra can broadly be interpreted as a stratigraphic sequence. Below sample 13, however, within the lower soil horizon, such assumptions cannot so readily be made, and the heightened deterioration and pollen losses possibly render these spectra uninterpretable.

The spectra within the turf-line show a simple pattern of change during its development. The landscape was open throughout, with no suggestion of woodland or scrub near the site. The basal turf-line spectra are dominated by wild grasses (Gramineae < 8 μm anl-D). Whether the grassland was actively grazed is unknown. Although there are a high number of pastoral indicator herbs, including *Plantago* spp., all of these are recorded in the lower soil horizon and in the sediment, so that their contemporaneity with the turf-line cannot be demonstrated. In addition, the high proportion of undifferentiated Plantaginaceae, and plantains of maritime affinities, makes it difficult to be confident of ecological associations.

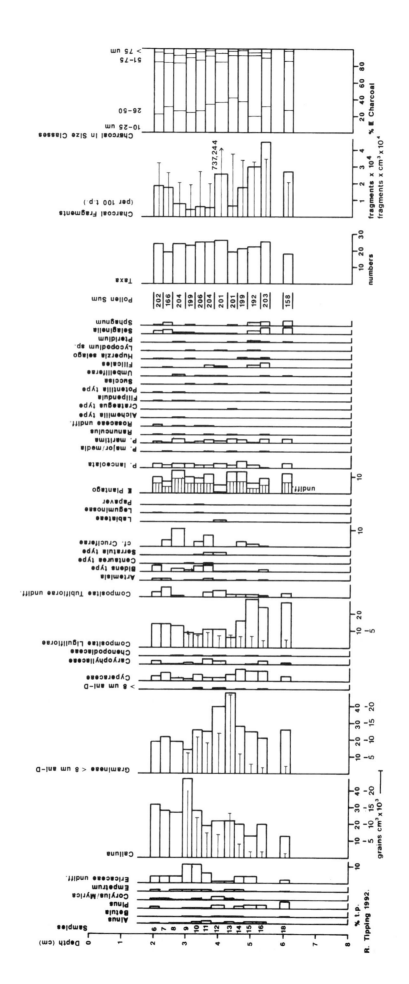

Illus 178   Pollen percentage data, concentrations of major taxa (inset within bars of *Calluna*, Gramineae <8 μm anl-D, Compositae Liguliflorae), pollen sums and microscopic charcoal counts

A similar problem is encountered with evidence for cereal growing, in the records of Gramineae > 8 μm anl-D, and associated arable 'weeds'. First, the intense deterioration of all large grass grains rendered closer identification impossible, so that it cannot be assumed that these grains are from cereals. Secondly, such grains are also recorded within the lower soil horizon, so that they may not have been contemporaneous with the turf-line. Thirdly, the indications from the site location, and the representation of pollen of *Plantago maritima* (above), make it likely that many disturbed-ground herbs could have been sited in natural coastal plant communities.

However, it is probable that the proportion of grassland declined through time, and that close to the time of burial by F1045, the site was covered by a heath community of *Calluna* (ling) and other heathers (Ericaceae undiff.). It is difficult to interpret this in terms other than of reduced grazing pressure. This in turn implies that the earlier spectra represent some indirect anthropogenic activity in the maintenance of open grassland.

Microscopic charcoal is abundant in all spectra. The decline in fragments per 100 t.p. within the turf-line does not represent a reduction in fire frequency, but merely that pollen was relatively more abundant as a result of higher concentrations. Charcoal concentrations are high throughout, and given the probability that the parent material of the soil, and the overlying sediment, is an ash, there is no requirement to assume any of the charcoal to be contemporaneous with the turf-line.

6.10 Diatoms

David G. Mann

6.10.1 Introduction, Material and Methods

Nineteen sediment samples were studied and all, except one, were taken from within or adjacent to Area 1 Sampling Column C (Illus 175). The remaining sample (F2036: B254, Phase 8) was of the post-roundhouse ash deposits on Area 2. The samples are listed in stratigraphic order in Illus 179.

Each sample was treated with boiling hydrogen peroxide (30 per cent w/w) for a few minutes, to oxidize organic material and disperse the sediment. This method was preferred to other, more vigorous methods of oxidation (such as with concentrated sulphuric and nitric acids), to minimize further breakage and erosion of the diatoms. The treated sediment was then washed five times with distilled water, by repeated centrifugation and removal of the supernatant. Finally, the cleaned sediment was resuspended in distilled water and aliquots of the suspension were dried onto circular cover slips; these were mounted permanently using the high refractive index mountant Naphrax and are held in the herbarium of the Royal Botanic Garden, Edinburgh.

Three cover slips were prepared per sample, the suspension being added at a density such that very few diatom frustules were obscured by other frustules or mineral debris.

Counts of diatoms and chrysophyte cysts were made in non-overlapping transects taken across the cover slip, using an immersion objective (N.A. 1.32). Generally, enough transects were completed to give a total diatom count, excluding chrysophyte cysts, of at least 100 valves, but the count was varied up or down according to the diversity of the assemblage. Thus, for context F1046 (B107, Phase 7) only 74 valves were identified, whereas 150 were identified for context F1040 (B103, Phase 8) which contained over three times as many taxa. Fragments of valves were identified and counted as whole units wherever the fragment contained a feature represented only once per valve, such as the central nodule of a raphid diatom. In every case the count was completed using just one of the three preparations made. The other preparations were then scanned at low power (×25 objective) for any taxa not recorded in the transects. All such trace taxa were given an arbitrary count of 0.01, to facilitate their inclusion in the tables (see archive report) and summary data. The taxonomy and nomenclature are those of Krammer & Lange-Bertalot (1986–91).

6.10.2 Results and Discussion

6.10.21 General features of the diatom assemblages

Diatoms are present in all of the samples, but abundance and state of preservation vary considerably. Context F1038 (B119, Phase 1) is particularly poor, with very small, eroded fragments of diatom, a few phytoliths and much mineral matter; the diatoms present in this material are species found more abundantly in overlying layers and their state of preservation is consistent with the hypothesis that they are not autochthonous, but have been transported downwards in the soil profile by invertebrates or water. Elsewhere, the state of preservation, with some unfragmented valves or even complete frustules, suggests that at least some of the diatoms were incorporated into the soil as it formed, with little subsequent movement vertically. For Blocks 103 and 104 (Phase 8), radiometric dates (Part 4.1) suggest that deposition of material was rapid and soil microstratification (Part 6.11) shows that there has been little reworking by invertebrates. Even so, it has been impossible even here to identify all the diatoms fully, because they are fragmentary, lacking diagnostic features; or because they have been deformed by heat, especially in material from Blocks 103 and 104 (Phase 8), but also, though in smaller numbers, in B107 (Phase 7), and B254 (Phase 8); or because they belong to as yet undescribed taxa.

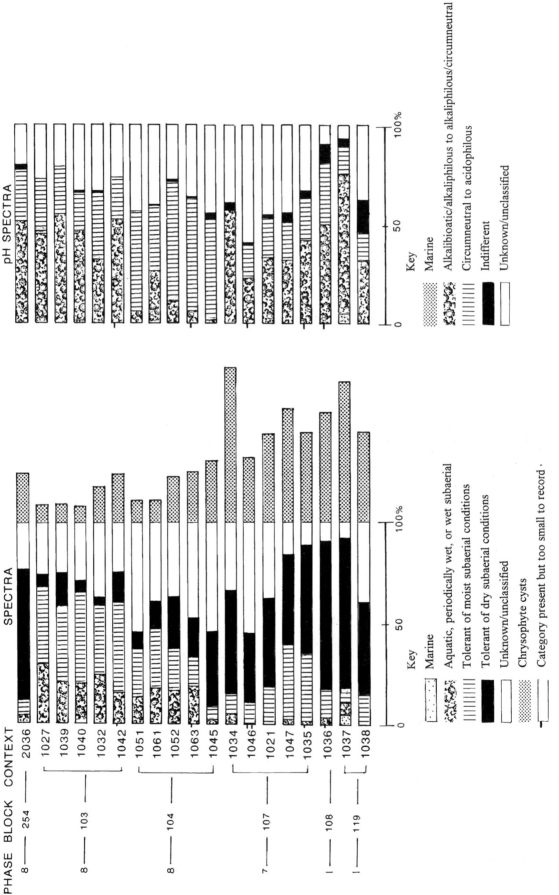

Illus 179   Diatom diagram

The diatom species fall into two main groups, which have been interpreted as having been derived from two kinds of habitat, using the ecological information in Lund (1946) and Denys (1992):

1. A terrestrial assemblage can be distinguished, where the species are mostly characteristic of neutral to somewhat acid soils or bryophyte mats, and known to be very tolerant of dry conditions (though active growth requires moisture). These species include *Eunotia* spp, *Hantzschia amphioxys*, *Navicula contenta*, *Pinnularia borealis*, *P. intermedia*, *P. lata*. There are also some species that are more characteristic of basic soils or turfs, such as *N. mutica* and *N. cincta*. In general, the terrestrial assemblage is better represented in B107 (Phase 7); B108 (Phase 1); B119 (Phase 1); and B254 (Phase 8), than in B103 and B104 (Phase 8).

2. There is also an assemblage that is more characteristic of periodically wet or semiaquatic conditions. The species in this group are mostly base-loving (alkaliphilic, alkalibiontic) and include *Caloneis bacillum*, *Cymbella aspera*, *Diploneis* spp. (*elliptica*, *ovalis*, *ovalis-oblongella*), *Navicula viridula*, *Mastogloia smithii*, *Nitzschia amphibia*, *N. sinuata*, *Rhopalodia gibba*. Similar assemblages have been described from seasonally flooded dune-slacks at Braunton, Devon (Round 1958), where the sand has a high pH as a result of high shell content; they also occur in water-logged sedge-moss carpets, again where the pH is fairly high (6–7). The semiaquatic assemblage is best developed in B103, though it is also quite abundant in B104. Within B104 there are also some species that again are characteristic of periodically wet or semiaquatic conditions, but which are acidophils, having pH optima between 5.5 and 7. These include *Navicula cocconeiformis* and *Nitzschia palustris*.

The two main assemblages are mixed together in most of the samples, and it is conceivable that they could have originated close together in a mosaic of habitats, some wetter, others drier. However, the large volume of ash dominated by Assemblage 2 in the upper 'farm mound' deposits (F1039 & F1040: B103) implies that the source material for this assemblage was distinct and easily separable from that yielding Assemblage 1.

Besides these two main elements of the diatom flora, there were also a few marine diatoms. These were found sporadically throughout the sequence, being particularly abundant in F1037 (B119, Phase 1) and F1040 (B103, Phase 8), where the epiphytic marine diatom *Rhabdonema arcuatum* was recorded. The frustules (cell-walls) of this species were intact and well preserved, and the simplest explanation for their presence in the soil is that they arrived attached to windblown seaweed, which then decayed. The same origin is possible for the few cells of *Grammatophora* spp found. The marine planktonic

genus *Coscinodiscus* was represented by a few fragments in F1035 (B107, Phase 7), F1036 (B108, Phase 1) and F1037 (B119, Phase 1), but this is not surprising in a coastal site, since the valves of many *Coscinodiscus* species are very robust and could arrive in wind-borne marine sediment or in sea spray.

A striking absence throughout is any convincing evidence of diatoms that are characteristic of highly acid habitats, such as ombrotrophic peats (e.g. from blanket bog); thus *Brachysira serians* and related species, *Frustulia rhomboides*, *F. saxonica* and *Peronia fibula* were not found. *Eunotia* and *Pinnularia* are two genera that are generally associated with acidic environments but few of the species identified in any of the samples were extreme acidophils. *Tabellaria binalis*, *T. flocculosa* and *T. quadriseptata* are further species that might be expected in wet, highly acid sites, but in all the samples only one girdle band was found of *Tabellaria*, among many thousand diatoms examined. It is concluded, therefore, that bog peat did not contribute to the soils or 'farm mound' deposits, unless all such peat was taken from below the bog surface, where any diatom shells might have been removed by dissolution.

There are relatively few freshwater epiphytes, e.g. from the genera *Cocconeis*, *Achnanthes*, *Cymbella* and *Gomphonema*, and no convincing evidence of freshwater planktonic diatoms. From this it seems clear that the diatom assemblages were derived from very shallow water, waterlogged moss carpets or turf, and not from the marginal vegetation of lakes or other open waters.

There is one main criticism that can be levelled against using the diatom counts (Illus 179) as a basis for commenting on the nature of the palaeosols or 'farm mound' deposits. This is the high proportion of the total count attributable to taxa that either cannot be identified to species (and where the genus is not restricted to a particular pH or habitat type) or for which reliable ecological information is missing. In some samples, such as F1046 (B107, Phase 7), F1045 and F1051 (both B104, Phase 8) for habitat moisture; or F1046 (B107, Phase 7) for pH preference, more than half of the diatoms counted could not be classified according to their habitat preferences. However, it is not considered likely that this will bias the interpretations given. The majority of the diatoms giving rise to difficulty were *Eunotia* and *Pinnularia* fragments that could not be identified to species because of poor preservation; *Pinnularia* valves have a very robust and characteristic structure, which means that they can remain identifiable to genus even when fragmentary, with most of the silica dissolved away. As far as it is possible to judge, all the fragments observed could have come from *Eunotia* or *Pinnularia* species that are represented by better preserved and identifiable specimens found elsewhere in the same samples: fragmentary specimens were not assigned to species unless the identification could be made with some degree of confidence. There is no evidence for any source materials other than those mentioned above.

All samples contained other mineral matter, abiogenic and biogenic, besides diatom shells, but the quantities varied considerably. In B107 (Phase 7), B108 and B119 (both Phase 1) and in much of B104 (Phase 8), the diatoms were accompanied by large amounts of other mineral matter, including phytoliths and occasional sponge spicules, but in some contexts, especially F1039 and F1040 (both B103, Phase 8), diatoms and diatom fragments (pieces of valve and girdle band) were predominant. Here many of the diatoms were distorted by heat, yet clearly had been intact cells before firing. These samples appear to represent the ash from highly organic material, such as fen peat. The lowest sample in the sequence showing any real evidence of firing was F1021 (B107, Phase 7), where some distorted diatom frustules were found. Above this, distorted frustules were present in all samples, though they were much commoner in the 'farm mound' deposits (B103 & B104, Phase 8). There has been no systematic examination of the effects of heat on diatom frustules, but routine firing of diatoms at 550 °C for 0.5–1 hour, to obtain clean frustules for taxonomic studies, leads to less distortion and fusion of the wall than was observed in the St Boniface material. It is concluded, therefore, that some at least of the diatoms in the St Boniface ash deposits have been heated above 550 °C. Significant loss of diatoms through melting and fusion of the silica can be ruled out for the ash in F1040 (B103, Phase 8), since most of this deposit consists of recognizable diatoms or diatom fragments.

6.10.22 Comparisons between blocks

The primary sandy soil horizons (B108 & 119, Phase 1) and the Late Iron Age ash dumps (B107, Phase 7) are similar in their diatom composition, being dominated by terrestrial assemblages, especially by species preferring more neutral or basic conditions, e.g. *Navicula cincta*. Derivation of the diatoms from turf on mineral soil is quite likely. The presence of distorted frustules in the upper part of Block 107 deposits (F1021, F1046 & F1034) suggests inputs of ash, but the ash must then have been derived largely from the same rather dry, neutral or basic turfs as the undistorted diatoms.

There is a marked change between Block 107 (Phase 7) and Block 104 (Phase 8) with a decrease in the percentages of truly terrestrial species. In all of the contexts in B103 and B104 (Phase 8), except F1045 (B104), terrestrial species very tolerant of desiccation make up 25 per cent or less of the total count, whereas in B107 (Phase 7), B108 and B119 (both Phase 1) and B254 (Phase 8), the proportion varies between 35 per cent and 74 per cent. The lower percentages of terrestrial diatoms are accompanied by a decrease in the ratio of chrysophyte cysts to total diatoms, which is consistent with a change to more continuously wet conditions. Altogether, the evidence suggests that the ash in the 'farm mound' deposits was derived from turf, peat and soil from waterlogged habitats, together with some continuing input of material from drier sites. Context F1045 is anomalous in having a low percentage of diatoms characteristic of wet or periodically wet habitats, like the underlying deposits in B107 (Phase 7), but a pH profile that matches the other samples from B104 (Phase 8).

Within the 'farm mound' deposits, the primary deposits (B104) are characterized by higher proportions of acidophilous taxa than the secondary deposits (B103), both within the drier terrestrial assemblage and within the assemblage derived from wetter sites. Some change in the source of fuel, either geographically or stratigraphically (as might occur if, for example, more leached surface vegetation and peat were used first and then underlying organic deposits that had formed close to a base-saturated water table), is likely to have occurred between the two blocks. Contexts F1039 and F1040 (B103) are particularly rich in diatoms (see above), relative to other mineral material, but both here and elsewhere in B103 much of the diatom material is very highly fragmented, suggesting considerable processing by invertebrates or abiotic agencies after the death of the diatoms; whether this took place before or after firing cannot be determined.

Context F2036 (B254, Phase 8) does not match any of the 'farm mound' deposits in B103 and B104 (Phase 8). The percentage of terrestrial taxa able to withstand drought is very high (65 per cent), higher than in any other samples apart from F1037 (B119, Phase 1) and F1036 (B108, Phase 1), which also resemble F2036 in being dominated by alkaliphils. Distorted frustules are present, indicating inputs of ash, but the source material seems to have been a turf on fairly dry, basic soil, rather than the wetter material giving rise to the assemblages in B103 and B104.

6.11 Soil Micromorphology

Stephen Carter

6.11.1 Introduction

Soil thin-sections (STS) were selected primarily to answer questions relating to the composition and accumulation of the 'farm mound' and underlying sediments in Area 1. Comparative samples were also taken from the basal and uppermost deposits on Areas 2 and 3.

Three main types of sediment were identified during the excavation of Area 1. At the base of the section there were a number of sterile layers, interpreted as a pre-Iron Age soil (B118 & B119, Phase 1). These were overlain by up to 1.5 m of deposits containing occasional Iron Age artefacts and structures at the south end of Area 1. The top of these deposits was marked by an extensive layer

(F1011: B105, Phase 7), interpreted as a buried topsoil. This was overlain by up to 1.5 m of finely layered sediments dipping gently to the north (B103 & B104, Phase 8). They contained few diagnostic artefacts and were assumed to be of Norse or medieval date. The uppermost deposits represent the 'farm mound'.

Sixteen soil thin-sections were produced in order to answer questions arising from this initial interpretation of the stratigraphy:

1. What is the composition of the 'farm mound' and how did it accumulate? What is the difference between the 'grey' layers (B104, Phase 8) and the 'brown' layers (B103, Phase 8) in the mound?
2. Are there any differences in composition or depositional history between the 'farm mound' and the underlying Iron-Age sediments (B107, Phase 7)?
3. What is the nature of the pre-Iron Age soil (B118 & B119, Phase 1)?

6.11.11 Samples

Sixteen 5×7.5 cm thin-sections were produced from four groups of samples:

1. Area 1, Sample Column C, STS samples 102–111. Ten sections of the 'farm mound' and underlying Iron Age sediments (Illus 175 for location);
2. Area 1, Sample Column A, STS samples 100 and 101. Two sections of the pre-Iron Age soil (Illus 44 for location);
3. Area 3, STS samples 27 and 28. Two sections of the pre-Iron Age shell sand deposits under the roundhouse (Illus 53 for location);
4. Area 2, STS samples 31 and 32. Two sections of sediments overlying Iron Age structures, similar to the Area 1 'farm mound' (Illus 118 for location).

6.11.12 Methods

The soil thin-sections were examined and divided into areas of uniform composition and structure with up to five areas in some sections. The micromorphology of these areas was described using the methods and terminology of Bullock *et al* (1985). Full descriptions are contained in the project archive. These descriptions concentrated on aspects of micromorphology which are particularly relevant to the understanding of these sediments:

1. Basic mineral and organic components (composition of the sediment);
2. Sediment fabric (mode of deposition).
3. Microstructure and pedofeatures (post-depositional processes).

6.11.13 Results

The thin-section descriptions are summarized in Tables 41 and 42. They are supported by quantitative data for carbonized peat fragments (Tables 43 & 44). In addition, the results of the routine soil analyses (pH, loss on ignition and calcium carbonate) and particle size analyses provide complementary quantitative data (Table 45).

6.11.2 The 'Farm Mound' (B103 & B104, Phase 8)

Soil thin-sections (STS): 111, 102, 103, 104, 105. Contexts: F1050, F1032, F1042, F1043, F1110, F1045.

6.11.21 Basic mineral and organic components (Table 41)

The 'farm mound' sediments are very dominantly mineral, with organic components contributing less than 10 per cent by weight (loss-on-ignition results: Table 45). The coarse mineral material consists of silt and sand-sized grains of quartz with a few sedimentary rock fragments (mudstone, siltstone and fine sandstone) and rare bone and marine shell fragments. The fine mineral material is a mixture of quartz and mica grains with various types of biogenic silica (phytoliths, diatom frustules and chrysophyte cysts).

The organic components are dominated by fragments of carbonized peat with a few carbonized plant stem and root fragments. The peat appears in section as black amorphous organic matter with occasional laminated plant remains and fungal tissue and a variable concentration of mineral grains. In addition to the carbonized material, there are rare fragments of uncarbonized peat and thin laminations of humified organic matter in some thin-sections.

6.11.22 Fabric and microstructure (Table 42)

The 'farm mound' was seen to be finely layered in the field and was divided into extensive contexts, *c.* 5–20 cm thick. In thin-section, most of these contexts, notably F1110 (B104, Phase 8), were subdivided for the purposes of description into distinct areas *c.* 1–5 cm thick. Therefore, at both the macro- and meso-scale, the fabric of the 'farm mound' is strongly banded. At the micro-scale, three fabrics were observed:

1. Banded: areas with a few horizontal divisions *c.* 1–10 mm thick, ranging from amorphous organic bands *c.* 1 mm thick to coarse mineral bands with a random fabric;

TABLE 41: SUMMARY OF MICROMORPHOLOGICAL CHARACTERISTICS (A) COMPOSITION (RELATIVE ABUNDANCE: * FEW, ** FREQUENT, *** ABUNDANT)

			BASIC MINERAL COMPONENTS COARSE MATERIAL FINE			MATERIAL		BASIC ORGANIC COMPONENTS	
Section	*Zone*	*F no./Block*	*Quartz*	*Rock frags*	*Phytoliths*	*Diatoms*	*Chrysophytes*	*Carbonized peat*	*Amorphous laminations*
111	1	1050/103	***	*	**	*		**	*
	2	1050/103	***	*	**	**	*	**	
	3	1032/103	***	*	**	*		*	*
	4	1042/103	***	*	**	**	*	**	
102	1	1043/103	***	*	**	*		*	*
	2	1110/104	***	*	***	**	*	**	**
103	1	1110/104	***	*	**	*		**	
	2	1110/104	***		***	*	**	*	***
	3	1110/104	***	*	**	*		**	
	4	1110/104	***		***	*	*	*	***
	5	1110/104	***	*	**	*		**	
104	1	1110/104	***	*	**	*	*	**	
	2	1110/104	***	*	***	*	*	**	**
	3	1110/104	***	*	**	*	*	**	
	4	1110/104	***	*	**	**	**	**	**
	5	1045/104	***	*	**	*	*	**	
105	1	1045/104	***	*	**	*	*	**	*
	2	1011/105	***	**	?	?	?	**	**
106	1	1011/105	***	**	?	?	?	**	
	2	1034/107	***	*	*			*	
107	1	1034/107	***	*	*			*	
	2	1046/107	***	*	*			*	
108	1	1046/107	***	*	*			*	
	2	1021/107	***	*	*			**	
109	–	1048/107	***	*	**	*		*	
110	–	1035/107	***	**	**	*		*	
31	–	2057/254	***	**	**	*	*		
32	–	2036/254	***	**	**	*		*	
100	1	1084/116	***	**	*			*	
	2	1085/118	**	**	*			*	
101	–	1085/118	**	**	*			*	

TABLE 42: SUMMARY OF MICROMORPHOLOGICAL CHARACTERISTICS: (B) FABRIC, MICROSTRUCTURE AND PEDOFEATURES (RELATIVE ABUNDANCE: * FEW, ** FREQUENT, * ABUNDANT)**

Section	Zone	F no./Block	Coarse fabric	Microstructure	PEDOFEATURES			
					Texture	Phosphate	Carbonate	Excrement
111	1	1050/103	Banded	Crumb-granular		*		***
	2	1050/103	Clustered	Crumb-granular				
	3	1032/103	Banded	Crumb-granular			*	***
	4	1042/103	Clustered	Crumb-granular		**		***
102	1	1043/103	Clustered	Channel + crumb				**
	2	1110/104	Banded	Channel + crumb			*	**
103	1	1110/104	Clustered	Channel				*
	2	1110/104	Laminated	Channel				*
	3	1110/104	Clustered	Channel				*
	4	1110/104	Laminated	Channel				*
	5	1110/104	Clustered	Channel				*
104	1	1110/104	Clustered	Channel				*
	2	1110/104	Laminated	Channel				*
	3	1110/104	Clustered	Channel				*
	4	1110/104	Laminated	Channel				*
	5	1045/104	Clustered	Channel				*
105	1	1045/104	Banded	Channel	*			*
	2	1011/105	Banded	Channel-spongy				*
106	1	1011/105	Random	Spongy-crumb				**
	2	1034/107	Random	Spongy-crumb		*		***
107	1	1034/107	Random	Spongy-crumb				***
	2	1046/107	Clustered	Massive-channel				*
108	1	1046/107	Clustered	Massive-channel				*
	2	1021/107	Random	Spongy-crumb		*		***
109	–	1048/107	Random	Channel-spongy		*		***
110	–	1035/107	Random	Spongy-crumb				***
31	–	2057/254	Banded	Crumb-granular	*		*	***
32	–	2036/254	Banded	Crumb-granular			*	***
100	1	1084/116	Random	Channel	**			
	2	1085/118	Random	Channel-spongy	**			**
101	–	1085/118	Random	Channel-spongy	**			**

2. Laminated: areas with very fine parallel layering (*c*. 50–500 mm) of amorphous organic matter, biogenic silica and quartz;

3. Clustered: areas with no horizontal divisions but the coarse material has a very heterogeneous distribution with individual components clustered together.

The microstructure of the 'farm mound' changes systematically down the sequence from a complex crumb-granular structure with high porosity close to the modern surface to a channel structure with low porosity deeper in the mound. The crumb-granular structure is created by soil ingesting invertebrates and the highest section (STS111) consists largely of excrement. This declines in abundance with increasing depth and, from STS103, the structure is created by the growth of fine roots with only rare invertebrate burrows and excrement.

6.11.23 Composition and sources of the 'farm mound' sediments: part 1

The results of the chemical and physical analyses (Table 45) indicate that, at the scale of the context, the 'farm mound' sediments are all similar. They are slightly calcareous, non-humose sandy silt loams. These results, however, mask the variation within contexts that is seen in the thin-sections. Three main types of sediment were identified in thin-section:

1. Mineral sediment with carbonized organic matter;
2. Laminated mineral and uncarbonized organic sediment;
3. Uncarbonized organic matter bands.

6.11.231 Mineral sediment

The predominantly mineral sediment constitutes the majority of the deposits, forming the thicker layers (1–5 cm) with a clustered or banded fabric. The main components are coarse quartz grains, biogenic silica and carbonized peat fragments. Of these three, only the carbonized peat directly indicates a source of the sediment: there is at least some fuel ash. Very rare fragments of coniferous wood charcoal demonstrate that driftwood was burnt too.

The majority of peat used as fuel would have been totally oxidized during burning and therefore reduced to a mineral residue. This residue will contain mineral grains and biogenic silica bodies, particularly phytoliths that were present in the peat. It is therefore possible to create a sediment consisting of mineral grains, biogenic silica and carbonized peat simply by burning peat.

Other lines of evidence may be used to support this interpretation of the sediment source. When viewed in oblique incident light, areas of abundant fine material are seen to be highly reflective with orange/red colours. This is characteristic of material that has been heated. There are rare fragments of fused ash, quartz grains set in a glassy matrix, that are the product of silica melting at high temperature (>500 °C). These fragments may be related to the frequent clusters of coarse quartz grains that give this sediment its distinctive fabric. The clusters appear to be coherent fragments although they have not totally fused and they may have formed at lower temperatures or in brief periods of high temperature. There is therefore good evidence for the majority of the sediment having been burnt.

An analysis of the carbonized peat fragments confirms that they are a possible source for the mineral material in the sediment. The percentage

TABLE 43: ANALYSIS OF BURNT PEAT FRAGMENTS LARGER THAN 1 mm IN STS 102–111 (AREA 1, SAMPLE COLUMN C) AND STS 31–32 (AREA 2):

(a) Total number in 5 × 7.5 cm section, fragment length (% in each size class) and total length in 5 × 7.5

				PERCENTAGE IN SIZE CLASS			
Section	*Context*	*Block*	*Total*	*no. 1–2 mm*	*2–5 mm*	*>5 mm*	*Total Length (mm)*
111	1050/1032/1042	103	44	77	18	5	97.2
102	1043/1110	103/104	47	79	21	0	77.2
103	1110	104	58	81	19	0	87.6
104	1110/1045	104	27	52	41	7	57.4
105	1045	104	55	79	21	0	88.7
105/106	1011	105	28	92	8	0	37.6
106/107	1034	107	11	–	–	–	15.4
107/108	1046	107	5	–	–	–	8.4
108	1021	107	42	68	29	3	80.7
109	1048	107	27	89	11	0	39.2
110	1035	107	7	–	–	–	8.4
31	2057/2036	254	8	–	–	–	11.4
32	2036	254	8	–	–	–	12.2

TABLE 44: ANALYSIS OF BURNT PEAT FRAGMENTS LARGER THAN 1 mm IN STS 102–111 (AREA 1, SAMPLE COLUMN C) AND STS 31–32 (AREA 2):

(b) Percentage mineral content and maximum grain size of minerals (% in each class)

| Thin-Section Context | Block | MINERAL CONTENT | | | MAXIMUM GRAIN SIZE | | | | |
		<2%	2–10%	>10%	None	63µm	250µm	500µm	2000µm
111	1050/1032/1042	103	25	39	36	2	16	68	14	0
102	1043/1110	103/104	12	47	41	6	9	68	13	4
103	1110	104	25	53	22	3	11	79	7	0
104	1110/1045	104	41	44	15	0	26	59	15	0
105	1045	104	51	36	13	15	27	42	16	0
105/106	1011	105	75	25	0	4	46	50	0	0
106/107	1034	107	–	–	–	–	–	–	–	–
107/108	1046	107	–	–	–	–	–	–	–	–
108	1021	107	64	36	0	32	22	39	7	0
109	1048	107	82	7	11	26	33	33	8	0
110	1035	107	–	–	–	–	–	–	–	–
31	2057/2036	254	–	–	–	–	–	–	–	–
32	2036	254	–	–	–	–	–	–	–	–

and the maximum grain size of mineral grains in peat fragments larger than 1 mm was determined (Tables 43 & 44). Almost all fragments contained some mineral grains up to a maximum of *c.* 50 per cent; the maximum grain size was fine sand in most peat fragments with less than 20 per cent containing larger grains. This corresponds with the overall sediment texture (Table 45) which is dominated by silt and fine sand. Biogenic silica was not visible in the carbonized peat because it was obscured by the blackened organic matter. However, in rare fragments of uncarbonized peat, phytoliths and a few diatoms were present together with the quartz grains.

So far in this discussion, the term 'peat' has been used in a general sense, meaning any sort of organic sediment that could have been used as a fuel. Most, if not all, of the peat used in Orkney at present is blanket peat which has a negligible mineral grain content. The majority of the carbonized peat fragments from the 'farm mound' are therefore not blanket peat. There is no blanket peat in Papa Westray at present but two alternatives are available: peaty surface horizons to gleyed and podzolized soils (turves) and organic alluvium or lake mud. The burning of peaty turves would have created large volumes of ash containing mineral grains and phytoliths as well as mineral-rich carbonized fragments. Freshwater organic alluvium and lake muds would yield an ash containing mineral grains and abundant biogenic silica, particularly diatom frustules and chrysophyte cysts. Fragments, up to 2 mm across, of pure biogenic silica dominated by diatoms are present in STS 111 (Zones 2 & 4); chrysophyte cysts are present throughout the 'farm mound'.

Other possible sources of fuel that are not excluded by the available evidence include herbivore dung, which would yield an ash of phytoliths and diatoms, and seaweed. It is impossible to assess the relative abundance of all the fuel types that may be present from the thin-section data.

6.11.232 Laminated organo-mineral sediment

This sediment forms the areas of laminated fabric which constitute less than 10 per cent of the thin-sections. It consists of microlaminated amorphous organic matter, fine fragments of carbonized peat, fine quartz grains and biogenic silica in bands up to 1 cm thick. The organic laminations are brown, 50–500 µm thick and up to 2 mm long. Some of the thicker laminations contain sheets of phytoliths but the majority of the biogenic silica occurs between the organic laminations. Phytoliths are the most abundant type in all of the laminated bands with diatoms and chrysophytes varying from rare to common.

6.11.233 Uncarbonized organic bands

In areas with a banded fabric (STS 111, Zones 1 & 3: STS 105, Zone 1) the main bands of mineral sediment are separated by well-defined individual horizontal organic bands up to 1 mm thick and up to 2 cm long. The organic matter is yellow and amorphous with rare iron pseudomorphs of cell structure. Mineral inclusions consist of frequent phytoliths, sometimes organized in continuous horizontal layers and rare diatoms. There is one example of an organic band with calcium oxalate crystals and the bands in STS 111 (Zone 3) contain single grain micritic calcite. With the exception of the diatoms, all of this mineral material is derived

TABLE 45: RESULTS OF SOIL PHYSICAL AND CHEMICAL ANALYSES FROM SELECTED CONTEXTS

Context	Thin Section	pH	Loss on ignition (%)	CaCO$_3$	PARTICLE SIZE ANALYSIS (% weight in size class)			
					500–2000μm	250–500μm	63–250μm	<63μm
AREA 1 Column A								
1084	100	8.9	3.1	0	5.1	12.8	25.3	56.8
1085	100/1	8.9	2.2	0	2.8	17.2	26.2	53.8
AREA 1 column C								
1001	–	7.1	10.0	0	1.2	6.1	37.0	55.7
1017	–	8.1	7.1	0	1.9	5.8	33.1	59.1
1030	–	8.5	6.3	1	1.2	6.2	28.3	64.3
1039	–	8.4	3.8	2	1.6	5.6	28.5	64.3
1050	111	8.4	5.0	1	4.3	8.0	24.6	63.1
1032	111	8.1	4.9	1	2.8	8.6	30.7	57.9
1042	111	8.5	4.2	2	2.0	5.9	33.5	58.6
1043	102	8.6	2.4	1	1.4	9.2	43.2	46.2
1110	102/3/4	8.2	5.7	2	3.0	7.0	30.7	59.4
1045	104/5	8.6	4.9	0	2.2	6.8	30.4	60.6
1011	105/6	8.4	6.3	0	3.1	9.4	28.3	59.2
1034	106/7	8.8	5.5	0	4.1	10.4	36.4	49.1
1046	107/8	8.9	4.6	0	3.8	10.4	32.2	53.6
1021	108	8.5	6.5	1	4.9	8.7	30.2	56.1
1048	109	8.8	6.0	0	2.8	9.5	35.4	52.4
1035	110	9.0	3.5	0	2.9	6.9	28.5	61.8
1049	–	8.8	3.3	0	5.7	12.6	34.7	47.0
1037	–	9.1	2.7	0	8.8	18.7	37.5	35.0
1038	–	9.1	2.4	0	4.7	31.2	28.4	35.7
1006	–	9.1	1.1	0	3.5	11.7	37.8	47.0
AREA 2								
2057	31	8.6	4.4	0	3.3	7.6	28.6	60.5
2036	31/2	8.8	2.7	0	1.4	5.8	29.4	63.4
AREA 3								
3014	27	8.9	2.4	1	1.9	28.7	31.9	37.6
3015	27	9.3	1.6	4	4.0	42.0	27.9	26.1
3018	28	9.1	1.5	4	7.1	63.5	20.6	8.8

from the tissues of higher plants and therefore this type of organic band appears to be the highly humified remains of relatively large plant fragments.

6.11.234 Other components

There are some other rare mineral components that demonstrate the presence of other materials in both the mineral and organic 'farm mound' sediments. Fish bones were noted in most thin-sections and marine shells are present in two of them. Both classes of material were recovered from bulk samples and are dealt with in detail elsewhere. Rounded sand-sized fragments of marine shell were recorded from two thin-sections (STS 102, Zone 2 and STS 105, Zone 1). In each case a horizontal scatter of occasional fragments was present. Two possible sources for this material are calcareous beach sand or dune sand and there are extensive deposits of the latter to the south of the site.

6.11.235 Conclusion

It is clear that the dominant component of the 'farm mound' sediments is ash, derived from the burning of peat and 'peat substitutes'. The ash contributes almost all of the mineral components and all of the carbonized organic components. Uncarbonized organic components are a minor part of the sediments but this is partially the result of post-depositional decay leaving only the highly humified amorphous residues of much bulkier plant tissues. It is not possible to identify this material in thin-section and therefore its origins remain unknown.

6.11.24 Composition and sources of the 'farm mound' sediments: part 2

Block 103 and 104 sediments have been identified as ash. The sediments contain carbonized fuel fragments, and biogenic mineral residues identified in thin-section may be used to identify the sources of this fuel. Modern reference samples of fuel were collected in Orkney for comparison with the archaeological material.

6.11.241 Modern reference samples

A wide range of sediments may be used as fuel, all containing a significant combustible component. Samples of organic- and organic matter-rich sediments were collected in Orkney from areas with sediment parent materials similar to the site at St Boniface. They include both blanket and raised bog peats, peaty turf and peaty alluvium.

Blanket peat from Stenness (HY 315 098, 150 m OD) Three samples of peat from the bank of Mr Peter Leith, Appiehouse, Stenness. The peat is roughly 1 m deep and the vegetation is currently dominated by *Calluna vulgaris* (heather) and *Eriophorum* spp. (bog cotton). This bank is cut in three steps and peats from each step have characteristic burning properties:

Top: Good-quality, fibrous peat;
Middle: Poor-quality, very fibrous peat;
Bottom: Very high-quality, amorphous peat (some soil adhering).

Peaty turf from Stenness (HY 301 112, 30 m OD) A sample of O horizon and underlying mineral Ag horizon from a peaty gley, classified as Olrig Series, Thurso Association. The vegetation is dominated by *Calluna vulgaris* (heather), *Erica cinerea* (bell heather) and *Scirpus caespitosus* (deer grass).

Valley sediments from Durkadale, Birsay (HY 302 248, 35 m OD) The floor of Durkadale contains an extensive valley bog with base-rich alluvium, peaty alluvium and acidic raised bog peat. Three samples were collected from the north end of the bog:

1. Peaty alluvium with a vegetation cover dominated by *Caltha palustris* (kingcup), *Potentilla palustris* (marsh cinquefoil), *Filipendula ulmaria* (meadowsweet) and *Menyanthes trifoliata* (bog bean);
2. Marl, underlying the peaty alluvium at 0.5–1.0 m depth;
3. Raised peat with a vegetation cover of *Calluna vulgaris* (heather), *Erica cinerea* (bell heather) and *Scirpus caespitosus* (deer grass).

6.11.242 Methods

The samples were air dried and then sub-samples burnt under oxidizing and reducing conditions. Samples were oxidized by heating over a gas burner until the material was totally turned to ash. Samples were reduced by wrapping tightly in foil and heating at 200 °C until carbonized. The oxidized ash and reduced (carbonized) fragments from each sample were impregnated with resin and thin-sections made by the Department of Environmental Science, University of Stirling. The thin-sections were described using the methods and terminology recommended by Bullock *et al* (1985).

6.11.243 Results

The relevant characteristics of the carbonized samples are summarised in Table 46. The figures for percentage mineral content range from zero up to almost 100 per cent but this underestimates the variation within some samples. The Stenness blanket peat and turf O horizon samples have a uniformly low mineral content consisting of silt and fine sand-sized quartz. The turf Ag horizon and the base of the blanket peat profile, which is, in effect, also an Ag horizon, contain a much higher proportion of quartz which is poorly sorted and occurs as grains up to medium sand size. These terrestrial samples may be contrasted with the Durkadale alluvial samples. The peaty alluvium has a highly variable mineral content which at the lower end approaches the composition of the Durkadale peat. These two samples can be seen as two parts of a continuum from pure peat through to pure mineral alluvium. The mineral grains are moderately sorted with dominantly silt-sized quartz and there are variable concentrations of biogenic silica (phytoliths, diatoms and chrysophytes).

The marl is very different from the other sediments as it contains very little organic matter and consists largely of authigenic calcium carbonate.

The basic organic components are equally varied. In the Stenness blanket peat there is a clear progression from well-preserved organic residues at the top through poorly preserved organic to amorphous residues at the base. This decomposition is matched by compression of the structure into parallel layers with reduced pore space. This range of preservation and structure is seen within the Durkadale raised bog peat sample. The terrestrial soil samples from Stenness contain amorphous organic matter with some roots and the structure tends to granular. This contrasts with the peaty alluvium which has amorphous organic matter but a massive, low porosity structure.

6.11.244 Comparison with archaeological material

The results presented in Table 46 show that carbonized organic sediments may be classified by the quantity and type of mineral components, type and preservation condition of organic components, and microstructure. In the thin-sections of Area 1 sediments (B103, B104 & B107), carbonized fuel fragments larger than 1 mm were classified according to size, percentage mineral content, and maximum

TABLE 46: MODERN REFERENCE SAMPLES OF ORGANIC SEDIMENTS: SUMMARY TABLE OF MICROMORPHOLOGICAL CHARACTERISTICS OF CARBONIZED RESIDUES

	% mineral	Basic mineral components	Basic organic components	Structure	% voids
STENNESS					
Top peat	<1	Silt and fine sand sized quartz	Dominant, well preserved organ residues with common amorphous residues	Convoluted layers	40–60
Middle peat	<1	Silt and fine sand sized quartz	Very dominant poorly preserved organ residues	Convoluted layers	40–60
Bottom peat	<1	Silt and fine sand sized quartz	Dominant amorphous residues with frequent elongate, parallel tissue residues	Sub-parallel layers	5–20
Bottom peat / Ag horizon	20	Silt to medium sand sized quartz	Amorphous residues	Granular to channel	20
Turf O horizon	2	Silt and fine sand sized quartz	Amorphous residues	Granular	20–30
Turf Ag horizon	90	Silt to medium sand sized quartz	Common organ residues and amorphous residues	Spongy to granular	20–50
DURKADALE					
Peaty alluvium	20–80	Dominant, moderately sorted silt sized quartz with frequent clay and fine sand, few diatoms and very few chrysophytes and phytoliths	Frequent organ residues and dominant amorphous residues	Massive to low porosity channel	5–10
Marl	99	Dominant microsparite with common diatoms, few phytoliths and chrysophytes and very few silt sized quartz grains	Tissue residues	Massive to low porosity channel	5
Peat	0–10	Dominant silt sized quartz with frequent phytoliths, diatoms and chrysophytes	Varies from very dominant well preserved organ residues to very dominant amorphous residues	Convoluted layers to parallel layers	10–80

mineral grain size (Table 44). Comparison of the results from archaeological and reference material may indicate the types of organic sediment represented in the Area 1 sediments.

6.11.245 Percentage mineral content

In Area 1, the mineral content of carbonized fragments increases up through the stratigraphy, from Block 107 which is dominated by fragments with less than 2 per cent up to Block 103 which is dominated by fragments with over 2 per cent. Less than 2 per cent mineral components corresponds to either blanket and raised bog peats or soil O horizon, essentially horizons of pure organic matter. Results greater than 2 per cent correspond to alluvium or soil

Ag horizon. Fragments from Block 103 rarely exceeded 30 per cent mineral matter, suggesting peat-rich alluvium and peat/soil interface.

6.11.246 Basic mineral components

In Area 1, the only recorded mineral component of carbonized fragments was quartz. In Block 107 this was generally silt or fine sand sized but maximum grain size increased up the sequence to Block 103 where most had fine sand. The relative absence of fine sand lower in the sequence could result from the low percentage mineral content of the fuel fragments there, rather than an actual change in mineral components. The lack of biogenic silica in the Area 1 fuel fragments appears to indicate a blanket peat or peaty turf source rather than peaty alluvium. The Area 1 sediments did contain abundant biogenic silica in the groundmass and this may be interpreted in two ways. It could derive from a fuel that, because of its combustion properties, has consistently oxidized and therefore not produced carbonized fragments. Alternatively, it could be present in the carbonized fragments but be invisible in thin-section. The latter interpretation is favoured because it matches the observation in the reference samples that biogenic silica was generally visible only in oxidized residues.

6.11.247 Basic organic components

The organic components of the carbonized fragments in the Area 1 thin-sections were generally too small to be confidently identified. For example, small fragments of highly decomposed organic residues will appear to be amorphous. The few large fragments (> 5 mm) consisted of amorphous residues, well-preserved tissue residues and decomposed organic residues. Detailed comparison with the reference samples is not possible.

6.11.248 Structure

Structure, as in the case of the organic components, cannot be consistently identified in small (1 to 2 mm) fragments of carbonized fuel. The larger fragments contained examples of layered structure, similar to the peat reference samples, massive low porosity structure similar to the peaty alluvium, and granular structure, similar to the turf structure.

6.11.249 Discussion

Comparison of the archaeological and modern reference material is hindered by the small size of most of the carbonized fragments from the archaeological sediments. Results for percentage mineral content clearly demonstrate that both peat, from blanket peat, peaty turf or raised bog, and turf or alluvium are present. More precise identification of the type of peat depends on analysis of the organic components and structure and this is not possible in most cases. However, it is apparently more abundant in Block 107 sediments than in Blocks 103 and 104. Abundant biogenic silica is only a feature of the alluvial reference samples. The abundant biogenic silica in the fine fraction of Block 103 and 104 sediments, therefore, may indicate an alluvial source for much of that fuel. This contrasts with Block 107 where biogenic silica is rare.

Comparison is inevitably limited to those reference sediments that have been sampled. Comparison, therefore, cannot be made, for example, with a peaty podzol turf or organic lake mud. Examination of these two sediment types in thin-sections from other areas suggests that the podzol turf will resemble gley turf and the lake mud will appear amorphous and rich in biogenic silica.

6.11.2410 Conclusion

Comparison of the carbonized fuel fragments with modern reference material indicates that much of the fuel from the 'farm mound' (B103 & 104, Phase 8) originates in an alluvial or lacustrine environment. The closest match is with a peaty alluvium. The Late Iron Age sediments (B107, Phase 7), that underlie the 'farm mound', differ in that they appear to contain fuel dominantly from a truly terrestrial source, much of it a peat with very little mineral matter.

6.11.25 Accumulation of the 'farm mound'

The topographical survey clearly shows that the Area 1 section face cuts through the western flank of the mound and the results of coring indicate that the centre of the mound may be twice as deep as the 1.5 m exposed in the cliff-section. Therefore the part of the mound that was sampled is relatively shallow and peripheral to the centre of deposition. Analysis of the basic components of the mound led to the conclusion that it consists largely of ash. The banded and laminated fabrics of the sediments show that they must have accumulated by the deposition of numerous small volumes of sediment. The overall dip of these sediments in the section face indicates that this process started at the south end, where the mound is deepest, and then extended northwards.

The extent of an individual deposit is unknown because the contexts recorded in the field incorporate numerous discrete layers. However, they are clearly very thin, even relative to their minimum surface area, and do not represent undisturbed dumps of sediment. The processes most likely to produce the observed fine parallel stratification are wind and water erosion; an unconsolidated mound of ash in Papa Westray would be susceptible to both. It is therefore suggested that the sampled 'farm mound' deposits are wind- and water-borne sediments derived from higher parts of the mound and redeposited on the lower slopes. There is very little evidence in the section face for gully erosion but this may have occurred higher on the mound. Sheet wash appears to have been the dominant process with the deposition of thin but extensive sediments. This would have led to size sorting of the sediments as finer particles were transported further down the mound. The relatively thick, coarse-grained mineral sediments on the one hand, and the thin, fine-grained, laminated organo-mineral sediments on the other, could be the coarse and fine fractions created by this process.

Between the pre-'farm mound' buried soil (F1011: B105, Phase 7) and the modern surface, there was no field evidence for major breaks in sediment accumulation represented by soil formation. This is supported in the thin-sections by the changes in microstructure. A crumb-granular structure created by prolonged high biological activity is found associated only with the modern ground surface. This soil structure has developed in the top 0.9 m of the mound at Sample Column C and the sedimentary stratigraphy has been destroyed in the top 0.4 m by biological activity. Below this zone of modern topsoil formation, the channel microstructure is the product of very limited root and invertebrate penetration. It is unclear whether this reflects a very low level of modern activity or, alternatively, restricted vegetation growth and invertebrate burrowing contemporary with the accumulation of the mound. Uncertainty on this point has a bearing on the interpretation of the bands of organic matter identified in thin-section. They can be interpreted as either plant material dumped on the mound with the other waste, or isolated plants growing on the mound which were buried by further dumping. Both interpretations are plausible and a total lack of plant growth would seem to imply a remarkably rapid rate of sediment accumulation.

6.11.26 Comparison of Blocks 103 and 104 (Phase 8)

The 'farm mound' was separated into two blocks of contexts on the basis of sediment colour. Block 103 consists of relatively brown sediments and overlies Block 104 which consists of relatively grey sediments. In Sample Column C the boundary of these two blocks lies between F1043 (B103) and F1110 (B104) in thin-section STS102. The boundary in thin-section is poorly defined and does not mark a significant stratigraphic break.

Comparison of the basic components found in Block 103 sediments (STS111 and STS102, Zone 1) with those in Block 104 (STS102, Zone 2: STS103: STS104: STS105, Zone 1) reveals only two differences (Table 48). Phosphatic pedofeatures are present as very rare impregnative nodules in Block 103 (STS111, Zones 1 & 4). The crystalline vivianite (iron phosphate) has impregnated fragments of uncarbonized and carbonized peat, presumably after deposition of the sediment. Phosphate levels are high throughout the 'farm mound' and the significance of this difference is not clear.

TABLE 47: SUMMARY OF BIOLOGICAL COMPONENTS IN SELECTED BLOCKS FROM AREA 1.

Results derived from wet sieving and flotation, standardized to 10 l sample volume and expressed as weight in grams or frequency

Block	Mammal Bone	Fish Bone	Marine Shell	Fuel Ash Slag	Burnt Peat	Charcoal	Cereal Grain	Other Seeds
103	24	71	68	8	2	1	38	7
104	42	108	162	1	5	2	31	6
107	22	4	23	7	1	1	6	2
119	11	2	<1	1	<1	<1	1	3

TABLE 48: SUMMARY OF BIOLOGICAL COMPONENTS IN BLOCKS 103 AND 104 FROM THE FOUR SAMPLING COLUMNS.

Results derived from wet sieving and flotation, standardized to 10 l sample volume and expressed as weight in grams or frequency. Blocks did not occur in all columns.

Block	Mammal Bone	Fish Bone	Marine Shell	Fuel Ash Slag	Burnt Peat	Charcoal	Cereal Grain	Other Seeds
103 C	96	392	516	50	11	4	211	15
103 D	111	234	125	19	5	4	124	38
104 A	199	235	296	3	6	11	80	4
104 B	75	388	562	6	21	9	138	34
104 C	18	104	206	<1	8	1	28	13

The second difference is that fragments of diatom-rich, pure biogenic silica occur in Block 103 (STS111, Zones 2 & 4). These were interpreted as ash derived from freshwater alluvial or lacustrine sediments. It is therefore possible that the colour change from Block 104 to Block 103 reflects a change in fuel used on the site and therefore a different ash on the mound.

6.11.27 The 'farm mound': conclusions

The section face in Area 1 cut through the western flank of the 'farm mound' where it was up to 1.5 m deep. Analysis of thin-sections from Sample Column C reached the following conclusions:

1. The visible portion of the mound consists almost entirely of ash derived from the burning of peat, peaty turves and other organic materials;
2. Other minor components are bones, marine shells and plant tissue.
3. The sediment was derived from higher on the mound by water and wind erosion and was deposited in thin layers and very fine laminations;
4. Accumulation occurred without any major breaks and the mound surface did not become fully vegetated until the dumping of ash ended. Scattered plants may have grown on the mound during its accumulation;
5. Limited evidence suggests that the colour change between Blocks 104 and 103 may reflect changing sources for fuel used on the site.

6.11.3 The Late Iron Age Sediments (Block 107, Phase 7)

Soil thin-sections (STS): 106, 107, 108, 109, 110.
Contexts: F1034, F1046, F1021, F1048, F1035.

6.11.31 Basic mineral and organic components

These sediments are dominantly mineral with organic components contributing less than 10 per cent by weight (loss-on-ignition results: Table 45). The coarse mineral material consists of silt and sand-sized quartz grains with few to frequent sedimentary rock fragments and rare bone and marine shell fragments. The fine mineral material is a mixture of quartz, mica, phytoliths and diatom frustules. The organic components are dominated by fragments of carbonized peat with a few carbonized plant stem or root fragments. Uncarbonized organic matter includes rare peat fragments.

6.11.32 Fabric and microstructure

The fabric of the coarse material in these sediments is random except in F1046 (STS 107 & 108) where it is clustered. The microstructure of F1046 is also exceptional, being practically massive with a very low porosity. The other sediments have varied, but related, microstructures which reflect the degree of porosity and aggregate development. They range from channel structure with relatively low porosity and no distinct aggregates, through spongy to crumb structure with high porosity and common crumb aggregates. This sequence of microstructures reflects an increasing level of biological activity.

6.11.33 Comparison of the composition and accumulation of the 'farm mound' (Blocks 103 & 104) and the Late Iron Age sediments (Block 107)

Comparison of the basic components that constitute the 'farm mound' and the underlying Late Iron Age sediments reveals a great similarity in composition and, in most cases, differences are a matter of degree only. In the mineral components, chrysophyte cysts were not recorded in the Late Iron Age sediments but they were present in most of the 'farm mound' layers. In the organic components, amorphous laminations were not recorded in the Late Iron Age sediments. The similarity in composition is also reflected in the results of the particle size analysis (Table 45) which show no change in texture between the two types of sediment. In contrast to the similarity in composition, fabric and microstructure display major differences. The sedimentary banded and laminated fabrics of the 'farm mound' are absent in the Late Iron Age deposits which are almost all random. Similarly, the channel microstructure of the lower layers of the 'farm mound', not affected by recent pedogenesis, contrasts with the spongy and crumb structures of the Late Iron Age deposits.

The similarity of composition suggests that the Late Iron Age sediments, like the 'farm mound', largely consist of ash. The absence of chrysophytes, which form part of the ash, implies that there may be differences in the types of fuel used and this possibility is supported by the analysis of carbonized peat fragments (Tables 43 & 44). The carbonized peat fragments in the 'farm mound' contain, on average, more mineral material and this has a larger maximum grain size. The microstructure and fabric of the Late Iron Age sediments indicate high levels of biological activity in all contexts except F1046. This indicates that, in contrast to the 'farm mound', the rate of sediment accumulation has been slow and these contexts may be described as a sequence of buried soil A horizons. The biological reworking of the fabric has destroyed the original stratification and therefore the mode of deposition is unclear. Only F1046 preserves its original fabric and it appears to be a dumped sediment, rather than a soil layer formed *in situ*. F1046 is a layer of pure ash, dominated by fused quartz and vitrified silica fragments which indicate a high temperature during burning. It forms a well-defined horizontal layer, 4.9 m long and up to 10 cm thick. The lack of root and invertebrate penetration is probably caused by the fused nature of much of the ash and this has preserved the dump intact.

In conclusion, Block 107 consists of *in situ* ash dumps, deposited infrequently, with intervening periods of soil formation. Soil formation has largely destroyed the original stratigraphy of the dumps. The top of this block of sediments is defined by a final soil (F1011: B105, Phase 7).

6.11.4 The Late Iron Age Buried Soil (Block 105, Phase 7)

Soil thin-sections (STS): 105, 106.
Context: F1011.

6.11.41 Micromorphology

STS 105 spans the upper boundary of F1011 with the base of the 'farm mound' (F1045: B104, Phase 8). The junction is sharp but complex and the two layers are interleaved with lenses of F1011 extending for *c.* 2 cm up into F1045. The lower boundary of F1011 with F1034 (B107, Phase 7), STS 106, is a less well-defined horizontal zone *c.* 1 cm wide.

The basic components of F1011 in thin-section are similar to those of the underlying Block 107 sediments (Table 41) although, in the coarse mineral material, rock fragments are considerably more abundant. The fine material is largely obscured by abundant organic pigment which is responsible for the dark appearance of this layer in the field. The top 2 cm of F1011 (STS 105, Zone 2) contain significantly more uncarbonized organic matter than the rest of the layer. The most prominent components are horizontal, amorphous organic laminations, *c.* 100 µm thick and up to a few millimetres long. These are abundant at the upper surface of the layer but are rare below 1 cm. Amorphous organic matter is also common in the fine material of these top 2 cm.

The distinctiveness of the top 2 cm is maintained in the fabric and microstructure. The presence of the organic laminations give it a banded fabric, in contrast to the random fabric of the rest of the layer. Similarly, it has a low porosity channel structure which becomes spongy as pore space increases with depth and some areas at the base of the layer have a crumb structure.

6.11.42 Interpretation

F1011 was identified in the field as a buried soil horizon. It formed a distinctively dark, continuous layer, 10 cm to 20 cm thick, along most of the Area 1 section face. The appearance of the layer in thin-section confirms and amplifies this interpretation.

The organic laminations at the upper surface are the highly decomposed remains of the *in situ* vegetation, buried by the 'farm mound'. The preservation of these undisturbed humified plant remains reflects the rapidity and depth of burial under the mound of ash. The low porosity of the top of F1011 and its interleaving with the overlying sediment F1045 (B104, Phase 8) are both interpreted as evidence of trampling as the mound started to accumulate in this area. The higher porosity and spongy/crumb structure of the remainder of F1011 are typical of an uncultivated soil A horizon.

It is concluded that F1011 is a well-developed soil A horizon which had a stable vegetated surface at the time of burial under the 'farm mound'. Interpretation of the underlying Block 107 sediments identified four other soil A horizons (F1034, F1021, F1048, & F1035: B107, Phase 107). They were not distinctive in the field and this seems to be the result of a different burial history. The Block 107 soils were buried by shallow sediments and remained within the zone of biological activity, forming the base of the new overlying soil. They have therefore lost the fine organic matter and pigment that was preserved by rapid deep burial in F1011 and gave it a distinctive colour.

6.11.5 The Pre-Iron Age Buried Soil

Soil thin-sections (STS): 27, 28, 100, 101.

Contexts:	F1006:	(Till)
	F1037, F1038 & F1049:	(B119, Phase 1)
	F1085:	(B118, Phase 1)
	F3014, F3018:	(B310, Phase 1)
	F3015:	(B305, Phase 3)

In all areas of the St Boniface cliff-section, the earliest man-made features were seen to overlie sediments that represent a pre-Iron Age soil. Flagstone bedrock underlies the site and this is covered by a shallow and irregular layer of till (F1006). In Areas 2 and 3 the till is overlain by up to 0.5 m of sand but in Area 1 there is up to 0.4 m of sandy loam.

Chemical and physical analyses of the sand in Area 3 (Table 45: F3014, F3018, B310, Phase 1; and F3015, B305, Phase 3) showed that it is a calcareous, moderately well-sorted medium sand. Two thin-sections (STS27 & STS28) were produced of this sand. It consists of a mixture of sand-sized single-grain quartz, sedimentary rock fragments and marine shell with limited evidence for sedimentary banding. This is clearly a windblown shell sand. A cemented iron/manganese pan is present in STS27. This was recorded in the field extending under the structures in Area 3. It follows archaeological boundaries and must have developed at least after the early human burial here. F3014 (B310, Phase 1) became decalcified after the pan had formed and the upper part of F3015 (B305, Phase 3) was also decalcified, presumably at the same time. There is no evidence to suggest that the upper horizons of a soil profile are present in Areas 2 and 3 and the sediments are interpreted as an eroded shell-sand accumulation that has partially decalcified in the Iron Age.

Chemical and physical analyses of the sandy loam in Area 1 (F1037, F1038, & F1049: B119, Phase 1) show that it is a non-calcareous, poorly sorted sandy loam. There are no thin-sections of these layers but an equivalent context, F1085 (B118, Phase 1) was sectioned (STS100 & STS101). Basic mineral components consisted of frequent quartz and sedimentary rock fragments with a fine fraction of quartz, mica and very few phytoliths. Organic components consisted of very few small carbonized fragments. The rarity of biogenic silica contrasts with its abundance in the ash-derived sediments in Area 1. Overall there is very little evidence for burning in this layer and it is interpreted as a local till-derived sediment. The fabric and microstructure of F1085 (B118, Phase 1) are the product of biological activity and this supports its interpretation as a soil layer. There are frequent textural coatings but these clearly derive from the overlying archaeological sediment (F1084: B116, Phase 5) and therefore post-date the burial of the soil.

The results of particle size analysis (Table 45) indicate that F1037 and F1038 (B119, Phase 1) are relatively deficient in fine sand and rich in medium sand when compared to the underlying till F1006. This pattern is reinforced by the thin-sections of F1085 (B118, Phase 1) where medium sand is also relatively abundant. The presence of moderately sorted medium sands only a few metres to the south in Area 3 suggests that this medium sand enrichment is due to a windblown sand component in the Area 1 sediments. The Area 1 sediments are non-calcareous. The presence of marine shell sand cannot, therefore, be used to confirm or refute this suggestion. However, a simple analysis of the medium sand in a selection of sediments does support it. In addition to marine shell fragments, the medium sand in Area 3 consists of sand-sized single-grain quartz and fragments of mudstone and siltstone. The proportions of these types in Area 3 sand F3018 (B310, Phase 1) are 45 per cent quartz and 55 per cent rock fragments. These figures may be compared with F1110 (B104, Phase 8) in the 'farm mound', which has no windblown sand content, where there is 94 per cent quartz and 6 per cent rock fragments. The pre-Iron Age soil layer F1085 has 67 per cent quartz and 33 per cent rock fragments. This result is consistent with the addition of windblown sand.

There are a number of possible interpretations of the windblown sand in the Area 1 soil. It could reflect the mixing by invertebrates or cultivation of a thin surface layer of sand into the till-derived soil profile. Alternatively, a sand layer equal to the 0.5 m recorded in Area 3 could have been eroded largely as a result of human disturbance around the Early Iron Age settlement, with some mixing into the soil.

The site lies at the north end of a large area of windblown sand on the west side of the island which has been developing since at least the Neolithic period (Ritchie 1983). Immediately south of the site, the modern soil profile contains some sand mixed into a till-derived soil and is therefore similar to the buried Area 1 profile. This situation supports the suggestion that the 0.5 m of pure sand under Area 3 is a fragment of a more extensive deep sand cover which has been destroyed by erosion.

It is concluded that the pre-Iron Age soils around the site were developed in a shallow layer of calcareous windblown sand. Human disturbance and natural erosion in the Iron Age has removed most of the sand except where it was protected by buildings, leaving soils developed in till with some added decalcified sand.

6.11.6 'Farm Mound' Type Sediments on Area 2

Soil thin-sections (STS): 31, 32.
Contexts: F2057 & F2036: B254, Phase 8.

Sediments which resembled the Area 1 'farm mound' (B103 & B104, Phase 8) were also recognized on Area 2. Thin-sections were prepared of F2057 overlying F2036. F2057 was interpreted on site as a possible ground surface.

6.11.61 Micromorphology (Tables 41 & 42)

The boundary between F2057 and F2036 could not be identified in STS31. Coarse mineral components were dominated by sand-sized quartz grains with frequent sedimentary rock fragments. The fine mineral material consisted of quartz and mica with common biogenic silica (phytoliths with some diatoms). There were rare fragments of diatom-rich sediment and fragments of linked phytoliths. Organic components consisted of few carbonized peat and plant stem or root fragments and rare uncarbonized peat fragments. The fine material was highly reflective with orange and red colours in oblique incident light, indicating that it had been heated. It is clear that F2057 and F2036 consist of ash.

The fabric of both STS31 and STS32 is banded, with rock fragments, diatom-rich fragments and amorphous organic matter showing an indistinct banded distribution. This banding is poorly defined because of the high level of biological reworking of the fabric. There is a poorly developed crumb-granular microstructure created by partially coalesced invertebrate excrement. This indicates that a soil has developed in these sediments. The biological mixing has almost destroyed the original sediment stratigraphy which consisted of more horizontal layers than are now apparent in the field.

6.11.62 Comparison with the Area 1 sediments

The similarities between F2057 and F2036 (B254, Phase 8) and the Area 1 'farm mound' (B103 & B104, Phase 8) and underlying Late Iron Age sediments (B107, Phase 7) are clear. In all cases, the source of the material is fuel ash. However, given the uncertainties about the precise identification of the fuels involved, it is difficult to associate the Area 2 ash with either the 'farm mound' or the underlying Block 107 ash. The absence of chrysophyte cysts in thin-sections from the Area 2 ash can be paralleled in the Block 107 ash but the presence of diatom-rich fragments is paralleled only in Block 103, the upper part of the 'farm mound'. It is therefore not possible to match confidently the ash deposits on Areas 1 and 2 on the basis of the soil thin-section evidence alone.

PART 7

Discussion

7.1 'Farm Mounds' and the Formation of the Area 1 Sediments

Stephen Carter

7.1.1 Introduction

The section face in Area 1 cut through up to 2.5 m of relatively stone-free sediments which were interleaved at the south end with the northern limit of the structures (Structure 22) associated with the Iron Age settlement. Prior to excavation, these sediments had been described as 'dark brown loamy earth with a little shell-midden material, showing that the feature is a typical "farm mound"' (Lamb 1983a, 18). Given the functional and chronological assumptions implicit in the term 'farm mound' (Bertelsen 1979: Part 1.2), it is proposed to discuss the Area 1 sediments in terms of their composition, source, age and mode of deposition, to determine to what extent the sediments correspond to the monument type which has been ascribed to them.

7.1.2 Area 1 Sediments

The aim of this section is to bring together the relevant evidence from a range of specialist reports in order to summarize our understanding of the Area 1 sediments. The following sources of evidence have been utilized:

- Stratigraphy (layer depth and extent, boundary form)
- Soil physical and chemical properties
- Soil micromorphology
- Diatoms
- Carbonized plant remains
- Carbonized wood
- Pollen
- Shells
- Fish bone
- Mammal and bird bone
- Artefacts
- Radiocarbon dates

The individual specialist reports on these subjects should be consulted for more details or justification of a particular interpretation. Here, the sediments will be discussed in terms of their composition, source, mode of deposition and the degree of post-depositional alteration.

The sediments in Area 1, excluding the structures at the south end, have been divided into nine blocks. Of these, the key blocks which are discussed below comprise: B119 (Phase 1 soil), B107 (Phase 7 sediments), B105 (Phase 7 soil), and B103 & B104 (Phase 8 sediments). Other blocks contain only a few contexts and do not add further information.

7.1.21 Stratigraphy and extent

7.1.211 Introduction

The 'farm mound' is defined, for the purposes of this discussion, as those sediments assigned to Blocks 103 and 104 in excavation Area 1. The base of Block 104 is marked by the well-developed Late Iron Age buried topsoil F1011 (B105, Phase 7). Therefore the 'farm mound' consists, at least in Area 1, of all those sediments overlying the Late Iron Age ground surface. The depth and extent of archaeological sediments was recorded in an auger survey and this recorded 'farm mound' type sediments over an area of at least 60 m by 90 m at the north end of the site. Unfortunately, the auger survey did not detect the buried soil and therefore failed to distinguish between the 'farm mound' sediments and those in Block 107 which underlie the buried soil (B105). These sediments would appear very similar in an auger sample as their main differences are in structure and not in composition (Part 6.11). Calculation of the extent of the 'farm mound' cannot, therefore, simply be based on the results of the auger survey. A more rigorous approach involves the reconstruction of the pre-'farm mound' palaeotopography, using the available information, and comparison of that with the modern surface.

7.1.212 Development of the site topography

The natural topography can be determined by interpolation from levels on the surface of the glacial till at various points around the margins of the site

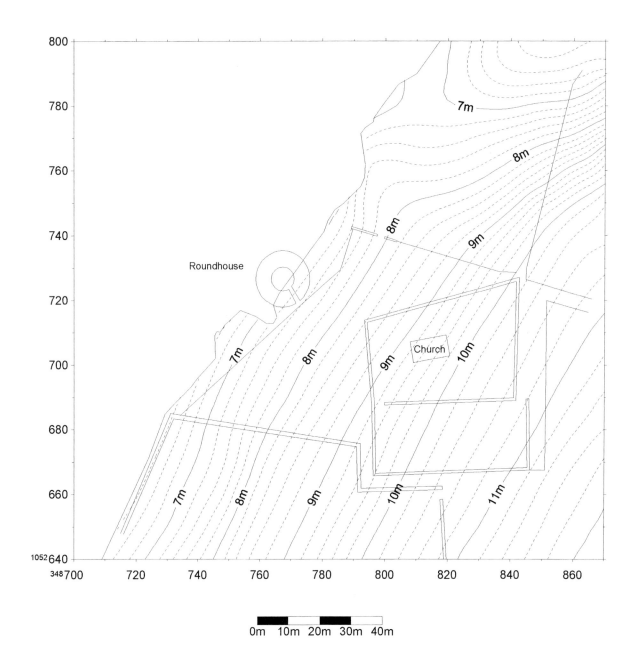

Illus 180   Contour model of natural surface of till

(Illus 180). On average, roughly 0.5 m of soil (B119 and related Phase 1 deposits) was recorded over the till. Augering failed to reach the till at any point through deep archaeological sediments. From the south end, a slope of uniform gradient runs parallel to the coast and then turns inland, steepening slightly. At the north end of the site, the land rises at the coast to enclose a shallow depression. This is interpreted as a storm beach shingle ridge so may not have been present throughout the history of the site.

The depth and extent of Iron Age sediments is only certain on the coast where they are well exposed. Inland, they were too stony to auger and partially buried by later sediments and structures. The focus of the settlement was the roundhouse and there are up to 3 m of rubble and stone structures around it. This enclosed settlement extends for roughly 70 m in the cliff-section and its southern limit is visible running inland for 30 m. Comparison with similar sites, such as Gurness (Hedges 1987, ii, fig. 2.1) or Howe

(Ballin Smith 1994, Illus 23), indicates that the enclosure is likely to be roughly circular with the roundhouse located off-centre within it. The surviving part of the main settlement mound at St Boniface is therefore reconstructed as a 70 m diameter semicircle and this places it entirely on the seaward side of the present church (Illus 181). The sediments recorded in Area 1 as Block 107 are also Iron Age in date and demonstrate the existence of a halo of shallower, less stony sediments around the settlement mound. In Area 1 they extend for at least 30 m north of the mound but to the south they were not investigated and it is therefore not known if they encircle the mound. On the assumption, however, that this is the case, then they may be represented by a series of deepened, relatively stone-free soil profiles which were recorded to the east and south of the modern graveyard. When this information is plotted (Illus 181), it indicates a large area of sediments 1–1.5 m deep under the site of the modern graveyard. Dry-stone structures have been revealed during grave digging to the south of the church (Part 1.2). They are of unknown age but may be part of a Late Iron Age settlement, contemporary with the sediments of Block 107 in Area 1.

The accumulation of the Iron Age settlement mound and its peripheral sediments altered the topography of the site and the contours plotted on

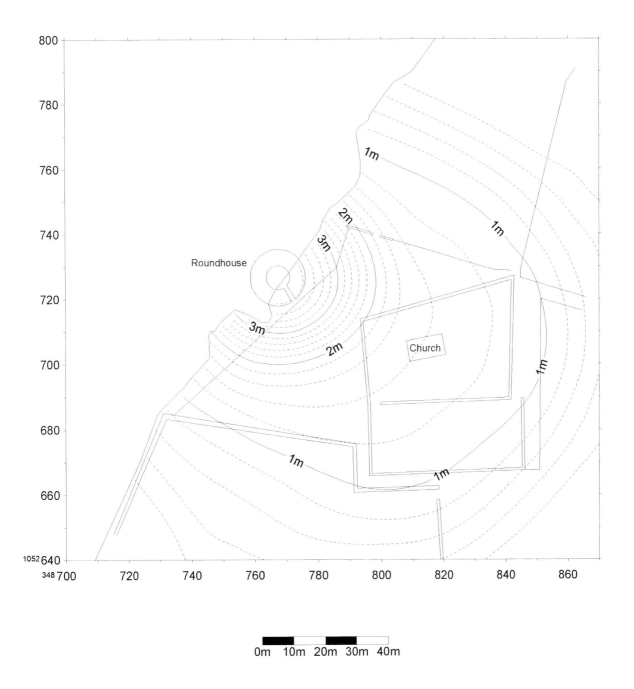

Illus 181   Contour model showing depth of LIA and earlier deposits

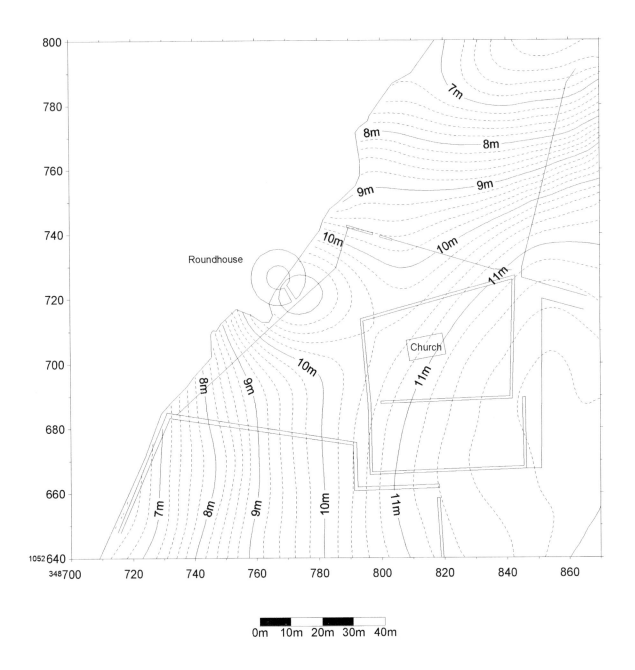

Illus 182   Contour model of the LIA ground surface

Illus 182 are considered to approximate to the Late Iron Age ground surface. Two main changes are apparent. The mound has created a ridge of higher ground, projecting out towards the coast with steep slopes to the north and south. In addition, the peripheral sediments have reduced the gradient on the slope inland of the mound to create an area of almost level ground.

The difference between the Late Iron Age and modern ground levels is plotted on Illus 183 and this is presented as a representation of the depth and extent of sediments of Norse and later date.

7.1.213 Depth and extent of the 'farm mound'

In Illus 183, three centres of sediment accumulation are apparent: the main mound in the centre and two smaller mounds to the north and south. The 'farm mound', represented by Blocks 103 and 104 in excavation Area 1, forms the main, central mound. The results of the topographic survey and augering (Part 2.2) demonstrate clearly that the southern mound incorporates a rectangular stone building on its summit. No clear structural evidence could be discerned on the northern mound, which forms a

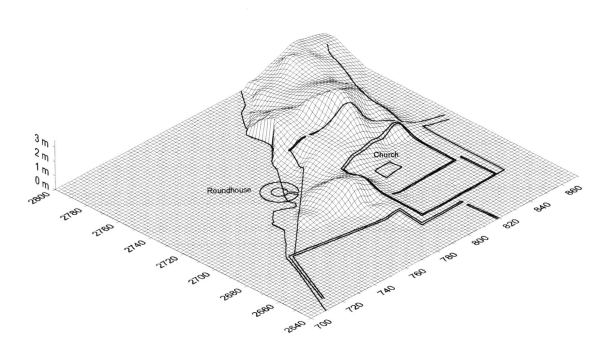

Illus 183   Orthographic projection showing depth of Norse and later deposits

subrectangular or roughly square artificial platform. Test-pitting of one side of the platform indicated that it appears to overlie sediments of the 'farm mound'.

The 'farm mound' covers the north-facing slope to the north of the Iron Age settlement. Its western limit has been destroyed by marine erosion but projection of the surviving contours suggests that it only extended for a further 20 m or so to the west. The northern limit of the mound is obscured by a series of relatively deep sediments, below and to the north of the north platform, which fill a natural depression in the till surface (Illus 180). It is not known whether these are part of the 'farm mound' or a much earlier fill of the depression, although the sediments are similar in character to the mound. On the east side, the mound has been truncated by cultivation, forming a step up to 1 m high (Part 2.2). The southern limit of the 'farm mound' is currently marked by the north wall of the graveyard. The graveyard, however, has clearly been levelled and the mound may have originally extended further south. There is also evidence of recent quarrying of the 'farm mound', adjacent to the graveyard (Part 2.2). Despite the various erosional losses and sources of uncertainty noted above, it appears that the greater part of the 'farm mound' has survived. Its maximum dimensions could have been 60 m north to south and 90 m transversely.

Sediments are deepest at the top of the slope, in excess of 3 m, where there is a pronounced knoll 1.5 m high. This knoll has, at least in part, been accentuated by quarrying adjacent to the graveyard wall. Auger penetration of the main mound was variable, indicating that there are some stones scattered throughout these sediments. On the south side of the mound, immediately north of the graveyard wall, stone was consistently encountered within 0.5 m of the surface. The mound clearly has a different composition in this area and may include stone structures. These may represent a focus of Norse or medieval buildings associated with the mound or, alternatively, they may be of Late Iron Age date and indicate an otherwise unrecognized settlement.

7.1.214 Summary

Block 119 and related natural sediments in other Phase 1 blocks probably underlie the whole site in a layer up to 0.5 m deep. Block 107 (Phase 7) is assumed to form a halo, 1–1.5 m deep and roughly 30 m wide around the Iron Age settlement mound. In the area of the present graveyard it appears to have a markedly different character as stone structures have been recorded. The Late Iron Age soil (B105, Phase 7) is probably present wherever subsequent deep burial has occurred and, therefore, its extent will be similar to the 'farm mound' sediments (B103 & B104, Phase 8). The results of an auger survey

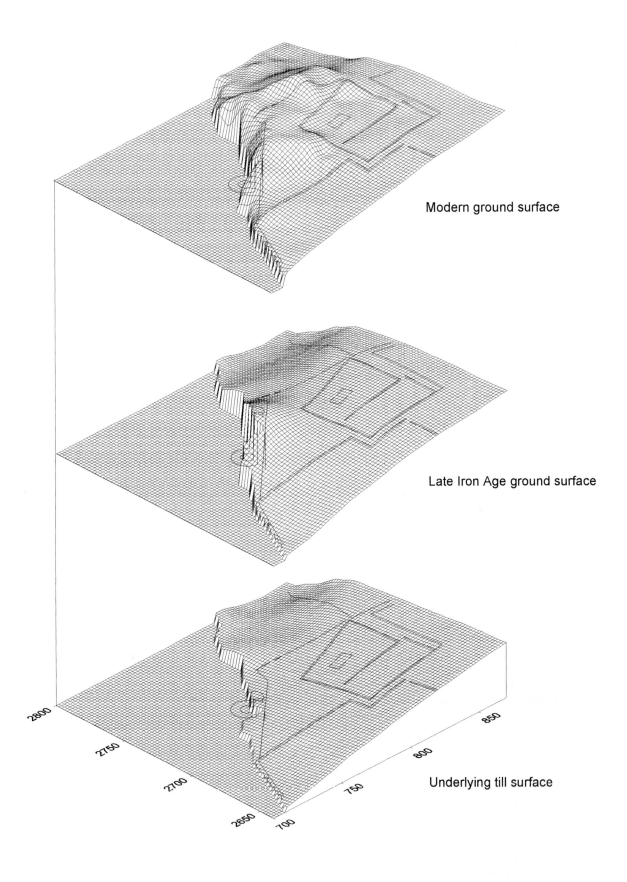

Modern ground surface

Late Iron Age ground surface

Underlying till surface

Illus 184   Expanded view of past and present ground surfaces suggest that the 'farm mound' sediments were deposited on the slope to the north of the Iron Age settlement mound and covered an area roughly 60 m north to south and 90 m east to west. They are deepest at the top of the slope, where they are in excess of 3 m. An expanded view of present and past ground surfaces is presented in Illus 184.

7.1.22 Composition

The components that constitute the sediments may be divided into two main groups: the mineral grains that make up the bulk of the sediment and the biological or cultural materials that are minor inclusions in these sediments. Composition of the main blocks is summarized in Table 47.

7.1.221 Mineral grains

The particle size distribution of the mineral grains was determined by wet sieving and the grain shape and mineralogy examined in thin-section. Particle size distribution is remarkably uniform in all sediments, with one exception (B119), and they can be classified as sandy silt loams. Block 119 sediments, with a greater abundance of medium sand grains, are classified as sandy loams.

7.1.222 Biological and cultural components

Macroscopic components larger than 1 mm were collected through a programme of systematic wet sieving and flotation. Microscopic components (pollen, diatoms, phytoliths and the smaller carbonized plant remains) were observed in soil thin-sections and specifically prepared slides.

The distribution (Part 4.3) of macroscopic biological components in Blocks 103 and 104 (Phase 8), B107 (Phase 7) and B119 (Phase 1) is summarized in Table 47. Three classes of animal remains have been quantified. Mammal bone is present in uniformly low concentrations (10–40 g/10 l) but fish bone is exceptionally abundant in Blocks 103 and 104. No other block exceeds 17 g/10 l concentration. Marine shell is relatively more abundant in Blocks 103 and 104 (Phase 8) but these concentrations are low compared to the shell-rich dumps in Phase 5 and Phase 6.2, where they exceed 4 kg/10 l. Four classes of carbonized plant remains have been quantified. Burnt peat includes fragments of amorphous or largely amorphous carbonized organic matter. Charcoal includes recognizable fragments of stem tissue of woody shrubs and trees and there is a high degree of correlation between burnt peat and charcoal concentrations in the results, with highest values in Block 104 (Phase 8). For grain and other seeds, both Blocks 103 and 104 have relatively high concentrations. The one remaining class of material, fuel ash slag, is vitrified mineral material derived from the burning of organo-mineral

sediments. It is relatively abundant in Block 103 (Phase 8) and Block 107 (Phase 7), but rare in Block 104 (Phase 8) and Block 119 (Phase 1).

Concentration of microscopic biogenic silica (phytoliths and diatoms) was assessed semi-quantitatively. Phytoliths are frequent to abundant in Blocks 103 and 104 (Phase 8), and Block 107 (Phase 7), but rare in Block 119 (Phase 1). Diatoms are frequent in Blocks 103 and 104 (Phase 8), rare in Block 107 (Phase 7), and very rare in Block 119 (Phase 1). Classification of the diatoms according to their ecological ranges indicates that, although there is a degree of overlap between blocks, a dominant habitat is present in each block. Most taxa in Block 107 (Phase 7) derive from terrestrial, neutral to acid soils; in Block 104 (Phase 8), from acid and alkaline, wet or semiaquatic sediments, and in Block 103 (Phase 8), from alkaline, wet or semiaquatic sediments.

Artefacts were rare in all of the blocks under discussion despite the wet sieving programme. Blocks 103 and 104 (Phase 8) contained a few small fragments of copper alloy, two iron objects and a strap handle from a vessel of medieval type. Block 107 (Phase 7) contained six sherds of pottery and a fragment of a bone comb. Two small flakes of flint (SF71 & SF161) were the only artefacts recovered from, respectively, Block 105 (Phase 7) and Block 119 (Phase 1).

7.1.23 Sources

Source can be discussed in terms of the ultimate natural origin of the sediment and also, in many cases, the immediate human process that brought it to the point of deposition. Both of these are of relevance in determining the formation processes controlling the Area 1 sediments.

The sandy silt loam texture of the bulk of the sediments is inherited from the main sediment parent material on the island, a glacial till derived from mudstones, siltstones and fine sandstones. Therefore, this texture does not in itself define a particular soil or sediment source. The exceptional sandy loam texture of Block 119 (Phase 1) is interpreted as the product of mixing windblown sand and a sandy silt loam, till-derived sediment.

The key evidence for the sources of the bulk mineral sediments comes from the analysis of diatoms contained within them. Classification of the diatoms according to their ecological ranges indicates the following dominant sources:

Block 107 (Phase 7): terrestrial, neutral to acid soils (turves?);
Block 104 (Phase 8): acid and alkaline, wet or semiaquatic sediments;
Block 103 (Phase 8): alkaline, wet or semiaquatic sediments (base-rich flushes, fen peat?).

The abundance of diatoms suggests that Block 103 (Phase 8) derives from more highly organic sediments while Block 104 (Phase 8) and Block 107 (Phase 7) contain progressively more mineral-rich sediments. The abundance of carbonized and vitrified residues in Blocks 103 and 104 (Phase 8) and Blocks 105 and 107 (Phase 7) indicates that the organo-mineral source sediments were burnt before deposition and, therefore, are fuel ashes. Variation in the proportions of vitrified and carbonized residues in these sediments is a product of the different fuel types and their combustion properties. Block 119 (Phase 1), in which such residues or any other anthropic inputs are rare, is clearly not derived from fuel ash. It is interpreted as an *in situ* soil with some occupation debris mixed into its upper surface.

Interpretation of the bulk of the sediments in Blocks 103 and 104 (Phase 8) and Blocks 105 and 107 (Phase 7) as fuel ash, however, does not necessarily provide an explanation for the source of the other plant and animal residues. Analysis of the abundant fish bone (Part 6.3) in Blocks 103 and 104 (Phase 8) has demonstrated that it is the waste from the filleting of white fish, primarily saithe and cod. Most of this fish was apparently not eaten on the site but the much less abundant mammal and bird bone is probably refuse from food that was consumed there. The small numbers of marine mollusc shells could also be human food waste but fishing bait or seabird food waste are equally likely sources for the shells. The very few artefacts in Blocks 103 and 104 (Phase 8) emphasize the rarity of what might be considered normal domestic refuse. Block 107 (Phase 7) is somewhat different in that fish bone is not abundant and appears simply to be part of the mix of a low concentration of food refuse.

7.1.24 Mode of deposition

7.1.241 Blocks 103 and 104 (Phase 8)

These two blocks of sediment were deposited by the same processes and are discussed together. There is little evidence for post-depositional mixing of these sediments, except towards the top of Block 103, and the original sedimentary structure is clear. It is clear (Part 7.1.213) that they form an extensive mound on the north slope of the Iron Age settlement mound. They were deposited as a sequence of thin, extensive layers and very thin laminations, dipping northwards from a centre of deposition on the south side of the deposits. The fine layering, which is apparent in soil thin-sections, has been explained as the result of redistribution of sediment from the top of the slope at the south side by the action of wind and water. It is assumed that the fuel ash that constitutes these blocks was dumped in heaps which were unstable and susceptible to erosion. The ash was then washed or blown to form thin, stable low-angle sheets of sediment. It was assumed that this process would lead to size sorting downslope, leaving coarse, proximal sediments at the top and finer distal sediments at the bottom. Particle size analysis failed to detect any such effect but this may reflect the

location of the sampling columns: all four columns (A–D) were clustered within a distance of only 10 m in the centre of the 60 m long mound slope. They did not, therefore, sample either the top or bottom of the slope where the greatest impact of sorting is to be expected. Quantification of the biological components in Blocks 103 and 104 for each column (Table 48) shows that many become less abundant downslope (columns C & D). This pattern could result from deposition of these components (bone, shell, charred fuel, grain) at the top of the slope followed by partial redistribution. However, there are a number of exceptions, indicating that other (unknown) processes of deposition may have been operating at the same time.

The rate of accumulation of Blocks 103 and 104 appears to have been rapid. The lack of post-depositional mixing in these sediments indicates rapid, continuous burial.

7.1.242 Blocks 105 and 107 (Phase 7)

Block 105 is a soil developed in the top of the Block 107 sediments and, therefore, has a common mode of deposition. Analysis of soil thin-sections showed that, throughout most of Block 107, nothing remained of the original sedimentary fabric. It is, therefore, unclear how these sediments were deposited. One discrete deposit, a fused ash (F1046: B107) which forms an extensive layer up to 0.1 m deep, has survived. There is therefore some support for the discontinuous deposition of relatively large volumes of sediment. The large area covered by these shallow sediments suggests the deliberate spreading of the material. Block 107 is horizontal and therefore cannot be explained as the product of redistribution as is the case proposed for Blocks 103 and 104.

7.1.243 Block 119 (Phase 1)

The main source identified for sediments in this block is the underlying till and therefore they form a soil developed *in situ*. The sand component is seen to be part of an extensive deposit of windblown sand that survives as a layer 0.35 m deep elsewhere on the site (B247, B248, B250, B305: Phase 3, and B251, B308, B310, B312: Phase 1) where it has been protected by Phase 1 and Phase 5 structures.

7.1.25 Volume ratio of organic fuel to ash deposits

7.1.251 Introduction

The ratio between the volume of fuel burnt on the site to the volume of ash deposited in Area 1 may be calculated from estimates of the bulk density and organic matter content of the original fuel and bulk density of the resultant ash. The key variable in this calculation is the nature of the original fuel. It is clear that a number of different fuel types were used, ranging from fen peats with a high organic matter content to turves with a medium to low organic matter content. In view of this variation, a range of ratios has been calculated for a variety of possible fuels to illustrate the possible range of results.

7.1.252 Materials and methods

A range of possible fuels was collected in Orkney (Part 6.11). They are summarized as follows:

Blanket peat from Ward Hill, Stenness
• Top peat
• Middle peat
• Bottom peat

Peaty gley turf from Stenness

Valley sediments from Durkadale, Birsay
• Peaty alluvium
• Marl
• Raised bog peat

The samples were oven dried (105 °C) and the dry bulk density determined by weighing blocks of known volume. The ash content (weight) was determined by loss-on-ignition and this ash was then compressed into a container of known volume to give a compressed ash dry bulk density.

7.1.253 Results

The results are presented in Table 49. The ratio between the volume of fuel to ash is presented in column 5 where the volume of ash is presented as a percentage of the volume of dry fuel.

TABLE 49: RATIO OF FUEL BULK DENSITY TO ASH BULK DENSITY FOR A RANGE OF ORGANIC SEDIMENTS FROM ORKNEY

	1.	2.	3.	4.	5.
Stenness					
Top peat	707	96.1	27.6	325.0	8.5
Middle peat	394	97.7	10.6	236.5	4.0
Bottom peat	900	94.1	53.1	562.5	9.4
Turf (O horizon)	240	55.9	105.8	587.5	18.0
Turf (Ag horizon)	1064	55.9	469.2	587.5	79.9
Durkadale					
Peaty alluvium	937	30.1	655.0	712.5	91.9
Marl	890	4.7	848.2	762.5	111.2
Peat	684	90.0	68.4	412.5	16.6

1 = fuel dry bulk density (g/l);
2 = loss-on-ignition (%);
3 = weight of ash (g) per litre of dry fuel;
4 = compressed dry bulk density of ash (g/l);
5 = ash volume as a percentage of dry fuel volume.

7.1.254 Discussion

The proportion of dry fuel surviving as ash varies from only 4.0 per cent in the fibrous blanket peat up to 91.9 per cent in the peaty alluvium. In general, the true peats produced only 5 to 15 per cent ash by volume indicating a reduction of 10 or 20:1 during burning. The top of the peaty turf also yielded a low volume of ash but the lower mineral part of the turf left almost 80 per cent of its volume. For the whole turf and peaty alluvium, a volume reduction of 2:1 or less seems probable. The result of 111.2 per cent from the Durkadale Marl implies an increase in volume after burning and this reflects a failure to pack the ash as tightly as the original sediment. With a loss-on-ignition as low as 4.7 per cent, the marl would not have been useful as a fuel.

7.1.255 Conclusion

Fuels like turf or peaty alluvium can create ten times as much ash as more or less pure organic peats. The large volume and prominence of the 'farm mound' are the result of the use of fuels with a high ash content.

7.1.26 Volume and rate of accumulation of the 'farm mound'

The total surviving volume of the 'farm mound' may be calculated from the sediment depths shown in Illus 183. These give an approximate volume of 5,650 cu m and losses could account for an additional 10 per cent to 20 per cent. The rate of sediment accumulation may be calculated from estimates of total sediment volume and duration of accumulation. Of these two variables, a reasonable estimate of total volume can be calculated but duration is extremely uncertain. Radiocarbon dates from Blocks 103 and 104 allow a timespan of a few decades up to more than two centuries for the accumulation of those sediments (Part 4.1). In addition, it is assumed, given the position of Area 1 on the periphery of the 'farm mound', that these sediments are neither the earliest nor the latest in the mound. The thin-section evidence for only limited biological disturbance suggests rapid accumulation and, on this basis, an estimate of decades rather than centuries seems appropriate for the formation of the 'farm mound'.

On the assumption of a total volume of 6,000 cu m and a duration of deposition of between 20 and 100 years, accumulation rates would lie between 120 and 600 cu m of compressed ash *per annum*. 6,000 cu m of ash represents the residue from the burning of 60,000 to 120,000 cu m of dried peat or roughly 12,000 cu m of dried peaty alluvium.

7.1.27 Post-depositional alteration

Composition and evidence for the mode of deposition can be affected by post-depositional processes. These may involve the loss or introduction of materials and the reorganization of existing components. These processes must be clearly identified in order that the original composition and stratigraphy of the sediments may be determined.

7.1.271 Chemical processes

Routine soil and thin-section analyses both provide evidence for changes in the chemical composition of the Area 1 sediments. The sediments in all blocks are now highly alkaline, non-calcareous to slightly calcareous with high levels of easily available phosphate. It is clear that the basal soil (B119, Phase 1) was decalcified prior to burial because the shell component of the windblown sand has been dissolved. The most likely source of calcium carbonate for the recalcification of the sediments is Block 103 (Phase 8), which derives from base-rich, semi-aquatic sediments and perhaps Block 104 (Phase 8) also. It is suggested that Blocks 105 and 107 (Phase 7) were neutral to acidic when deposited and pollen evidence for heath vegetation indicates that the soil (B105, Phase 7) was acidic when buried by the primary 'farm mound' sediments (B104, Phase 8). High phosphate levels in the basal soil and even the underlying till are also a product of post-burial movement, probably from Block 107 sediments which are rich in ash and organic refuse.

7.1.272 Physical processes

Physical disruption of sediments by plant root growth and invertebrate activity has been identified at various depths in the stratigraphy. Block 119 (Phase 1) and Blocks 105 and 107 (Phase 7) have sediment microstructures created entirely by post-depositional biological activity. Block 104 (Phase 8) and the lower part of Block 103 (Phase 8) are largely unaffected and retain their original sedimentary structure but the top of Block 103 has been partially mixed by biological activity at the modern ground surface.

In general, this type of disruption decreases away from the ground surface and therefore it is most pronounced in sediments that have remained close to a surface for long periods. This relationship can be demonstrated in Area 1 using estimates of the rate of accumulation of sediment obtained by statistical evaluation of radiocarbon dates. The *in situ* soil (B119, Phase 1) remained at the surface from its formation until late in the first millennium BC and therefore became a well-developed soil with a biological structure. It was buried by the sediments of Block 107 (Phase 7). Dates from the top and bottom of this block show that there is a 69 per cent probability that it took 45–270 years to accumulate the 0.5–1.0 m of sediments that constitute Block 107 (Phase 7). Similar analysis of Block 105, the soil that developed in the top of Block 107, suggests that it existed for 310–525 years (69 per cent probability). Taken together, these figures suggest that the

sediments of Block 107 remained close to the ground surface for at least 400 years. This is sufficient time for total biological mixing. In contrast, dates from the top and bottom of 1.5 m of sediment assigned to Blocks 103 and 104 (Phase 8) are very close and there is a 69 per cent probability that the sediment accumulated in less than 160 years. This relatively rapid accumulation is also indicated by the survival of the original structure except where the top of Block 103 approaches the modern surface. A calibrated date of cal AD 1010–1280 (GU-3069c) from the top of Block 103 indicates that the modern soil has developed over at least 700 years.

7.1.28 Conclusions (Table 50)

By combining the information available about sediment composition, source, mode of deposition, rate of accumulation and post-depositional alteration it is possible to construct an approximate dated sequence of development for Area 1. The 'farm mound', as it was originally envisaged by Lamb (1983a), is now known to consist of two distinct accumulations of sediment separated by a long-standing soil.

The whole site is underlain by a shallow glacial till which formed the parent material for a soil (B119, Phase 1) which developed during the first 5000 years of the Holocene. At an unknown date this soil was covered by at least 0.35 m of windblown shell sand, part of a large area of sand-blow which also covered the Neolithic site of the Knap of Howar 1 km to the south. The chronology provided by that site (Ritchie 1983) suggests that sand was deposited after 3500 cal BC. The earliest date from deposits overlying the sand in Area 3 shows that it was present at St Boniface by 2700 cal BC (AA-9561). In Area 1, where the sand was not protected by Bronze Age buildings of Phase 2 and Phase 4, it was partially eroded, and then decalcified and mixed into the underlying soil. This process occurred during the 1800 years between 1300 cal BC and cal AD 500 and was probably promoted by disturbance from the adjacent settlement. Some occupation debris was incorporated into the top of the soil at this time.

The mixed sand and till-derived soil was finally buried by the accumulation of the sediments of Block 107 (Phase 7), between roughly AD 500 and 750. These consisted of fuel ash derived primarily from the burning of turves mixed with some general domestic refuse. Subsequent biological mixing has destroyed the original stratigraphy and it is therefore uncertain how this was deposited; however, the extent of the sediments suggests that this is more than a dump of refuse. Cultivation is one possible mechanism for the spreading of the deposits but this cannot be confirmed with the evidence available. Deposition of Block 107 (Phase 7) subsequently ended and a soil (B105, Phase 7) developed in its surface. This ground surface existed from roughly cal AD 750 to 1100. The soil supported a *Calluna*-rich heath vegetation by the time it was buried, indicative of long-term stability and lack of human disturbance.

TABLE 50: SUMMARY OF SEDIMENT FORMATION IN AREA 1

Date	Block	Event
8000–3000 BC	119	Development of soil in glacial till
3000–1500 BC	119	Accumulation of windblown sand over soil
1300 BC–AD 500	119	Bronze Age and Iron Age activity, mixing and decalcification of windblown sand in soil.
AD 500–750	107	Slow accumulation of fuel ash and other domestic waste forming 0.5–1.0 m of well-mixed sediments
AD750–1100	105	Development of soil in top of Block 107 sediments
AD 1100–1200	103/104	Rapid accumulation of fuel ash, fish processing waste, and some other refuse forming up to 3.0 m of highly stratified sediments
AD 1200–present	1/102	Development of soil in top of Block 103 sediments. Marine erosion of west side of Area 1

Deposition started again in approximately AD 1100 with the accumulation of Block 104 (Phase 8). Sediments were dumped on the north slope of the Iron Age settlement mound and then redistributed by natural processes down the slope in a series of shallow layers and lenses. These started at the south end of Area 1 and gradually extended northwards as more sediment was deposited. Block 104 (Phase 8) consisted of fuel ash derived from the burning of turf and other organic sediments, mixed with abundant fish processing waste and a little domestic refuse. The rapid accumulation of Block 104, taking a few decades at most, was continued by the equally rapid accumulation of Block 103 (Phase 8). Differences between these two blocks appear to result from a change in the source of fuel to a base-rich and more organic sediment and there is no change in the abundance or nature of the fish processing waste. The rapid rate of sediment accumulation is evidence of a high level of activity on the site but it is difficult to explain this in terms of a normal settlement. The evidence is consistent with the use of the site by a specialist fishing enterprise, solely for the processing of freshly caught white fish to produce wind-dried fillets (stock fish). The fuel ash is interpreted as the product of fires used to render down the fish livers for oil. This is discussed further in Part 7.2.

The date for the ending of deposition of Block 103 (Phase 8) is uncertain as the latest sediments lie inland of the exposed section and were not sampled. A date of *c*. AD 1200 is possible. Since that time there has been no significant accumulation of sediment in Area 1 and the loss of an unknown volume of sediment by marine erosion.

7.1.3 The Farm Mound in Orkney

7.1.31 Summary of previous research

The Area 1 sediments at St Boniface were identified as a 'farm mound' during a re-survey of the island in 1982 by Lamb (1983a). The identification of this site and six other 'farm mounds' in Papay was, in part, the result of a previous survey of Sanday and North Ronaldsay (Lamb 1980) where twenty-two settlement mounds, referred to as tells, were identified. Between these two surveys there were two important shifts in interpretation. In Sanday and North Ronaldsay, all large man-made mounds were given the general description of tells, mounds of accumulated settlement debris following the Near Eastern model with no implied age for the sites. By the time that Papay was surveyed, only mounds characterized by brown loamy earth were referred to as 'farm mounds', a Norwegian term for a medieval site type in Arctic Norway. Mounds consisting of superimposed stone structures, such as King's Craig (Lamb 1983a, No.16), were specifically excluded. This change in interpretation is discussed by Lamb in the introduction to the Papay survey (1983a, 7):

When the Sanday and North Ronaldsay list was compiled, the farm mounds of those islands had been observed but not studied in detail. The exposure of stone structures, by sea-erosion at Hookin and by farmyard clearance at How, suggested that the mounds resulted from the repeated replacement of structures after the manner of oriental tells. Work by Dr D.A. Davidson and Mr I. Simpson of Strathclyde University has since shown that their composition characteristically is a fairly uniform organic deposit. The mounds therefore are closely parallel to the *gårdshauger* of Arctic Norway.

The research work referred to by Davidson and Simpson (Davidson *et al* 1983; Davidson *et al* 1986) concentrated on three of the mounds in Sanday: Langskaill, Westbrough and Skelbrae. Radiocarbon dates were obtained, indicating that these three mounds were initiated in the Late Iron Age and Norse periods and, with the exception of the basal peats at Westbrough, consisted of peat ash and turves with some domestic refuse (Davidson *et al* 1986, 56–8). Although these researchers accepted the interpretation of farm mound they failed to detect specific structures or buildings forming part of the farm. In Orkney, where buildings are constructed almost exclusively of stone, this seems a curious result even from their relatively small sampling pits. One further important point is that, despite the remark by Lamb quoted above, the sediments were generally mineral in content with only 2 to 9 per cent loss-on-ignition (Davidson *et al* 1986).

7.1.32 The Norwegian farm mounds

The Norwegian farm mounds (*gårdshauger*) have been noted since the late nineteenth century but detailed archaeological investigations began only in the 1960s (Bertelsen 1979). Recent research excavations by Bertelsen (1984, 1989) and Holm-Olsen (1981) have provided a large body of information about their distribution, age and composition. The mounds occur in Norway north of the Arctic Circle and are most abundant in the counties of Nordland and Troms. Radiocarbon dates from the bases of mounds generally fall in the range AD 900–1500 (19 sites) but two dates from the first millennium BC have also been obtained (Bertelsen 1979). The relationship between these very early dated strata and the overlying mound is not known as the results derive from test pits only. The composition of the mounds has been the subject of much discussion but current opinion (Bertelsen 1989) is that the key component is turf derived from turf and timber houses. The repeated construction and disintegration of these structures is the main source of sediment in the mound. Other contributing materials include domestic refuse (food refuse, ashes and artefacts) and animal dung. The farm mounds are therefore closely related to the Near Eastern tell in that they have formed primarily by the accumulation of fine mineral sediments, introduced as house building material. It may be concluded that the distribution of farm mounds corresponds to the area in which permanent settlements of turf-built structures were established, apparently in the medieval period.

7.1.33 Comparison of the evidence from Norway and Orkney

The equation of the Orkney mounds with the Norwegian farm mounds was based on the observed lack of stone structures in the mounds investigated in Sanday and the appropriate radiocarbon dates (Davidson *et al* 1983; Lamb 1983a). Subsequent analysis of the composition of three of the Sanday mounds by Davidson *et al* (1986) appeared to reinforce this link as they identified turf, ash and other domestic refuse as the main components. However, if the comparison is taken a stage further, to the question of formation processes, then differences begin to emerge.

Davidson *et al* (1986, 45), in a summary of their findings, stated:

It is suggested that these materials accumulated from the ash of domestic hearths as well as from the residues of bedding material from the byres (cattle sheds). Turves (vegetation plus some underlying soil) would have been cut, dried, and then used in the byres and such turves would have retained a significant mineral content. The implication is that the inherent fertility of the island made it unnecessary for the farmers to spread the dung over the fields.

This interpretation was related to an earlier theory of Norwegian mound formation by Munch (1966). He proposed that a shift from arable agriculture to stock fish production occurred in the eleventh to thirteenth centuries AD. The mounds were thought to consist largely of animal dung no longer spread on the fields. Subsequent excavation results in Norway have played down the importance of dung as a component of the mounds and this theory is now thought not to explain either the available dating or distribution evidence (Bertelsen 1984). The current Norwegian interpretation, namely the decay of turf-built structures, is hard to reconcile with the Orkney results because of the general lack of evidence for structures within the Sanday mounds. In the cases of the investigations at Westbrough and Skelbrae, this could reflect the limited size of the sample pits, but at Langskaill the mound has been half removed by the sea exposing a complete section. In over 100 m of section, up to 4.5 m deep, the only structure noted was 'some crude walling low down near the N extremity' (Lamb 1980, 17). This may be related to a layer of flagstones noted by Davidson *et al* (1986, 53) in the same area. Therefore, on the evidence available to date there is no reason to believe that these Sanday mounds contain the complex stratigraphy typical of a settlement mound.

This conclusion compares well with the results from St Boniface where both the Norse and Late Iron Age elements of the supposed farm mound (Blocks 103/104 & 107) are similarly lacking in evidence of structures. The St Boniface results highlight one further contrast with the Norwegian data: the absence of artefacts in the Orkney mounds. The Norwegian mounds were initially dated using their abundant artefact assemblages but very little has been recovered from the Orcadian mounds. Wet sieving of 727 l of sediment from Blocks 103 and 104 at St Boniface produced only two iron objects and a few items and scraps of copper alloy. No artefacts are reported by Davidson and Simpson from Sanday and, in his survey, Lamb (1980, 17) specifically noted that no artefacts were visible in the long Langskaill cliff-section. Indeed, Lamb was able to propose a very early prehistoric date for that mound because of the absence of artefacts. It seems, therefore, that the Orkney mounds that have so far been investigated belong to a class of stratified ash mounds, largely lacking any structures or other evidence of occupation on the mound. Therefore, they are not farm mounds *sensu strictu*, in the manner in which that monument type is defined in its Norwegian homeland.

7.1.34 Formation of the Orkney mounds

Clearly the Orkney mounds represent a major focus of activity in the Late Iron Age and Norse periods. The key requirements for the formation of mounds of this type appear to be:

- a process that uses large quantities of fuel;
- a fuel with a high ash content;
- no reuse of the ash after burning.

At St Boniface it is proposed that the process responsible for the use of fuel in the Norse period is the processing of fish liver oil but in the Late Iron Age no such specific explanation can be proposed. The use of a fuel with a high ash content may provide an explanation for the limited distribution of the mounds in Orkney which have only been recognized on Papay, Sanday and North Ronaldsay. These islands lack peat deposits, now and in the past, and therefore their inhabitants would have used alternatives like turf and organic sediments, rich in mineral matter. Use of blanket peat, which is widely available elsewhere in Orkney, will generate perhaps only 10 per cent of the ash present at St Boniface and a 3 m high mound would be reduced to an insignificant 0.3 m deep layer. Failure to use the ash, primarily as an agricultural fertilizer, has been discussed by Davidson *et al* (1986, 45) who proposed that it reflected the natural high productivity of those islands with mounds. An alternative explanation, appropriate for the Norse period at St Boniface, is that the producers of the ash, being specialist fishermen, were not involved in arable agriculture and therefore had no need for fertilizers.

The four mounds dated so far in Orkney have all produced dates in the range AD 500–1400. Given the three requirements listed above, it might be assumed that this restricted timespan reflects the currency of processes leading to the accumulation of ash. However, there is evidence from an excavated settlement site for much earlier ash accumulation. At Pool, also in Sanday, excavations have revealed a Neolithic settlement mound consisting primarily of ash dumps with the foundations of numerous stone houses. The mound has been partially destroyed by marine erosion but it appears to have originally covered an area roughly 50 m in diameter with sediments at least 1 m deep in the centre. The fuel that generated the ash has been identified as a freshwater organic sediment, probably dug from an adjacent lake basin (Hunter *et al* forthcoming). There is therefore no reason to expect that all deep ash accumulations will prove to be early medieval in date. However, the site at Pool is a settlement mound with numerous stone buildings and this highlights the most distinctive feature of the medieval Orkney ash

mounds, which is their lack of structures. Therefore, on the basis of the available evidence, it is proposed that these mounds do form a distinctive site type of early medieval date, but one that is not related to either the Norwegian *gårdshauger* or the stone settlement mounds of Orkney.

7.2 The Settlement Complex: Discussion and Overview

Christopher Lowe

7.2.1 Introduction

The aims of the excavation assessment (Part 2.1.2) of the cliff-section at St Boniface Church were to clarify the nature, date, quality and extent of the archaeological deposits and features at the site. These objectives were realized as a result of the rigorous and fully integrated programme of fieldwork and post-excavation analysis. The key tool in this work was the creation of a complete stratigraphic hierarchy which spans, with varying degrees of detail and definition, some 4000–5000 years in the development of the site, from the earliest times to the present day. This was achieved in spite of the logistical and topographical problems which the cliff-section presented prior to excavation (Part 2.1.3).

The success of the project, however, has not been simply restricted to providing some answers to those questions which were posed at the outset. Other research themes, unanticipated at the start, have arisen as the project developed. These, together with an overview of the site and its development over time, are discussed in roughly chronological order.

7.2.2 The Second Millennium BC and Earlier

The earliest structural remains on the site comprise the funerary monuments of Phase 1 and the fragmentary buildings of Phase 2. They can be dated not later than the middle of the second millennium BC and, as indicated by the radiocarbon dates from contexts at and near the base of the section, could be considerably earlier. No diagnostic Neolithic material, however, was recovered from the site. Nonetheless, the early third millennium BC date from cattle bone in the primary sand horizon is presumably indicative of Neolithic settlement in the area. The earliest identifiable pottery from the site is of Late Bronze Age type.

The change in the use of the site from funerary to domestic, possibly by Phase 2 but certainly by Phases 4 and 5, can be paralleled at Howe (Ballin Smith 1994), Pierowall (Sharples 1984), Quanterness (Renfrew 1979) and at Calf of Eday Long cairn (Davidson & Henshall 1989, 107–9). In each case, Iron Age structures, demonstrably early structures in the cases of Howe, Pierowall and Quanterness, were constructed on or adjacent to Neolithic chambered tombs. A similar sequence has tentatively been advanced at Pool (Hunter 1990, 178) and examples of a similar imposition of Iron Age over Neolithic structures have also been noted at Clettraval and Unival on North Uist (Hingley 1992, 16).

In each of the cases where dating is available, the 'restructuring' of the earlier monument has been a feature of the Early Iron Age period. At St Boniface, on the other hand, the reuse of an earlier funerary focus can be assigned to a period not later than the Late Bronze Age settlement of Phase 4. Hingley's (1992, 16, 41–2) recent reappraisal of Iron Age society in Scotland, stressing 'the significance of ideology and ritual in defining, perpetuating and contradicting dominant systems', has suggested that appropriation of earlier sites, funerary or domestic, was a mechanism whereby prestige and status could be enhanced. Clearly, this kind of model is relevant to the later development of the site, in the transition between the Late Iron Age and Early Christian periods (Part 7.2.42). Here, however, at the opposite end of the chronology, the enhancement of status, which appropriation of an earlier focus could offer, seems not to have been accorded to the builders of the Early Iron Age site, but rather to the predecessor settlement of the Late Bronze Age or earlier. In other words, it is at this period, in the last quarter of the second millennium BC, that the settlement continuum, occupying broadly the period 1250 BC to AD 1250, seems to have begun.

The fragmentary remains of the Late Bronze Age settlement of the late second millennium BC (Phase 4) lay immediately to the north of the later roundhouse. The best preserved of the buildings of this phase, Structure 4, was a thick-walled, free-standing cellular building. Although only partially exposed in both plan and section, it resembles structures of the type associated with the Late Bronze Age phase at Jarlshof (Hamilton 1956) or, in general, the Calder-type 'Neolithic/Bronze Age' houses of Shetland (Calder 1956; Calder 1964; Lowe forthcoming). Rubble deposits beneath the later roundhouse may represent further remains of buildings of either this or an earlier period of settlement.

The poorly preserved remains of Structure 3, to the north of Structure 4, and Structure 5, which was built over and between the earlier buildings, were the only upstanding remains attributed to this phase. The concentration of buildings, within the area that was later enclosed, and significantly none was found outwith this limit, would indicate a nucleated settlement, of the type revealed in the Jarlshof sequence. There is no evidence that the settlement of Phase 4 was enclosed and, insofar as this settlement phase was represented on site, no substantial or 'pre-eminent' buildings appear to have been present. Although substantial parts of the Phase 4 or earlier settlement were levelled as a result of the construction of the roundhouse, Structures 3 to 5 remained intact and presumably continued to be occupied into this later phase (Phase 5). The construction and occupation of Structure 5 may lie wholly within this later phase.

7.2.3 The Iron Age Settlement

7.2.31 Introduction

The construction on the site of a substantial thick-walled roundhouse appears to mark a significant change in the nature of the settlement, in terms of the monumentality (Barrett 1981, 215; Armit 1990b, 92) of the building itself which was to dominate the settlement and the local landscape for the next 1500–2000 years. If the status or prestige of the earlier phase settlement had been enhanced by association with, or proximity to, the earlier funerary focus, it is interesting to reflect upon how much more this would have been enhanced by the very act of incorporating the earlier cairn and settlement remains into the wall-fabric of the roundhouse itself and sealing the other funerary features beneath its floor. The construction of the roundhouse on a sand and rubble subsoil betokens confidence, if not arrogance, on the part of the builders. Those builders, like those at Howe who strove against gravity to build the Phase 5 roundhouse 'halfway up a clay mound' (Ballin Smith 1994, 39), however, were not the builders of Mousa, arguably a late building (Fojut 1981, 227), but the Late Bronze Age or Early Iron Age inhabitants of the site.

7.2.32 The roundhouse

The large circular building (Structure 2) at St Boniface was constructed sometime in the period between 1610–1320 cal BC (AA-9560) and 800–390 cal BC (GU-3059c & GU-3271c). A date within the second quarter of the first millennium BC, given the presence of Late Bronze Age/Early Iron Age pottery types in the wall fabric of the building, seems the most likely period for its construction. Other, similarly early buildings, described as roundhouses, have been discovered in Orkney in recent years (Tables 51 & 52), including the buildings at Bu (Hedges 1987, i) and Quanterness (Renfrew 1979), both on Orkney Mainland, and Pierowall, Westray (Sharples 1984) and Tofts Ness on Sanday (Dockrill 1988; Hunter et al forthcoming). An early date for Crosskirk broch, in Caithness, although discounted by its excavator (Fairhurst 1984, 165), has also been revived by Armit (1991, 188).

In terms of Armit's (1991, 182–3; 1992, 18) classification, Structure 2 at St Boniface could be defined as a complex atlantic roundhouse:

> the *simple atlantic roundhouses* are those which, although they may be massively built, lack evidence for the use of the specific traits of *broch architecture*; the *complex atlantic roundhouses* employ some or all of these traits in their construction and include those structures previously classed as *broch towers*. This latter term will be used to describe structures with palpable evidence of multi-storey construction (MacKie's brochs (1983)) but does not imply a typological distinction.
>
> (Armit 1991, 183)

TABLE 51: RADIOCARBON DATES FOR EARLY IRON AGE ROUNDHOUSES IN ORKNEY AND CAITHNESS

	Uncalibrated	*Calibrated*
Bu, Mainland		
GU 1228 primary occupation of roundhouse	2470±95 bp	830–385 BC
GU 1154 primary occupation of roundhouse	2460±80 bp	810–390 BC
Quanterness, Mainland		
Q 1465 primary occupation of roundhouse	2570±85 bp	915–465 BC
Q 1464 primary occupation of roundhouse	2440±85 bp	810–380 BC
Tofts Ness, Sanday		
(all samples were taken from later deposits associated with the secondary roundhouse)		
GU 2183	2990±100 bp	1515–950 BC
GU 2207	2510±140 bp	985–370 BC
GU 2288	2470±50 bp	805–410 BC
GU 2544	2470±50 bp	805–410 BC
St Boniface, Papa Westray		
GU 3059c shell midden, TAQ roundhouse	2830±50 bp	800–390 BC
GU 3271c shell midden, TAQ roundhouse	2850±50 bp	800–390 BC
Pierowall, Westray		
GU 1580 occupation deposit, TPQ roundhouse	2510±80 bp	830–395 BC
GU 1581 occupation deposit, TAQ roundhouse	2425±60 bp	780–385 BC
Howe (Phase 5), Mainland		
GU 1789 construction of roundhouse rampart	2405±70 bp	800–385 BC
Crosskirk broch, Caithness		
SRR 266 construction of broch floor (TPQ)	2380±50 bp	770–400 BC

References: Ballin Smith 1994; Fairhurst 1984, 162; Dockrill pers comm; Hedges 1987, i; Renfrew 1979; Sharples 1984

The radiocarbon dates have been calibrated with respect to their calendrical age in accordance with the procedures described by Dalland (1993), using software which incorporates the Belfast calibration curve (Pearson *et al* 1986). The dates have been adjusted, where necessary, for the marine effect. The 'Long Continuous Range' dates, quoted here, are equivalent to the 2-sigma level of confidence.

Structure 2, clearly of massive construction and arguably of circular form, certainly has the appearance of a broch. Among the specific traits of broch architecture could be included the checked entrance, bar-hole and 'guard cell', and the presence of an external settlement, the later phases of which were laid out in respect of the building. Although preserved to a height, externally, of up to 3 m, the interior face of the building was much reduced, standing only 1 m high or less, well below the 1.8 m or so where a scarcement level might be expected (Hedges 1985; 1987, iii, 10). Nor was there any trace of an intra-mural stair or passage, although such would have most likely lain in the 9 o'clock to 3 o'clock position in the circuit (the entrance lying at 6 o'clock), or, in other words, in that part of the building which has been lost to erosion.

On the basis of MacKie's (1983, 125; 1987; 1991; 1994) strict classification, regarding the absence of a high hollow wall with superimposed intra-mural galleries and, moreover, the proposition that 'no true broch can be older than about 50 BC', Structure 2 could not be classified as a broch. It is interesting to reflect, however, that the St Boniface building, when identified as the Castle of Bothikan (Lowe 1994), was included in MacKie's distribution map as a 'probable broch' (MacKie 1965, fig.1). In Hedges' (1987, iii, 50) survey of the brochs of Orkney, the Castle of Bothikan was catalogued in the list of authenticated broch sites, in the category of 'known brochs'. It is unfortunate, therefore, that the unwitting re-excavation of the building should have found not a broch but a roundhouse! In part, this is a problem of terminology and classification and it is a

TABLE 52: EARLY IRON AGE ROUNDHOUSES IN ORKNEY AND CAITHNESS

(All dimensions in metres)

Site	External Diameter	Internal Diameter	Wall Thickness
St Boniface	17.6	10.6	3.2–3.8 (Primary)
	17.6	7.5	4.9–5.3 (Secondary)
Quanterness	8.8	7.0	0.8–1.4 (Primary)
	10.2	7.0	2.1 (Secondary)
Pierowall	>16.0	?10.0	3.1
Howe (Phase 5)	?16.0	?8.0	?4.0
Bu	20.0	9.0–10.1	4.8–5.7
Tofts Ness	8.4–9.6	5.2	1.6–2.2
Crosskirk, Caithness	18.3	9.5	4.3–5.8

References: Ballin Smith 1994, 31–2; Fairhurst 1984; Dockrill pers comm; Hedges 1987, i; Renfrew 1979; Sharples 1984

subject which has been ably discussed, most recently, in the various writings of Armit, Hedges and MacKie. The neutral term 'roundhouse' has been employed here.

7.2.33 Structural development and use of space

The structural sequence which has been revealed at St Boniface carries both echoes and discordances with other, excavated Iron Age sites. It is a sequence which progresses from an unenclosed to enclosed site. Throughout this development the roundhouse was associated with a series of extra-mural structures, each major phase of building superimposed upon another. It is a sequence which begins in the second quarter of the first millennium BC and continues, seemingly unbroken, through to at least the first quarter of the first millennium AD.

The primary roundhouse phase (Phase 5) witnessed the construction of the roundhouse and its insertion among the buildings of a pre-existing settlement, elements of which were left upstanding and presumably continued in occupation through the Phase 4/5 interface. Other structural elements of the Phase 4/5 extra-mural settlement are considered to be represented by the deep rubble horizon which accumulated over the buildings of Phase 4, against the exterior of the roundhouse and on which the buildings of Phase 6.1 and later were subsequently constructed. Structure 22 may represent an outlying part of this settlement, albeit a relatively late building in the sequence. No evidence for the enclosure of the Phase 4/5 settlement was located. Notable deposits of this phase included a number of a large shell

middens. The presence of limpets, in quantity, was also a feature of the Early Iron Age levels at Pierowall (Sharples 1984, 91).

Clearly, Structure 2 at St Boniface is not the 'isolated roundhouse' (Hedges 1985, 167; Foster 1989, 35; 1990) which, on the basis of its dating, might have been imagined; nor is its extra-mural settlement a late feature on the site. It is not known if the outbuildings associated with the primary roundhouse settlement were arranged on a radial or non-radial basis (Foster 1989, 36) since few extant structural features of this phase (Phase 5) were exposed on plan. Much will depend upon the extent to which the surviving buildings of Phase 4 continued to exercise an influence upon the design and layout of the settlement and this is unknown.

The change from unenclosed to enclosed site (Phase 6.1), effected for whatever reason, signifies a radical change in the development of the site and in the perceptions of the inhabitants of the site. Whether the enclosure was occasioned by concerns about defence or status is not known. It is apparent, however, that the presence of an enclosure would enable control over the movements of people in and out of the settlement to be more effectively exercised. The primary enclosure of the settlement is attributed to the period in or around the last quarter of the first millennium BC or possibly slightly earlier. The enclosure comprised a stone-revetted ditch and wall, pierced on the north-east by a gateway through which a causeway extended to the north of the site. The radical misalignment of the roundhouse and enclosure entrances, to the south-east and north-east respectively, is an unusual feature of enclosed Iron Age sites. The misalignment at St Boniface can be explained by the chronological relationship of the two structures and the assumption that the requirements of the builders of the enclosure differed, in some unquantifiable way, from those which concerned the earlier builders of the roundhouse. Perhaps changes in the immediate landscape or resource needs occasioned what appears to have been a reorientation of the later settlement. Further entrances through the enclosure may exist elsewhere on the circuit. No parallels for such an arrangement are known at present, although there are few sites where the enclosure has been examined, or survives sufficiently complete to be examined by fieldwork.

A series of buildings was constructed in the area between the enclosure and the roundhouse. Access between both was seemingly conducted via the extra-mural passage which extended around the roundhouse. Such buildings as survive, and the implications of the relationship between the enclosure entrance and the extra-mural passage around the roundhouse, would suggest that the settlement of Phase 6.1 was laid out on an organized radial plan. The position of Structure 6, opposite the enclosure entrance, however, seems anomalous (Part 4.6.2). This building could form part of the structural assemblage of Phase 5 (Illus 12).

Phase 6.2, attributed to the first quarter of the first

millennium AD, witnessed the recutting of the enclosure ditch and the refurbishment of the structures at and around the entrance into the enclosure. The ditch terminals, not traced during the excavation, are assumed to have lain closer to the external causeway than was the case with regard to the primary enclosure ditch. The use of transverse stone buttresses to support the revetted sides of the ditch can be paralleled at the Broch of Gurness (Hedges 1987, ii, 46).

Further buildings (Structure 10 and, possibly, Structure 12 later) expanded across the space between the enclosure entrance and the roundhouse, interrupting access to the latter via the passage around its walls. Access to the roundhouse via this passage was ultimately blocked by the insertion of a series of cross-walls and external buttresses. Phase 6.2, prior to the subsequent abandonment of the enclosed site, seems to be typified by a relative breakdown of the radial pattern previously established, leading to an infilling of space within the enclosure. Stone-robbing, represented by the debris left *in situ* in the passage prior to its final blocking, also occurred. Overall, the impression of Phase 6.2 is that of a settlement in decline.

The creation of what might be termed 'ritual deposits' (Part 7.2.34) are accredited to this relatively late phase of occupation. The presence of 'burnt mound material' (*sensu* Barber 1990), in association with burnished pottery, is also a feature of this phase. Burnished ware was also recovered from spreads of burnt mound material at Kebister, Shetland (Owen & Lowe forthcoming).

7.2.34 Ritual aspects

Barrett (1981, 215) has commented, in the context of the brochs, that 'the very acts of their construction contain the recognition of, or submission to, an authority continually seeking to assert its own natural validity'. Ritual aspects of monumentality, in the context of the insertion of the roundhouse into an earlier settlement and its construction over earlier funerary structures, have been considered elsewhere (Part 7.2.3). This early example aside, the formation of what could be considered as ritual deposits appears to represent a relatively late phenonmenon in the development of the site. Both examples, the deposition of human remains in the primary sediments of the secondary enclosure ditch and the burial of an arthritic cat beneath secondary paving levels in the enclosure entrance, belong to Phase 6.2. Both deposits are concentrated within the area of the secondary gateway. This phase has been typified as one of incipient decline and breakdown in the order and organization of the settlement.

Human remains were recovered from the enclosure ditch which surrounds the broch at Torwoodlie, Selkirkshire (Piggott 1951, 105). Four burials were found on the line of the disused palisade at Dryburn Bridge, East Lothian (Triscott 1982), and fragments of two skulls were recovered from the enclosure

ditch at Rispain Camp, Wigtonshire (Haggerty & Haggerty 1983). Human remains were also found beneath the threshold of one of the buildings at Wag of Forse (Curle 1947, 21) and Campbell (1991, 141–7) has highlighted a series of ritual pit deposits, containing articulated and cremated animal bone, beneath the floor of the wheelhouse at Sollas. The radiocarbon dates for this activity at Sollas calibrate, roughly, to the first quarter of the first millennium AD. The burial of a seated arthritic old man beneath the floor of Enclosure I at Crosskirk is also a relatively late feature in the sequence at that site. Bone from the skeleton has been radiocarbon dated to 430 cal BC–cal AD 140 (2 sigma: Fairhurst 1984, 86–8). An interesting point is that these ritual deposits, if so considered and where dated, seem to be associated with immediate pre-abandonment sequences and/or a Middle Iron Age date.

7.2.4 The Early Medieval Ecclesiastical Site (see Part 1.2.3)

7.2.41 Introduction

Historical notices of an early ecclesiastical settlement at St Boniface church, whether of a monastic and/or episcopal structure and organization, have not survived. Lamb (1993, 265; 1995) has suggested that a Pictish bishopric was established at St Boniface by around the middle of the eighth century. Certainly the presence of such an establishment may be inferred for around the middle of the ninth century, on the basis of the documentary evidence contained in the *Life* of St Findan and, possibly also, on the basis of the saga reference to Rognvald Brusison's burial on the island in AD 1046 (*Orkneyinga Saga* cap.xxx; Taylor 1938, 185). That some form of early ecclesiastical establishment existed on the site, possibly from the eighth century, is most clearly represented in the local toponymy and in the material assemblage which has been previously recovered. The latter comprises two cross-inscribed stones and a stone panel from a composite corner-post shrine. These have been dated, on art-historical grounds, to the eighth century or, more broadly, to the last quarter of the first millennium AD.

The cross-inscribed stones were found during grave-digging on the north side of the church. On the assumption that the stones functioned as grave-markers, this clearly indicates that the early medieval and post-twelfth-century cemeteries on the site were spatially coincident to a greater or lesser degree. The early medieval church is assumed either to underlie its later successor or to have been located to one side of it, possibly to the north in the area now overlain by the 'farm mound'. This is an area where stone was consistently encountered close to the surface during the course of the auger survey. The possible settlement focus, thus located (Part 7.1.213), could represent the site of the early church at St Boniface, its contemporary cemetery lying to the south of it. It may be significant, in this context, that the local folk tradition, recorded by Marwick (1925, 34: Part 2.2.4) and still just traceable today (Lamb 1983a, 18), seems to have preserved some memory of an ecclesiastical building in this area. The identification of a second mound, to the west of the churchyard, which clearly has the remains of a subrectangular building on its summit, is discussed elsewhere (Part 2.2.4).

7.2.42 The spatial association of Iron Age and ecclesiastical sites

The reconstruction of the palaeotopography of the site (Part 7.1.212), proposed on the basis of the auger survey and by analogy with excavated broch sites in Orkney, suggests that the early ecclesiastical site and its successor were established on the fringe of the Iron Age settlement. This is an interesting location and is quite different from sites, such as St Tredwell's chapel on Papay (Lowe 1994, Illus 6), Marykirk at Grimeston in Harray (Lowe 1987, ii, figs. 18–19), the chapel at Houseby in Birsay (Lowe 1987, ii, fig. 22), Peterkirk in Evie (Lowe 1987, ii, fig. 21), and possibly Kirkaby on Unst, Shetland (Lowe 1987, ii, fig. 32) and many of the lochside Iron Age promontory sites which have later ecclesiastical associations (Lowe 1987, i, 26), where the ecclesiastical focus has been established directly over the Iron Age settlement mound, frequently over the broch itself. Parallels for a fringe location, on the other hand, appear to be less common, although this may be an artefact of preservation and survival. Examples include Crosskirk in Caithness (Fairhurst 1984) and, from Orkney, Tammaskirk in Rendall (Lowe 1987, ii, pl. 47b), Lyking chapel in Sandwick (Lowe 1987, ii, fig. 20), St Mary's church at Culbinsbrough on Bressay, Shetland (Lowe 1987, ii, fig. 39), and possibly the *Monker Green* site at Stromness cemetery (Bell & Dickson 1989).

The frequent association of ecclesiastical and Iron Age sites in the Northern Isles, particularly in Orkney, is a well-known phenomenon and has been discussed elsewhere (Lowe 1987, i, 287–327). It was first noted by the compiler for the *New Statistical Account* (1842) for Sanday and reiterated by Marwick (1923, 27) in his examination of the monuments of that island. Clouston (1918, 105), like Marwick, concluded that 'this was simply for the utilitarian purpose of securing a handy quarry [of building stone]'. This association, considering brochs as secular centres of power in the traditional landscape, however, may suggest a situation which was not guided by strictly utilitarian considerations. Lamb (1973a, 196–7; 1976, 151; 1979, 2; 1983b, 178), for example, has suggested that the frequent association of ecclesiastical sites with Late Iron Age domestic settlements may represent an important element of continuity. The sites may have been gifted to early ecclesiastics by secular patrons in much the same way that the reuse and reoccupation of Roman

sites, particularly forts, is evidenced in Anglo-Saxon England, a phenomenon which has been discussed by Cramp (1976, 212–15), Rigold (1977) and Richard Morris (1983, 40–5). The reuse of elevated, enclosed, fortified sites, donated by princely or royal patrons seeking to extend and ensure their political influence, is also a feature of the sites and monuments of the eighth-century Anglo-Saxon mission in Central Germany (Parsons 1983). The establishment of ecclesiastical sites on Iron Age settlements in Orkney may have served an existing Christian community, on the site or in the vicinity, or have facilitated its conversion. Some such process was suggested by Scott (1926, 48) in his discussion of the ecclesiastical artefacts from the Broch of Burrian on North Ronaldsay. More recently, Lamb (1993; 1995) has discussed the phenomenon in the context of facilitating the expansion of Pictish royal power in Orkney in the eighth century and has drawn attention to a network of Petrine dedications which may reflect the head churches of this early ecclesiastical organization.

No firm conclusions can be drawn solely in respect of the location of St Boniface church and its spatial relationship to the earlier Iron Age settlement. A fringe location, however, could be considered to be more indicative of an attachment to an existing settlement than establishment of the church directly over the settlement mound itself. It is not known if the early ecclesiastical site at St Boniface was associated with an extant settlement or whether it was established among its abandoned ruins; this is discussed further below. Certainly the indications, from the excavated cliff-section (Phase 6.3), are that the core area of the Iron Age site had been long abandoned prior to the eighth century. The roundhouse itself, however, may have still been standing at this time (B217, Phase 8).

No structural evidence for the early ecclesiastical site was recovered from the excavated cliff-section. The fragmentary late buildings (Structures 14, 15 & 21) on Area 2, which have been assigned to Phase 8, like the subrectangular building (Part 2.2.4) which lies immediately to the east, relate to a poorly defined late post-roundhouse or medieval occupation on the site and are of uncertain association. The stone shrine panel, which was recovered from the beach in 1992, is unprovenanced. It may suggest that ecclesiastical structures were present on this part of the site. Equally, it could have derived as rubble from later building works in the vicinity.

7.2.43 The plaggen soil: an 'ecclesiastical artefact'?

The best possible evidence, from the cliff-section, for Early Christian activity on the site could come from Area 1. It may be represented by the formation of the deep plaggen soil (B107, Phase 7) outwith and to the north of the enclosed Iron Age settlement. The results of the soil thin-section analysis (Part 6.11) indicate that these sediments consisted of *in situ* ash dumps, deposited infrequently, with intervening periods of soil formation. Cultivation has been proposed as a possible mechanism for the spreading of the deposits. The base of the soil, overlying the old causeway which approached the enclosed site from the north, has been radiocarbon dated to cal AD 285–670 (GU-3063). The upper soil horizon, below the buried old ground surface, has been radiocarbon dated to cal AD 520–870 (GU-3065) and cal AD 620–880 (GU-3064c).

The historical and agricultural background to the formation of deep topsoils in Orkney has been discussed by Davidson and Simpson (1984), who noted a degree of correlation between deep topsoils and long established farms. A mid- to late Norse date for the initiation of deep topsoil formation has subsequently been proposed by Simpson (1993). Both works, however, have also proposed, after Barber (1981, 359–60) and in connection with his work on Iona, the possibility that the occurrence of deep topsoils may be associated with areas settled during the early monastic period. This would certainly be an appropriate context for the formation of the Late Iron Age sediments on Area 1. The upper range of the uppermost radiocarbon dates from this horizon can be safely accommodated within an Early Christian settlement chronology. The lower date (cal AD 285–670: GU-3063) from the primary soil horizon, as a *terminus post quem* for the accumulation of the deposits, would not be incompatible with such an interpretation.

Man-made soils in the vicinity of the abbey on Iona were introduced to the site over some time within, and possibly continuing throughout, the period between the seventh century AD and the medieval period (Barber 1981, 359). Barber (1981, 360) suggested that the introduction of man-made soils represented part of the 'economic package' of the early Church. It was considered, however, that it was probably not a feature of the earliest phase. The dating of the Late Iron Age sediments at St Boniface, unlike the evidence from Iona, however, provides a much tighter chronology for their introduction.

The chronology of Block 107 is dependent on the dating of the sediments of which it is composed, its fabric, microstructure and accumulation rate, and statistical analyses of the duration and formation periods of the buried ground surface which developed in the top of the sediments and the accumulation rate of the overlying ash mound (Part 7.1). The period AD 500–750 emerges as the most likely period for the formation of the plaggen soil. This, however, cannot be easily reconciled with an Early Christian chronology in Orkney. While such a chronology could, just conceivably, be accommodated within a seventh-century context, a sixth-century date would be more difficult to sustain. On the other hand, any restriction of the chronology, for example to the period AD 650–750, would have to reconcile the soil micromorphological evidence (Part 6.11) for a relatively slow and intermittent accumulation. This problem is exacerbated further if the soil is considered to be an artefact of an ecclesiastical establishment which was founded under Pictish royal control not earlier than AD 715. Lamb (1993, 265), for example, has suggested a date *c.* AD 750 for the establishment of a Pictish bishopric in Orkney.

Historical evidence for a sixth- or seventh-century ecclesiastical presence in Orkney is slight. Radford (1983, 14) has drawn attention to a passage from the *Life* of St Ailbe, an early sixth-century bishop of Emly, in Ireland, who:

> volens fugere homines . . . ad insulam Tile in occiano positam navigare decrevit, ut ibi viveret Deo secrete solus
>
> (*Vita Sancti Albei* cap.xli: Plummer 1910, 61)

> wishing to flee from men . . . he resolved to sail to the island of Thule set in the ocean, that he might live alone with God
>
> (Radford 1983, 14)

Identifying Thule with Shetland, Radford (1983, 14) has claimed this as 'the first Christian reference to the northern isles of Britain'. Cormac's voyage and sojourn in Orkney, to seek 'a desert place in the ocean' (herimum in oceano), reported in the *Life* of St Columba (Anderson & Anderson 1961, 441, 443), represents another early ecclesiastical reference to the Northern Isles. This event is usually attributed to the last quarter of the sixth century (Wainwright 1962a, 112; Radford 1983, 14). A case can also be made that Book VII.14 of Dicuil's *Liber de mensura orbis terrae* (Tierney 1967, 75), written on the Continent in AD 825, may also refer to the establishment of eremitical groups or individuals on Orkney in the eighth century and possibly earlier (Lowe 1987, i, 15–18). The relationship of the eremitic or anchorite tradition to the early missionary church, however, is unclear. Lamb (1973b, 85) has suggested that the movement that founded the eremitic monasteries was 'either completely separate from, or else an off-shoot of, the missionary activity'. A more recent article implies a ninth- or tenth-century context for this activity in the Northern Isles (Lamb 1993, 268).

It is difficult to reconcile fully the introduction of man-made soils at St Boniface with an Early Christian chronology, unless a special pleading is made for the radiocarbon dates, or the model of soil development which is proposed here, or for a very early ecclesiastical, and eremitical, presence on the site. In the present state of knowledge it would be extremely difficult to postulate early eremitical activity at the site.

Economy of interpretation would therefore suggest that the introduction of man-made soils on the site represents an indigenous development which was undertaken by the Late Iron Age inhabitants of the settlement. Structural remains of this period were not located in the excavated cliff-section. The Late Iron Age settlement, therefore, is assumed to lie outwith the enclosed site, within the outer zone of settlement which has been postulated in the reconstruction of the palaeotopography of the site (Part 7.1.212). The final phases of the soil formation, perhaps the period AD 700–750, or slightly earlier and slightly later, almost certainly coincide with an ecclesiastical presence on the site and only in this sense could the formation of Block 107 be considered as an 'ecclesiastical artefact'.

The interpretation of the Block 107 sediments as part-indigenous, part-ecclesiastical in origin would contradict the hypothesis, previously advanced (Barber 1981), that the introduction of man-made soils formed part of the 'economic package' of the Early Church. This interpretation, however, has another, perhaps more far-reaching, implication for the site in particular. It implies that there is continuity between the Late Iron Age and Early Christian phases of settlement and, moreover, raises the possibility that the early ecclesiastical site was established at St Boniface to serve, convert and control, at the behest of a secular power, an extant, local population.

7.2.44 The buried ground surface

The subsequent period in the development of the ecclesiastical site coincides with the development of a long-standing ground surface (B105, Phase 7) in the upper horizon of the plaggen soil. Cultivation ceased and this area was effectively abandoned. In a sense, the buried soil represents as much, if not more, of an 'ecclesiastical artefact' as the underlying soils from which it was formed.

At the time of its burial by the ash mound, *c.* AD 1100, the ground surface supported a *Calluna*-rich heathland, indicative of long term stability and a lack of human disturbance. Statistical analysis (Part 4.1) indicates that there is a 69 per cent probability that the ground surface developed over a period of between 310 and 525 years. The extent to which other parts of the settlement may have also been abandoned is not known.

Historically within the period AD 750–1100 would belong, possibly the shadowy figure of 'Bishop Bercham', the events surrounding St Findan around the middle of the ninth century and, towards its end, the burial of Rognvald Brusison in AD 1046. Artefactually, the cross-inscribed stones and the shrine panel could also be of this period. Although no structures unequivocally of this period were located in the cliff-section, the presence of lumps of impressed mortar in the primary ash mound constitutes good evidence for an earlier mortared building on the site. It is all the more ironic, therefore, that these fragmentary pieces of evidence should have to be set beside evidence, from the cliff-section, of what appears to represent a major period of inactivity on the site.

The nature and physical extent of this abandonment phase can only be speculated upon. If it was as total and long-lasting as may be inferred on the basis of the chronology of the old ground surface, it would imply that all of the extant archaeological assemblage, including the cross-inscribed stones, the shrine panel fragment and the postulated mortared building, would have to be accommodated within the eighth century. This seems perhaps a little unlikely, as does the burial of Rognvald Brusison in among the ruins of a long-abandoned site which would have been so short-lived as to have hardly been remembered, some 300 years on, as a place of sepulture. The refounding or refurbishment of the church in the twelfth century and the early episcopal claims which have been made for the site in the period prior to this (Lamb 1993; 1995: Part 1.2.24) would also be difficult to reconcile with a site which had been abandoned for such a long period. Likelihood alone, therefore, suggests that continuity between the earlier and later periods of ecclesiastical use of the site is more likely than not.

The causes of the abandonment are similarly unknown but it seems curious, given the labour and energy which had previously been expended in developing the soils of this area, that the abandonment, at least on this part of the site, should have been so seemingly total and long-lasting. While its immediate cause could be attributed to raids of the early Viking period, it is difficult to see how this abandonment horizon could have persisted across several centuries without recourse to other, unknown, mechanisms or processes. Whether this has any relevance to Marwick's (1925, 36) suggestion that the absence of primary Norse settlement names on Papay implies that 'the Celtic missionaries were, for the most part, left undisturbed' is not clear. It is clear, however, that there is no evidence, from the excavated cliff-section, of Viking settlement at the site.

7.2.5 *The Later Medieval Ecclesiastical Site* (see Part 1.2.2)

7.2.51 Introduction

It has been suggested that there is a greater likelihood, than not, of continuity between the earlier and later phases of ecclesiastical use of the site. In part, this emerges as a result of the very tight radiocarbon chronology for the dating of the plaggen soil, the buried ground surface and the overlying ash mound. None of these features, of course, is 'ecclesiastical' in itself, yet their dating implies some measure of contemporaneity with an ecclesiastical presence on the site. Continuity can also be inferred on the basis of the spatial relationship between the earlier and later cemeteries. Nonetheless, there are real problems in trying to reconcile the excavated evidence with the implicit historical model which is dependent on inferences and hypotheses about the development of the site from a possibly quasi-episcopal centre in the eighth century through to the establishment of a parish church in, perhaps, the twelfth century. This problem becomes exacerbated, given that the twelfth-century attributes of the site, such as the hogback and the structural form of the medieval church, are based on deductions which derive from stylistic and art-historical sequences.

The later medieval ecclesiastical site is considered within the context of the historical record of Rognvald Brusison's burial on the island in AD 1046, the early fabric and design of the standing church of St Boniface, the hogback stone, and the fish-processing station which was established adjacent to the site *c*. AD 1100.

7.2.52 Ecclesiastical monuments of the eleventh century

Orkneyinga Saga (cap XXX: Taylor 1938, 185) records the burial of Earl Rognvald Brusison on Papa Westray in AD 1046. On the basis of the clear political connection between Rognvald's family and the Outer Isles in general and, seemingly, Papa Westray in particular, as evidenced in Rognvald's burial on the island, this study has postulated (Part 1.2.24) an association between Rognvald Brusison and the site of St Boniface church. On the basis of the evidence presented here, it is assumed that Rognvald would have been buried within the cemetery of the early phase ecclesiastical settlement, the Northumbrian-inspired bishopric church of the eighth-century mission. The church within or beside which Rognvald was buried is assumed, on the basis of the fragments of impressed mortar which were recovered from the primary levels of the ash mound, to have been of mortared construction. Given this possible association, it is surprising that the hogback-type monument, although seemingly stylistically later than the eleventh century, should not have been associated, if only in popular tradition, with Rognvald himself. A break in tradition, however, could be explained by the stone's apparent loss and its subsequent rediscovery *c*. AD 1800 (Part 1.2.23).

A possible model of the ecclesiastical repercussions of Rognvald's defeat by Thorfinn and the subsequent establishment of the Orcadian bishopric at Birsay has been presented elsewhere (Part 1.2.24). These events could have led to the demise or abandonment of the ancient episcopal centre on the site and its later refurbishment or restoration as a parish church. Whether the fish-processing site falls between or overlaps with an ecclesiastical presence on the site is not clear. Its initiation, however, could be contemporary with the decline in the fortunes of Rognvald Brusison's line.

The implications of this model for high-status secular settlement in the vicinity of the site are unclear. Certainly none was identified in the excavated cliff-section and, with the possible exception of the single brooch pin from the ash mound, diagnostic artefacts of a Norse cultural milieu, such as specific comb or pin types or pottery, were notable by their absence. Steatite vessels and artefacts were similarly absent.

It would have to be assumed that any related Norse settlement lay some distance from the excavated cliff-section. Proximity to the church might be indicated by analogy with the arrangements which can be discerned at Tuquoy, on Westray (Owen 1993), the earldom farm at Orphir (Johnston 1903; Batey & Morris 1992) and, possibly, also the earldom centre at Birsay, regardless of whether Thorfinn's Christchurch and the earl's and bishop's palaces were located in the village or on the nearby Brough of Birsay (Lamb 1974; 1983b). Against this, however, at St Boniface, would have to be placed an absence of any recognizable surface remains of such a settlement, unless they are largely buried beneath the later ash mound. It would also be difficult to explain the absence of any traditional memory of such an earldom or high-status association. In mitigation, however, it is clear that no traditions or memory of a high-status settlement at Tuquoy survived and it could be argued that Orphir would have been similarly forgotten but for the saga reference to the earl's feasting hall and the events which accompanied the Christmas revelries there in AD 1135. Both sites, however, demonstrably contain mortared ecclesiastical buildings of some architectural merit (Lowe 1993b) and it is these elements of those sites which reflect the status of the secular patron on whose lands the buildings were erected. Whether a similar, high-status Norse settlement lay adjacent to, or in the vicinity of, St Boniface church is not known, and its earldom associations can only be postulated. The rise to prominence, albeit temporary, of the episcopal seat at Birsay and the fortunes of the earldom line under Thorfinn and his descendants, however, could have effectively erased any memory of an earlier stratum of an early earldom or ecclesiastical centre on Papay.

7.2.53 Ecclesiastical monuments of the twelfth century

The evidence for twelfth-century ecclesiastical activity on the site, like that for the eleventh, is fragmentary and diverse in kind. To this period can be assigned, possibly, the hogback-type monument and the medieval fabric of the nave and chancel church which underlies the eighteenth-century building. The dating of both monuments, however, depends on stylistic considerations, concerning art-historical, and structural or architectural developments. Bicameral churches in the Northern Isles and the use of 'Romanesque' round-arched openings, for example, are not normally dated earlier than the twelfth century. This, however, may need to be revised in the light of the recovery of mortar, as discard material, from what is clearly an early twelfth-century context.

A twelfth-century date has also been proposed for the formation of the ash mound and the establishment on the site of what was effectively a fish-processing station. These chronologies, in combination with the historical reconstruction which has been proposed for the eleventh century, could be accommodated within one of three possible models for the development of the site in the twelfth century. The ash mound could be contemporary with either the early phase and/or the later phase church, accepting continuity in the ecclesiastical use of the site. Alternatively, the ash mound could occupy a brief period in the development of the site, between a postulated abandonment or demise of the early ecclesiastical site and the establishment of its medieval successor parish church. Such a chronology, perhaps represented by an ecclesiastical hiatus in the period c. AD 1050–1150, could accommodate the historical and archaeological evidence and models presented in this study. Contemporaneity between the fish-processing site and the church, however, would not be without its mutual benefits.

7.2.54 The fish-processing station

The ash mound immediately north of St Boniface church has been interpreted as the only surviving remains, above ground, of an early fish-processing station. The mound was formed on an area of ground which had previously been cultivated but which, at the time of mound initiation, supported an acidic heathland flora. The radiocarbon, pollen and soil micromorphological evidence concur to suggest that accumulation was rapid, intensive and of relatively short duration. The presence of lumps of a hard, impressed mortar in the primary deposits of the primary mound indicate that a high-status building, most probably a church, was demolished, or its ruins disturbed, at this time. Whether this coincides with the refurbishment or construction of a new church on the site, possibly the medieval bicameral church which was altered in the eighteenth century, is not known.

Large assemblages of fish-bones have been recovered from other Norse sites in northern Scotland, such as Freswick Links and Robert's Haven, both in Caithness, where commercial fish-processing has either been implied or proposed (Batey 1989, 226; Barrett 1993; Morris, Batey & Barrett 1993; Simpson & Barrett forthcoming). The evidence from St Boniface, however, would suggest that the bones of the fish and the meat that it provided are only half the story and that the key to fully understanding this phase in the development of the site lies with the mineral ash sediments in which the bones were recovered. The ash mound has been interpreted as an artefact of fish liver oil production, the residues derived from the firing of cauldrons in which the fish livers were boiled and the oil extracted.

The importance of fish liver oil for lighting, as a lubricant and for other domestic purposes in pre-industrialized societies should not be underestimated. Oil was certainly used in Shetland in the sixteenth century as a commodity in which *skats* (taxes) could be paid (Balfour 1859, 15–16, 34,

53), together with butter and *wadmel* (cloth). In Orkney, where *skat* payments were normally made in butter or malt, oil too, nonetheless, is occasionally mentioned in the rental of c. AD 1500, in two instances in connection with Papa Westray itself (Peterkin 1820, 86).

The ash mound at St Boniface church probably provides the best evidence, to date, of what an eleventh or twelfth century fish-processing station would have looked like. Topographically, in addition to the mound which survives, such activity would predicate the existence of features which are no longer in evidence on the site; most notably, a suitable landing place for the delivery of the fish and the uplift of the products created at the site. Ethnographic parallels would imply that the landing site would have most likely comprised a stony beach or ayre, on which the fillets would have been laid to dry (Smith 1984, 48–9).

Artefacts associated with oil production would have included iron cauldrons, in which the livers were boiled, ladles, to skim off the oil as it rose to the surface, and wooden barrels, most probably of oak (Anne Crone, pers comm), in which the oil would have been transported. Artefacts associated with fishing would include iron fishing hooks and stone line-sinkers. None, however, was recovered. The structural requirements of oil production are not clear but may have included buildings for the storage of equipment and produce. The boiling of the fish livers, meanwhile, would have most likely been an open-air activity. The overall impression is that such a site, with the exception of the ash mound itself, could have been to a large extent deficient in both structures and artefacts.

The location of the settlement, from which the fish-processing site was operated, is not known. The most likely site, however, if not seaward of the mound and thus lost to erosion, would probably be within or around the adjacent church and cemetery. The relatively late subrectangular buildings on Area 2 and the ground to the west of the present graveyard may represent the site of this settlement. For what it is worth, the folk traditions recorded by Marwick (1925, 34: Part 2.2.4), concerning the old woman who lived on the site and baked bread on Sundays, or the tradition that the service in St Boniface church was once interrupted by 'folks singing . . . a short distance away', could represent a corrupted folk memory of this early processing site.

The nature of this settlement, like its relationship to the church, is uncertain. It is clear, however, that cultivation continued throughout the period of the mound's accumulation and that grain, whether burnt during the drying process or deliberately discarded where it showed evidence of sprouting or insect attack, was incorporated into the ash mound. The mound was relatively rich in carbonized cereal grains (Table 16) and the introduction of both oats and flax appears to be associated with its formation (Part 4.3.84). Artefacts were rare. With the exception of a possible iron sickle, a single iron nail and a strap handle from a jug of medieval type, the few remaining artefacts from the mound were of copper alloy. These comprised an incised ring, a decorated strip, a pin, a possible rivet and several pieces of copper alloy sheet and other fragments. This is an odd assemblage and while some could relate to personal ornaments, which were either lost or discarded on the mound, others, such as the strip and the fragments of copper alloy sheet, are of unknown provenance and the manner of their deposition in the mound is uncertain. The artefactual evidence would suggest that domestic refuse was not normally deposited on the mound.

The depth and extent of the ash mound, and the rapidity with which it accumulated, are indicative of intensive fish exploitation on a commercial scale. The stock-fish trade (Part 1.2.42), to which could now be added the export of fish liver oil, emerges as the most likely historical context for the site. Whether this trade was conducted directly with the markets of Britain and Continental Europe or via the Bergen entrepôt is not known, although the latter is probably the more likely. Whether the church at St Boniface was directly associated with this activity is also unknown but it is not difficult to appreciate the financial benefits that would have been generated through some involvement in the trade. Trade in this period would also have been facilitated by the organizational structure which the Church could have provided. The association, therefore, of church and processing site may not necessarily be as mutually exclusive as might first appear. It would, however, imply that the ecclesiastical site was something rather more than just a parish church.

The fish-processing station appears to have been of relatively short duration. The twelfth century may have witnessed both its formation and abandonment. The reasons for its abandonment are not known but it appears to have been abrupt. Possibly the landing site and drying beach were lost at this time, the result of catastrophic erosion. Alternatively, political changes, related to the increasing 'Scottification' (Wainwright 1962b, 190) of the secular and ecclesiastical powers in Orkney from the thirteenth century onwards, may have interrupted or restricted access to Norwegian markets. In any event, the site was abandoned and forgotten and the settlement complex contracted around the parish church and graveyard of St Boniface, the only medieval church, aside from the cathedral in Kirkwall, still in ecumenical use today, but one, moreover, which almost certainly has a longer and more varied past.

7.3 Conclusion

Christopher Lowe

One of the broader remits for the St Boniface Coastal Erosion project was to develop a methodology and approach which could be utilized at other eroding coastal sites. The fieldwork strategy and the multi-disciplinary approach which was adopted, both in the field and during the post-excavation analyses, have been presented in this report. Much new information on the development of Iron Age sites and, particularly, new light on the Orkney 'farm mounds' has been generated as a result of this work which, by its very nature, was only minimally destructive of the archaeological deposits. Clearly, great potential also exists for clarifying the Late Iron Age/Early Christian interface and medieval occupation on the site.

The nature of the assessment has stressed the vertical dimension rather than the horizontal plane and it is this which has facilitated appreciation of the development of the settlement through time. Of necessity, some phases of the site's development are more clearly defined than others. The key to the project, however, has been the recording of sequence.

Beverley Ballin Smith (1994, 291), in a postscript to the Howe report, has commented that:

> total excavation of the site was the only feasible means of recovering useable information. With these factors in mind, excavation of similar sites in the future will not be cheap, if the reliability of the data is to be ensured.

Although total excavation of a site will always remain highly desireable, the strategy and approach adopted on the St Boniface cliff-section may provide an appropriate and cost-effective response to meeting the challenges which coastal erosion presents.

The estate of the Traills, the old lairds of Papay, was broken up and sold to its former tenants in the early part of this century. In the light of the serious threat that coastal erosion poses, not only to the site at St Boniface church but also elsewhere in Orkney and Scotland, Hugh Marwick's (1925, 37) advice to the newly independent proprietors of the island is as relevant today as it was then:

> They may well be proud of their heritage, and it is to be hoped they will do all in their power to preserve from destruction the numerous relics that survive to tell of their various ancestors who lived and loved and fought so long ago where they live and move and have their being today.

Bibliography

Adam of Bremen's History of the Archbishops of Hamburg-Bremen: see Schmeidler 1917 & Tschan 1959.

Ambrosiani, B. & Clarke, H. (eds) 1993 *Developments around the Baltic and the North Sea in the Viking Age* (Proceedings of the Twelfth Viking Congress, Stockholm, 1994).

Anderson, A.O. & Anderson, M.O. 1961 *Adamnan's Life of Columba*, London.

Anderson Smith, W. 1883 'Curing and preserving fish at home and abroad' in Herbert, D. (ed.) 1883, *Fish and fisheries: a selection from the prize essays of the International Fisheries Exhibition, Edinburgh, 1882*, 93–104, Edinburgh.

Armit, I. (ed.) 1990a *Beyond the brochs: Changing perspectives on the later Iron Age in Atlantic Scotland*, Edinburgh.

—— 1990b 'Monumentality and elaboration in prehistory: a case study in the Western Isles of Scotland' *Scot Archaeol Rev* 7, 1990, 84–95.

—— 1991 'The Atlantic Scottish Iron Age: five levels of chronology', *Proc Soc Antiq Scot* 121, 1991, 181–214.

—— 1992 *The later prehistory of the Western Isles of Scotland*, Oxford (BAR Brit. Ser., 221).

Arnold, C.J. 1975 'Fragments of bone combs from Papa Westray, Orkney', *Proc Soc Antiq Scot* 106 1974–5, 210-11.

Balfour, D. 1859 'Oppressions of the sixteenth century in the islands of Orkney and Shetland' *Abbotsford and Maitland Clubs* 31, 1859, Edinburgh.

Ballin Smith, B. (ed.) 1994 *Howe: four millennia of Orkney prehistory*, Society of Antiquaries of Scotland Monograph Series, 9, Edinburgh, 1994.

Barber, J. 1981 'Excavations at Iona, 1979', *Proc Soc Antiq Scot* 111, 1981, 282–380.

—— 1990 'Burnt mound material on settlement sites in Scotland' in Buckley, V. (ed.) 1990, 92–7.

Barrett, J.C. 1981 'Aspects of the Iron Age in Atlantic Scotland: a case study in the problems of archaeological interpretation', *Proc Soc Antiq Scot*, 111, 1981, 205–19.

Barrett, J.H. 1993 *Robertshaven: an archaeological investigation of rural economy in the medieval earldom of Caithness* (privately distributed pamphlet).

Bass, W.M. 1987 *Human Osteology: a Laboratory and Field Manual*, 3rd edn, Columbia: Missouri Archaeological Society.

Batey, C.E. 1989 'Recent work at Freswick Links, Caithness, Northern Scotland', *Hikuin*, 15, 1989, 223–9.

Batey, C.E. & Morris, C.D. 1992 'Earl's Bu, Orphir, Orkney: excavation of a Norse horizontal mill' in Morris & Rackham (eds) 1992, 33–41.

Batey, C.E., Jesch, J. & Morris, C.D. (eds) 1993 *The Viking Age in Caithness, Orkney and the North Atlantic* (Proceedings of the Eleventh Viking Conference, Kirkwall, 1989), Edinburgh.

Bell, B. & Dickson, C.A. 1989 'Excavations at Warebeth (Stromness Cemetery) Broch, Orkney', *Proc Soc Antiq Scot* 119, 1989, 101–31.

Benediktsson, J. (ed.) 1968 *Islendingabók and Landnámabók* 2 vols: (Islenzk Fornrit I), Reykjavík.

Berry, J. 1985 *The Natural History of Orkney*, London.

Bertelsen, R. 1979 'Farm Mounds in North Norway: a Review of Recent Research', *Norwegian Archaeological Review* 12, 1, 1979, 48–56.

—— 1984 'Farm Mounds of the Harstad Area: Quantitative Investigations of Accumulation Characteristics', *Acta Borealia* 1, 1984, 7–25.

—— 1985a 'The Medieval Vågan: an Arctic urban experiment?' *Archaeology and Environment* 4, 1985, 49–56 (Department of Archaeology, University of Umeå).

—— 1985b 'Artifact pattern and stratificational units', *American Archaeology* 5, 1, 1985, 16–20.

—— 1989 'Gårdshaugene I Nord-Norge', *Hikuin*, 15, 1989, 171–82.

—— 1990 'A north-east Atlantic perspective', *Acta Archaeologica* 61, 1990, 22–8.

Bertelsen, R. & Lamb, R.G. 1993 'Settlement Mounds in the North Atlantic' in Batey, Jesch & Morris (eds) 1993, 544–54.

Bertelsen, R. & Urbanczyk, P. 1988 'Two perspectives on Vågan in Lofoten', *Acta Borealia* 6, 1988, 98–110.

Beveridge, E. 1931 'Excavation of an Earth-house at Foshigarry, and a Fort, Dun Thomaidh, in North Uist', *Proc Soc Antiq Scot* 65, 1931, 299–357.

Bond, J.M. & Hunter, J.R. 1987 'Flax-growing in Orkney from the Norse period to the 18th century', *Proc Soc Antiq Scot* 117, 1987, 175–81.

Bowman, A. 1990 'Boat naust survey on Papa Westray, Orkney', *International Journal of Nautical Archaeology and Underwater Exploration* 19.4, 1990, 317–25.

Boycott A.E. 1936 'The habitats of freshwater Mollusca in Britain', *J Anim Ecol* 5, 1936, 116–86.

Boyd, W.E. 1988 'Cereals in Scottish antiquity', *Circaea* 5, 1988, 101–10.

Boyle, P., Pierce, G. & Watt, J. 1992 *Guide for the identification of premaxillae and vertebrae of the fish from the North Sea*, University of Aberdeen, Department of Zoology.

Brand, J. 1701 *A Brief Description of Orkney, Zetland, Pightland Firth and Caithness*, Edinburgh.

Brothwell, D. & Dimbleby, G. (eds) 1981 *Environmental Aspects of Coasts and Islands*, Oxford (BAR Int Ser, 94).

Brothwell D., Bramwell D. & Cowles G. 1981 'The relevance of birds from coastal and island sites', in Brothwell & Dimbleby 1981, 195-206.

Buckley, V. (ed.) 1990 *Burnt offerings: international contributions to Burnt Mound archaeology*, Dublin.

Bullock, P., Federoff, N., Jongerius, A., Stoops, G. & Tursina, T. 1985 *Handbook for soil thin-section description*, Wolverhampton.

Bunting, M-J. 1993 Environmental History and Human Impact on Orkney, unpublished PhD thesis, University of Cambridge.

Calder, C.S.T. 1956 'Report on the discovery of numerous stone age house-sites in Shetland', *Proc Soc Antiq Scot* 89, 1955–6, 340–97.

—— 1964 'Cairns, Neolithic houses and burnt mounds in Shetland', *Proc Soc Antiq Scot* 96, 1963–4, 37–86.

Campbell, E. 1991 'Excavation on a wheelhouse and other Iron Age structures at Sollas, North Uist, by R J C Atkinson in 1957', *Proc Soc Antiq Scot* 121, 1991, 117–74.

Caulfield, S. 1978 'Quern replacement and the origins of brochs' *Proc Soc Antiq Scot* 109, 1977–8, 129–39.

Clapham, A.R., Tutin, T.G. & Moore, D.M 1987 *Flora of the British Isles*, 3rd edn., Cambridge.

Clark, J.G.D., 1947 'Whales as an Economic Factor in Prehistoric Europe', *Antiquity* 21, 1947, 84–104.

Clarke, D.V. & Sharples, N. 1985 'Settlement and subsistence in the Third Millennium BC' in Renfrew (ed.) 1985, 54–82.

Clouston, J.S. 1918 'The Old Chapels of Orkney', *Scot Hist Rev* xv, 58, 1918, 89–105 & xv, 59, 1918, 223–40.

Clucas, I.J. & Sutcliffe, P.J. 1981 *An Introduction to Fish Handling and Processing*, (Tropical Products Institute) G143. London: Overseas Development Administration.

Clutton-Brock, T.H. & Albon, S.D. 1989 *Red deer in the Highlands*, Oxford.

Colgrave, B. & Mynors, R.A.B. (eds) 1969 *Bede's Ecclesiastical History of the English People*, Oxford.

Colley, S. 1982 Interim Report on the fish remains from Tuquoy, Westray, Orkney, unpublished.

—— 1983 'Interpreting prehistoric fishing strategies: an Orkney case study', in Grigson, C. & Clutton-Brock, J. (eds), *Animals and Archaeology: 2 Shell Middens, Fishes and Birds*, Oxford (BAR Int Ser, 183), 157–71.

—— 1989 'The Fish Bones', in Morris (ed.) 1989, 248–59.

Cramp, R.J. 1976 'Monastic Sites' in Wilson, D.M. (ed.) 1976 *The Archaeology of Anglo-Saxon England*, 201–52, Cambridge.

Cramp S. *et al* 1985 *Handbook of birds of Europe, the Middle East and North Africa : The birds of the Western Palaearctic*, Vol. 4, Oxford.

Crawford, B.E. 1983 'Birsay and the early earls and bishops of Orkney' in Thomson (ed.) 1983, 97–118.

Curle, A.O. 1939 'A Viking Settlement at Freswick, Caithness', *Proc Soc Antiq Scot* 73, 1939, 71–110.

—— 1947 'The excavation of the wag or prehistoric cattle-fold at Forse, Caithness, and the relationship of wags to brochs, and implications arising therefrom', *Proc Soc Antiq Scot* 80/81, 1945–7, 11–25.

Curle, C.L. 1982 *Pictish and Norse Finds From the Brough of Birsay, Orkney 1934–1974*, Society of Antiquaries of Scotland Monograph Series, 1, Edinburgh.

Dalland, M. 1993 'Calibration and Stratigraphy', in Barber, J.W. (ed.) 1993, *Interpreting Stratigraphy*, 27–35, Edinburgh.

Dalland, M. & MacSween, A. forthcoming 'The Coarse Pottery', in Owen & Lowe forthcoming.

Davidson, D.A. & Simpson, I.A. 1984 'The formation of deep topsoils in Orkney', *Earth Surface Processes and Landforms* 9, 1984, 75–81.

Davidson, D.A., Harkness, D.D. & Simpson, I.A. 1986 'The Formation of Farm Mounds on the Island of Sanday, Orkney', *Geoarchaeology* 1,1, 1986, 45–60.

Davidson, D.A., Lamb, R. & Simpson, I.A. 1983 'Farm Mounds in North Orkney: A Preliminary Report', *Norwegian Archaeological Review* 16, 1, 1983, 39–44.

Davidson, J.L. & Henshall, A.S. 1989 *The chambered tombs of Orkney*, Edinburgh.

Denys L. 1992 'A check-list of the diatoms in the Holocene deposits of the western Belgian coastal plain with a survey of their apparent ecological requirements I. Introduction, ecological code and complete list', *Service Geologique de Belgique, Prof Pap* 1991/2, No. 246, 41 pp.

Dickson, C.A. 1983 'The macroscopic plant remains', in Hedges 1983, 114.

—— 1987 'The macroscopic plant remains', in Hedges 1987, i, 137–42.

Dickson, C.A. & Dickson, J.H. 1984 'The botany of the Crosskirk broch site' in Fairhurst 1984, 147–55.

Dickson, J.H. 1992 'North American Driftwood, especially *Picea* (spruce) from archaeological sites in the Hebrides and Northern Isles of Scotland', *Review of Palaeobotany and Palynology*, 73 (1992), 49–56.

Dicuili Liber de Mensura Orbis Terrae: see Tierney 1967.

Dixon D. forthcoming 'Petrological Report on the Pottery from Tofts Ness' in Hunter *et al* forthcoming.

Dockrill, S.J. 1988 'Tofts Ness', *Discovery & Excavation in Scotland*, 1988, 29.

Donaldson, A.M. 1986 'Carbonized seeds, grain and charcoal' in Hunter 1986, 216–20.

Donaldson, A.M., Morris, C.D. & Rackham, D.J. 1981 'The Birsay Bay project: preliminary investigations into the past exploitation of the coastal environment at Birsay, Mainland, Orkney', in Brothwell & Dimbleby (eds)1981, 67–85.

Driesch, A. von den 1976 *A guide to the measurement of animal bones from archaeological sites*, Peabody Museum Bulletin 1, Harvard.

Edlin, H.L. 1973 *Woodland Crafts in Britain*, Newton Abbot.

Evans J.G. & Vaughan M. 1983 'The molluscs from the Knap of Howar, Orkney' in Ritchie 1983, 106–14.

Fairhurst, H. 1984 *Excavations at Crosskirk Broch, Caithness*, Society of Antiquaries of Scotland Monograph Series, 3, Edinburgh.

Fairhurst H. & Taylor D.B. 1971 'A Hut-circle Settlement at Kilphedir, Sutherland', *Proc Soc Antiq Scot* 103, 1971, 63–99.

Fenton, A. 1973 'Craig-fishing in the Northern Isles of Scotland and notes on the poke-net', *Scott Stud* 17, 1973, 71–80.

—— 1978 *The Northern Isles: Orkney and Shetland*, Edinburgh.

Fojut, F. 1981 'Is Mousa a broch?', *Proc Soc Antiq Scot* 111, 1981, 220–8.

Foster, S. 1989 'Transformations in social space: Iron Age Orkney and Caithness', *Scot Archaeol Rev* 6, 1989, 34–54.

—— 1990 'Pins, combs and the chronology of Later Atlantic Iron Age settlement', in Armit (ed.) 1990a, 143–74.

Graham, A. 1952 'Spruce and Pine timber in Two Scottish prehistoric buildings', *Arch Newsletter* 4, 1952, 133–7.

—— 1971 *Synopses of the British Fauna (New Series) No. 2: British Prosobranch and other operculate gastropod molluscs*, Linnean Society of London.

Graham-Campbell, J. 1980 *Viking Artefacts: A Select Catalogue*, London.

Gray, H. 1977 *Anatomy Descriptive and Surgical*, American edition revised from the 15th edition by Pickering Pick, T. & Howden, R., New York.

Greig, J.R.A. 1991 'The British Isles', in van Zeist, W., Wasylikowa, K. & Behre K-E. (eds), *Progress in Old World Palaeoethnobotany*, Rotterdam, 299–334.

Gudmundsson, F. 1965 *Orkneyinga Saga* (Islenzk Fornrit XXXIV), Reykjavík.

Haddan, A.W. & Stubbs, W. 1873 *Councils and ecclesiastical documents relating to Great Britain and Ireland* ii, (i).

Haggerty, A. & Haggerty, G. 1983 'Excavations at Rispain Camp, Whithorn 1978–1981', *Trans Dumfriesshire Galloway Natur Hist Antiq Soc* 58, 1983, 21–51.

Hamilton, J.R.C. 1956 *Excavations at Jarlshof, Shetland*, Edinburgh.

—— 1968 *Excavations at Clickhimin, Shetland*, Edinburgh.

Hamilton-Dyer, S. forthcoming 'The bird bones from Viking Tuquoy, Westray, Orkney' in Owen forthcoming.

Hedges, J.W. 1983 'Trial excavations on Pictish and Viking settlements at Saevar Howe, Birsay, Orkney', *Glasgow Archaeol J* 10, 1983, 73–124.

—— 1985 'The Broch Period' in Renfrew, C. (ed.) 1985, 150–75.

—— 1987 *Bu, Gurness and the Brochs of Orkney* (3 vols), Oxford, (BAR Brit Ser, 163–165).

Hewitson, J. 1996 *Clinging to the Edge: Journals of an Orkney Island*, Edinburgh.

Hillman, G.C. 1981 'Reconstructing crop husbandry practices from the charred remains of crops' in Mercer R.J. (ed.) 1981, *Farming Practices in British Prehistory*, Edinburgh, 123–62.

—— 1984 'Interpretation of archaeological plant remains: the application of ethnographical models from Turkey' in van Zeis, W. & Casparie, W.A. (eds) 1984, *Plants and Ancient Man: Studies in Palaeoethnobotany*, Rotterdam, 1–41.

Hingley, R. 1992 'Society in Scotland from 700 BC to AD 200', *Proc Soc Antiq Scot* 122, 1992, 7–53.

Hodkinson, B. 1987 'A reappraisal of the archaeological evidence for weaving in Ireland in the Early Christian Period', *Ulster J Archaeol* 50, 1987, 43–53.

Holder-Egger, O. 1887 'Vita Findani', *Monumenta Germanicae Historica* XV, 1, 502–6.

Holm-Olsen, I.M. 1981 'Economy and settlement pattern 1350–1600 AD, based on evidence from farm mounds', *Norwegian Archaeological Review*, 14, 2, 1981, 86–101.

Hunter, J.R. 1986 *Rescue excavations on the Brough of Birsay 1974–82*, Society of Antiquaries of Scotland Monograph Series, 4, Edinburgh.

—— 1990 'Pool, Sanday: a case study for the Late Iron Age and Viking periods' in Armit (ed.) 1990a, 175–93.

Hunter, J.R., Bond, J.M. & Smith, A.N. 1993 'Some aspects of Early Viking settlement in Orkney' in Batey, Jesch & Morris (eds) 1993, 272–84.

Hunter J.R., Dockrill, S.J., Bond, J.M. & Smith, A.N., (eds) forthcoming *Archaeological Investigations on Sanday*.

Jensen, H.A. 1979 'Seeds and other diaspores in medieval layers from Svendborg', *The archaeology of Svendborg Denmark* 2, Odense, 1–101.

Johnston, A.W. 1903 'Notes on the Earl's Bu at Orphir, Orkney, called Orfjara in the sagas, and on the remains of the round church there', *Proc Soc Antiq Scot* 37, 1902–3, 16–31.

Jones, A.K.J. 1991 The fish remains from Freswick Links, Caithness, unpublished PhD thesis, University of York.

Kenward, H.K., Hall, A.R. & Jones, A.K.G. 1980 'A tested set of techniques for the extraction of animal and plant remains from waterlogged archaeological deposits', *Science and Archaeology* 22, 1980, 3–15.

Kerney M.P. 1976 *Atlas of the non-marine mollusca of the British Isles* Institute of Terrestrial Ecology, Cambridge.

Kerney M.P. & Cameron R.A.D. 1979 *A field guide to the Land Snails of Britain and north-west Europe*, London.

Kirkness, W. 1921 'Notes on the discovery of a coped monument and an incised cross-slab at the graveyard, St Boniface church, Papa Westray, Orkney', *Proc Soc Antiq Scot* 55, 1920–1, 131–4.

Kolsrud, O. 1913 'The Celtic bishops in the Isle of Man, the Hebrides and Orkneys', *Zeitschrift für celtische Philogie* IX, 1, 1913, 357–79.

Krammer K. & Lange-Bertalot H. 1986–91 'Bacillariophyceae' in Ettl H., Gerloff J., Heynig H. & Mollenhauer D. (eds) 1986–91, *Süsswasserflora von Mitteleuropa* 2 (1–4), Stuttgart & New York.

Krogman, W.M. & Iscan, M.Y. 1986 *The Human Skeleton in Forensic Medicine*, Illinois.

Lamb, R.G. 1973a Coastal Fortifications and Settlements of North Atlantic Britain, unpublished PhD thesis, University of Birmingham.

—— 1973b 'Coastal Settlements of the North', *Scot Archaeol Forum* 5, 1973, 76–98.

—— 1974 'The Cathedral of Christchurch and the Monastery of Birsay', *Proc Soc Antiq Scot* 105, 1972–4, 200–5.

—— 1976 'The Burri Stacks of Culswick, Shetland and other paired stack-settlements', *Proc Soc Antiq Scot* 107, 1975–6, 144–54.

—— 1979 Church Archaeology in Orkney and Shetland (privately distributed pamphlet).

—— 1980 *The Archaeological Sites & Monuments of Sanday and North Ronaldsay* (RCAHMS List No.11).

—— 1983a *The Archaeological Sites & Monuments of Papa Westray and Westray* (RCAHMS List No.19).

—— 1983b 'The Cathedral and the Monastery' in Thomson (ed.) 1983, 36–45.

—— 1993 'Carolingian Orkney and its transformation' in Batey, Jesch & Morris (eds) 1993, 260–71.

—— 1995 'Papil, Picts & Papar' in Crawford, B.E. (ed.) *Northern Isles Connections: essays from Orkney & Shetland presented to Per Sveaas Andersen*, 9–27, Kirkwall.

Lang, J.T. 1974 'Hogback monuments in Scotland', *Proc Soc Antiq Scot* 105, 1972–4, 206–35.

—— 1988 *Viking-Age Decorated Wood*, Dublin.

Lowe, C.E. 1987 Early Ecclesiastical Sites in the Northern Isles and Isle of Man: An Archaeological Field Survey, (2 vols), unpublished PhD thesis: Department of Archaeology, University of Durham.

—— 1990 'Excavations at St Boniface Church, Papa Westray, Orkney', *Discovery & Excavation in Scotland* 1990, 45–7.

—— 1992 Sample taphonomy and the radiocarbon dating programme for the St Boniface excavation (internal report to Historic Scotland, May 1992).

—— 1993a 'Preliminary results of the excavation assessment at Munkerhoose cliff-section and farm mound, St Boniface Church, Papa Westray, Orkney', *Northern Studies* 30, 1993, 19–33.

—— 1993b 'Crosskirk survey' in Owen 1993, 321–4.

—— 1994 'George Petrie and the "brochs" of Papa Westray', *Proc Soc Antiq Scot* 124, 1994, 173–87.

—— forthcoming 'The Shetland prehistoric house sequence' in Owen & Lowe forthcoming.

Lund J.W.G. 1946 'Observations on soil algae I. The ecology, size and taxonomy of British soil diatoms', *New Phytologist* 45, 1946, 196–219.

Macan T.T. 1977 *A key to the Fresh- and Brackish-water Gastropods with notes on their ecology*, Freshwater Biological Association, Scientific Publication No. 13 (4th edn).

McCormick, F. 1981 'The animal bones from Ditch 1' in Barber 1981, 313–18.

—— 1984 'Large mammal bone' in Sharples 1984, 108–11, Fiche 2, D10–F2.

—— forthcoming a 'The animal bones from Cnip, Lewis'.

—— forthcoming b 'Calf slaughter as a response to marginality'.

MacDonald, A.D.S. 1977 'Old Norse papar names in N and W Scotland' in Laing, L. (ed.) 1977, *Studies in Celtic Survival*, BAR (Brit Ser 37), 107–11 (also published in *Northern Studies* 9, 1977, 25–30).

—— 1992 *Curadán, Boniface and the early church of Rosemarkie* Groam House Lecture, 1992.

MacGregor, A. 1974 'The Broch of Burrian, North Ronaldsay, Orkney', *Proc Soc Antiq Scot* 105, 1974, 63–118.

—— 1985 *Bone, Antler, Ivory and Horn*, London.

MacKie, E.W 1965 'The origin and development of the broch and wheelhouse building cultures of the Scottish Iron Age', *Proc Prehist Soc* 31, 1965, 93–146.

—— 1983 'Testing hypotheses about brochs', *Scot Archaeol Rev* 2, 1983, 117–28.

—— 1987 'Impact on the Scottish Iron Age of the discoveries at Leckie broch', *Glasgow Archaeol J* 14, 1987, 1–18.

—— 1991 'The Iron Age semibrochs of Atlantic Scotland: a case study in the problems of deductive reasoning', *Archaeol J* 148, 1991, 149–81.

—— 1994 'Gurness and Midhowe brochs in Orkney: some problems of misinterpretation', *Archaeol J* 151, 1994, 98–157.

MacKinley, J.M. 1914 *Ancient Church Dedications in Scotland (Vol 2: Non-scriptural dedications)* , Edinburgh.

MacSween, A. forthcoming a 'The Pottery from Tofts Ness', in Hunter *et al* forthcoming.

—— forthcoming b 'The Pottery from Pool', in Hunter *et al* forthcoming.

—— 1990 The Neolithic and Late Iron Age Pottery from Pool, Sanday, Orkney, unpublished PhD Thesis, Department of Archaeological Sciences, University of Bradford.

Maltby, J.M 1981 'Iron Age, Romano-British and Anglo-Saxon animal husbandry – a review of the faunal evidence' in Jones, M. & Dimbleby, G. (eds) 1981, *The Environment of Man: the Iron Age to the Anglo-Saxon Period* (BAR Brit Ser, 87), 155–204.

Mann, R.W. & Murphy, S.P. 1990 *Regional Atlas of Bone Disease*, Illinois.

Martin, A.C. 1946 'The comparative internal morphology of seed', *American Midland Naturalist* 36, 3, 1946, 513–660.

Marwick, H. 1923 'Antiquarian Notes on Sanday', *Proc Orkney Antiq Soc* 1, 1922–3, 21–9.

—— 1925 'Antiquarian Notes on Papa Westray', *Proc Orkney Antiq Soc* 3, 1924–5, 31–47.

Moore, P.D., Webb, J.A. & Collinson, M.E.S. 1991 *Pollen Analysis*, Oxford.

Morris, C.D. 1985a 'Viking Orkney: a survey' in Renfrew, C. (ed.) 1985, 210–42.

—— 1985b 'Skaill, Sandwick, Orkney: preliminary investigations of a mound-site near Skara Brae', *Glasgow Archaeol J* 12, 1985, 82–92.

—— (ed.) 1989 *The Birsay Bay Project, Volume 1, Brough Road Excavations 1976–1982*, University of Durham, Department of Archaeology monograph series no. 1, Durham.

Morris, C.D. & Rackham, D.J. (eds) 1992 *Norse and Later Settlement and Subsistence in the North Atlantic*, Department of Archaeology, University of Glasgow Occasional Paper Series no.1.

Morris, C.D., Batey, C.E. & Barrett, J.H. 1993 'The Viking and Early Settlement Archaeological Research Project: past, present and future', in Ambrosiani & Clarke (eds) 1993, 144–58.

Morris, C.D., Rackham, J. & Young, R. 1989 'Overall assessment' in Morris (ed.) 1989, 102–7.

Morris, R. 1983 *The Church in British Archaeology* (CBA Res Rep No.47), London.

Munch, G.S. 1966 'Gårdshauger I Nord-Norge', *Viking* 30, 1966, 25–54.

Mykura, W. 1976 *British regional geology: Orkney and Shetland*, Edinburgh.

New Statistical Account, Edinburgh, 1842.

Nicholson, R.A. 1991 An investigation into variability within archaeologically recovered assemblages of faunal remains: the influence of pre-depositional taphonomic processes. Unpublished Ph.D. thesis, University of York.

Nilsson, O. & Hjelmqvist, H. 1967 'Studies on the nutlet structure of south Scandinavian species of *Carex*', *Botaniska Notiser* 120, 1967, 460–85.

Noddle, B. 1977 'The animal bones from Buckquoy, Orkney' in Ritchie 1977, 201–9.

—— 1979 'A brief history of domestic animals in the Orkney Islands, Scotland, from the 4th millennium BC to the 18th century' in M. Kubasiewicz (ed.) 1979, *Archaeozoology*, 286–303, Szczecin.

—— 1983 'Animal bone from Knap of Howar' in Ritchie 1983, 93–103.

Nye, S. & Boardman S.J. forthcoming 'The botanical remains from Tuquoy' in Owen forthcoming.

O'Connor, A. & Clarke, D.V. (eds) 1983 *From the Stone Age to the 'Forty-Five*, Edinburgh.

Omand, C.J. 1986 (transl.) 'The Life of Saint Findan' in Berry, R.J & Firth, H.N. (eds) 1986 *The People of Orkney*, 284–7, Kirkwall.

Orkneyinga saga: see Gudmundsson 1965 & Taylor 1938.

Ortner, D. & Putschar, W.G.J. 1987 *Identification of Pathological Conditions in Human Skeletal Remains*, Washington DC.

Ovrevik, S. 1985 'The second millennium and after' in Renfrew, C. (ed.) 1985, 131–49.

Owen, O.A. 1993 'Tuquoy, Westray, Orkney: a challenge for the future?' in Batey, Jesch & Morris (eds) 1993, 318–39.

—— forthcoming *Excavations at Tuquoy, Westray, Orkney*.

Owen O.A. & Lowe C.E. forthcoming *Excavations at Kebister, Shetland*, Society of Antiquaries of Scotland Monograph Series.

Parsons, D. 1983 'Sites and Monuments of the Anglo-Saxon Mission in Central Germany', *Archaeol J* 140, 1983, 280–321.

Pearson, G.W., Pilcher, J.R., Baillie, M.G.L., Corbett, D.M. & Qua, F. 1986 'High precision 14C measurement of Irish oak to show the natural 14C variation from AD 1840 to 5210 BC', *Radiocarbon* 28, 2B, 1986, 911–34.

Peterkin, A. 1820 *Rentals of the Ancient earldom and Bishoprick of Orkney*, Edinburgh.

Petrie, G. 1863 MS Notebook 7 (SAS 550: MSS 26).

Piggott, S. 1951 'Excavations in the Broch and Hillfort of Torwoodlie, Selkirkshire 1950', *Proc Soc Antiq Scot* 85, 1950–1, 92–117.

Plummer, C. 1910 *Vitae Sanctorum Hiberniae*, Oxford.

Rackham, D.J. forthcoming 'The animal bones from Tuquoy, Westray' in Owen forthcoming.

Radford, C.A.R. 1962 'Art and Architecture: Celtic and Norse', in Wainwright 1962c, 163–87.

—— 1983 'Birsay and the spread of Christianity to the North' in Thomson 1983, 13–35.

Renfrew, C. 1979 *Investigations in Orkney*, (Soc Antiq London Rep Res Comm, 38), London.

—— (ed) 1985 *The Prehistory of Orkney: 4000 BC–AD 1000*, Edinburgh.

Renfrew, J.M. 1974 'A report on the cereal grains at Dun Mor Vaul' in Mackie, E.W., *Dun Mor Vaul: An Iron Age Broch on Tiree*, Glasgow, 210–13.

Rigold, S.E. 1977 'Litus Romanum: the Shore Forts as Mission Stations' in Johnston, D.E. (ed.) *The Saxon Shore* (CBA Res Rep 18), 70–5.

Ritchie, A. 1977 'Excavation of Pictish and Viking-Age Farmsteads at Buckquoy, Orkney', *Proc Soc Antiq Scot* 108, 1976–7, 174–227.

—— 1983 'Excavation of a Neolithic Farmstead at Knap of Howar, Papa Westray, Orkney', *Proc Soc Antiq Scot* 113, 1983, 40–121.

Roes, A. 1963 *Bone and Antler Objects from the Frisian Terp Mounds*, Haarlem.

Round, F.E 1958 'Observations on the diatom flora of Braunton Burrows, N. Devon', *Hydrobiologia* 11, 1958, 119–27.

Ross, A. 1994 'The Pottery [from Howe]' in Ballin Smith (ed.), 1994, 236–56.

RCAHMS 1946 *Inventory of the Ancient Monuments of Orkney and Shetland*, 3 vols, Edinburgh.

Sandnes, J. 1977 'Mannedauen og de overlevende' in Mykland (ed.) *Norges historie* 4, 1977, 75–247.

Schmeidler, B. (ed.) 1917 *Gesta hammaburgensis ecclesiae pontificum*, Hanover & Leipzig.

Scott, A.B. 1926 'The Celtic Church in Orkney', *Proc Orkney Antiq Soc* 4, 1925–6, 45–56.

Serjeantson, D. 1988 'Archaeological and ethnographical evidence for seabird exploitation in Scotland', *Archaeozoologia* 2, 1988, 209–24.

—— forthcoming 'The bird bones', in Hunter *et al* forthcoming.

Sharples, N. 1984 'Excavations at Pierowall quarry, Westray, Orkney', *Proc Soc Antiq Scot* 114, 1984, 75–125.

—— forthcoming *Excavations at Upper Scalloway, Shetland*.

Silver, I.A. 1969 'The ageing of domestic animals' in Brothwell, D. & Higgs, E. (eds) 1969, *Science in Archaeology*, 283–302 London.

Simpson, I.A. 1993 'The chronology of anthropogenic soil formation in Orkney', *Scot Geogr Mag* 109, 1, 1993, 4–11.

Simpson, I.A. & Barrett, J.H. forthcoming 'Interpretation of midden formation processes at Robert's Haven, Caithness, Scotland using thin-section micromorphology', *J Arch Science*.

Sjovold, T. 1974 *The Iron Age settlement of Arctic Norway*, Norwegian Universities Press.

Skene, W.F. 1867 *Chronicles of the Picts and Scots*, Edinburgh.

Small, A., Thomas, A.C. & Wilson, D.M. (eds) 1973 *St Ninian's Isle and its Treasure*, 2 vols, Aberdeen University Studies Series no. 152.

Smith, A.N. forthcoming 'The worked bone from Tuquoy, Westray, Orkney' in Owen, forthcoming.

Smith, C. 1994 'Animal bone report' in Ballin Smith 1994, 139–53.

Smith, D.H. 1984 *Shetland life and trade 1550–1914*, Edinburgh.

Snæsdóttir, M. 1990 'Stóraborg: an Icelandic farm mound', *Acta Archaeologica* 61, 1990, 116–19.

Southern, R.W. 1953 *The Making of the Middles Ages*, London.

Stevenson, R.B.K. 1955 'Pins and the chronology of brochs', *Proc Prehist Soc* 21, 1955, 282–94.

Stockmarr, J. 1971 'Tablets with spores used in absolute pollen analysis', *Pollen et spores* 13, 1971, 615–21.

Storm, G. (ed.) 1880 *Monumenta Historica Norwegiae*, Christiana.

Taylor, A.B. (ed.) 1938 *The Orkneyinga Saga: a new translation with introduction and notes*, London.

Tebble, N. 1976 *British Bivalve Seashells*, 2nd edn, Edinburgh.

Thomas, A.C. 1971 *The Early Christian archaeology of north Britain*, Oxford.

—— 1973a 'Sculptured stones and crosses from St Ninian's Isle and Papil, Shetland' in Small, A., Thomas, A.C. & Wilson, D.M. (eds) 1973, 8–44.

—— 1973b *Bede, archaeology and the cult of relics*, The Jarrow Lecture, 1973.

—— 1983 'The Double Shrine 'A' from St Ninian's Isle, Shetland' in O'Connor, A. & Clarke, D.V. (eds) 1983, 285–92.

Thomson, W.P.L. (ed.) 1983 *Birsay: a centre of political and ecclesiastical power*, Orkney Heritage, vol. 2, Kirkwall.

—— 1986 'St Findan and the Pictish-Norse Transition' in Berry, R.J. & Firth, H.N. (eds) 1986, *The People of Orkney*, 1986, 279–83.

—— 1987 *History of Orkney*, Edinburgh.

—— 1996 *Lord Henry Sinclair's 1492 Rental of Orkney*, Kirkwall.

Tierney, J.J. (ed.) 1967 *Dicuili Liber de Mensura Orbis terrae*, (Scriptores Latini Hiberniae VI), Dublin Institute for Advanced Studies, Dublin.

Tipping, R., Carter, S. & Johnson, D. 1994 'Soil Pollen and Soil Micromorphological Analysis of Old Ground Surfaces on Biggar Common, Borders Region, Scotland', *J Archaeol Science* 21, 1994, 387–401.

Triscott, J. 1982 'Excavations at Dryburn Bridge, East Lothian' in Harding, D. (ed.) 1982, *Later Prehistoric Settlement in Southeast Scotland*, 1982, 117–24, Edinburgh.

Tschan, F.J. (ed.) 1959 *Adam of Bremen's History of the Archbishops of Hamburg–Bremen*, New York.

Veen, M. van der 1987 'The plant remains', in Heslop, D.H. (ed.) 1987, *The excavation of an Iron Age settlement at Thorpe Thewles, Cleveland, 1980–1982* (CBA Res Rep 65, 93–99), London.

Vita Sancti Albei: see Plummer 1910.

Vita Sancti Columbae: see Anderson & Anderson 1961.

Vita Sancti Findani: see Holder-Egger 1887 & Omand 1986.

Wainwright, F.T. 1962a 'Picts and Scots' in Wainwright 1962c, 91–116.

—— 1962b 'The Golden Age and after' in Wainwright 1962c, 188–92.

—— (ed.) 1962c *The Northern Isles*, Edinburgh.

Wheeler, A. & Jones, A.K.G. 1989 *Fishes*, Cambridge Manuals in Archaeology, Cambridge.

Wilson, D.M., 1983. 'A bone pin from Sconsburgh, Dunrossness' in O'Connor & Clarke (eds) 1983, 343–9.

Withrington, D.J. & Grant, I.R. (eds) 1978 *The (Old) Statistical Account, 1791–1799: vol XIX Orkney & Shetland*, Edinburgh.

Young, A., 1956 'Excavations at Dun Cuier, Isle of Barra, Outer Hebrides', *Proc Soc Antiq Scot* 89, 1956, 290–328.